An Appetite for Power

Buthelezi's Inkatha and South Africa

An Appetite for Power

Buthelezi's Inkatha and South Africa

Gerhard Maré and Georgina Hamilton

Ravan Press, Johannesburg
Indiana University Press, Bloomington and Indianapolis

First published 1987
by Ravan Press, PO Box 31134, Braamfontein, 2017 South Africa,
and
Indiana University Press, Tenth and Morton Streets,
Bloomington, IN 47405, USA

Maré Gerhard
    Appetite for power: Buthelezi's Inkatha and South Africa.
    1. Inkatha — History
    I. Title II. Hamilton, Georgina
    323.1'1963 DT878.Z9

Library of Congress Cataloging-in-Publication Data

Maré, Gerhard
    An appetite for power.

    Includes index.
    1. Inkatha (Organization: South Africa)
2. Kwazulu (South Africa) — Politics and government.
3. South Africa — Politics and government — 1978-
4. Buthelezi, Gatsha. I. Hamilton, Georgina.
II. Title.
JQ1998.I54M37   1988   324.268'093   87-21527

1   2   3   4   5   92   91   90   89   88

ISBN 0 86975 328 2 Ravan (cased)
     0 86975 313 4 Ravan (pbk)
     0 253 30812 7 Indiana (cased)

Trade distribution in Britain:
Third World Publications Ltd
151 Stratford Road, Birmingham B11 1RD, Tel. 021-773 6572

Typeset by Russell Press Ltd, Gamble Street, Nottingham NG7 4ET
Printed in England by Villiers Publications,
26a Shepherds Hill, London N6

CONTENTS

List of illustrations, maps and diagrams   vi
Abbreviations used in text   vii

Preface   1

1. Introduction   5

2. The Availability of the Past   15

3. The Institutions of Apartheid   27

4. Inkatha Re-formed: Traditions Revived   45

5. Inkatha's Structure   61

6. 'A Pinch of African Communalism'   97

7. The Politics of Pragmatism and Populism   135

8. Picking up the Gauntlet   181

9. Conclusion   217

Appendix 1:Inkata   227
Appendix 2:'The Statement of Belief' issued to branches of Inkatha   228
Appendix 3:Description of the Mace of the KwaZulu Legislative
             Assembly and its Symbolic Significance   229
Appendix 4:KwaZulu Regulations for Chiefs and Headmen   230

Bibliography   233

Select Index   257

ILLUSTRATIONS, MAPS AND DIAGRAMS

Illustrations

King Solomon kaDinuzulu with his headmen	47
Mounted bodyguard at Solomon's installation	48
Buthelezi at his installation as chief	51
Buthelezi with King Goodwill	52
Shaka Day celebrations 1985	*Between pp. 118 and 119*
The launch of UWUSA, May Day 1986	
Barney Dladla and Harriet Bolton	122
Inkatha's Soweto Day rally 1986	*Between pp. 150 and 151*
Buthelezi with the *amabutho*	
Buthelezi with PFP leaders	
Buthelezi receiving an honorary degree at Witwatersrand University	
Buthelezi as chancellor of the University of Zululand	
Buthelezi at the KwaZulu-Natal Indaba	*Between pp. 182 and 183*
Buthelezi with US business leaders	
Inkatha impis in Lamontville	
Prince Gideon Zulu in disturbances in Umlazi, Shaka Day 1985	
Inkatha impis pursue mourners at memorial service for Victoria Mxenge	*Between pp. 214 and 215*
Thomas Shabalala	
Chief Buthelezi	223
Buthelezi with Kaizer Matanzima	224

Maps

South Africa and Neighbouring States	*facing p. 1*
Regional Map of Natal Province	14
Political Map of Natal Province	180
Durban Metropolitan Region	190

Diagrams

Genealogy of the Zulu Kings	16
The Buthelezi Family Tree	22
Khulani Holdings	114

ABBREVIATIONS USED IN TEXT

For abbreviations of publication titles and other sources see p.235.

AALC	— African American Labour Centre
ABI	— Arnold Bergstraesser Institute
ABRECSA	— Alliance of Black Reformed Churches of South Africa
AFL-CIO	— American Federation of Labour — Congress of Industrial Organizations
ANC	— African National Congress
ANCYL	— African National Congress Youth League
ASB	— Afrikaanse Studentebond
AZACTU	— Azanian Congress of Trade Unions
AZAPO	— Azanian People's Organization
AZASO	— Azanian Students Organization
BAC	— Black Advisory Council
BAD	— Bantu Affairs Department
BAWU	— Black Allied Workers Union
BC	— Buthelezi Commission
BCC	— British Council of Churches
BCMSA	— Black Consciousness Movement of South Africa
BEPA	— Bureau for Economic Planning and Analysis
BIC	— Bantu Investment Corporation
BOSS	— Bureau for State Security
BPC	— Black People's Convention
BUF	— Black Unity Front
CC	— (Inkatha) Central Committee
CED	— Corporation for Economic Development
CIA	— Central Intelligency Agency
COSAS	— Congress of South African Students
COSATU	— Congress of South African Trade Unions
CoT	— Committee of Ten (Soweto)
CRC	— Coloured Persons Representative Council
CUSA	— Congress of Unions of South Africa
DBSA	— Development Bank of South Africa
DET	— Department of Education of Training
DTA	— Democratic Turnhalle Alliance
FOSATU	— Federation of South African Trade Unions
GC	— (Inkatha) General Council
HRA	— Hambanathi Residents Association
IIE	— Institute for Industrial Education
JORAC	— Joint Rent Action Committee
KDC	— KwaZulu Development Corporation
KFC	— KwaZulu Finance and Investment Corporation
KLA	— KwaZulu Legislative Assembly
KSC	— KwaZulu Shoe Company
LC	— Lombard Commission
LMF	— Luthuli Memorial Foundation
LP	— Labour Party of South Africa
NATU	— Natal African Teachers Union
NC	— (Inkatha) National Council
NCM	— National Convention Movement
NECC	— National Education Crisis Committee
NF	— National Forum
NIC	— Natal Indian Congress
NISMAWU	— National, Iron, Steel, Metal and Allied Workers Union
NP	— National Party

NPC	— Natal Provincial Council
NRP	— New Republic Party
NSC	— National Statutory Council
NSRAIEU	— National Sugar Refinery and Allied Industries Employees Union
NUSAS	— National Union of South African Students
NUTW	— National Union of Textile Workers
OAU	— Organization of African Unity
PAC	— Pan Africanist Congress
PC	— President's Council
PFP	— Progressive Federal Party
PNDB	— Port Natal Development Board
PRP	— Progressive Reform Party
RP	— Reform Party
SAAWU	— South African Allied Workers Union
SABA	— South African Black Alliance
SABC (TV)	— South African Broadcasting Corporation (TV)
SACC	— South African Council of Churches
SACTU	— South African Congress of Trade Unions
SADF	— South African Defence Force
SAIC	— South African Indian Council
SAP	— South African Police
SASA	— South African Sugar Association
SASO	— South African Students' Organization
SCA	— Soweto Civic Association
SEIFSA	— Steel and Engineering Industries Federation of SA
SPCC	— Soweto Parents' Crisis Committee
SPRO-CAS	— Study Project on Christianity in Apartheid Society
TUACC	— Trade Union Advisory and Co-ordinating Council
TUCSA	— Trade Union Congress of South Africa
UBC	— Urban Bantu Council
UCASA	— Urban Councils Association of South Africa
UDF	— United Democratic Front
UF	— Urban Foundation
UN	— United Nations Organization
UNIP	— (Zambian) United National Independence Party
UP	— United Party
UTC	— Umlazi Trading Company
UWUSA	— United Workers Union of South Africa
WB	— (Inkatha) Women's Brigade
WCC	— World Council of Churches
WITCO	— Western Industrial and Trading Company
WRAB	— West Rand Administration Board
YB	— (Inkatha) Youth Brigade
YSC	— Youth Service Corps
ZTA	— Zululand Territorial Authority

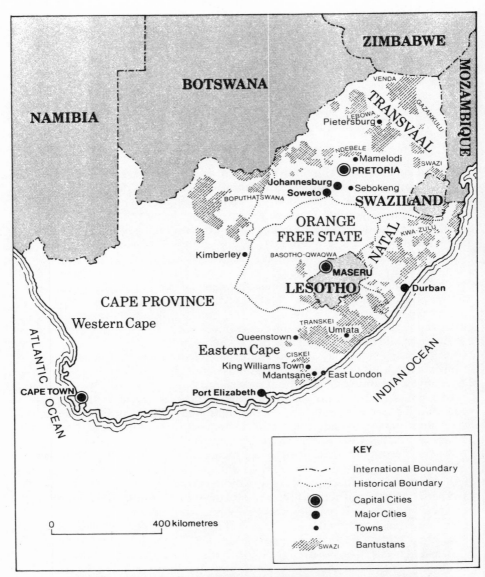

SOUTH AFRICA AND NEIGHBOURING STATES

Preface

Chief Gatsha Buthelezi's Inkatha movement now lays claim to an important role in the determination of South Africa's future. Over the past decade Buthelezi has enjoyed a prominence in the media — initially coloured by notoriety, but now smacking of hagiography — which surpasses that accorded to any other black South African leader. In addition to growing veneration by South Africa's media and promotion by the government, Buthelezi has received much favourable attention from Western governments, notably those of the USA, the UK and West Germany. There has been a tendency, verging on conspiracy, to ignore dangerous trends in Inkatha, trends that seem to be anti-democratic and are certainly against the long-term objectives of the South African working class.

A recent instance was when Buthelezi, guarded by his KwaZulu Police (a bantustan segment of the national police force), was the only prominent black leader to be allowed to hold a meeting on June 16, the tenth anniversary of the Soweto uprising, a few days after the state had declared a national emergency and following hundreds of deaths and thousands of detentions over the last two years. The irony of this meeting and the state's stamp of approval for Inkatha's role in these events has drawn no comment from Buthelezi's backers in the press, in white politics, in business locally and internationally. This is not unexpected, but these supporters must then share responsibility for the past, present and future actions and aims of Inkatha's leadership and some of its members.

This book arose out of the need for a critical examination of Inkatha at a crucial period of the history of South Africa, and particularly of Natal. Not only is Buthelezi vying for a decisive stake in national power-sharing but he has already travelled a disturbing distance towards securing the predominant role in ruling the province's future, as is manifest in the deliberations of the Natal Indaba.

Certain attacks on Inkatha and Buthelezi have been shallow, merely reflecting a moral rejection based on immediate events. We have attempted a deeper historical analysis of opposition in South Africa and in the Natal region.

This study has been shaped by the society in which we live in several ways. Access to information and the means to disseminate ideas and news are extremely restricted. The racial categorization and separation that have remained the essence of South Africa even during reform, have meant that many case studies of the day-to-day experience of African people in Inkatha-controlled KwaZulu and Natal remain to be done in order to flesh out our wider and more structural investigation. Hence we do not pretend here to grapple with the nature and organization of the Inkatha movement in a definitive way. This book is primarily an examination of the way in which Buthelezi projects and sells himself and his movement, and of how they have acted and responded to the competitive terrain of South African politics over the past decade.

1

Within these limits our work has been further circumscribed by detentions and the fear of reprisal which require the anonymity of some of the people we spoke to, and have probably prevented others from speaking to us at all. We have also been aware that 'white society' protects us to some extent from the threats and fears which engulf Africans in their communities.

Most of the written material on which this study is based has been collected by one of the authors. We wish to thank the many individuals and institutions who helped us, especially the libraries at the University of the Witwatersrand, the University of Natal (Killie Campbell), the Inkatha Institute, the Ecumenical Resource Centre in Durban and the South African Research Service in Johannesburg. A special word of thanks to the three researchers (DC, TR and LM) who undertook the task of finding, cataloguing, reading and indexing the hundreds of speeches Chief Buthelezi has delivered; to KH, who made some sense of the often contradictory and incomplete press coverage of the events of August 1985 around the city of Durban; to the students whose unpublished research material was made available to us, and to all the individuals from church, legal and community organizations we spoke to, called on and whose resources we used. We take full responsibility for how we have used the material they offered.

In South Africa it is regrettably necessary to use different words to refer to people classified by the state as being Indian, coloured, African and white, because the classification is the foundation of a policy that has given people vastly different life chances. It has forced them to live in different areas, to be able to do only certain kinds of work, to marry only approved people, to have extensive or no political rights at all, and in some cases to live or to die.

The state has changed its terminology to refer to Africans as 'blacks', no doubt partly influenced by the solidarity that 'black' has come to signify among oppressed people who reject the categorization into Indian, coloured and African groups. In this text, 'black' will be used to refer to this solidarity in oppression, and not to Africans only. Obviously terms used within quotations have been respected. Chief Buthelezi, for example, nearly always uses 'black' in the official government sense as referring to Africans.

It has also been necessary to refer to ethnic divisions within the African population, not because the official description of such divisions or the state policies flowing from them are accepted, but because they have an administrative reality (they form the foundation of the bantustan policy) and they have an ideological reality. They have been accepted by many people, both the manipulators of the ethnic sentiment and often the manipulated, as having a validity in describing conflicts and justifying actions. According to state policy there are ten African 'ethnic nationalisms' in South Africa, each one allocated to a bantustan: Xhosa to both the Transkei and the Ciskei for some reason, Zulu to KwaZulu, Tswana to Bophuthatswana, etc.

Postscript, June 1987

This book was completed in late 1986. While it is tempting to try for immediacy in writing contemporary history, it was not intended as a journalistic contribution to an understanding of struggle in South Africa.

Much has happened over the past eight months, but little need be added to our conclusions. On the contrary, events have rather confirmed the arguments we advocate.

While Inkatha has held back from involvement in the latest attempt by P.W. Botha to get negotiations with moderate African leaders under way through the National Statutory Council, the same reticence has not been shown in maintaining control over the regional population. At the passing out parade of KwaZulu police in 1987, Buthelezi praised South Africa's ex-spymaster and Commissioner of Police, General Johann Coetzee:

> I have never hidden the fact that I have a high regard for General Johann Coetzee, both as the highest officer in the South African Police Force and as a fellow South African.

KwaZulu has also been able to realize its goal of taking control of the important police stations in the major townships of KwaMashu and Umlazi. This is no victory for 'liberation' as it has been unambiguously stated by Buthelezi that the bantustan police are in the forefront of the struggle against the 'politics of intimidation' practised by the African National Congress and its 'surrogate' the United Democratic Front. Buthelezi asked Law and Order Minister A.J. Vlok, in 1987, that they

> . . . be put in a position where we can better defend that which so badly needs to be defended . . . I sincerely hope . . . that the South African Government will not continue to tie my hands at this level of my leadership [as KwaZulu minister of police] simply because I am an opponent of apartheid.

Furthermore, the KwaZulu police will now be allowed to stop and search any vehicle without a warrant and to seize any article. People suspected of involvement in, or withholding information about theft, violence or illegal possession of firearms and ammunition can now be detained for 90 days. This legislation was passed in the KwaZulu Legislative Assembly and without apparent pressure from the central government.

Politically, too, Inkatha is stepping up areas of control over Africans in the region while those who oppose the state suffer under the state of emergency. The attempt to establish a multi-racial and multi-cultural conservative legislature in the Natal region — the Indaba — has given tentative political form to an alliance between some large capitalist interests and the aspiring 'Zulu' capitalism within Inkatha. The 'Ngotshe Cooperation Agreement', between Inkatha and the white farming community of a politically sensitive border district in Northern Natal, gives the movement unprecedented access to a very large rural African population outside of KwaZulu, people notoriously inaccessible whether as farm labourers, or as 'squatters', In exchange Inkatha is to keep COSATU and other unions out (except possibly Inkatha's United Workers Union of South Africa), help prevent ANC infiltration, and keep control over the African workforce and those living on white-owned 'labour farms'.

Whereas previously KwaZulu employees had been asked for pledges of loyalty, a 1987 Act in the bantustan makes an oath of allegiance a condition of service in any section of its public service. The pledge also requires that no civil servant should 'directly or indirectly vilify, denigrate or in any manner speak in contempt of the Chief Minister, the Cabinet, members of the KwaZulu Legislative Assembly and all persons in authority in the KwaZulu Government service'. This is an oath of loyalty to a bantustan government, created under the apartheid policy, in which Buthelezi has claimed he is participating under duress, and primarily as a strategy.

Further confirmation that Inkatha perceives as hostile all activity that it does

3

not itself initiate, came when Buthelezi prorogued the KLA. He justified his action as enabling members to return to their constituencies and counter what he termed a declaration of 'war' in the stayaway call supported by progressive organizations in protest at the May 1987 whites-only general election.

In the propaganda field, Inkatha has revived a direct hold on the mass media that it lost when its own newspaper, *The Nation*, closed down. It has recently bought the Zulu-language newspaper *Ilanga* (founded by the first ANC president John Dube early in the century) from the Argus Company. Journalists who refused to work for a political party were sacked and the paper was kept going by seconded KwaZulu government staff.

There is a distressing silence from the media and from Inkatha's local and international political and economic supporters about the involvement of members of the movement in violence against opponents of the state. Instead, Buthelezi receives praise for his support for capitalism, his 'Christianity', and his 'moderation'. Their support also implicitly and explicitly extends to the ethnic belligerence that characterizes an increasing number of speeches by Buthelezi and King Goodwill, under the banner of 'Zulu renaissance' and the revival of the 'Zulu nation'.

At a time when organizations striving for a democratic South Africa struggle to overcome the racial and ethnic divisions that have served apartheid South Africa so well, Inkatha continues to exploit these differences and mobilize under ethnic calls.

Gerhard Maré
Georgina Hamilton

1. Introduction

On 1 May 1986 the Inkatha movement launched a pro-capitalist trade union amid a media fanfare. The next day newspapers reported that a poll conducted by the University of South Africa in 1985 had shown that Pretoria businessmen preferred Chief Buthelezi to President P.W. Botha as leader. Clearly Inkatha's message was reaching one of its most coveted audiences. Buthelezi has not always been received so well, even by this obviously conservative audience, but through persistent effort he has managed to present a picture of himself as a man offering a commodity that is increasingly valued by certain interests — it is not for nothing that he has described himself as a politician of the 'marketplace'.

In the view of some very influential reformers the Inkatha movement has an essential role to play in a changing South Africa. This is partly due to the way in which Chief Buthelezi has made himself and his followers available to conservative reformers. It has also been brought about through the tremendous pressure of popular resistance and the organizational forms and demands of that resistance. Whereas ten years ago Buthelezi and the National Cultural Liberation Movement, Inkatha, were perceived to be part of the radical opposition to apartheid and his approaches for participation were scorned, today the same overtures, in the context of recent events, have gained a level of acceptance by the state and even by business that would have been unthinkable in the mid-1970s. It is not that Buthelezi's position has changed, but that under pressure there are more takers for what he has to offer. This book shows why Inkatha has become so desirable, even if only as the result of a reluctant process of changed perceptions among the power-holders.

The same Afrikaans-language newspapers that criticized Buthelezi as recently as 1983 when he opposed the new constitution now advise that reform is all but impossible without his participation. The state that castigated and threatened him, and repeatedly attempted to undermine his position in the bantustan it had created, now nods with approval at his local endeavours to ensure stability and profitability, and tentatively offers him a national role. Probably the US government and large-scale economic interests in South Africa have been most consistent in their support for Buthelezi and his actions over the years, especially over the past decade. They, and the media they control or influence, have given both the man and the position that he holds greater coverage than any other opposition politician.

However, the same pressures that have brought what Buthelezi has to offer into line with what a number of conservative interests now feel they need are also rapidly making those offerings, those political commodities, inadequate to the times. It is the fear that they may already be obsolescent that has made the business community scurry to Lusaka to confer with the African National

5

Congress, whose time is now closer than at any other time in the 75 years of its existence. While Buthelezi is not yet irrelevant, he is probably being forced to define his position too clearly too soon, to reveal too many of the compromises he has had to make, to associate with the wrong interests, when political survival now depends on lack of clarity, on greater ambiguity and on fewer open compromises.

Broadly speaking, Buthelezi and Inkatha stand today for a multi-racial capitalism untainted by apartheid; for the politics of non-violence towards the central state, and hence for negotiations with the current holders of power; for 'constituency politics', which increasingly have come to mean less democratic representation of interests and more control over members (an indispensable element in the politics of consociationalism that Buthelezi is engaged in). They represent 'stability', which in the current context has come to mean taking action against the many other organizations of resistance, and compromise, both in terms of the nature of the vote (away from demands for universal franchise) and of the structure of a future South Africa (away from a unitary state). It is clear that it is more in the detail than in the principles that the apparent gulf between Buthelezi and the state now lies.

In the political 'marketplace' there are many competitors offering their ideas about change and attempting to gather a following to boost the relevance of their wares. The big prize is acceptance within the 'reform' process, a future place in a South Africa that will not have been too radically altered. Who will be indispensable largely depends on the kind of future that can be shaped through reluctant and piecemeal concessions. Outside the 'marketplace' at present are the organizations carving a new South Africa through struggle, largely rejecting the new façades that still rest firmly on the old foundations (SARS [ed], 1983).

There are competing notions of what the struggle for transformation in South Africa is about. To struggle for the vague constituency, 'the people', defined simply by their common (if variable) experience of domination, at this stage in South Africa's history is not as simple as it might have been ten years ago. Even when populist mobilization succeeds its hold is tenuous, open to alternative views of what holds people together and what sets them apart, and of what 'post-apartheid' South Africa will look like. The specific role of the working class cannot be unproblematically collapsed into populist mobilization. Buthelezi's populism, clearly class-specific, is the populism of the dominant classes demanding a reordering of the alliances of capitalism rather than a populism directed against capitalism itself.

The Inkatha movement, inextricably tied as it is to the bantustan policy and the structures created under that policy, has been subject to the same buffeting and erosion by mass revolt that has been directed at the central organs and values of racist and capitalist South Africa. This has clarified many aspects of the movement, exposing what had been hidden, confirming what some had argued and suspected. Inkatha has also had to enter into new alliances as old ones fell away — the fickleness of opportunist politics does not make for long-term friendships. For some Inkatha offers the last hope for a peaceful, negotiated settlement. For the state it may be the most hopeful partner in the first tentative steps beyond or away from the bantustan policy, steps aimed at bringing African people into the central power structure while maintaining a policy based on 'power-sharing' between 'groups' — a plurality of minorities. For millions Inkatha is a sellout. For thousands of its members Inkatha, like any populist organization, represents many options — they may belong to the same organization, but they have not all joined for the same reasons.

To give substance to this analysis we have examined the political history of the region within which Inkatha was formed and where it has its strongest base, Natal and KwaZulu. The movement is also analysed in relation to the political dynamics of 1980s South Africa. Since there is no neutral high ground in this society from which to survey and evaluate Inkatha or any other organization, we have measured Inkatha against the criteria of transformation of a society that is beyond reform.

Reform is the name of the process that the state says it has initiated, and that business, local and foreign-based, would like to see more effectively implemented. In other words, it is a process that is under the control of the dominant forces in South Africa. In order to maintain their dominance these forces are agreed that new participants have to be brought in, even if these new allies were the enemies of yesterday.

Transformation of South African society, on the other hand, will entail the total rejection of the racial and ethnic divisions that have been implemented and manipulated to fragment opposition, the establishment of a democracy in which all can participate in decisions that affect them at all levels and a society that is non-exploitative both internally and in relation to its southern African neighbours. Does Inkatha hinder or help the process of struggle towards such a society? What vision does the leadership of Inkatha present, through their words and deeds, of a future South Africa? Does that vision advance sectional interests or the demands of the majority? These are some of the questions to which we will suggest answers.

Of central importance to understanding the path along which Inkatha leaders have steered the organization is the distinction that is made between *regional* and *national* involvement and aspirations. This distinction can take many forms, such as that between 'Zulu' on the one hand, and 'African' on the other, or between 'ethnic group' and 'nation', 'KwaZulu' and 'South Africa'. Chief Buthelezi expressed it like this in 1976:

> We must accept regional politics as a reality which existed long before we were conquered. The danger comes only when some people allow themselves to be blinded by regional involvement to the exclusion of any participation in the cause of all Blacks . . . [I]t is so much poppycock . . . for people to imply that, being involved in regional politics, one is necessarily undermining Black unity. The people in these Reserve areas have to exist and they should be helped by us, and we by them, in our attempts to eke out an existence, even within our dreary circumstances.
>
> This means that we have to face the fact that we have day-to-day goals, as we have to live for 365 days each year and every year. On the other hand, we must have long-term goals which are in the interests of our common Black struggle in the whole of South Africa. *I have never been confused about the line between these two phases* of our Black struggle [KLAD, 8:85-6, emphasis added].

This important statement draws attention to the tension between regional involvement (which Buthelezi equates with 'short-term day-to-day goals'), and national aspirations ('long-term goals'). This tension has brought about many apparent ambiguities in the role that Inkatha and Buthelezi play within South African politics, and has consciously been used to foster confusion. While Buthelezi claims never to have been confused about the distinction he drew, this study shows that the nature of his 'involvement in regional politics' irrevocably taints his claim to be involved in 'the interests of our common Black struggle'.

7

Inkatha, as an integral part of apartheid's ethnic separation, cannot be part of the successful transformation of South Africa. Neither can Buthelezi successfully hold what he claims to be a 'traditional' leadership role within the 'Zulu nation' and at the same time lead a struggle on behalf of all African people in South Africa. The content of Inkatha's 'national struggle' must also be examined.

The region within which Buthelezi has chosen to wage the 'day-to-day' struggle on behalf of the people living there is largely confined within the province of Natal. (Unless otherwise stated 'Natal', in this chapter, refers to the provincial boundaries, including KwaZulu). Natal is one of the four provinces that were created within the Union of South Africa in 1910. The Union brought together the Boer Republics that had been defeated in the Anglo-Boer war at the turn of the century and the colonies of the Cape and Natal. It also integrated the African, coloured and Indian populations without their participation in deciding the form or the content of the new state.

Natal occupies an area of some 91 355 km², or 8.1% of the total land area of South Africa,* but with 20% of the total South African population resident there it has a population density more than twice as high as the national average. The bits and pieces that make up the KwaZulu administrative area total about 38% of the province's land area, but account for 55% of its population.

Most of South Africa's Zulu-speaking African population is concentrated in Natal (75% of the total), while about 90% of Africans resident in the province are Zulu-speaking. The remainder are mostly Xhosa-speaking and live in and around the urban areas (BC Report, vol. 1, nd:69-72). The African population of Natal is about 4.7mn (or 77% of the total population of the province). Official figures allocate about 3.9mn to KwaZulu and all but 700 000 of these to 'rural' KwaZulu. With the enormous and rapid movement of people into 'informal settlements' — shanties, slums, squatter areas around the Durban/Pinetown and Pietermaritzburg industrial areas — this last figure is clearly a vast underestimate. Haarhoff (1985:39) argued that about 1.5mn Africans live in an urban environment in the Natal region, 65% of them in the Durban urban area.

Several processes are at work here. First, the state has attempted to relocate as large a part of the African population as is possible to the bantustans, and to confine them there except for periods during which they sell their labour within 'white' South Africa. The bantustan land areas were legally established through the 1913 and 1936 'Land Acts', and given ethnic and political identity under the National Party (NP) government through, for example, the Promotion of Bantu Self-Government Act of 1959. Control over movement from the bantustans was attempted through influx control — the 'Pass Laws' (recently abolished). Second, there are the Africans who have attempted to establish a legal presence outside the bantustans, through so-called 'section 10' rights. 'Section 10' of the Natives (Urban Areas) Consolidation Act spells out the strict conditions under which Africans may live outside the bantustans (see Horrell, 1978:174). In Natal these 'rights' were frequently abolished through the administrative incorporation of townships, such as KwaMashu, into KwaZulu. While the residents of these

---

*These official figures for 1985 exclude the so-called 'independent' bantustans. If these were taken into account Natal would account for an even smaller percentage of the total land area of South Africa. Official figures are notoriously unreliable in South Africa, and are qualified by the policy contortions of apartheid. For example, the populations and the land area of the 'independent' bantustans (the Transkei, Bophuthatswana, Venda and the Ciskei) are excluded from national statistics. It is therefore frequently necessary to refer to unofficial counts and estimates.

townships are within the jurisdiction of KwaZulu they have continued to live within commuting distance of the industrial areas situated within 'white' South Africa. The third process is the movement of people, in defiance of the law as it stood until recently, from the bantustans to live in 'white' South Africa in order to be with family or to find employment.

Finally there has been the conglomeration of people into the urban areas of Natal, but still within the boundaries of KwaZulu. This movement has been motivated by a number of factors, probably the most important of which has been the destitution of the outlying areas and the possibility (no matter how remote) of employment, or some other means of making money, closer to industrial and urban concentrations. In Natal it was possible without breaking the Pass Laws because of the proximity of pieces of KwaZulu land to industrial and urban areas. This in contrast to the western Cape, where squatter camps such as Crossroads are hundreds of kilometers from the nearest bantustans, the Ciskei and the Transkei, in the eastern Cape. The African residents of Crossroads were therefore always in contravention of influx control laws unless they had acquired 'section 10' status (see, for example, SPP, vol.3, 1983; Platzky and Walker, 1985).

The distribution of KwaZulu's land has also affected the number of people who commute to work daily, rather than migrate to industrial areas within the province. Of a total of 1 329 000 African migrant workers in South Africa in 1981, 280 000 (or 21%) were from Natal (obviously not all were migrating to jobs within the region). This compares with 384 200 commuters in Natal, or 52% of the national total of 'frontier commuters employed in "white" areas' Survey, 1983:138). The Indian population of the province, having arrived primarily as indentured labour for the fledgling sugar industry in the 1860s, today comprises about 11.3% of Natal's population. This makes them the second largest group, followed by whites (10%) and coloureds (1.5%).

Immediately after its annexation by the British in the mid-19th century, Natal lacked a viable base on which a settler economy could be built, and was starved of financial resources. This changed with the planting of sugar. The first public sale of the crop occurred in 1856, and by the end of the decade sugar was being exported to the Cape colony. It was also at this time (1860) that the labour needs of the sugar growers forced them to look beyond the colony and to import indentured labour from India (see p.19).

Both sugar and wattle, Natal's other main crop, were established and maintained over the years as extremely labour-repressive activities, with poverty wages and poor living conditions. This and the fact of foreign ownership have made both industries the subject of critical enquiries into wages and working conditions over the last 15 years.

African economic activity during the 19th century was not solely agriculturally based. As Etherington commented:

> By the time of the Anglo-Zulu war, African Christian communities had not only established a flourishing peasant economy, but had also embarked upon entrepreneurial capitalist ventures on a significant scale.

He suggests that measures taken by white settlers to curb the economic activities of Africans through legislation

> were not so much designed to safeguard Whites against potential Black competition, but aimed rather to undo progress which had already been made. Moreover, it is at least arguable that the rise of political activism and religious separatism at the end of

9

the nineteenth century owed more to the loss of valued economic opportunities than to a newly awakened desire to compete on equal terms in the dominant society [1985:265].

Defence or promotion of commercial interests by a petty bourgeoisie claiming a 'Zulu identity' came to the fore both in the 1920s and the 1970s around 'Zulu' political movements — both called Inkatha*. Agricultural activity became more and more difficult after the 1913 Land Act froze the acquisition of land by Africans. During the time of the first Inkatha it was largely around agricultural activity, based on mission land and freehold farms, that the petty bourgeoisie consolidated and sought to safeguard their 'valued economic opportunities'. In the 1970s, trading and services were the areas of most rapid expansion, largely through the involvement of the state's Bantu Investment Corporation (BIC).

In the 1920s the worries and the woes of the African petty bourgeoisie were on the periphery of the growth of capitalism in the region (except when they were needed as allies in labour recruitment for larger concerns). The centre was provided by the sugar industry and the concerns that grew up around it (Sitas et al, 1984:6). This made for a regionally specific economy, even if not an independent economy (see Marks, 1981:11), until the central state policy to stimulate a national capitalism started having its effects on Natal. After 1910, when the Union of South Africa came into being, 'the Natal bourgeoisie became part of a national bourgeoisie' (Marks, 1986:13). This was not a sudden event but a process, and for some time there was conflict over the flow of labour from the atrocious conditions of the sugar, wattle, and coal industries to the slightly better conditions of the Transvaal mines.

The process of incorporation through ownership and control took rapid strides during the decades starting from the 1960s. Sitas et al have discussed 'some of the linkages which ultimately subordinate a large proportion of Natal's industry to the control of large national or foreign corporations' (1984:22). They found that with concentration and centralization of ownership and control of capital in South Africa generally, employment was stabilized, but this stability applied to a smaller and smaller proportion of the work force. Manufacturing output increased during the 1960s by 8.51% while employment in this sector grew by 5.64%. During the 1970s output grew by 5.43% and employment by a mere 2.82% (quoted Sitas et al, 1984:24).

Natal has not been exempt from this trend that has thrown about 25% of South Africa's workforce (or 3 mn people) out of work (Thomas, 1986). Sitas et al argued that the maintenance of a relatively stable work force, linked to skill and length of employment, has occurred in Natal as well, with the concomitant unemployment on a fairly permanent basis especially of young entrants to the job market and people far removed from urban centres (1984:28; 48).

Productive activity remains regionally tied, though it is no longer correct to talk of a regionally specific capitalism. Access to the port, labour, water, decentralization subsidies, favourable climatic conditions, etc., all serve to favour one place against another for accumulation purposes. Probably the most important aspect of regional preference at present and in the foreseeable future is that of stability. It is in this context that the 'regional options' such as the KwaZulu/Natal 'Indaba' become central, and political and economic alliances with African economic interests are essential to a nationally controlled but

---

*See Appendix 1 for the meaning of *Inkatha*.

regionally based monopoly capitalism and its political representatives (on the Natal economy, also see Stanwix, 1983).

The policy of 'separate development' (as the so-called 'positive aspects' of apartheid came to be called) attempted to give dignity to the idea that South Africa is basically composed of 'First' and 'Third World' components, rather than the more directly racial categorization of backward African and advanced white segments of the population. The terminology was used to 'explain' and justify the stark contrasts (in living standards, educational and social facilities, incomes, health, etc) between white society and the African population. The 'Third World' is then given convenient geographic form through the enforced separation of Africans into the bantustans. Within this dualism everybody is 'developing' but has started from a different point and hence advances at a different rate. At some distant future point the existing inequalities will, so the argument goes, be overcome. Until then the slogan is 'patience'.

That was, and in many circles still is, the dominant argument in Natal, except that the clear geographic distinction does not exist to the same extent as elsewhere in South Africa and on certain levels, even if only administratively, an interrelationship between the racial groups has to be acknowledged. Artificial separation leads to instability. It was not for nothing that the report of the Buthelezi Commission was entitled *The Requirements for Stability and Development in KwaZulu and Natal*, taking that interdependence as a starting point. The same demands for stability and acknowledgement of the interwoven character of Natal revived interest in the 'KwaZulu/Natal Option'.

The interrelationship is, however, not only on the level of employment, residence, infrastructure, services, recreational facilities, etc.; another element is that the wealth that has been channelled into white hands originates from the poverty of the black, especially the African, population.

Nattrass wrote (1985:50) that

> South Africa enjoys the somewhat dubious distinction of having one of the most unequal distributions of income in the world. Not only is income unequally distributed here, but the inequality also has a racial overlay and is partnered by the continuance of significant poverty.

She compared the national picture with that of Natal, and concluded that

> Whilst KwaZulu/Natal region has a different demographic, ethnic and economic structure from that of the rest of the Republic, these differences have not had a marked impact on either the income distribution or the lifestyles in the region. White standards of living in this area are, on average, five times better than those of the Indian and Coloured communities and nearly 12 times greater than those of the Black regions, and within the Black community there is a gap emerging between urban and rural lifestyles.

In 1976, 56% of the economically active population of KwaZulu were employed outside the bantustan (SPP, vol 4, 1983:4). This has meant that in typical KwaZulu rural areas 'between 70 and 80 per cent of families have members away as migrant workers' (Nattrass, 1985:55). More than a third of the population of KwaZulu is landless, and it is therefore no wonder that migrant remittances far exceed KwaZulu's internal revenue creation. Nattrass refers to a study of three districts that showed that these remittances, even though a small percentage of the migrants' actual incomes (about 17%), still made up some 75% of total household incomes (1985:55). Apart from employment within the KwaZulu administration services (as public servants, nurses, labourers in the department of works, teachers, etc.), there are few jobs. In 1981 6122 people were employed in industrial undertakings in the bantustans. All except 700 of these jobs were at the Isithebe industrial 'growth point'. Some 30 000 new job-seekers enter the job market in the region every year (SPP, vol 4, 1983:4). By 1984 the number of employees at Isithebe had increased to 11 000, while another 1 200 people found work at Ezakheni, also within KwaZulu. 'Other things being equal,' said Corporation for Economic Development chair Professor S.P. du Toit Viljoen in 1977 at Isithebe, KwaZulu could become the 'Ruhr of South Africa' (FM special report on KwaZulu, 11 May 79). But of course 'other things' are not equal in South Africa, and one of those inequalities is the totally skewed power relations that have existed for so many years, both between races and classes.

KwaZulu, for which Chief Buthelezi has taken responsibility and in which he hoped to achieve some measure of development, cannot ever hope to feed its population, provide them with jobs, and improve the general standard of living in terms of basic facilities, infant mortality, education levels, employment, social and health services, etc. Under the existing structural power relationships, and even in some solutions for the future (see Giliomee and Schlemmer [eds], 1985), this inequality forms part of the whole. The rich are rich because the poor are poor. In 1982/3 the white-controlled Natal Provincial Administration spent four times as much on health facilities for all race groups as the KwaZulu authorities did. Pensions for whites far exceed those paid to blacks.

In fact KwaZulu is only a distinct region in that it is artificially maintained as such, reinforced through participation of some Africans in that maintenance, even if such participation is hedged with qualifications. The effect is that its existence, as with the other bantustans, serves to deflect responsibility from the central state and capital in South Africa on to the KwaZulu authority and on to the people who live there (the 'Third World' component). As recently as early 1986 parliament was told that 'South Africa's Third World component was too large for (the) housing goals' that would have to be met if influx control was truly scrapped, instead of being replaced with the euphemistically named 'orderly urbanization strategy' (National Party Member of Parliament, DN, 6 Feb. 86). A policy of blaming the victims, who are largely located in the bantustans, is all too common in South Africa.

Stanwix (1983:55) noted that the population in Natal is poorer than in South Africa as a whole (probably in large measure due to the relatively small white population in the province, which serves elsewhere to push up the average income). He also noted that in Natal 'there are severe inequalities between the KwaZulu component and the rest of the region as well as marked differences in their composition of economic activity'.

However, he warned that this does not prove the 'existence of two clearly differentiated sub-regions . . . [but rather these factors] reflect much more the integration of these components and the arbitrary (in economic terms) nature of the KwaZulu boundaries' (1983:55).

A glance at the map shows the fragmentary nature of KwaZulu, and also casts a great deal of doubt on Buthelezi's contention that his involvement in KwaZulu is partly justified by the need for regional development (that region being KwaZulu). KwaZulu exists as a separate entity in terms of administration and legislative control, and of ideology (to justify the vast inequalities between the races), but geographically there is little to justify it.

The rest of this book falls into into three sections. Chapters 2 and 3 provide background on the formation of Inkatha. Chapter 2 deals with the historical material without which it is impossible to understand the dynamics that allowed such a movement to arise and to grow to the prominence it has achieved. Chapter 3 takes up the history of Africans in Natal from 1948, the year in which the National Party (NP) came to power. The first legislation in the process of fragmentation of the African population that was to lead to the 'independence' of the Transkei 25 years later was the Bantu Authorities Act of 1951. This Act reaffirmed and redefined the role of chiefs and the 'tribe' as the base of an administrative pyramid. The bantustan legislative assemblies were to become the peaks of these pyramids. It was into this apartheid-affirmed stucture, and not (as he was to maintain later) simply into some idealized notion of traditional authority, that Chief Mangosuthu Gatsha Buthelezi stepped in the early 1950s, to take up his position as chief of the Buthelezi tribe.

In 1959 the Promotion of Bantu Self-Government Act made provision for the ultimate independence of the bantustans, and gave greater clarity to the other two layers within each ethnic pyramid, namely the regional authorities and territorial authorities (tribal authorities had already been provided for in 1951). The regional authorities were to supply the majority of members of the bantustan legislative assemblies — their 'parliaments'. This meant that chiefs always outnumbered elected members in these bodies. The territorial authorities became the legislative assemblies: for example, the Zulu Territorial Authority (ZTA), formed in 1970, became in 1972 the KwaZulu Legislative Assembly (KLA). Chief Buthelezi, although rejecting the state-envisaged final goal of 'independence' and having resisted the establishment of tribal authorities for a while during the 1960s, became head of the ZTA in 1970 and has since been in command of the KLA.

Chapters 4 and 5 deal with the formation (or re-formation) of the Inkatha movement in 1975 and with the structures of the organization. Chapter 4 examines the process of reformation, and the earlier origins of a specifically Zulu organization in the Inkatha of the 1920s of which King Solomon was the patron. Chapter 5 provides information on the constitution and constitutional changes that have taken place, on the Women's and Youth Brigades of Inkatha, and on membership and methods of recruitment.

Chapters 6-8 give content to the previous chapters by examining the Inkatha movement 'in action'. Chapter 6 deals with Inkatha's economic policies and relationships to capital, and labour. It discusses the early and increasing involvement of Inkatha in direct economic enterprises, albeit largely through development corporations and white-owned capital and spells out some of the implications of this involvement. Chapter 7 focuses mainly on the relationship between Inkatha and the ANC as it is this that illustrates and explains much of the movement's antagonism to opposition groups while it enjoys a fairly cordial relationship with white parliamentary parties. Chapter 8 deals with Inkatha's controversial role in suppressing such activities as schools boycotts and consumer boycotts — controversial because it appears to run counter to claims made by Inkatha leaders that it adheres strictly to a policy of non-violence and change through dialogue.

In the final chapter conclusions are drawn and points made in the text of the book are consolidated.

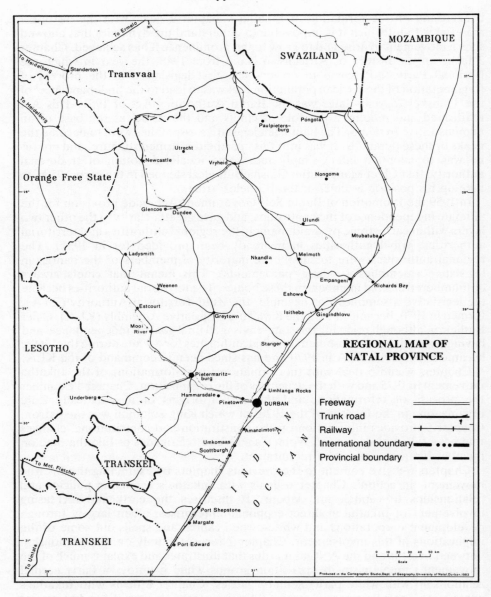

REGIONAL MAP OF
NATAL PROVINCE

Freeway
Trunk road
Railway
International boundary
Provincial boundary

2. The Availability of the Past

King Cetshwayo kaMpande . . . was my maternal great grandfather. I am the son of his granddaughter, Princess Constance Magogo Sibilile Matithi Ngangezinye kaDinuzulu, full sister to King Solomon Nkayishana kaDinuzulu, and of the Senior Prince Mshiyeni Arthur Edward, former Zulu Regent during the minority of King Cyprian Bhekuzulu Nyangavezizwe kaSolomon, father of our present Monarch, His Majesty King Zwelithini Mbongi Goodwill kaBhekuzulu. I am also proud of the fact that on my father's side my family has served the Zulu Kingdom for so many generations, and that my paternal great grandfather, Myamana Buthelezi was Prime Minister of the Zulu Nation during King Cetshwayo's reign and also Commander-in-Chief of the Zulu army.

With these words Chief Mangosuthu Gatsha Buthelezi, chief minister of KwaZulu, president of Inkatha and chairman of the South African Black Alliance, laid claim to a specific ethnic tradition within 1980s South Africa (see diagrams, pp.16,22). He was writing the foreword to a booklet on King Cetshwayo published by the KwaZulu Monuments Council (Laband and Wright, 1983).

Buthelezi continued with several references to the 'Zulu Nation', and placed the administrative capital of the KwaZulu bantustan, Ulundi, within that history: 'From this place of our forefathers, we are pursuing the ideals of establishing a free and open society . . .' (1983:xi). Chief Buthelezi is extremely aware of and sensitive about the historical tradition that underpins modern 'Zulu' identity and gives legitimacy to his participation in the politics of the 'Zulu Nation', as distinct from participation in the apartheid-created KwaZulu bantustan. This awareness is displayed in frequent tracings of his genealogy in his speeches (eg STb, 6 Nov. 83; Ngubane, 1976:121-22; BS, 26 Oct. 76:4-6, 7 Feb. 79:1).

However, it is not only Buthelezi's personal history that has given a measure of coherence to the ethnic identity of the Zulu-speakers of Natal, but also the history of Africans in south-eastern Africa since the late 18th century, and especially since the colonial occupation of Natal in the 1840s. It was in this period that the patterns of government, labour exploitation and land occupation were established that were subsequently to be given extreme expression under apartheid, with its massive population removals, racial separation, political exclusion, labour exploitation and allocation, and concomitant repression of the vast majority of the country's people.*

---

*This chapter relies heavily on Beall, et al, 1984, 1986; and Maré, 1982.

GENEALOGY OF THE ZULU KINGS

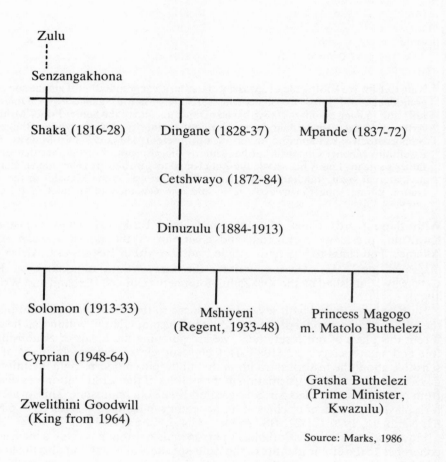

Zulu
⋮
Senzangakhona

Shaka (1816-28)   Dingane (1828-37)   Mpande (1837-72)

Cetshwayo (1872-84)

Dinuzulu (1884-1913)

Solomon (1913-33)   Mshiyeni   Princess Magogo
(Regent, 1933-48)   m. Matolo Buthelezi

Cyprian (1948-64)

Gatsha Buthelezi
(Prime Minister,
Kwazulu)

Zwelithini Goodwill
(King from 1964)

Source: Marks, 1986

In the early 19th century the strongest state yet seen in south-east Africa emerged under the leadership of Shaka Zulu. The formation of this state involved deep-seated changes in the social and economic structures of the productive units that made up the Zulu nation. As Peires has written (1981:8), the effect of all these changes was to produce 'one of the most arresting features of the Zulu state . . . its capacity to harness the energy of its subjects in its service'. This, in turn, meant that the Zulu state was able to withstand the political, military and, importantly, the economic pressures of colonialism until late in the century. The existence of such a definite and relatively long-lasting political entity, and its resistance to colonialism, has made available to Buthelezi, as it had to ethnic politicians before him, a rich tradition of symbols that could be used to mobilize a regional population.

The first penetration of the Zulu state by the forces of colonialism was through the agency of hunters, traders and missionaries, even while the political power of this state was wholly unchallenged. Later, while the area in which the Zulu kings continued to rule was drastically reduced through first Trekboer and then British colonial occupation of the area south of the Tugela river (see map), trade still did not fundamentally disrupt the economic and social organization of the kingdom. Trade between Natal and Zululand in the mid-19th century was mainly (except for firearms) in industrially produced goods that were already available in the pre-capitalist society, such as blankets, hoes and picks, even if the products from Europe might have been more efficient. Moreover,

> the trader gained possession of the surplus commodity already produced in the country (cattle or hides) and thus demanded no alteration to the process of production [Guy, 1982:15-16].

Zulu society was, therefore, left fairly intact under the economic pressure of merchant capital.

In colonial Natal the fact that colonialism made its effect felt in the form of finance capital (or speculative capital), also served (at least in part) to allow a measure of resistance on the part of the African population to the ravages of wage labour. Speculators bought up large areas of Natal in the hope that land prices would increase and profits could be made. By 1870 the land area held by speculators reached a high of nearly 30% of the land available in Natal (ie excluding Zululand) (Christopher, 1969:351). This land was used for what was known as 'Kaffir farming', or renting out to Africans, much to the disgust of colonial farmers, who felt that this practice was depriving them of labour. At this time the colonial administrative authority was not willing to use reduction in the land area available to Africans to force African labour to work on commercial farms. This does not mean that other methods, such as taxation, were not used. The local colonial authorities were:

> sufficiently aware of the realities of the situation to know that a frontal attack on the African way of life, and the appropriation of their land was not possible. He [Shepstone, the Secretary for Native Affairs in Natal] therefore supported the idea of leaving Africans in possession of large tracts of land, but, by gradually usurping political control, diverting the surplus products of labour created in African societies to support colonial systems of government [Guy, 1979:9; also Etherington, 1979].

The effects, first, of colonial demands for cheap administration and the inability to subdue militarily the Zulu kingdom north of the Tugela river, and, second, continued access to speculators' land, reserves or locations in Natal, and the land within Zululand proper, allowed the Zulu state to retain its essential autonomy. Africans in Natal generally were able to avoid having to labour for colonists — at least on a large-scale — until the last quarter of the 19th century. It was only in 1897 that the Zulu kingdom was incorporated into the colony of Natal, and only in the early 20th century that white occupation of land within Zululand took place, 'later than almost every other case in southern Africa' (Beall, et al, 1986). The effect was to leave a legacy of unconsolidated land occupied by Africans, and the symbols of continuity, resistance and apparent Zulu political and cultural coherence that could be used by subsequent regional leaders.

The availability of land was not only important in the avoidance of wage labour for a longer time than elsewhere, but also allowed the continuation, albeit under perpetually changing 'tribal' conditions, of 'traditional' authority structures — the chiefs and councillors. The system of indirect rule established in the mid-19th century, also as a result of demands for cheap administration in a poor colony, sought to transform the administrative power of the chiefs (both hereditary and appointed). As Justice Beaumont pointed out in 1905,

> In Natal you are undermining the authority of the Chiefs every day. Every act dealing with the Natives that is passed more or less undermines the authority of the Chiefs, and, on the other hand, you are trying to bolster them up to retain their position . . . [Marks, 1970:14].

The powers that were given to chiefs by the colonial authority were of a different nature to the powers they had had in independent pre-colonial societies; the effect was to undermine the legitimacy of their position because such absolute power would not have been countenanced. Furthermore,

> . . . The most fundamental prop of chieftainly power, the chief's power to grant his followers land and cattle, had been undermined by the pressures of population within the Reserves, and the severe cattle diseases which had decimated African-owned cattle in the colony at the turn of the century [Marks, 1970:41].

While the Zulu kingdom and Africans in Natal had been able to hold out against the demands of capitalism for labour and land for longer than most, when the inevitable collapse came it was as overwhelming as elsewhere in its impact on the economic, social and political life of Africans. It benefited white agriculturalists, industrialists and mining interests, who now had greater access to cheap labour. The turning point came with the Bambatha rebellion in 1906, the last major resistance of an African chief against capitalist encroachment, and, in the light of the 19th century history of the region, it was no surprise that it should have occurred in Natal, now including Zululand (for an excellent and full discussion of the events see Marks, 1970). Roux wrote that the rebellion distinguished

> between two periods in the history of the black man in South Africa: the early period of tribal wars against the white invaders . . .; and the second period, one of struggle for national and democratic rights within the framework of present-day South Africa where black and white intermingle in complex economic and political relationships [1964:87].

The rebellion was about labour, and specifically the £1 head tax imposed by the Natal Government in 1905 on every male over the age of 18. This tax, it was hoped, would both raise revenue and force Africans into wage employment. The rebellion of Chief Bambatha of the Greytown district drew the full wrath and military power of the colonial and settler authority because of fears it would lead to a consolidation of resistance under the Zulu King Dinuzulu. In a massacre in which British troops used machine guns against the warriors, between 3000 and 4000 of Bambatha's followers and those of the chiefs who had joined him were mown down in the Nkandla forests (Marks, 1986:29). Bambatha's head was cut off and displayed to prove that he was dead and the rebellion over. In the same year, 1906, John Dube, who was later to become the first president of the movement that was later called the African National Congress, started a newspaper in Natal called *Ilanga lase Natal*. This was to be the new direction of political action.

The population mix of modern-day Natal was also largely established in the 19th century. The African population had been scattered by the wars that accompanied the formation of the state under the Zulu people led by Shaka. It was this disruption that allowed Boers and British to settle south of the Tugela and then to contain many Africans within reserves (locations) in Natal on their return to their land.

Natal never attracted large numbers of colonial settlers, and there were several reasons for this. The threat that was continually felt to be posed by the unvanquished Zulu kingdom just to the north, the difficulty in finding crops that would provide an economic base for the various emigration schemes that were offered to people in Britain and the greater attraction of emigration to established colonies such as Canada all served to place Natal low on the list for potential settlers. It was on the Cape that the British first placed their hope for a viable colonial economy in southern Africa. However, the settlers who did arrive were largely of British stock, and many of the Boers who had preceded British occupation and ultimate annexation in 1845 left Natal to avoid the colonial system they had fled in the Cape colony (see, for example, Brookes and Webb, 1979).

The Indian community that now outnumbers the whites in the province owes its presence to the unwillingness of Africans in Natal to work for the wages and under the conditions that applied on the sugar plantations in the colony. About 90% of the Indians who came to Natal arrived as indentured labourers from 1860, and stayed on after the completion of their period of indenture. They remained as labourers, servants, in the fishing industry, as traders, professionals, market gardeners, farmers and in many other occupations. Today most of the economically active Indian population is employed in industry, filling many of the positions of supervision between white owners and unskilled African workers, but also working alongside Africans in all occupations and together belonging to worker organizations and political organisations such as the United Democratic Front (UDF) and the Azanian People's Organization (AZAPO).

In the 20th century the discriminatory practices established in Natal during the previous century were formalized. Land allocations were given legislative form in the 'Land Acts' of 1913 and 1936, allocating 35% of Natal and a derisory 13% of the total land area of South Africa to 80% of the national population. As the Surplus People Project (SPP) commented,

> By providing that only strictly defined areas would henceforth be open to African ownership and occupation, and by placing the power to determine and regulate these areas in the hands of the all-white Parliament, it put a stop to the previous very limited purchase of freehold land on the open market by Africans and furthermore made isolated African properties that had already been bought vulnerable to the charge that they were misplaced in white territory [SPP, vol 4, 1983:34].

Years later these 'isolated African properties' came to be called 'black spots' by the National Party government, and subject to forcible removal from the white-owned areas which surrounded them. After 25 years of the removals policy, the populations of these areas are still being added to the overcrowded land that is KwaZulu.

As in the rest of South Africa, the clearing of 'black spots' was not the only reason Africans were relocated into the reserves and later the bantustans (see Maré, 1980; SPP, 1983; Platzky and Walker, 1985). Whatever the reason, and they have all been racially discriminatory, the effects have been human misery, anger and a settlement pattern that has crowded the bantustans far beyond any possibility of subsistence production. The SPP (vol 4, 1983:53) estimated that between 1948 (when the National Party took power) and 1982 about 750 000 Africans, Indians and coloured people had been removed in Natal and relocated elsewhere, with another 600 000 Africans under threat of removal.

On a national scale this shift in population is illustrated in the table below (Roux, et al, 1982):

Geographic Distribution of the De Facto African Population:

	1960	1970	1980
Urban Areas	29%	28%	25%
Rural Areas	31%	25%	21%
Bantustans	40%	47%	54%

If we look at Natal we find confirmation of this population shift. In the Nqutu area of KwaZulu, infamous as a relocation site, the Tomlinson Commission, investigating conditions under which the African areas could be made economically (agriculturally) viable, recommended a population of 13 000. If implemented this would have meant that at the time (the early 1950s) about 5000 families would have had to be moved from Nqutu. Most of the people there could only live on their own produce for between five and seven months of the year. However, rather than decreasing, the population had risen to an estimated 200 000 people by 1979 (Maré, 1980:13). At that time '30% of the householders had no land at all to cultivate' (Clarke, 1978:11), while 70% of the economically active population of the area were forced to migrate in search of work (Barker, 1974:5). This example could be multiplied countless times in KwaZulu, and in other bantustans. The social and economic disintegration of these areas is enormous, and is integrally related to the affluence that characterizes most of 'white' South Africa and the profitability of capitalist production in the country.

On the administrative level a similar process of exclusion from central processes and the simultaneous maintenance of supposedly 'traditional' structures (such as the chiefs) occurred during the 20th century. The provincial system of second-tier government for whites within the Union of South Africa that was created in 1910 was in part a reaction from the other delegations to the demands for even greater autonomy by the Natal contingent to the pre-Union conference. White Natalians (Africans were totally excluded from the deliberations) wanted a federal system to allow the province freedom to give expression to its 'British tradition', which they felt would be lost under a centralized government. This the other delegates were not willing to grant, fearing the 'sort of plague spot and public danger' that Natal's administration of Africans had created in the region. The memory of the Bambatha rebellion was still fresh in the memory of the delegates. It was hoped that Natal's closer incorporation into the Union, as a province, would put an end to this 'mismanagement' (Marks, 1970:353). The provincial system was, therefore, a compromise between a unitary state and a federation. In a way similar to the manufacturing or maintaining of the tradition of the 'Zulu Nation', there has also been a made tradition of white Natalian ethnicity, with a set of values that bear little relation to the practice of this community. Language rights, 'liberalism', a more easy-going attitude to life in general and a less tense relationship with the African population are claimed to be important elements of these values.

As if their exclusion from the deliberation that led to Union was not enough, all anti-Union meetings by Africans in Natal were banned, and the few Africans who had the vote in the colony (three in 1903, six in 1909, and three in 1931) were later removed from all participation in a vote for central authority.

In 1936 two important Acts were passed: the Trust and Land Act, which added a 'quota' of land to the land 'scheduled' for African occupation in the 1913 Land Act (Horrell, 1978:203) but confirmed the principle of racial separation, and the Representation of Natives Act, which entitled Africans in Natal to elect, indirectly, a single senator to the central government. The elections were to take place through chiefs, local councils and advisory boards. The Act also established the Native Representative Council (NRC), on which one nominated and three representative members from Natal were to serve. The nominated member, until the NRC was disbanded in 1951, was Mshiyeni kaDinuzulu, acting paramount chief of the Zulus (see box, p.16). Other posts were filled by such people as John L. Dube, first president of the South African Native National Congress (later the African National Congress), and Chief Albert Luthuli, later to become president of the ANC until the organization was banned by the state in 1960. They were both involved in Natal as well as national politics.

The NRC was initially called the 'official mouthpiece of the African people' by the conservative president-general of the ANC, Rev S. Mahabane, who had been re-elected in 1937 (Walshe, 1970:127). For some years the ANC tried to make support for the NRC a major part of its policy. In the 1942 elections for the NRC the ANC gained 'an informal but real influence through at least seven of the 16-member Council' (Walshe, 1970:271). James Calata, secretary-general of the ANC from 1936 to 1949, said the Congress had 'succeeded in sending Congressmen to the NRC without saying so'. However, by 1944 some of these members were urging the government to abandon all segregationist legislation, and by 1946 a resolution was moved in the ANC proposing a boycott of the NRC. The futility of the previous policy of 'working within the system' was becoming clear. As Walshe wrote,

At this point [by 1948] Congress, with the Youth League in the vanguard, came to accept the need for non-collaboration in the NRC, the 'Programme of Action' and the systematic use of passive resistance as in the Defiance Campaign of 1952 [1970:370].

The NRC was eventually abolished by the National Party government in 1951. The Bantu Authorities Act of that year both did away with the NRC and made provision for tribal and regional authorities, redefining and re-emphasizing the resolve of white political authority to maintain control through untraditionally static and strong 'traditional tribal' structures. What must be borne in mind is that while the origins of these structures lie in the policies developed by the colonial authorities in Natal from the mid-19th century onwards, their purposes have

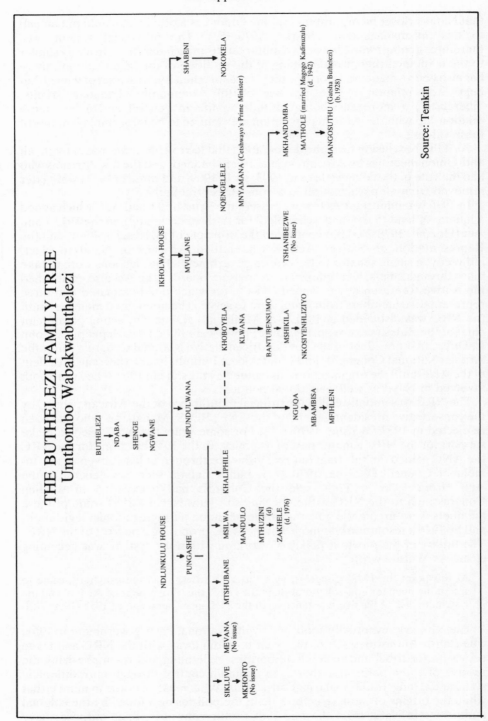

THE BUTHELEZI FAMILY TREE
Umthombo Wabakwabuthelezi

Source: Temkin

changed over time. Initially they served as an economic and political link between pre-capitalist society and colonial administrators. Today chiefs and tribal authorities (with some notable exceptions) form part of the control mechanisms over an African population superfluous in the long and short term to capitalist labour needs.

African politics in Natal, outside of state-created structures, is far too complex a subject to enter into in this book. A few general comments do, however, need to be made, especially in the light of the frequent references made by Chief Buthelezi, not only to his Zulu past but also to the specific ANC tradition within which he places himself and the Inkatha movement. The tradition is that of the 'founding fathers' of the ANC. In other words, it refers to an expression by the pre-1940s ANC of the 'need for equal opportunity for all, and hence the rights of educated and qualified Africans to advance in the modern sector of the economy and to participate in the provincial and parliamentary institutions of government' (Walshe, 1970:413). These sentiments — a fair share for those who deserve it (the educated and qualified) — are adequately encompassed by Buthelezi's 1970s and 1980s ideological stance.

His references to the ANC usually take the form of allegiance to '. . . the ideals of the African National Congress as propounded by the founding fathers in 1912, built on the solid rock of our Ubuntu-Botho* ideal' (BS, 18 May 80; also see, for example, 24 Sep. 83:6; 5 Nov. 83:5). As in the case of the early ANC, chiefs play a prominent role in Inkatha. In the ANC during the early years of its existence this was because of the organization's rejection of the 1913 Land Act which centrally affected chiefs and their control over land. Subsequently it was predominantly in Natal that the ANC managed to gain significant support in the rural areas: Albert Luthuli, Natal ANC leader from 1951 and later national president, was himself a chief. However, even here the banning of the organization prevented support from being converted into organizational strength (Lodge, 1983:290).

The similarities between the ANC in 1912 and the Inkatha movement in 1975 should not be stressed to the exclusion of fundamental differences — differences that increased as Inkatha gained confidence in its role in South Africa. The ANC was founded in 1912 in the self conscious desire of the 'founding fathers' to 'encourage a sense of supra-tribal unity' (Walshe, 1970:412), while Inkatha was born out of the 'tribal' or ethnic institutions of the apartheid state. It has tried to escape the legacy of that birth ever since, in repeated calls (with little success) for 'black unity' under the banner of Inkatha.

A fairly strong ethnic homogeneity, a 'Zulu identity', has been created in the region, particularly in the 20th century with increased urbanization and improved communication. This 'identity' has built on the history of political consolidation under Shaka north of the Tugela, and of decades of successful resistance to political domination. Because of the availability of this identity, and of the politicians to make use of it, social movements in the region have frequently taken a rather idiosyncratic and chauvinistic line towards national movements. This tendency is well illustrated by the political actions of such individuals as A.W.G. Champion, renegade in both the Industrial and Commercial Workers Union (ICU), a mass movement that had its origins 'in the early post-war attempts by

---

*'Inkatha strives for the promotion of African patterns of thought and the achievement of African Humanism otherwise commonly known in Nguni languages as Ubuntu and Sotho languages as Botho' (Bengu, Lecture 4, 1977:5).

white socialists to organize black labour in Cape Town' (Lodge, 1983:5), and the ANC in Natal, from which he was ousted by Albert Luthuli. 'An embarrassingly conservative colleague' is how Walshe described Champion as Natal president of the ANC in relation to Xuma, the national president. To strengthen its independence the Natal ANC even went so far as to seek more money from chiefs (Walshe, 1970:393-95; on Champion also see Marks, 1986).

It is ironic, as Brookes and Webb pointed out, that 'from conservative Natal and Zululand came the institution which for many years was for many Africans the symbol of liberation' (1979:296; Rich 1984:132-33). It says much that it should be from the Natal leaders and from the 'founding fathers' of the ANC that Inkatha should draw its claim of continuity with the ANC and its ideas. The tactics and the content of the demands made by the ANC started moving away from those of the 'founding fathers' with the formation of the ANC Youth League (ANCYL) in 1944. It is necessary to add that while Inkatha draws its claims to a radical political direction from the 'founding fathers', Buthelezi has never been shy of calling on a vast array of ANC leaders of subsequent generations to add credibility to his actions. As he told his audience when celebrating ten years of Inkatha existence:

> From my mother's knee onwards, I was drawn into politics. The great founding father of the ANC, Dr. Pixley ka Isaka Seme, was my uncle. I spent many a long hour on numerous occasions talking about the struggle for liberation with Chief Albert Luthuli. I knew people like Walter Sisulu, Nelson Mandela, Zami Conco, M.B. Yengwa, Oliver Tambo, J.K. Ngubane and Joe Mathews personally. I was a member of the ANC's Youth League. Thus both by hereditary right and by voluntary association, I was steeped in the struggle for liberation [BS, 29 Jun. 85].

The ANCYL saw the possibilities of mass organization, essential for pressure rather than petition politics, in the poverty of a rapidly growing African urban population increasingly severed from any contact with rural subsistence production. Lodge wrote:

> [It was] this recognition of the political opportunity presented by these popular outbursts [among the urban poor in the 1940s] that was the most important contribution made to the nationalist movement by the Africanists [in the ANCYL]. From such struggles they distilled a strategy of mass action, centred on the use of the boycott weapon . . . but also involving strikes, civil disobedience and non-cooperation [1985:22].

Such actions, rather than merely the threat of them, are largely anathema to Buthelezi and Inkatha and it is no wonder that the origins of the Inkatha movement should be sought in an era that predates the ANCYL, this despite Buthelezi's own brief membership of the Youth League while he was a student at the University of Fort Hare in the late 1940s.

In 1948 much of the social fabric of South Africa was fundamentally altered when the National Party came to power. The disappointment felt even by conservative African politicians that the relaxation of controls on urbanization and the increase in job opportunities forced by wartime demands for labour were not to be carried through by the Smuts government, was turned into firm knowledge that white South Africa had no intention of willingly sharing power, or ever submitting to majority rule. A barrage of legislation to crush opposition to the state was passed and ruthlessly used, as was the power of the repressive apparatuses (the army and the police). To confirm their exclusion separate political structures were being forced on the black population, and not only on

Africans. Gatsha Buthelezi, contentious heir to the Buthelezi chieftainship, became part of those separate structures in the 1950s. In the year that the National Party came to power he went to the University of Fort Hare in the eastern Cape, as so many of central and southern Africa's political leaders have done.

3. The Institutions of Apartheid

Administrative separation

As Chief Buthelezi told the Inkatha Annual General Conference in 1985, he became involved, not only in the 'struggle' as he would have it, but also in the structures of apartheid, both 'by hereditary right and by voluntary association' (BS, 29 Jun. 85:10-11). To understand the implications of involvement in the structures of the state, it is important to examine the nature of what the apartheid policy has been and still is. It can be seen as a series of *separations* (the word *apartheid* does, after all, mean 'separateness'), the most obvious of which are racial and territorial.

The previous chapter dealt with the racial separation of land areas and of administrative bodies in Natal and Zululand, as it developed during the 19th century. Centuries before the early European settlers at the Cape had already started the pattern of protecting what they had laid claim to, and excluding the indigenous population. This often occurred not for racial, but for religious or purely economic reasons, such as the fear of competition for land, and later for markets. However, the land they laid claim to was already inhabited by the existing African population. By the end of the 19th century, through the use of superior military technology, a 'divide and rule' policy, and the help of collaborators, the settlers had 'largely stabilized' territorial separation between settlers and the African population. This separation was given legislative force soon after the Act of Union, with some 13% of the total land area reserved for Africans (80% of the South African population); further acquisition by Africans of land outside these areas was prohibited.

Separate areas are important to justify separate administration. The 1913 Land Act continued not only the principle of territorial separation but also that of administrative separation. The Act was 'an important prerequisite for the establishment of separate government institutions for these [reserve] areas' (Kotze, 1975:25), as distinct from bodies established for Africans in 'white' South Africa.

There had been two possibilities for government over Africans. The first was to weaken the institution of chieftainship and rule through the colonial bureaucracy and a council that attempted to involve 'non-traditionalists' in government — this was the system attempted in the eastern Cape. The second was to rely on chiefs, appointed and hereditary, for (indirect) rule — the system developed in Natal. At first the first method was tried, and the council system was extended to all African areas through the 1920 Native Affairs Act. Whatever the reasons, the councils were never enthusiastically implemented and by 1948, when the National Party came to power, there were only three local councils in Natal (out of 25 outside the Transkei), while the sole general council, an umbrella body, existed in the Transkei.

In urban areas outside the reserves the state established native advisory boards (under the Native Urban Areas Act of 1923), with extremely limited and purely advisory functions. They were replaced in 1961 by the possibly even more despised urban bantu councils (the UBCs, or 'Useless Boys Clubs' as they were scathingly labelled). The UBCs were in turn replaced, first by the community councils (from 1977), and then by black local authorities (after 1983).

On a national level there had been extremely limited participation in central government allowed to Africans at the time of Union.* This representation was totally eroded under the National Party government. Even before the NP came to power the threat posed by black voters in a few marginal constituencies in the Cape set in motion a process that was to lead to the separation of voters' rolls in 1936. From then on Africans who had qualified for the vote would elect three (of 153) white members of the House of Assembly, while four indirectly elected senators would represent all Africans in the Union of South Africa. At the same time a Natives Representative Council (NRC) was established, but this proved totally inadequate to the increasingly militant demands for representation at central government level.

In 1948, when the National Party came to power, the ANC Youth League (ANCYL), formed in 1944 and making increasingly radical demands of the parent body, presented a Programme of Action around the idea of African nationalism and involving a mass organization, boycotts, strikes, and civil disobedience (Walshe, 1970:289). The pressure was for the ANC to move away from the negative strategy of reaction and to take the initiative. While the Congress was still wary of the left, it had by the early 1950s shifted slightly from the Africanist position that had characterized it during the 1940s (Lodge, 1983:37). The Programme of Action, adopted at the 1949 annual congress of the ANC, rejected white leadership and all forms of segregation. It led to the 'appointment of a council of action which would organize a boycott of all differential political institutions' (Lodge, 1983:26).

'Ethnic' separation

In 1951, with the passing of the Bantu Authorities Act, the National Party government started on the process of establishing or reinforcing separate political institutions for Africans. The Act made provision for three levels of administration — tribal, regional, and territorial authorities. The Minister of Native Affairs, Dr Hendrik Verwoerd, said this three-tier system of government would reintroduce traditional tribal democracy to African people. Kotze (1975:26) commented that only the first tier, 'consisting of tribal authorities, resembled the traditional system'. The next two levels, regional and territorial authorities, simply brought the local level bodies together on a spatial basis. The council system was to be replaced, and the focus shifted to ethnic fragmentation of

---

*Before Union there were 6633 Africans on the common voters roll in the Cape. In Natal there were at one time six. Africans in the Boer Republics (to become the Orange Free State and Transvaal provinces) never had any vote.

the African population, away from predominantly racial definitions and consequent racial administrative or advisory bodies. The NRC was also abandoned — partly because it was racially rather than ethnically based, largely because it was already a discredited body .

On the established territorial and racial base the new government, through the Bantu Authorities Act and then the Promotion of Bantu Self-Government Act in 1959, added administrative structures for what were now ethnically defined 'homelands'. The 1959 Act was introduced by the Minister of Bantu Affairs, De Wet Nel, who spoke of 'cultural nationalism' and 'ethnic particularities', attempting to move away, at least rhetorically, from racism. However, the tension between the racism of the apartheid policy and what Moodie called 'positive apartheid' or 'cultural pluralism', was there from the start:

> . . . Major public proponents of apartheid have tended to shift their ground depending on the argument, thereby creating an ideological system which is riddled with inconsistencies . . . cultural pluralism is a morally acceptable reality, whereas racism is not; and protagonists of apartheid tend to justify racism on the grounds of cultural pluralism [1980:275-6].

The apartheid policy, with its ethnic separation and ethnically based administration, was an attempt to defuse several pressures that were mounting against the central state. Growing worker militancy was reflected in the fourfold increase in the number of strikes involving African workers between 1950 and the mid 1950s. The South African Congress of Trade Unions (SACTU), later a member of the Congress Alliance which brought together most radical opposition to apartheid, was formed in 1955. Rapid urbanization of African people during the 1950s was making a racially exclusive political system more untenable by the day. Instead of exclusion from central power the state was attempting to shift the focus to separate political power. The 'winds of change' of African nationalism that swept through the continent after the second world war set an example as they forced aside the direct control of the colonial powers. Verwoerd acknowledged the effect of international pressure when he commented that 'we cannot govern without taking into account the tendencies in the world and in Africa'.

Internationally, too, South Africa was under pressure at the United Nations, and was soon to leave the Commonwealth. Moodie quotes the author of the book *Van Malan tot Verwoerd*, Beaumont Schoeman, as saying that Prime Minister Verwoerd told his cabinet that he 'wished to show the world something great and new which would confirm the just intentions of the government's policy, and also provide a basis for the western members . . . to prevent action against South Africa in the UN' (Moodie, 1980:264). This message was given just before the Transkei Constitution Act was passed (a direct result of the political path taken through the principles of the Promotion of Bantu Self-Government Act). Verwoerd had to persuade the other members of the cabinet of the necessity of the policy of 'separate development' as they perceived it as an undesirable extension of the autonomous power of African government.

The apartheid policy was designed to meet all these threats to white supremacy and exclusive control over wealth and political power. It fulfilled many other needs as well, most importantly the need to maintain separate areas for the social reproduction of the labouring class where increasing poverty and a criminal imbalance in resource allocation could be justified in terms of 'dual economies' and 'Third World' components rather than sheer greed and the necessities of capitalist development. From these separate areas labour could also be allocated to the politically powerful but economically weak agricultural sector, where wages were too low to attract workers from the mining sector and the by now dominant manufacturing sector.

More important for the present study, however, concerned as it is with the political consequences of apartheid on the regional political structures, is the attempt to create or rekindle *ethnic nationalisms*. 'Positive cultural nationalism' was to take the place of the wider African nationalism — 'the monster which may still perhaps destroy all the best things in Africa', as Bantu Affairs Minister M.C. de Wet Nel described it in 1959. He admitted that there were two bonds that kept the black population of South Africa together: 'their colour' and 'their hatred of the white man'.

'Cultural nationalism', on the other hand, meant that 'the Bantu too will be linked together by traditional and emotional bonds, by their own language, their own culture, their ethnic particularities'. Underlying the policy was not white social engineering, he argued, but the fact that:

> The Zulu is proud to be a Zulu and the Xhosa proud to be a Xhosa and the Venda is proud to be a Venda, just as proud as they were a hundred years ago. The lesson we have learnt from history during the past three hundred years is that these ethnic groups, the whites as well as the Bantu, sought their greatest fulfilment, their greatest happiness and the best mutual relations on the basis of separate and individual development . . . the only basis on which peace, happiness and mutual confidence could be built up [quoted Moodie, 1980:266].

In these words De Wet Nel presented the grand justification for a policy that was to cause untold misery in its implementation.

It was not only racial dominance that was to be safeguarded through apartheid. The system of cheap labour was to be continued with the added measure of greater control over the allocation of that labour. Verwoerd had said in 1956 that the opposition in Parliament

> . . . apparently did not understand the difference between one national economy and one State . . . The simple fact is that the opportunity of separate government, the opportunity of living separately, and the opportunity of developing separate tertiary industries for each of the race groups does not of necessity mean that the economic activities of the country should be split up [quoted in Davenport and Hunt (eds), 1974:49].

The single economy rested heavily on what has euphemistically been called 'the principle of impermanence'. This meant that Africans outside the bantustans were either there temporarily as migrants or commuters, or, if resident, would have no property or political rights, precious few amenities, and would be subject to the same humiliations of pass checks as all other Africans.

The 'principle of impermanence' meant that wages could be kept low on the by this time quite untenable ground that this income was supplemented by family agriculture in the bantustans. Union organization was also made very difficult with a migrant work force, and housing and other social facilities could be kept to the very minimum, away from the obvious contrast with the standard of living of white South Africa, and from industrial areas in case social unrest should spill out of the townships. Profits, however, were high in the 1960s. Sharpeville caused a brief scare and foreign capital flowed out of South Africa, but the trend was soon reversed as the state clamped down on opposition. The rate of return on United

Kingdom investment in South Africa in 1965 (by which time the post-Sharpeville outflow of capital had been reversed) was 12.1%, higher than in any other country in which Britain had substantial investment. The equivalent figure for US investment was 20.6%, as against 10.4% average return on investment for all other countries in which the USA was economically involved (see Maré, 1982:115; Seidman and Seidman, 1977; First, 1972).

As the apartheid policy has unfolded since 1951, and especially since 1959, racial categorization of people has continued: the present constitution of South Africa, with its claims to 'widen democracy', is essentially based on racial categorization, and racial domination — what has been 'widened' is the number of direct (reluctant or enthusiastic) participants in the structures and execution of the policy. For African people, however, the policy has meant further separation into state-defined ethnic groupings. These groupings have, furthermore, been elevated into political 'nationalisms', each one allocated to a land area fragmented in varying degrees. There are at present ten of these 'national states', four of which have been granted 'independence' from the rest of South Africa.

The Surplus People Project, in their investigation of population relocation in South Africa, documented some of the bitterness created between communities through the policy that defines access to social facilities, jobs, education, housing, medical services, etc, on the basis of allegiance to an unacceptable ethnic unit (see, for example, Platzky and Walker, 1985:23; SPP, vol 5, 1983).

The tragedy implicit in the policy of ethnic separation was clear from early on. In 1960 J.C.M. Mbata wrote a report for the South African Institute of Race Relations in which he commented on one area that he visited:

> The Tsonga admit that until the Bantu Authorities system was imposed, they had lived peacefully, and successfully together with both Venda and Sotho people . . . [T]here was . . . intermarriage on a large scale . . . no one in the past sought to impose his authority or way of life on the others . . . The Shangaan argue that the Bantu Authorities system has upset this delicate balance of co-existence.

He concluded most pertinently:

> It is clear that the fragmentation of South Africa *and its peoples* has had the effect of creating antagonisms where none existed, and opening up old wounds where these were healing. To 'unscramble' the population of the country is impossible, hence the failure of the Government to follow to the letter its policy of ethnic separation . . . [emphasis added].

What has happened in South Africa, especially since the introduction of Bantu Authorities, clearly illustrates a process in which 'cultural pluralism' becomes the politicization of tribal differences, to paraphrase John Saul.* In other words, pre-capitalist social, economic and political forms of organization are artificially maintained or recreated. However, they are in a distorted form, and in a context where they have very little relevance (other than to create antagonisms and to serve as a handy point of reference if conflict should arise) (see Saul, 1979:391-423).

---

*'For "tribalism" (the politicization of ethnicity which is all too characteristically a pathology of dependent Africa) does not spring primarily from the bare fact of the existence of cultural differences between people. Rather, it has been teased into life, first by the divide-and-rule tactics of colonialism and by the uneven development in the economic sphere which colonialism also facilitates, and secondly by the ruling petty bourgeoisie of the post-colonial period . . .' (Saul, 1979:309).

It comes as no surprise that over the years competition for scarce resources, whether educational facilities, jobs, most importantly land, and many other necessities, should often be defined in ethnic terms. The state hands over land, budgets, job allocations, infrastructural schemes, etc., on an ethnic basis to the various groups (or 'nations') created by the policy of apartheid. There have been many land disputes such as that between Bophuthatswana and QwaQwa in the Thaba 'Nchu area of the Orange Free State, between the Ciskei and the Transkei over Glen Grey and Herschel, between KwaZulu and the Transkei over Umzimkulu, between Lebowa and Gazankulu over the Bushbuckridge, Tzaneen and Phalaborwa region, between KwaZulu and KaNgwane and Swaziland over the state's intention to hand over the KaNgwane bantustan and the Ingwavuma region to Swaziland.

On a smaller scale the same 'ethnic' definitions have also lived on to define antagonistic groups. To take just KwaZulu: the conflict over land in southern Natal has been presented as a clash with the Transkei. Much of the continuing debate over the future of the Ingwavuma district is put in terms of age-old histories of conquest and allegiances and whether people are 'Swazi' or 'Zulu'. Clashes in the shanty towns surrounding the formal townships around Durban took on an ugly 'factional' mask as war between 'Zulu' and 'Pondo' at the end of 1985 and early in 1986. A small Sotho-speaking community near Nqutu has come in for criticism for wanting to hold on to their language in a Zulu-speaking area.

Buthelezi on the stage

Chief Gatsha Mangosuthu Ashpenaz Nathan Buthelezi was born on 27 August 1928 in Mahlabatini to Chief Mathole and Princess Constance Magogo Zulu.* Some five months earlier Inkata KaZulu had accepted a new constitution. This document, that of an 'organization designed by the Zulu aristocracy and the African petty bourgeoisie to gain state recognition for the king [Solomon]' (Marks, 1986:36), was to receive mention in the first constitution of the Inkatha movement revived by Chief Buthelezi 47 years later in 1975.

In 1948 the young Buthelezi arrived at Fort Hare, the university for black people in the eastern Cape that produced many southern African leaders of later years (see, for example, Beard, 1972:172-73). He studied for a BA degree, majoring in Bantu Administration, under Professor Z.K. Matthews, an important ANC figure. Buthelezi was 19 when he started his student days, and he was a member of the ANC Youth League from 1948 to 1950. He often refers to this fact, but does not give it the content which would enable his position within Youth League radicalism to be clarified (see, for example, Deane, 1978:24). An ANCYL-led boycott of the visit to Fort Hare by the Governor-General of the Union of South Africa, Brand van Zyl, in 1950, caused Buthelezi's expulsion for action taken by him and others against students who had welcomed the Governor-General. Buthelezi's biographer hinted that the 'heartbroken' Buthelezi might not have been guilty of any offence, and that he felt that he had failed in his duty towards his tribe, within which there had been some opposition to his university

---

*It is not clear why Chief Buthelezi should have decided in the last few years that he was not going to be known as Gatsha any more, but as Mangosuthu. His biographer, Temkin, called his book *Gatsha Buthelezi: Zulu Statesman*, and in the KLA he has been known by that name until recently. Whatever the reason the media, by now including the SABC, were quick to jump to the Chief's sensitivities.

career (Temkin, 1976:36-37). Tribal opposition had been in part directed at the 'radical' company that he had been keeping (such as then journalist Jordan Ngubane). To make matters worse, in 1949 Buthelezi, then in his second year of study, had helped in the offices of the ANC in Durban in attempts to calm the racial tension that had erupted between Indians and Africans (Temkin, 1976:36; see, for example, Webster, 1977, on the '1949 riots'). These events, as will be discussed below, have become a symbol of the racial form that social and economic tensions can take in South Africa's racially divided society.

It is not clear what Buthelezi's role was in the attempts by the Natal Indian Congress (NIC) and ANC to restore calm, but Temkin commented that, 'as a future chief, he had to play his politics in as low key as possible' (1976:34). 'Low-key' appears to be a fair description of Buthelezi's actions over the next few years. Having assured Senator Edgar Brookes 'that he would steer clear of politics for the time being', Buthelezi took his exams at Natal University but graduated at the University of Fort Hare. He was then interviewed by Dr W.W.M. Eiselen, secretary for Bantu Administration, and warned that if he wanted to become a tribal chief (as he was destined to become) he would have to '"wipe out" the Fort Hare episode' (Temkin, 1976:39). Temkin said that it was to achieve this cleaning of his slate that Buthelezi joined the Department of Native Affairs for nearly two years, instead of serving his articles, as he had planned to do, with Rowley Arenstein, 'a Durban lawyer, who was a self-confessed communist' (Temkin, 1976:39; BS, 24 Sep. 83:9; 24 Aug. 85:16).

Temkin noted Buthelezi's 'single-minded' approach to becoming chief, a post with little prestige and a small income, and adds that Buthelezi had been greatly influenced by Chief Albert Luthuli, who gave up teaching to become a chief at Groutville (Temkin, 1976:39). What Temkin fails to mention here is that Luthuli was never officially recognized as chief because of his decision to involve himself in national politics. He became ANC president in 1952. Lodge wrote of him:

A man of great dignity and courage, he was immediately at home in the world of popular politics . . . His experiences as a local administrator gave him an insight into the parochial worries and concerns of ordinary people. His religious faith and training brought to his politics a principled belief in non-violence and a remarkable optimism about the capacity of whites to undergo a change of heart. For him, passive resistance, even on a mass scale, held no fears [1983:61; also 68].

Lodge quotes Luthuli at this point in words that could easily have been uttered by Buthelezi years later:

'It [mass passive resistance] is not subversive since it does not seek to overthrow the form and machinery of the state but only urges for the inclusion of all sectors of the community in a partnership in the government of the country on the basis of equality' [1983:61].

There are many similarities of language (the claims to Christian values, adherence to non-violence, calls for equality and sharing without changing the system, and belief in mass action), but there are also important differences, such as Buthelezi's claims that his espousal of non-violence is simply a tactical move, his ambiguity towards Christian action, and, most important, his central involvement in purely 'Zulu' politics and state administrative machinery.

The Bantu Authorities Act was passed in 1951, during Buthelezi's period of employment with the Department of Native Affairs. In November 1952 the Buthelezi tribe decided that Buthelezi, who was 24 at the time and had married in

July, should become chief and take over from the regent, Chief Maliyamakhanda. In March 1953 he was installed as acting chief and four years later his position received government approval (Temkin, 1976:45). Temkin wrote that Buthelezi saw it 'as his role to help re-establish the paramountcy of the Zulu king' (1976:46), even though the king, as chief of the Usuthu* seemed to have decided to accept the Bantu Authorities system for his people (something which Buthelezi's people were apparently not willing to do). The 'single-mindedness' of Buthelezi's move towards chieftainship, in itself a fairly small prize, has already been mentioned. However, this particular chieftainship was also the source of 'prime ministers' to the Zulu king, a post that Buthelezi's father had held under King Solomon. It could thus expand the young man's political horizons considerably, but only if the king should be restored to something of his previous central position in Zulu society (this time as figurehead and not as an executive monarch). The similarities with what the Zulu 'elite' had hoped to do with the kingship of Solomon early in the century are striking (see Chapter 4).

A wide 'Zuluness' with a distinct political definition had therefore to be created (or recreated), but it had to be prevented from falling totally into the hands of the ethnic planners of the central state — which would have meant 'independence' for KwaZulu. It was not enough for Buthelezi to remain at the level of tribal authorities, with its extreme fragmentation. Natal has been divided into more than 200 'tribes'. A larger unit had to be accepted, the political entity that later became the KwaZulu Legislative Assembly, claiming to speak for all 'Zulus'. In the same way, at the ideological level, Buthelezi 'was also doing his best to restore the pride of the Zulu in their nation', setting up a committee to honour Shaka, 'the founder of the nation' (Temkin, 1976:48). On 23-25 September 1954 celebrations were held at Stanger, where Shaka lies buried. Temkin claims that Luthuli, on behalf of the ANC, donated the largest ox to the celebrations (1976:116).

Jordan Ngubane, who had been requested by the paramount chief to write on the Stanger ceremony, wrote to Buthelezi, congratulating him on the role he was establishing for himself — 'once more [we are going to] employ all our resources for our own good as people'. He said that it was only because of Buthelezi's position that he would write about the ceremony. That the king would be the 'rallying point' and Buthelezi the 'premier' is what 'many Zulu intellectuals' hoped would happen, according to Temkin (1976:49).

During a 1955 visit to Natal by Hendrik Verwoerd (then Minister of Native Affairs), when he addressed some 300 chiefs and other leaders at Nongoma, Buthelezi 'welcomed the government's promise to retain the chieftainship' and asked that the position of the king (Cyprian) be changed: '"Most people resent the fact that the king is only used as a tool whenever there is trouble and they want him to have more of a say in our affairs"' (Temkin, 1976:51; Survey, 1955/6:66). Buthelezi was to change his mind on the position of the king once he had consolidated his own position within the bantustan structures, and had gained greater confidence and support. Verwoerd confirmed the position of Cyprian as head of the nation, but this was 'not acceptable to all the Zululand tribes, some of whom felt that the authority of the Zulu king did not extend to them' (Temkin, 1976:56-7). It is difficult, even today, to see to what extent the king (now

---

*The term 'Usuthu' came to be applied to the followers of Cetshwayo, one of the sons of the Zulu king Mpande (see diagram, p.16), in their struggle against the followers of another son, Mbulazi, who were known as the Gqoza, in 1856 (Guy, 1982a:13; 96, note 34; 246).

Goodwill) has served as a 'rallying point for the nation', or to what extent he has fragmented the African people in Natal through the inappropriateness of his position as 'traditionally' a figure of specific Zulu *tribal* allegiance.

On 6 September 1957 Buthelezi was officially installed as chief. He had steered clear of the pass protests that his wife and mother had been involved in so as not to jeopardize official recognition of his position. Luthuli, who could not attend the ceremony because of illness (says Temkin, although Luthuli could hardly have done so with the ANC opposition to Bantu Authorities) sent a letter (which arrived late, wrote Temkin) in which he restated ANC rejection of Bantu Authorities, because chiefs would become 'official mouthpieces' (1976:59). The director of the Institute of Race Relations, Quintin Whyte, who attended the ceremony, wrote that 'while leaders such as Buthelezi had no part in making the laws, they had to administer them. Buthelezi and others could only do their best to reduce the harshness of these laws and to develop their people within their framework' (Temkin, 1976:61).

Working within the system

With this reference to Whyte's comments, Temkin sets the scene for a frequently repeated explanation, or justification, of Buthelezi's involvement in state policy over the next three decades.

At a meeting of the Mashonangashoni Regional Authority in 1968, before the Authority had been formally established, Buthelezi as chair justified his participation in the Bantu Authorities system. This meeting is said to have signified capitulation to the state's political plans in Natal. Buthelezi said that 'co-operation was not acceptance of the apartheid system but evidence of a desire to progress within whatever system was imposed upon them' (Temkin, 1976:118). This idea is repeated at least 15 times in Temkin's biography of Buthelezi, reflecting the chief's undoubted sensitivity to accusations of working within the system. This justification also extends to obeying the laws and authority of the land: for example, when Buthelezi opened the first session of the Zulu Territorial Authority in 1970 he pointed out that '"essentially" they [the Zulu people] had co-operated "as subjects with whichever government . . . [was] in power"' (Temkin, 1976:127).

While much has been made in the political rhetoric of bantustan politics in Natal of resistance to the imposition of Bantu Authorities during the 1960s, the basis of that opposition is not clear. Nor is it clear whether chiefs and commoners opposed the move for the same reasons. There are vague reports that some 'tribes' wanted to wait and see how the implementation would work elsewhere, and that people resisted simply because they had not been consulted by the state.

There is some suggestion that oppostion at local level from the chiefs (the lynchpins of the policy) could have been conservative rather than a rejection of the state's attempts at greater and more efficient control through reintroduced 'traditionalism'. Temkin (1976:63) and Hill (1964:89) suggest that the chiefs feared changes in the degree of local autonomy they had over such matters as the fines that they imposed. It is possible that suspicion about loss of income and authority was behind their reluctance to accept the system.

Buthelezi, however, asked for the system to be made compulsory, long before the state made it clear that the initial element of choice had been removed. At the time of the Promotion of Bantu Self-Government Act (1959) Buthelezi wrote to a 'white political friend':

> I have stated at public meetings in the presence of my tribe that it would seem that the best thing would be to co-operate with it [the Bantu Authorities Act] since my cousin who is the Paramount Chief has done so. The people have not rejected the Act as far as I am aware. All that they have said is that I am trying to rush them despite the choice given by the government — that they are watching it in operation in the Usuthu ward [that of the Paramount Chief].

> I am not the person standing in the people's way to acceptance. I am prepared to abide by any Act passed by Parliament. Parliament has chosen to make this particular one permissive. My suggestion is that it should be compulsory like Bantu Education and other Acts of Parliament [quoted Temkin, 1976:72; similar sentiments were expressed in DN, 28 Apr. 64].

This remarkable letter was quite correct in that acceptance was voluntary at that time. However, with the ANC opposing the system, there must have been a fair degree of popular resistance to it, for different reasons from that offered by the chief (see Temkin, 1976:89). As late as 1965 the Minister of Bantu Administration and Development said in parliament that 'under no circumstances would I allow a Bantu Authority to be forced upon any tribe', and that the Act stated that consultation had to take place (Survey, 1965:133). At the same time Bantu Affairs Commissioners (white district officials functioning as magistrates) said that it was 'consultation, not acceptance, that was called for' (ST, 18 Apr. 65: see also Buthelezi, 1972:7; Temkin, 1976:93-96).

In 1974, looking back on this period in the 1960s, Buthelezi told the KLA 'Mr Oltman, who is a member of my department here,' and Mr Otto (the magistrate at Nongoma) had told his tribe that there was no option. He alleged Otto had said that 'magistrates were wrongly instructed when they told tribes and chiefs that they had an option in the matter. There was no such option. I complied because I am a law-abiding non-citizen of South Africa' (KLAD, 4:214; also Survey, 1969:131).

Buthelezi said at the time that he was relieved to hear that acceptance was unnecessary, that he did not believe that the system was the answer to South Africa's problems, but that he would co-operate. Little time was wasted and under a Government Gazette notice in September 1965 a tribal authority was established for the Mahlabatini tribal area, consisting of Buthelezi and 67 councillors.

It would seem that Buthelezi was not the centre of resistance. In 1966 107 tribal authorities had been established for the 282 government-recognized 'tribes' in Natal, and 12 regional authorities were functioning (Survey, 1966:147). By the next year only a further 12 tribal authorities had been established, amid continuing resistance, and early in 1968 there were still 135 to be created. However, during this year no less than 50 were formed. It was also in 1968 that Chief Cyprian Bhekuzulu (the Paramount Chief of the Zulus) died and Buthelezi became head of the Mashonangashoni regional authority in the Mahlabatini district.

In 1969 Prince Israel Mcwayizeni became regent until Prince Goodwill should come of age and marry. A rift developed between Buthelezi and Prince Israel, who apparently wished to ask for a Territorial Authority for the Zulus, while Buthelezi claims that he did not want it to be initiated from within the royal family or by him. This was the beginning of the rift between the royal family and Buthelezi that was to absorb much regional African political energy over the next few years, a conflict that the central state was quite willing to fan during its initial opposition to Buthelezi's loyal resistance.

Whether he was going to initiate moves to establish a Zulu Territorial Authority (ZTA) or whether he was simply going to go along with its creation, there is little doubt that Buthelezi benefited politically from this apartheid structure. If his accession to chieftainship had been perceived by observers like Jordan Ngubane in the 1950s as enabling the mobilization of Zulu society by the use of traditional authority in a modern context, he lost that advisory role as prime minister to the royal house after the death of Cyprian (at least for several years). The 'prime ministerial' role of the Buthelezi clan to the Zulu royal house dates back to the prominent role of Nqengelele under Shaka, and especially to the 'prominence in Zulu affairs' accorded to the Buthelezi chiefdom with Nqengelele's son Myamana being prime minister to Cetshwayo (see Buthelezi, 1978; Marks, 1970:31; Guy, 1982:46).

Brenda Robinson, one of the local journalists in the English-language press who had kept Buthelezi's name and image in the public eye in an extremely sympathetic way, wrote at the time, shortly after Cyprian's death:

> In 1968, after the death of Cyprian whom he had served for sixteen years, Buthelezi was elbowed out of Zulu royal affairs in a manner far from subtle. But to elbow him out of the public eye or the Zulu people's esteem proved a simple impossibility [STb, 16 Jun. 70, quoted in Temkin, 1976:121].

Ironically, it was the creation of the ZTA (based on the state's definition of 'traditional' society) that enabled him to continue to play a central role. Apartheid saved the chief from possible obscurity.

Temkin offers reasons for Buthelezi's decision to enter into the highest level of the administrative system devised for Africans by the NP government since 1951. It was suggested that he was 'reluctant', but that his friends and political mentors of many years standing, Bishop A.H. Zulu and the journalist Jordan Ngubane, urged him to enter. However, despite his alleged 'resistance' and indecision it must be clear that this was simply the latest step on a road of prior participation in government structures (whatever the justification) on which he had started many years earlier.

Why did Buthelezi feel it worthwhile to participate here as well? First, he would have a 'platform' from which he 'could draw attention to the iniquities and inequalities of the system', wrote Temkin (1976:123; 216). The plausibility of this reason is diminished when one recalls that this 'system' had been in existence for nearly two decades, and its 'iniquities and inequalities' had been shown up and rejected times without count. It would hardly seem necessary to expose the disastrous effects of a system that prosecuted hundreds of thousands of people under the pass laws, that relocated as many into the hellholes of the 'resettlement' camps (see, for example, Desmond, 1970), that banned organizations of resistance, and condemned thousands to a life of migration. Participation in the bantustan structures carried such a taint as to negate any value it might have had.

In an interview with the *Financial Mail* (14 Feb. 75) Buthelezi was asked if he had any regrets about working within the 'framework of separate development'. His reply was as superficial as the earlier justifications: 'No. If the government does not deliver the goods, it only proves that I was right in the first place. And if I have exposed certain fallacies and frauds in the system I have accomplished something' (also see Langner, 1983:11). As will be argued later, this circular 'Have your cake and eat it' argument does not hold if at the same time a clear political direction is claimed.

A second claim was that participation would offer 'some hope for the Zulu' if a 'Zulu homeland' was effectively led. Third, his 'abstaining could have a destructive effect on the Zulustan government' (Temkin, 1976:123). After 16 years of the ZTA and then the KwaZulu Legislative Assembly under the leadership of Gatsha Buthelezi, the bantustan is having to screen pensioners as they cannot all be paid, a fraction of the jobs have been created that are necessary to absorb the unemployed, let alone new workseekers, and there are frequent complaints of mismanagement, corruption, and totally inadequate infrastructural and health facilities. Buthelezi and his administration may not have directly caused this situation, but participation in a system that has these and other 'iniquities and inequalities' as its inevitable and sometimes conscious effects entails some responsibility for them — especially when Buthelezi and his administration claim credit for small victories that allegedly arise out of their participation.

On 9 April 1970 a meeting of chiefs eventually decided upon the establishment of a Territorial Authority (Survey, 1970:141). Proclamation 139 of 22 May set out the regulations for the ZTA. As elsewhere, chiefs and their 'traditional councillors' formed the basis of the Authority, the head of which had to be a chief. Buthelezi was unanimously elected the chief executive officer. Two out of five of the other executive members also had to be chiefs. At this stage there were 188 tribal authorities (out of 282 'tribes') and 22 regional authorities.

Buthelezi, replying to the Minister of Bantu Administration and Development, who opened the first meeting at Nongoma on 9 June 1970, assured him that reservations about the system had not meant 'disloyalty or "communism"', and he called for a speeding up of the process that had been set in motion — 'we cannot be expected to move towards self-determination and self-realization at ox-wagon pace' (Survey, 1970:143).

Buthelezi was now 'on the national stage'. He turned down an invitation to open the National Union of South African Students (NUSAS) congress, 'because he believed it better to avoid such a possibly controversial engagement so soon after his election' (Temkin, 1976:129). He did take part in 'controversial' political events during the early 1970s, but possibly the memory of student clashes with police in the general protest at detentions during 1969 and 1970 was too immediate during the year that the ZTA was formed. NUSAS had also been the target of several state threats of direct action against the movement.

It must be kept in mind that both white and black opposition groups and individuals perceived the newly-formed bantustan structures and some of the individuals who occupied places within them in a far from unfavourable light. To take just some examples: Dr Richard Turner, a radical Natal University lecturer who was very influential in both black and white student circles, wrote in an early 1973 postscript to his book, *The Eye of the Needle*, written in 1971, that

> In a sense, black consciousness has certainly furthered the development of black solidarity in South Africa, But it is people like Chief Buthelezi who are recognised by the bulk of Africans as their present leaders, while the BPC [Black People's Convention] is probably known by a relatively small percentage of predominantly middle-class blacks. [Turner, 1980:127]

While voicing caution about the future, the liberal-oriented Study Project on Christianity in Apartheid Society (SPRO-CAS), commented in 1973 that

Chief Gatsha Buthelezi has led the way among Bantustan leaders in voicing demands that could be satisfied only by a substantial modification of, or indeed by the abandonment of, separate development [SPRO-CAS, 1973:39]

In 1973 there occurred what was described by SPRO-CAS director Peter Randall as an event that 'may serve as a turning point in the history both of Black Solidarity and of Coloured-white relationships'. Clashes between students and university authorities at the University of the Western Cape for coloured students led to several mass meetings being called. At one Chief Buthelezi, Fatima Meer (the Durban sociologist with whom Buthelezi was subsequently to clash vehemently), and other leaders appeared together. Randall wrote that 'significantly enough, the SASO [the black consciousness student organization that had split from NUSAS in 1969] President was prepared to share the platform with a homeland leader . . .' (Randall, 1973:32).

One strand of Buthelezi's justification for involvement in first Bantu Authorities and then the next stage of the apartheid structure — the pragmatic, realistic argument — is well captured in his first report to the ZTA:

We as a people need development more than any other race group, and, for this reason, we say to those who have these reservations that a negative attitude will deprive us of the development that is available to our people within the framework of the policy.

Let us, therefore, unite as a people as whites are united and glean whatever development is allowed us in our lifetime, for the benefit of posterity.

What will be more gratifying to us as we close our eyes on our deathbeds than to think that we did our best in the circumstances and to the very limit of what was possible . . . Let us make mistakes and learn by them instead of folding arms.

Temkin comments that this approach of 'doing the best within the legal limitations' (while condemning the limitations) has been Buthelezi's 'standpoint to the present time' (1976:131). There are several criticisms of this approach. Some have already been mentioned. There is also more than a hint that 'legality' is equated with participation in state structures.

The second strand can be called one of 'moral affront'. It goes something like this:

Each and every person in South Africa, white or black, is willy-nilly working and living within the system imposed by oppressors on all of us. Vociferous black spokesmen who thrive on reiterating these cliches live in the native townships under WRAB [the West Rand Administration Board] and other administration boards to which they pay rent. They are educated in black schools that are financed directly by the Department of Education and Training. They attend separate black universities financed by the Government [St, 14 Jul. 78, reporting on Buthelezi's address to the Inkatha central committee meeting; also CT, 10 Apr. 78].

The argument is that there is no difference between simply living in South Africa as a black person, and actively participating in the structures of that society. To call those who opt for participation 'stooges' or 'puppets' is, according to this argument, totally wrong. Once more Buthelezi wants to have it his way while denying that it is his way. There is a very big difference between living in apartheid South Africa — carrying a pass, attending schools, living in group areas set aside for different racial groups, etc — and becoming part of the structures that have been set up for the maintenance of the society in this form. Becoming part of ethnically fragmented bantustan administrations, running an ethnic police force, fighting battles with other ethnically defined units over resources, is a far cry from doing those things that apartheid society enforces, doing them under pressure and, more and more often since the 1970s, dying while resisting apartheid. To equate these two aspects to justify participation in the apartheid structures reflects a measure of unease and sensitivity about such participation.

The third strand in Buthelezi's justification is that regional development and regional administration will always be necessary in South Africa, and that he is doing no more than participating in this technical task. In this vein Buthelezi told Justice and Police Minister Jimmy Kruger in 1977 (Inkatha, nd:7), when the latter called him in to warn him against taking non-Zulus into the Inkatha movement: 'In fact, the Ulundi thing as far as I am concerned is nothing more than local administration of the Zulu people . . . we are just a section of the South African people.' In 1976 he told the KLA (KLAD, 8:85-6) that the 'people in these Reserve areas have to exist and they should be helped by us, and we by them, in our attempts to eke out an existence . . . This means that we have to face the fact that we have day to day goals, as we have to live for 365 days each year and every year. On the other hand, we must have long-term goals . . .'.

Fourth, participation is justified in terms of the continuity of pre-capitalist political and cultural traditions. This is probably the most frequently used explanation of why Buthelezi has chosen the path of 'separate development', not because it is the policy of the central state but because it is primarily the historical continuity of 'Zulu' society and of Gatsha Buthelezi.

Buthelezi stated this position in an article written after the referendum results in 1983 (STb, 6 Nov. 83):

> I was the traditional Prime Minister to my first cousin, King Cyprian for 16 years, long before there was any KwaZulu Legislative Assembly. I never thought that the Prime Minister was so politically illiterate to the extent of him being unaware that I am not Chief Minister of KwaZulu by the grace of the Nationalist Government.

And in remarkably similar language he wrote in the *Sunday Times* (16 Jan. 83):

> I do not owe my political power to the KwaZulu Legislative Assembly or to Pretoria. King Shaka never owed his political eminence to any colonial power. The solidarity of the Zulu people was not dependent on white-created institutions when they defeated the might of the British Army. White South Africa observes a so-called Day of the Vow as testimony to the fact that the people I now lead have their own will and their own sense of destiny. An act of history made us South Africans and South Africans we are and will remain.

Here is a restatement of that short-term and long-term strategy that Buthelezi referred to in the KLA. The former is expressed in this version in terms of a separate 'Zuluness', and a specific history that dates back to pre-colonial south-east Africa. That in itself is fairly trite. What is remarkable is that this specific local history should be used in the last quarter of the 20th century to justify involvement in a policy as divisive and generally abhorrent as that of apartheid. Temkin, in trying to justify Buthelezi's participation, effectively condemns him, through pointing to the 'heads I win, tails you lose' basis of the argument: 'Homeland's [sic] policy has been superimposed on Buthelezi's own position: his mandate does not require acceptance of the policy, only its exploitation and conformity to its statutes' (1976:357).

It is probably a measure of discomfort with this justification that makes Buthelezi call upon the legitimating approval of certain ANC figures for the path that he has chosen. In a letter to the *Daily News* (28 Mar. 79) he wrote, in response to something that Natal University sociologist Professor Fatima Meer had said about him:

> . . . I want to know whether the suggestion is that I should abandon my people at the Buthelezi tribal level, and also at the Zulu ethnic group level in order to be passed by her [Fatima Meer] as the authentic voice of my people? Must I leave the Zulus to the wiles of BOSS-sponsored ambitious characters so that they can lead them to Pretoria's pseudo-independence? Neither Chief Albert Luthuli, Nelson Mandela or Walter Sisulu (and some leaders in exile), have ever told me that there was any conflict in serving my people at home and the black liberation struggle in which I am engaged on a wider basis.

In an interview with Graham Watts (SE, 1 Jul. 84) Buthelezi said that '. . . when he was a young man, he was advised by ANC leaders Chief Albert Luthuli, Nelson Mandela and Walter Sisulu to take up his hereditary position of chief minister of the Zulus'. He added that this was before the 'homeland policy' and that he did not choose to work within 'the system'. (There might not have been a 'homeland policy' when the young Buthelezi took up his chieftainship, but the Bantu Authorities system had been created and the role of chiefs within the system of indirect rule had been in existence for nearly a century, albeit initially outside Zululand.)

These claims were somewhat soured when in 1983 Albert Luthuli's eldest daughter, Dr Albertinah Luthuli (living in Zimbabwe at the time) said: 'I ask myself where Buthelezi went wrong. I remember so well years ago at my home in Groutville when he used to visit my father and he was a youth member of the ANC . . . And now he stands for the very things my father opposed . . .' (St, 16 Sep. 82). Buthelezi's legitimating use of an ANC tradition is discussed in more detail in Chapter 6.

The system develops

Political development in KwaZulu did not take place at the 'ox wagon pace' that Buthelezi had feared, and by 1972 the KwaZulu Legislative Assembly was created to replace the Zulu Territorial Authority. This was a major step forward in the state's constitutional planning for the bantustans, giving limited legislative as well as executive powers to these regional administrations. The Act under which the KLA was created, the Bantu Homelands Constitution Act of 1971, makes provision for 'Chapter 1' and 'Chapter 2' powers. During the first stage, which started for KwaZulu in 1972, an executive council is allowed, which becomes a cabinet in the next stage (Chapter 2). Excluded from 'Chapter 1' powers are important areas, such as establishment of townships and business undertakings, the appointment and dismissal of chiefs, and educational syllabuses. This means that the bantustans are forced to move to the next stage, even if they should reject the 'final' stage of 'independence', as KwaZulu has done (see Horrell, 1978:52-53).

In 1972, then, a constitution was drafted for KwaZulu which contained two aspects worth mentioning. First, the king had been 'downgraded' to a figurehead position, at the insistence of Buthelezi and the other executive councillors. This occurred against the wishes and petitions to the central state of such royalists as Prince Clement Zulu who had wanted an executive paramount chief (king) (Kotzé, 1975:55-58; Schmahmann, 1978:93; Butler et al, 1977:40). There is also a pledge of 'respect' for 'all laws applicable in the area of the KwaZulu Legislative Assembly' (Temkin, 1976:149).

The issue of the constitutional role of the king is of central importance to the detail of 'Zulu' politics. Buthelezi's tactics have rested on occupying a commanding position in KwaZulu that could not be challenged by an alternative tradition, such as that of the king, with the potential or actual backing of the central state. Powerful forces were trying to set up a system of government similar to that in Swaziland, another monarchy but with an executive king. These forces were operating not only within Zulu society, but also found allies in the state, and later amongst a disgruntled petty bourgeoisie. Their allies within the state did not want a sometimes rebellious Buthelezi running the bantustan for the largest ethnic group in South Africa, a showpiece if they did take 'independence'. Buthelezi tried to delay the installation of Goodwill as king of the Zulus. This was interpreted by some as a tactic to get the constitution for the KLA passed first, with its clauses defining a non-executive role for the king. This interpretation is rejected by Temkin, but on somewhat unconvincing grounds (1976:140).

Both parties in this conflict for the political power (real or imagined) of the king drew heavily on 'tradition' to justify their particular claims (see, for example, Temkin, 1976:139-46). It comes as no surprise that the first debate within the ZTA should have referred so often to the idea of a 'Zulu nation'. The ambiguities of this message when read together with rejection of the South African government's policy of trying to create a 'Zulu nation', are clear. Within that 'nation' and its cultural history there were at the time, and for a long time into the 1970s, two interpretations. One came from Buthelezi and the politicians (many of them ex-members of the ANC in Natal) and economic interests that perceived their place to be best served with a less direct involvement of the king. However, they were not stepping away from the specifically 'Zulu' element in the rules of this political game, simply redefining the rules of 'Zuluness': Schlemmer and Muil (1975:125) said that moves by the king and his advisers were opposed because 'they violated custom'. On the other side were a mixed bag of security police agents, black apartheid apostles, another brand of 'Zulu traditionalists' proposing an *executive* king (which they claimed was historically correct), and trading interests who felt threatened by the close links that Buthelezi and those around him had built up with 'white' (especially monopoly) business.

The KLA constitution provided for 24 September to be an official public holiday in KwaZulu to be known as King Shaka Day. The KLA would comprise a personal representative of the king, three chiefs (or chairs of community authorities) appointed by each of the 22 existing regional authorities, and 55 elected members (elections were not held until 1978). A comment by Butler et al (1977:41) draws attention to a point that has been mentioned in connection with Buthelezi's denial that he participated in apartheid:

> It is important to emphasize the limited nature of the changes in the constitutions of the homelands. The legislation of 1970 and 1971 [the Bantu Homelands Citizenship Act and the Bantu Homelands Constitution Act] provides no major break with the system established in the Transkei in 1963, the roots of which go back to the Bantu Authorities Act of 1951. What has been achieved *constitutionally* in recent years is the extension of Transkei-type models to the other former reserves.

A further concession that Buthelezi won was the right to select members of his own executive council, although the names still had to be presented to the KLA for approval.

The status achieved in 1972 was that of Stage 1 self-government. The Zulus were one of the last of the originally envisaged ethnic groups to get to this point. Buthelezi has fairly consistently come out against the final step, as envisaged by the political planners in Pretoria, and the KwaZulu bantustan will probably never become one of the 'independent national states' (of which there are four at present) recognized only by each other and by the South African state. Some of Buthelezi's early statements might have been read as leaving the way open for this totally false independence, especially those that made demands for a consolidated KwaZulu, something that had been ruled out by the inadequate consolidation proposals made by the state (see Temkin, 1976:165).

The KwaZulu Government Diary (1974:10) carried a 'statement of policy' in Buthelezi's foreword:

> We believe that it is in the interests of the Zulu nation that we gear our approach towards full political rights with the least political delay and that means nothing less but unqualified independence.

> We will therefore in terms of our constitution from time to time ask that more and greater powers and more comprehensive duties in respect of KwaZulu matters be handed over to us that we can orderly develop towards full autonomy.

This is followed by another statement which, although vague, seems to refer to protection, on an ethnic basis, of certain resources, such as trading facilities that were to become a major issue during the mid-1970s. This point reads as follows:

> We firmly reject any policy or move which could have the tendency and/or ultimate result that the wealth, resources and commercial opportunities of KwaZulu would no longer be reserved and developed exclusively for us.

To be fair to Buthelezi, the speech on which he based this foreword (quoted above) was given in the KLA the previous year (KLAD, 3:168-9). Here the phrase 'unqualified autonomy' rather than 'unqualified independence' was used. It would be correct to say that while one may find such instances where he envisaged 'independence' under certain conditions, generally he has rejected the climax of the bantustan policy. When *Drum* magazine wrote (December 1982) that he had seen the establishment of the ZTA as a 'step towards eventual independence', Inkatha secretary general Oscar Dhlomo was quick to respond that 'it was blatantly untrue to allege that there was ever a time when Chief Buthelezi ever contemplated taking so-called "independence"' (*Drum*, February 1983). This reply may say more about the sensitivity of the issue and the people involved than about Buthelezi's views.

During 1974 the KLA asked to move into the next phase of self-government (with greater legislative powers) in terms of the Bantu Homelands Constitution Act. The Minister of BAD replied sympathetically but said that it would have to await elections in KwaZulu. This was a pointed reference to the delay in holding elections in the bantustan because of the KLA's reluctance to use 'reference books', the notorious pass-book, and the decision that KwaZulu 'citizenship certificates' were to be issued (Langner, 1983:51). Greater status and power were again requested in 1976, and were finally granted in February 1977, still without elections and with KwaZulu divided into as many fragments as before.

Internal bantustan politics have not changed greatly except that the level of direct repression has escalated dramatically (for example, Haysom, nd; 1986). However, the changing political climate in South Africa as a whole has fundamentally altered the position originally envisaged for these regions. The KwaNdebele 'homeland' was due to gain its 'independence' at the end of 1986, but popular resistance has forced the South African state and African supporters of 'independence' for KwaNdebele to back down and postpone plans for further fragmentation of South Africa. Fewer attempts are being made to force the remaining five into 'independence'. Instead, a greater measure of incorporation of these bantustans is on the cards (see, for example, Cobbett et al, 1986). This new policy, only in its initial stages, has meant that it has become counter-productive to find a way of circumventing Buthelezi or forcing him into 'independence'. As the lines are being drawn ever more clearly in class rather than just racial terms, so the traditional opposition from the state and NP-controlled media has changed. Gone are the days when every session of the KLA was dominated by revelations and accusations about Department of Information and security policy involvement in KwaZulu politics in attempts to replace Buthelezi with someone more pliant. Even business had, in the early 1970s, wanted Buthelezi and other bantustan politicians to be legislatively excluded from the labour field. The name and face of Buthelezi is now frequently to be found making a point that supports the state's new direction, or attacking the enemies of 'reform' in South Africa. In this new definition of a common South Africa, albeit still composed of 'minorities', there is certainly a place for Buthelezi. The question is simply where. How can concessions be made without opening the doors to majority rule?

It is in this context that the federal option, advocated by Buthelezi for so long, is demanding serious consideration from politicians and academics. It has already been given the stamp of approval by business leaders in Natal, through their participation in deliberations of the Buthelezi Commission and now in the discussions for a joint administration and legislature in Natal between the Provincial Council and the KLA (known as the 'KwaZulu-Natal Indaba' or consultation). Buthelezi and Inkatha are turning the weakness, on an ideological level, of being part of the bantustan system, into a strength through making the bantustan and its politics a central part of regional and hence national politics. The presence in force of KwaZulu police, armed with automatic weapons, at the 1986 May Day launch of Inkatha's trade union in the heart of 'white' Durban is surely a sign of the future.

4. Inkatha Re-formed: Traditions Revived

Parallels from the past

On 22 March 1975 Inkatha YaKwaZulu was revived at KwaNzimela Diocesan Centre near Melmoth in northern Natal. More than 100 delegates were present from Natal, the Orange Free State and the Transvaal. The gathering represented 18 of the 26 regional authorities in Natal, the KwaZulu executive councillors, most of the members of Ubhoko (an interim preparatory body) and prominent Zulu women (see Langner, 1983:20).

The first constitution of this 'new' Inkatha not only used the term 'Zulu' (i.e. made the movement ethnically exclusive at its start), but also referred to the first Inkata*: a bracketed reference at the head of the first constitution read '(Founded in 1928 — by King Solomon ka Dinuzulu)'. Langner claims that by the time the first copies of the Inkatha constitution were published, 'Inkatha YaKwaZulu' had been altered to read 'Inkatha Yesizwe' ('Inkatha of the nation', rather than 'Inkatha of the Zulu people') (1983:21). This ambiguity of being caught between the 'Zulu nation', on the one hand, and national aspirations on the other continues to haunt the movement.

This was not the first attempt to revive the Inkatha movement in Natal since King Solomon's times. In an interview Zephaniah Mahaye, a Mtubatuba businessman, said there had been an attempt in 1943 (KCAV, no number). Langner cites an interview with Chief Buthelezi as his source for the claim that Chief Albert Luthuli, then president of the ANC, tried to revive Inkatha even before the ANC was banned (Langner, 1983:12). Buthelezi, then the 30-year old chief of the Buthelezi tribe, allegedly supported this move. Paramount Chief Cyprian Bhekuzulu, apparently after being dissuaded by the Department of Native Affairs, opposed the revival and claimed that it was just a vehicle for Buthelezi to establish a power base outside formal structures as his (Buthelezi's) tribe had rejected the Bantu Authorities system. Buthelezi's biographer, Ben Temkin, denies this and says that Buthelezi went as far as calling a 'conference of leading Zulu' at the insistence of 'many of the older Zulu, including a number of

---

*The spelling used in the press at the time has been retained to distinguish the 1920s Inkata from the Inkatha of the 1970s and 1980s.

45

ministers of religion'. This meeting was, however, 'gatecrashed' by C.B. Young, Secretary for Bantu Administration. Bishop A.H. Zulu, the first black Anglican bishop in South Africa and a close friend of Buthelezi, wrote a letter to Buthelezi in which he said he knew that the chief

> did not want this thing . . . The conference must certainly not meet if it will be interpreted as your attempt to create a counter-attraction to Bantu Authorities. If some people in Zululand and Natal want to view this matter from that angle you can be sure Pretoria will do so as well [quoted Temkin, 1976:75].

As it turned out, Buthelezi established himself firmly in the Bantu Authorities structures and in the KwaZulu bantustan before forming Inkatha in 1975.

Further 'attempts to revive Inkatha by the ANC in the 1940s and by Buthelezi in the 1960s' are referred to in a dissertation completed in 1977 (Bernstein, 1977:122). It is not clear whether these are references to the same moves that have already been mentioned. What is clear is that the conservatism and Zulu 'nationalism' or ethnic consciousness that had characterized much of Natal African politics during the 20th century also lay behind attempts to revive Inkatha. The first Inkata was the creation of the African petty bourgeoisie in Natal in the 1920s, which had seen the possibilities of using Zulu 'traditionalism' as a political tool and a means of economic advancement.

While the first Inkata became effective in 1924, arising out of a prior 'Zulu National Fund', it was the rejuvenation of the organization in 1928 that has received most frequent mention. A new constitution was written in 1928, hence the reference to the 'founding' in that year by Solomon in the 1975 constitution. While this explicit attempt at continuity was dropped, because it would interfere with the 1970s movement's national political aspirations, it does draw attention to the ironies of history. To paraphrase Marx, history repeats itself — the first time as farce and the second time as tragedy. If the farce of the 1920s was to be found in the overt misuse of Inkata funds collected from the poverty-stricken population of Natal to maintain King Solomon in a style that included large liquor debts (he was an alcoholic) and ostentatious motorcars, the tragedy of the 1970s lies in the effects on national and local political struggle of the Zulu chauvinist and ultra-conservative elements in Inkatha and their actions.

It is worth mentioning some of the continuities and ironies of the links between the two Zulu-based movements.* First, the 1928 constitution, presented by Buthelezi as an element in a tradition of Zulu politics, was drawn up by a white Durban-based lawyer at the instigation of sugar interests in Natal. George Heaton Nicholls, in the mid-1920s member of Parliament for Zululand and President of the South African Planters' Union and its affiliate, the Zululand Planters' Union, and a strong segregationist, instructed J.H. Nicholson to draw up the 1928 constitution, a document that ensured that the interests of the conservative African petty bourgeoisie and tribal elites were firmly entrenched in Inkata.

The whites who influenced Inkata at this time operated behind the scenes, and explicitly kept their names out of any link with the movement. This has a parallel in the later Inkatha, which, despite Buthelezi's hypersensitive denials, has also collected a number of advisers coming from similar agricultural and industrial

---

*This section could not have been written without personal communication with Nicholas Cope, who has produced a study of the Inkata of the 1920s and Zulu politics during this period (Cope, 1986). We wish to thank him for his help. Other references are given in the text.

BILLY PADDOCK

King Solomon kaDinuzulu of the Zulus (pointing) with his iziduna (headmen).

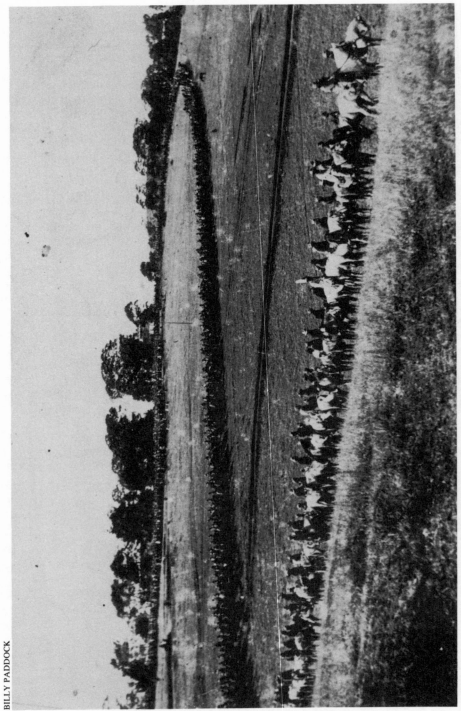

BILLY PADDOCK

Mounted ceremonial bodyguard (abaxualusi) at Solomon's installation in 1916.

backgrounds (such as Chris Saunders and Tony Ardington), from academic institutions (such as Professor Schlemmer of Natal University), from the press, where a long line of journalists have ensured that Buthelezi and the Inkatha movement have been kept in a very uncritical focus for many years now (people such as Tim Muil, Brenda Robinson, Roy Rudden, Suzanne Vos, and Arthur Konigkramer), and of course Walter Felgate (social anthropologist, businessman, and the least publicized personality in this constellation despite the frequency with which his name crops up in conversation) and Rowley Arenstein (recently unbanned lawyer and long-time friend and acquaintance of Buthelezi). Inkatha has maintained links with white political personalities (such as Ray Swart, now of the Progressive Federal Party) and parties, but this has been on a much more overt level.

In 1928 Heaton Nicholls went so far as to write a speech for King Solomon (in which the Industrial and Commercial Workers Union, the ICU, was attacked). Through the mouth of Solomon, but from the pen of Nicholls, the traditional virtues of the Zulu people were extolled. Temkin makes the claim, implausible if only because of the number of speeches given every year, that Buthelezi 'researches and writes all his own speeches — in longhand — . . .' (1976:4). It appears that the process is at present somewhat more sophisticated, using modern technology to transmit, if not write, the chief's speeches.

Second, it was not only white interests that shaped the 1928 constitution, but also specific class interests (white and Zulu). It suited both sugar planters and white commercial farming interests to 'retribalize' Zulu society, and to attempt to cement close links with the tribal elite and, especially, with the Zulu royal family (offers were, for example, made to repay King Solomon's large debts). While Solomon had not been accepted as paramount chief of all Zulu (Africans in Natal) by South African government officialdom (out of fear of a revival of Zulu political and military might), he had been acknowleged as chief of the royal tribe, the Usuthu. At the same time his acceptance in Zulu society stretched far beyond the measure of official recognition he had gained.

Such 'retribalization' at a regional level, already part of the national strategy of the state through the 1927 Native Administration Act, was perceived by regional agricultural interests to be a necessary step to secure what was being lost to the mining industry — sufficient, cheap Zulu labour, disciplined in production, as well as through tribal structures and values.

As early as 1916, when Solomon was officially installed as Paramount Chief, the limit of formal recognition, the motivation was that he could be used for 'administrative purposes'. The most important of such purposes was to recruit labour for the war effort in 1917 (Marks, 1986:33-34). Sugar producers in the 1920s wanted to use Solomon, through Inkata, to preserve Natal labour. More than five decades later Chief Buthelezi was being 'used' in a similar function as labour recruiter, but now by the mining industry, reflecting the changed economic circumstances. It was no longer possible to talk of purely regional business interests, and in any case there was probably enough labour to take jobs in Natal even at the low wages being paid.

In November 1981 Buthelezi 'dedicated' the new administrative building of The Employment Bureau of Africa (TEBA) in Ulundi, the KwaZulu 'capital'. The need to recruit mine labour locally, i.e. in South Africa, had been forced on the industry by a number of factors, including the liberation of Mozambique. In 1974 only 22% of the mines' labour force came from South Africa, while by 1981 a full

60% were recruited within the country. Buthelezi welcomed this change, and was especially 'glad to see Zulus return once again to mining'. Buthelezi told the gathering at the TEBA office that the mining industry provided skills to young workers and opened the door to other employment and that it served to make a 'young rural man . . . a more useful South African after he has subjected himself to the discipline of labour'. He continued, after reminiscing about his own visit to a gold mine:

'I have thought of it, that such work situations with their heavy demands on discipline and endurance are a far better training ground than any of the so-called guerilla camps outside the country, in making us men among men' [quoted in Gordon, 1982:30].

An article written by Dennis Gordon on the recruitment of Zulu-speakers for the mines, in the Chamber of Mines journal *Mining Survey*, offers a fascinating glimpse into the manner in which ethnicity is used to attract labour as late as the 1980s. Buthelezi was described as 'Chief Minister of the partially self-governing state of KwaZulu . . . also a Prince of the Zulu Royal Family, leader of the Inkatha movement . . . and one of Africa's most influential voices'. Bill Larkan, district manager of TEBA, was described as having a 'deep commitment to the Zulu nation', sharing a Christian commitment with Chief Buthelezi and even being called upon to open a KwaZulu cabinet meeting with prayer. Trevor Nel, in charge of TEBA operations south of the Tugela, 'believes that the traditional discipline to which rural Zulus are still subjected through the tribal structure of chiefs and headmen fits men for work on the Mines' while TEBA's Nongoma representative 'appeals to the highly-developed Zulu sense of humour by broadcasting facetious remarks as he travels the seasonally dusty or muddy roads' (Gordon, 1982).

In the 1920s Inkata conservative petty bourgeois interests were well personified in John Dube, president of the ANC from its formation in 1912 to 1917 and then, 'virtually for the rest of his life . . . to run the Natal provincial branch of Congress virtually as an independent fief' (Marks, 1975:163). A point made by Marks, that Dube's apparent later conservatism did not mean 'that he had changed from an earlier radicalism, . . ., but that the world around him had changed' (1975:165), applies in large measure also to Chief Buthelezi and the present-day Inkatha movement. Dube, by his 'avoidance of violence . . . his deeply ingrained desire for law and order . . .' and other attributes (such as a stress on self-help and the value of education), prefigures the present Inkatha leadership. However, most 'prophetically', Dube, in his close alliance with large-scale (sugar) producers in Natal, set a pattern that was to be repeated half a century later. Marshall Campbell, the sugar baron, apparently provided financial aid for Dube's educational institution (Marks, 1975:174). Today the Mangosuthu College stands as a monument to the close relationship between Buthelezi and the Anglo American Corporation.

Third, the use made of 'tradition', and especially of Solomon as effective (if not formal) king, finds an echo in the initial direct use made of King Goodwill as patron of the 1975 Inkatha. Even the term 'patron' was used of both Solomon and Goodwill, both relegated to (powerfully) symbolic positions as 'figureheads' of the ship of the 'Zulu nation'. The 'Zulu nation' as a term of political mobilization is still available to contemporary African politicians (as it was in the 1920s), but has come to be associated with the most conservative of political interests, partly because it carries with it the baggage that the apartheid policy has attached to it. It

The uses of tradition (1): Buthelezi (in horned cap) at his installation as chief in 1957, left King Cyprian (father of present King Goodwill), right Prince Isaiah Bhayisikili.

BILLY PADDOCK

BILLY PADDOCK

The uses of tradition (2): King Goodwill watched by Buthelezi as he looks at his new KwaZulu 'citizenship' card (1972).

does not just stand for a history of resistance, as was argued above, but also for the fragmentation of a national struggle in South Africa, and is linked to racial domination and economic exploitation.

A difference between the political and ideological struggle of 1928 and of 1975 lies in the central role that Buthelezi has taken upon himself to ensure continuity of Zulu tradition. This is not really surprising as the 'prime ministerial' role that Buthelezi has inherited from his paternal great grandfather, Mnyamana Buthelezi, 'prime minister' to King Cetshwayo, grandfather of Solomon (see the genealogy of the Zulu royal house, p.16), was only being reinstituted under Solomon. Solomon married several women from the Buthelezi tribe to resolve the tensions that had built up over the years between them and the Zulu royal family. He also married one of his sisters, Magogo (Chief Buthelezi's mother, who died in 1985), to Mathole, chief of the Buthelezi. Buthelezi managed to shift the king, Goodwill, into a subsidiary position, both in regard to the KLA and to Inkatha, while at the same time drawing as much legitimacy as possible from his own direct blood relationship with the royal family and from his ancestors' political relationship with the royal house (see for example, Buthelezi, 1978; Laband and Wright, 1983).

Fourth, the 1928 constitution and reconstruction of Inkata was not only to advance the direct interests of the classes involved, but also to counter the threat posed at the time by the large grassroots support that the Industrial and Commercial Workers Union (the ICU) was gaining in Natal. Ironically this was happening under the leadership of, amongst others, A.W.G. Champion, another Zulu leader who had to a large extent broken away from the national body within which he was functioning, as Dube had.

The speech referred to above, written for King Solomon by Heaton Nicholls, was aimed at attacking the ICU and bringing the weight of royal displeasure to bear on those who supported the movement. The ICU was drawing support because of the intense pressures exerted on the African rural population through changing conditions in agriculture — pressures such as land hunger because of the rising value of agricultural land, and the need for labour as the importation of indentured Indian labour had come to a halt. The supporters of Inkata, specifically the sugar industry's Heaton Nicholls, saw a segregationist policy and 'retribalization' as a counter to class-based politics. These were the themes of the speech Solomon delivered in 1928, the year in which 'an emotional pitch', unsurpassed by anything 'since the days of the native rebellion of 20 odd years ago' swept the small Natal Midlands town of Greytown, brought on by the real and exaggerated threat posed by the ICU in the district (Bradford, 1984:128).

Fifty-eight years later Inkatha has engaged in a process of trying to crush the COSATU unions and establish its own union instead, the latter arising out of a non-antagonistic relationship to capital and support for continued foreign investment. Nicholls, through Solomon, called the ICU leaders a 'noisy band of self-seekers'. Today Buthelezi, in relation to COSATU, refers to 'celebrity leaders who prance and posture as real leaders' (BS, 18 Mar. 86:5).

The campaign by the alliance of business interests, the conservative African petty bourgeoisie and the tribal elite during the 1920s was given publicity by the editor of the *Ilanga* newspaper, John Dube. In 1985 *Ilanga* journalists went on strike in protest at the pro-Inkatha editorial bias of the newspaper.

The analogies between the two periods could be expanded, but the point should be clear: the tradition of the 'founding fathers' of the ANC and of the first Inkata to which the contemporary Inkatha leadership appeals is a very conservative tradition with strong elements of anti-popular and anti-worker rhetoric and action.

Inkatha in the 1970s

The African National Congress was formed in 1912, when 'several hundred of South Africa's most prominent citizens: professional men, chieftains, ministers, teachers, clerks, interpreters, landholders, businessmen, journalists, estate agents, building contractors and labour agents, met in Bloemfontein (Lodge, 1983:1). In 1975 the formation (or re-formation) meeting of Inkatha was attended, in the words of Chief Buthelezi, by 'the cream of the elite Zulus in this province (Natal), from the Transvaal and the Free State' (KLAD, 7:772). Sixty-three years had passed, but it appears that the two groups were remarkably similar, if not in occupational composition then in class interest and aspiration. What distinguished the two meetings and the immediate concerns of those present was that the 1912 gathering aimed to create a *national* movement, to work against the exclusion and fragmentation strategies of the state that was formed in 1910 out of the Boer Republics and British Colonies (under the slogan of white unity — 'Ex Unitate Vires'). The 1975 gathering met to form an ethnic organization within a state-created administrative region of an already enormously divided South Africa.

The first president of the ANC was the Reverend John L. Dube, educationalist and editor of *Ilanga lase Natal*, who was seen as the man 'to weld the supra-tribal unity Congress had set itself to achieve' (Walshe, 1970:35). More than 60 years later Buthelezi was to appeal repeatedly to the personal and ideological links that Inkatha supposedly had with the early ANC, a link that carries little of the radicalism and direct resistance that is usually associated with the ANC as political symbol.

The process during the early 1970s that led to the formation of Inkatha is not all that clear. There are several references to the existence of a body called 'Inkatha' predating the official formation in March 1975. So, for example, in 1972 Buthelezi told the KwaZulu Legislative Assembly (KLAD, 1:10) that the first Inkata was something that Solomon kaDinuzulu had 'dreamed up', to promote the economic development of the Zulu people (we have already seen whose economic interests were served by the 1920s Inkata, and it was certainly not those of the ordinary 'Zulu people'). He stressed that what he was talking about was not a political party but a 'national movement'. He continued:

> As Chief Executive Councillor I would like to propose that this 'Ibandla' is not a party when we call ourselves 'Inkatha Ka Zulu' so that whoever has ambitions will be outside this 'Inkatha kaZulu'. That is something that was bequeathed to us by our late King Solomon ka Dinuzulu. I wish to stress that this is not a party. It is a national movement, but I would imagine that we of this Government when elections come we shout 'Inkatha' and they will say 'Ka Zulu'.

In 1973, the year after this rather cryptic reference, Buthelezi distributed the 1928 constitution to members of the KLA (Bernstein, 1977:117; KLAD, 3:281). Buthelezi repeated an earlier reason for the revival of Inkatha, namely 'economic upliftment' (KLAD, 3:174); 'We should not stop to do anything to improve our economic situation . . . Once we have a measure of economic power our battle will be half-won. That is why we should all support Movements such as Inkatha kaZulu and the Black Bank.' During the next session of the KLA Buthelezi said that he had received a telegram from a 'Mr Madlala of Johannesburg', who is 'the Chairman of Inkatha KwaZulu' (KLAD, 4:101). Wentzel (1977:6) wrote in the introduction to her interview with Dr Nyembezi and John Mavuso, chair and executive member of the Black United Front respectively, that:

> Inkatha had started in Dr Nyembezi's house in 1974 while a public meeting was being organized to receive Chief Gatsha Buthelezi and introduce members of his government to the Soweto public. The organizers of the meeting felt they would like to establish something more permanent and asked Chief Buthelezi for a name. He suggested the name Inkatha be revived . . .

> In 1974 [sic] the revived Inkatha was officially launched.

While the name was certainly around, and may have had several organizational forms before the formal reconstitution of Inkatha in 1975, what is clear is that the immediate fore-runner was a group known as 'Ubhoko' (a walking stick). Langner wrote that according to Dr Alpheus Zulu, a group of 'leading Zulus' began meeting during the early 1970s 'functioning as a "think tank" to try to work out a strategy for founding a national movement to halt the divisive effect of separate development and at the same time to act as a vehicle for the evolution of Black cultural patterns and self-reliance' (1983:17). This body developed into Ubhoko.

According to Langner, Buthelezi has claimed that the revival was his idea, with support from Bishop Zulu. In 1972 he started punctuating his speeches with the cry of 'Inkatha! kaZulu!'. Interestingly enough, in the light of the origins of the 1920s Inkata in the Zulu National Fund, Buthelezi also opened a trust fund:

> which would be used for the development of KwaZulu and its people and in particular in the fields of industry, commerce, agriculture, education, public relations and communication. He said the money could be used, for example, for the formation of a company to run a newspaper, a public relations office, and a planning and development body [Langner, 1983:17].

Ubhoko was formally constituted in February 1974, a year before Inkatha was formed.

In the KLA Buthelezi presented Ubhoko as a vehicle for the KwaZulu cabinet for 'liaison with the Zulu public and access to all those celebrities to advise us on any matter informally in the interests of the Zulu nation' (KLAD, 5:63). Members of Ubhoko included church figures such as Bishop Zulu (chair), members of the Zulu royal family such as Prince Gideon Zulu, academics such as Otty Nxumalo of the University of Zululand and Professor C.L.S. Nyembezi, and businessmen (Edward Ngobese, R.S. Ngobese) and professionals (Langner, 1983:18). One of the tasks of Ubhoko was to decide on a constitution for the planned Inkatha and in particular to examine the United National Independence Party Constitution of Zambia. Buthelezi had been impressed with this document during a 1973 visit. The UNIP constitution, with minor changes, was adopted by Ubhoko for Inkatha.

Buthelezi had also been a member of 'the group of leading politicians and academics of all races and parties who meet regularly and who are known as "Synthesis"' (introduction by E.S. Munger to Buthelezi, 1972). This must have been at the time when the idea of Inkatha was first seriously discussed, but whether there was any link is not known. 'Synthesis' is an exclusive and apparently influential discussion group composed of representatives of, for example, monopoly capital, sympathetic academics and some politicians, who invite speakers from a wide range of perspectives to brief them on contemporary issues that might have bearing on the decisions they have to make. It is not the kind of body that one reads about in the press.

Before we look at the kind of organization that was created in 1975, it is necessary to say something about the immediate reasons for the creation of Inkatha. Late in 1973 nearly all the bantustan leaders met in Umtata (Venda and QwaQwa were not represented). This meeting decided that an interview with Prime Minister B.J. Vorster would be sought early in 1974. It also asked for more money from taxes that were generated in the 'white' areas, and the repeal of the influx control legislation (Survey, 1973:164-5). Buthelezi claimed that this meeting showed the solidarity that could be achieved through the state policy.

The eight existing bantustans (two more were still to be created) met with the Prime Minister in 1974 in a 'spirit of goodwill' and it was agreed that further meetings would take place. After a meeting early in 1975 it was reported that Vorster had not agreed to any of the major requests made by the bantustan representatives, although minor concessions were made, such as the inclusion of Africans on the boards of bantustan development corporations. Consideration would be given to the return of non-communist exiles, and the recognition of trade unions for Africans could be discussed with the Minister of Labour. Buthelezi took exception to the suggestion that bantustan leaders meet with Department of Bantu Administration and Development officials to discuss the 'easing of the hardships caused by influx control regulations' (Survey, 1975:26).

Langner argues that the last straw before the formation of Inkatha was this 'homelands' leaders conference with Prime Minister Vorster in 1975. Eight days after a report-back meeting that was addressed by Buthelezi in Umlazi, Inkatha was formed in Zululand. This might be stretching the events somewhat, as the process of re-forming Inkatha was already well under way, but, as another example of the frustration of the bantustan leaders that dates back much further, it would have influenced the decision to go ahead with the formation meeting at KwaNzimela.

According to Langner, the motivation for Inkatha lay in attempts, first, to oppose the divisive effects of the apartheid policy, and, second, to stimulate self-reliance (1983:33). On a political level Buthelezi must have realized that he had reached the end of the road of what the apartheid policy had to offer. Without taking 'independence', an act that would have meant political suicide for anyone with sights higher than regional politics, he had to open options beyond the KLA. However, Inkatha's potential as a vehicle for achieving national goals only became clear later. At first the movement was locked into regional and ethnic politics, both in structure and in motivation. When Inkatha was discussed in the KLA for the first time during April 1975 (shortly after its formation), Buthelezi made the claim that the organization was the 'base from which to plan our liberation . . . I said in the past we need liberation even from such things as ignorance, poverty and disease. It was for this reason that I announced . . . that we were reviving "Inkatha", a National Cultural Liberation Movement founded by King Solomon ka Dinuzulu in 1928' (KLAD, 5:134). Not only was it to concentrate, in conception, on issues that would in effect only be resolved through participation in the bantustan stuctures (the same justification was earlier offered for taking part in the regional administration of KwaZulu), it was also initially for Zulus only.

When Buthelezi re-emphasized that Inkatha was not a political party he continued:

> In other words, all members of the Zulu nation are automatically members of Inkatha if they are Zulus. There may be people who are inactive members as no one escapes being a member as long as he or she is a member of the Zulu nation [KLAD, 5:134].

Probably Buthelezi never again stated this position as clearly, and would not have done so outside the confines of this ethnic administrative institution, the KLA, but these sentiments are of direct relevance to the apparent ambiguities of the Inkatha movement. To oppose Inkatha was to oppose the 'Zulu nation', was the message that he gave. To form any other organisation was to break the unity that Inkatha gave, to criticize Inkatha and its leadership was to meddle in the Zulu nation. The first national council and general conference meetings of Inkatha, held in July 1975, accepted Buthelezi as the '"unchallenged leader of the 4½ million Zulus in their struggle . . .", and he was empowered to speak on behalf of all Zulus' (Langner, 1983:25).

To unravel the complexities of what is meant by the 'Zulu nation' is beyond the scope of this book (for historical discussion of similar issues, see Wright, 1983; Hamilton and Wright, 1984). On a political level an appeal to Zulu 'nationhood' has had profound impact. The stress on a separate Zulu identity, excluding those outside the 'Zulu nation', started very early on in the life of the ethnically defined KwaZulu authority. Whgen the ceremonial mace was received by the chairman of the KLA from the Minister of Bantu Administration and Development in 1973, he reassured the minister that '. . .it will be kept as a token of the cordial relationship and good neighbourliness between our respective nations in this country' (KLAD, 3:1). Buthelezi, proposing that Shaka Day should replace Settlers Day as a public holiday in KwaZulu, said that '. . . he [Shaka] united all the tribes which is depicted on those strands of "inkatha" of our Mace, each strand representing a tribe in the KwaZulu area, and amalgamated these tribes into one nation' (KLAD, 4:334-5). In 1974 the positive, inclusive expression of Zulu nationalism was given form around the figure of the king. Buthelezi told the KLA that:

> The young man who was sitting here a few days ago, King Zwelithini Goodwill kaCyprian, is the King of 4¼ million Zulus in South Africa and when we are now being moved in the area of separate nationhoods as a nation, I think that he deserves such a place befitting a King of 4¼ million in South Africa . . . [Buthelezi was arguing for expenditure of R300 000 on a palace for the king — authors]. This House in fact belongs to the Zulu nation itself . . . If the Zulus want a monarchy, they must pay for it . . . If we are going to be independent, Sir, I think it is known that the King is a future head for the Zulu nation. I mean, for instance, just across here the King of Swaziland has not only one palace, but a number of them. And the Swazi nation, with all due respect to them, is a smaller nation than the Zulu nation . . . [KLAD, 4:360; also 5:56; 7:889].

In the early 1970s Buthelezi answered a question with the opinion that the 'Zulu nation' was, at the time, 'more united than it has been for the past 100 years' (Buthelezi, 1972:10).

Buthelezi has argued consistently in this vein. There are many instances when he refers to the policy of the National Party as divisive and argues for a wider South Africanism, but the strong element of ethnic identity remains, within which the Zulu people are the largest group in South Africa. In an interview in 1980 Buthelezi said that 'We in Inkatha recognize cultural identity . . . — we cannot wish it away. But I think most blacks would agree with me that cultural identity has been abused under the separate development policy' (St, 19 Aug. 80). In the same year, however, Inkatha secretary general Oscar Dhlomo wrote that the 'Zulus are not a tribe; they are a nation . . .' (NW, 7 Feb. 80). Also in 1980, Buthelezi distinguished between 'national groups' (of which the Zulu is one) within 'the nation of South Africa' (Buthelezi, 1980:3). On Soweto Day (16 June) in 1986 two of the very few meetings allowed to continue under the state of emergency in South Africa were addressed by Chief Buthelezi and by King Goodwill. The latter told his audience that 'Zulus' should 'root out those among them who are undermining their national unity'. He warned against '"new-fangled"' political organizations which 'propagated values which were total anathema to Zulu pride and culture' (DN, 17 Jun. 86).

There is a degree of fluidity attached to the terms 'tribe', 'ethnicity', 'nation', etc. What is clear is that the audience and the event shape the strength of the 'nation' appeal to Zulu speakers — the clear references to the nation quoted above were addressed to the KLA, composed solely of chiefs at that time, when the identity of this body had yet to be created in many ways. When addressing the Luthuli Memorial Foundation meeting, the stress was placed on the 'African nation', composed of a rich variety of ethnic (cultural) groups (see Bernstein, 1977:145-6; Langner, 1983:133 Booysen, 1982:160).

Without the clarity of commitment to a single 'nation' in South Africa (no matter how broadly inclusive), the appeals to a separate Zulu identity, within the context of the state's policy of a quarter of a century, are potentially very dangerous. The incidents described later in this book (see pp.189ff.) show how easily they can lead to violent conflict. Unscrupulous manipulators of ethnic sentiments feed on the tensions that have been created under the apartheid policy, ready to direct antagonisms for their own aims. 'Ethnic nationalism' also does not bode well for a future united South Africa, where regional politicians and the remnants of the old apartheid order are sure to attempt ethnic mobilization.

There are several cases where opposition to Buthelezi, the KLA and KwaZulu administration, and to Inkatha, have been labelled in racial and ethnic terms. For example, the celebration of historical figures in a regional past (so necessary for political mobilization) has on occasion taken on a reactionary tone. Shaka Day celebrations are held all over South Africa. In 1981 Dr F.T. Mdlalose addressed 1000 Inkatha followers in Soweto, and Buthelezi, who appealed to employers to let their workers off for the day, spoke at Stanger, a town with a mainly Indian population on the northern Natal coast. The Stanger Businessmen's Association had called for the closure of shops during the Shaka Day celebrations, mindful of the 'disturbances' that occurred in the town during these celebrations the previous year, when 'many stalls were looted and owners assaulted for not allowing their workers the day off'. It was suggested that 24 September be declared a public holiday in Stanger as well as in KwaZulu proper (*The Leader*, 25 Sep. 81). Buthelezi told the 10 000 people assembled that Indians had a great future, but that they should share 'their gifts with Africans', and in his familiar indirect style reminded them that '"It will be a sad day if I have to advise my people not to buy from these [Indian-owned] shops"' [NM, 25 Sep. 81].

The speakers in the KLA who followed Buthelezi's introduction to the movement in 1975, took up the theme of continuity with the 1920s Inkata. Chief O. Sithole, councillor for agriculture and forestry, reminisced:

> I was still a young boy when King Solomon inaugurated this movement. Our fathers were very much determined about this thing.

> A man from the Royal clan named Matshe used to collect contributions up in my area. Whenever this man addressed our people in our area, he would tell my people that there was so much money at the Royal Kraal Mahla, that he used to indicate a mealie tank that stood next to my father's house, a very big tank, which contained about 60 bags of mealiemeal. He would tell us that, out at Dlamahlahla kraal, there were six tanks full of money. People were very impressed by this, and this man used to go back to the Royal Kraal with many herds of cattle and a lot of money in his pocket. He would come not only once, but time and again he would come to collect . . .

> . . . Let us sacrifice and give all that we have, let us fill the six tanks with money [KLAD, 5:195].

The KLA debate was dominated by the themes of the 'Zulu nation' and how it was to form the base for the new Inkatha, references to the first Inkata and the need for sacrifice, as the romanticized version of that early history demanded, and Inkatha fees. What is striking is that, while several pages of transcribed debate were devoted to the issue of the amount of the contributions to be demanded from KLA members and Inkatha membership fees, in contrast there was very little discussion about the principles and aims of the new organization — '. . . you have to pay if you want to become free' was the message (KLAD, 7:710). Even the unemployed were not excluded. Buthelezi argued that unemployed people should pay according to their means, but that people 'must not stay at home. This is another liberation that I mention here, the liberation from slothfulness' (KLAD, 7:716).

The one issue, other than membership contributions, that raised debate was the relationship between the KLA and Inkatha. The first constitution stated that, should there be conflict between a decision of the Inkatha central committee and the KLA cabinet, the decision of the former should prevail. Buthelezi said hesitantly that '. . . we feel that this is African participatory democracy. I think it is a new form of constitutional law . . . I do not think that it is constitutional law, I think it is African participatory democracy' (KLAD, 7:721-2; also see Buthelezi, 1975:15). His confusion about how to justify this measure, which would have taken power away from the chief-dominated KLA, must have been apparent for it offered one of the few examples of members challenging his wishes. Paul Sibeko queried the idea of 'African democracy', to which Buthelezi retorted with '. . . African democracy is democracy expressed through the medium of African culture, as evidenced by the people who make up the nation . . .' (KLAD, 7:723). As a career politician himself, Buthelezi is probably as much of a stranger to some of the more 'philosophical' or theoretical issues of political practice as that other career politician for whom he has at times expressed respect, P.W. Botha.

Later in the debate Buthelezi amended the contentious section, and asked whether it would be in order to say that the cabinet would 'seriously consider' the views of Inkatha. This was agreed.

This revived Inkatha was not only placed squarely within Zulu ethnicity and even 'nationhood', but also based itself on the authority of chiefs in the rural areas, or in areas in which the power of chiefs held sway. A suggestion was made early on that branches should coincide with the area of authority of indunas (headmen or councillors to the chief). For urban areas branches would be formed in voting wards for the bantustan's elections. Regions in rural areas would then coincide with regional authority areas. To ensure rapid membership increases this strategy made a lot of sense: not only could pressure be applied by the chiefs on people subject to them in a range of ways, but pressure could also be applied on the chiefs through the KLA and the KwaZulu administration generally. So, for example, during the same year (1975), while Inkatha committees to run the planned elections (which in the event did not occur before 1978) were being discussed, Buthelezi said that he was '. . . distressed to find that the districts here in KwaZulu — for instance here in Nongoma . . ., Inkatha is almost dead. It is a dead duck' (KLAD, 7:921). The blame was laid squarely on the shoulders of obstructionist chiefs, who were called to account in the KLA. The assembly was already being used to advance the Inkatha movement because, in effect, the two could not be distinguished. It was only later, when Inkatha was established and national political considerations became more important, that it became important to deny the symbiotic relationship between the two bodies.

This debate also made it clear that the decision to form Inkatha had been taken by 'the cream of the Zulu elite', and that at grassroots level there had been very little knowledge, and certainly no consultation. For example, a representative from the Hlanganani Regional Authority complained that this thing was being done in a great hurry and he wanted time to go back and inform the people. The KLA chair assured him that he would '. . . be given the opportunity to go back to your people and to tell them what is going on' (KLAD 7:801). Inkatha had been formed, to represent all the Zulu people, a couple of months earlier.

It was not only the chiefs that appeared to be reticent in certain areas. The month after the formation of Inkatha Buthelezi was already complaining that civil servants ('. . . some of them are in this House'), were 'running down' the Inkatha constitution (KLAD, 6:350), an accusation that was to be repeated over the years, but with an ever larger number of people being included in the anti-Inkatha conspiracy.

Inkatha was formed in 1975 within the KwaZulu bantustan and it is clear that, whether as a matter of strategy or less self-consciously, it defined its issues at that stage within the bantustan. It was clearly necessary for gaining membership that an appeal should be made to the most immediate constituency, that over which administrative responsibility had already been accepted. However, there seems to be a similar 'inevitability' about the politicization of tribalism that went hand in hand with this mobilization. Inkatha arose as a 'Zulu' organization, inextricably tied to the bantustan structures of KwaZulu, and has never been able to escape this past in any significant way. As a 'Zulu' body it was able to mobilize readily, and as a bantustan movement it was protected from state action during its early years, but these apparent advantages have since become serious hindrances as the general mood in the country has changed.

5. Inkatha's Structure

The Inkatha constitution was modelled largely on that of the Zambian United National Independence Party (UNIP). KwaZulu interior minister Dr F.T. Mdlalose commented: 'We took several ideas from the 1928 Inkatha structure, but obviously it was defective in a number of ways', and that is why they turned to the UNIP constitution (KCAV, 157 and 176). In 1979 Inkatha secretary general Oscar Dhlomo told Inkatha youth delegates that the constitution 'grew out of the Lusaka Manifesto drawn up in 1969 by 14 African states and adopted by the United Nations Assembly by 113 votes to two' (NM, 26 Mar. 79).

The Lusaka Manifesto committed the 14 signatory states in eastern and central Africa, and later the members of the United Nations General Assembly, to work towards the abolition of racial discrimination and the right of all people in southern Africa to participate in their own government (see Brownlie (ed), 1971:526-33). It was totally inappropriate that Dhlomo should attempt to place the struggle of the Inkatha movement in the context of the Manifesto, as it states that peaceful change is preferable, but '. . . while peaceful progress is blocked by actions of those at present in power . . ., we have no choice but to give to the peoples of those territories (Mozambique, Angola, Portuguese Guinea, Namibia, Rhodesia, South Africa) all the support of which we are capable in their struggle against their oppressors'. On South Africa the Manifesto advocated actions even further removed from what Inkatha has always stood for:

> South Africa should be excluded from the United Nations Agencies, and even from the United Nations itself [Buthelezi has opposed this]. It should be ostracized by the world community. It should be isolated from world trade patterns . . . [Brownlie (ed) 1971:532, article 22 of the Lusaka Manifesto].

As has been mentioned, the first constitution stipulated that the Inkatha president also had to be the chief minister of KwaZulu (something as difficult to defend in a national liberation movement as the stipulation about Zulu predominance). Patrick Laurence, writing some years after the change in the constitution in 1979, argued that this clause was put in to 'guard against the contingency of an unprincipled opportunist taking over as Chief Minister and concluding an independence agreement with Pretoria' (1984:271). This might be true but it is one of many features confirming that the Inkatha movement grew out of, and within, the KwaZulu bantustan.

The movement has a 'well organized pyramidical structure', leading up from individual members, branches, regions, to the various top decision-making bodies and conferences. The *national council* (NC) is the policy making organ. The NC has 300 members on average, although, as Langner wrote, this body, like the general conference (GC), differs in actual composition from the provisions of the constitution. It is composed of the central committee, the KLA members who are also members of Inkatha, four representatives of the regions, members of the brigades' executives, one representative from each affiliated organization, and the organization's administrative officials. Inkatha has 'absorbed' the KLA through the NC, so that it can be regarded as in practice 'the legislative arm of Inkatha' (Langner, 1983:71). The NC can, in fact, propose legislation to the KLA. Schmahmann, commenting on the 'absorption', wrote that 'If not elitist, the movement has potential for being authoritarian . . . The potential for abuse by those who control the movement is . . . great. Intermingling the Legislative Assembly with the National Council and the Cabinet with the Central Committee precludes the growth of effective opposition political parties' (1978:285). The NC meets at least twice a year and, except for the opening, sessions are held in camera (Langner, 1983:79).

It appears that the *general conference* would consist of all NC members, along with two or three representatives of every branch. In the early 1980s there could, thus, have been 2300 delegates to the GC. Langner comments that 'provision for the representation of other interest groups on the General Conference (and the National Council) is negligible'. This provision had been copied from the UNIP constitution. Whatever the reason for its inclusion, in practice 'it is an effective preventive measure against the forming of pressure groups by these affiliated organizations' (Langner, 1983:80). It is at this level that constitutional provision is made for the representation of trade unions, amongst others. The GC can amend the constitution, by a two-thirds majority, and can 'consider, review or change' any policy. The GC has to meet annually to discuss a programme prepared by the central committee (CC), and approved by the NC. Voting is by secret ballot.

The *central committee* is responsible for 'programming' and implementation of policy. It must have a minimum of 25 members (the president, secretary general, 20 members elected by the GC every five years, and members nominated by the president in consultation with the CC). The number of nominated members has increased dramatically. While in the pre-1979 constitution provision was made for only three such members, a year after the constitution was changed (i.e. in 1980) the president had appointed 20 members, and the CC had 46 members. It has been suggested that these positions serve to co-opt local (community level) strong-men and warlords in KwaZulu whom it would be preferable to have within the organization rather than organize opposition from without. Presidential appointment, with the approval of the CC, also avoids clashes in the NC and GC where some of the appointees might be controversial. One such person, for example, is Mandla Shabalala of the Lindelani 'informal settlement' outside Durban (see map), who arose as a powerful local person, apparently outside the formal KwaZulu and Inkatha structures. Shabalala has featured prominently in allegations of vigilante involvement in the 1985 unrest in the Durban area and since then.

It may be an acknowledgement that the strategy of co-opting people on to the CC for political reasons has made it unwieldy in terms of its tasks, that an 'inner council' (shades of the central state's State Security Council) has been formed. For example, in 1980 it was reported that certain decisions had been taken by the 'newly-created inner council of the movement's central committee. It has been created to deal with urgent business' (St, 24 Dec. 80). Langner confirms the existence of the inner council, but says it was only formed in February 1981 (1983:86).

A member of the CC has to be over 21, have no criminal record (a stipulation that can be waived by the CC), and must be a 'disciplined person'. The 1980 CC had, among others, eight chiefs, six women and seven people from outside Natal as members, while fewer than half were also members of the KLA (Langner, 1983:83). On elections to the CC Langner writes that there is 'apparently much control over the candidature and it almost looks as if the outcome of the elections can be regarded as a foregone conclusion', but that democratic provisions do exist. The composition of the CC changes as well, with only 11 members of the first CC still in office in 1981. The CC is extremely powerful, both in the movement and also in KwaZulu politics. Internally the CC has 'overall control of the activities of the Inkatha and shall ensure that discipline in the Inkatha is maintained throughout the country'. Externally, the CC controls the selection of candidates for 'Parliamentary and Local Government Elections'.

The CC functions through a series of sub-committees, whose members are appointed from the CC and the NC by the president:

1. defence and security committee (12 members);
2. political, constitutional, legal and foreign affairs committee (10);
3. economic and finance committee (5);
4. social and cultural committee (9);
5. elections, publicity and strategy committee (8);
6. appointments and disciplinary committee (6).

What is clear even from the constitution, not merely from the practice of Inkatha in KwaZulu, is that at several levels the movement is part and parcel of the bantustan administrative structure. The NC incorporates the KLA, the CC decides on candidates for KwaZulu elections (that is the only 'Parliament' and 'Local Government' it participates in, at least at this stage), and the president has to qualify 'to be Head of Government in any government which the Movement, by virtue of having attained a victory at a General Election or for any other reason, is entitled to form'. The Inkatha president is also the only candidate which the movement will support for the post of head of government (Langner, 1983:82; Inkatha, nd(a)). Until Inkatha is drawn into a revised system of government in South Africa it means that, as was the case before the constitution was changed, the president of Inkatha must belong to the Zulu ethnic group. Gibson Thula, in charge of publicity for Inkatha for a time, said after the 1979 constitutional change, surely with his tongue firmly in his cheek, that it was now possible 'for a non-Zulu to become president of Inkatha and thus also chief of the Zulus' (*Frontline*, 1, 1, 1979). This would, of course, make nonsense of the KwaZulu bantustan constitution and Buthelezi's claim to sole legitimacy in the traditional position of prime minister to the Zulu king.

Inkatha is at present, in one of its aspects, simply another bantustan political party. In terms of the distinction drawn by Buthelezi between short- and long-term involvement, Inkatha is firmly located in the former as the ruling party within the KwaZulu bantustan.

It was probably wishful thinking that made Temkin write in 1976 that the presentation by Buthelezi of Inkatha as a *national* liberation movement to *overseas* audiences, rests on:

the already overwhelming and enthusiastic response with which it has been met in towns and cities all over the country . . . Inkatha is above black suspicions. It is not a government institution nor is it an institution arising even indirectly from official policy. There is no taint of apartheid attaching to it [1976:334].

Apart from the qualification of being able to head a government in which Inkatha has come to power, the president of the movement must be over 35 years of age. He (because of the 'tradition' appealed to by the KwaZulu leaders there is little doubt that the president will be male) has been given wide, but not free, rein. Article 14 of the Inkatha constitution lists the powers of the president, which include that of giving instruction 'on any matter affecting the Movement', to appoint committees and to take disciplinary action against any member, and provides that he will be the principal spokesman for Inkatha.

Langner's comment on the powers of the president are probably correct:

> There is no doubt that the power of Buthelezi's personality is a dominant factor within Inkatha, and superficially it seems as if he has unlimited powers in certain instances. But Buthelezi and Inkatha acknowledge that the President can only act within the precincts of the 'will of the people' and that he can be removed if his orchestration of the affairs of the movement are not acceptable [1983:93].

What needs to be added, though, is that Buthelezi has made the movement and his own personality virtually synonymous, which makes any overturning of his decisions difficult to imagine. Langner acknowledges that the president could 'entrench himself in a virtually unassailable position', as could members of the CC. Inkatha has argued that because consensus rules, the loopholes in the constitution should not present any problem:

> He [Buthelezi] says a matter is discussed until agreement has been reached. When asked in which way it becomes clear that there is consensus, he simply said: 'We know.' He pointed out that nowadays they might vote by show of hands, but traditionally — and even today — they *knew* when consensus had been reached [Langner, 1983:103].

Buthelezi operates by caucusing beforehand, 'planting' ideas rather than deciding. The liberal journal *Reality* (7,5,1975:3) commented editorially after an interview with the first Inkatha secretary general, Dr S.M.E. Bengu, that this type of consensus might mean that the 'dissident voice' will not be heard, a fear that has to some extent been borne out by a KLA request to the central government that opposition parties not be allowed to exist within KwaZulu. While the main reason was a legitimate concern about the involvement of the central state security apparatuses within KwaZulu opposition politics in the early 1970s, it was also stated that opposition parties were an unnecessarily divisive force. The KLA did not have the powers under the first stage ('Chapter 1') of self-government to implement this wish for trouble free internal politics. Minister M.C. Botha turned down the request for legislation to give effect to the proposal in 1975. Once Inkatha had been formed the NC rejected the formation of opposition parties. As 'Zulus were still bound in chains', they had a primary objective 'to free the nation of these chains'. The motion concluded that 'Therefore we can see no reason for the formation of political parties in KwaZulu' (DN, 16 Jan. 76). This line of argument makes sense if it is kept in mind that Inkatha presents itself, and its leaders perceive it, as reflecting the will of 'the people', of 'the oppressed', of the 'Zulu nation'.

Inkatha branches

It is important to look at the spread of branches and membership because it is on the basis of these that Inkatha claims to be a national, cross-ethnic movement, going beyond the state's policy of fragmentation. 'Non-Zulu' allegiance to

Inkatha and Chief Buthelezi has been a very sensitive issue with the Inkatha leaders, and maybe even more so with politicians and academics who favour the solution that the movement is said to hold for South Africa.

Inkatha's branches have to have a minimum of 30 members, a committee of eight members, and a 'branch executive committee' of 14 members. Langner wrote that it is not clear why there should be provision for two committees (1983:75). The large number of committee positions, relative to the minimum size of a branch, has also drawn comment. Venter (1982:37) suggested that it shows a concern not only with effectiveness, but also with status and 'elite formation'. This view was supported by a member of the Inkatha Institute in interview, who also referred to a similar structure in churches. Kiernan (1982:169), writing on Zulu Zionist churches, said it had been suggested that 'the emergence of elaborate hierarchies serves the purpose of maximizing opportunities for the exercise of leadership, thus compensating "for the loss of such leadership opportunities in the political and administrative spheres".' If this is indeed true of Inkatha it would indicate a very manipulative and paternalistic approach to membership. A more sympathetic, if not necessarily accurate, interpretation would be that in the case of a political movement such as Inkatha the abundance of committee seats could serve as a training ground for members in the procedures of the organization. If this was the case, it has not worked that well as one of the more recent activities undertaken by the Inkatha Institute is to train members and establish branch procedures.

A month after the formation of Inkatha in 1975 it was reported that ten branches had already been formed in townships around Durban. Nomathemba Sithole (secretary with the United States Information Service in Durban) was elected organizing secretary of the interim committee. Buthelezi said that branches had to be formed in consultation with the KwaZulu urban representative, a civil servant (DN, 26 Apr. 75) — no time had been lost in making use of the facilities offered by the bantustan. Early in 1977 there were 300 branches (200 rural and 100 urban) in existence, 18 of these outside Natal (Schmahmann, 1978:277-78). Professor Schlemmer, academic and Inkatha spokesman, said on SABC-TV (3 Dec. 84) that nearly a third of branches were in the Transvaal urban areas in 1984. Schmahmann made an early claim for Inkatha branches in the western Cape, where the African population comes mainly from regions inhabited by Xhosa-speaking people (the eastern Cape).Reference to these western Cape branches, placed specifically in the townships of Langa, Nyanga and Guguletu, have been made uncritically since then (see, for example, *Frontline*, 1, 1, 1979; NM, 21 Feb. 80; Langner, 1983:71). However, researchers in Cape Town have not been able to discover these branches.

A thesis submitted in 1983 mentioned 1000 branches of the movement in 20 regions — more than 90% of them in Natal (including KwaZulu) (Langner, 1983). However, Kane-Berman, writing a year earlier, claimed 1200 branches and placed 30 of these in Soweto (1982:155). Despite the contradictory figures, and despite the primary reason for quoting branch numbers and location — to show national membership — observers accept that Inkatha is predominantly a Natal and Zulu organization. Schlemmer admitted that branches outside the province reflected a Zulu-speaking presence in those areas, that even though ethnic affiliation does not appear on membership forms, the mass of its members are Zulu-speaking (over 95%), and that it is basically rurally based (1980:115). This Zulu and rural bias correlates very well with organizational patterns of Inkatha, at least during the first five or so years of its existence. In rural areas constituencies coincide with chiefs' areas of authority (Schlemmer, 1980:115; and above), and Inkatha regions take the same boundaries as the regional authorities in Natal established in terms of the 1951 Bantu Authorities Act. It comes as no surprise then that the movement's 'spectacular growth' can 'in large measure' be ascribed to the 'active co-operation of tribal chiefs' (Schlemmer, 1980:116). John Kane-Berman, ex-journalist, director of the South African Institute of Race Relations and also vice-chairman of the KwaZulu/Natal talks in Durban, wrote that Buthelezi confirmed this in that he 'has insisted that traditional authority be respected and that chiefs, as patrons, should exercise a watching brief over local branches' (1982:154). As far as could be established Inkatha has never claimed branches in any other bantustan.

Inkatha's brigades

While membership of Inkatha proper is restricted to 'persons' over the age of 18, 'female persons of not less than eighteen years of age' enroll in the Women's Brigade, while 'persons' who are under the age of 18 and 'those people who are accepted by the Youth Population as Youth' join the Youth Brigade. The latter provision regarding Youth Brigade membership was one of the additions to the constitution in 1979, while an amendment removed the Youth Brigade from the jurisdiction of the CC and placed it directly under the president (the Women's Brigade remained under CC control).

The Women's Brigade functions in parallel with the 'main constituencies, branches and other units' of Inkatha. It is supposed to play an 'instructive role in the mobilization of the womenfolk and upbringing of children towards the objectives of the Movement'. The Youth Brigade is allocated a less supportive role. It is to function as the 'reserve of the Movement and shall play the vanguard role of upholding and consolidating gains of the Movement'. It too exists side-by-side with the main structures. The chairs of both brigades are appointed by the president in consultation with the national women's council in the one case, and with the CC in the case of the Youth Brigade.

The Women's Brigade was inaugurated at the Inanda Seminary at the end of May 1977, and its first conference was held at Ulundi in October of that year. As with the other sections of the Inkatha movement, the conferences of the Women's Brigade are usually attended by large numbers of people. In 1978, for example, it was claimed that 1000 delegates attended (RDM, 5 Sep. 78), and they elected Anastasia Thula (wife of CC member Gibson Thula) as secretary.

Ella Nxasana, Women's Brigade executive member, said in 1979 (KCAV, 194) that the tasks of the members were, for example, ploughing, gardening and sewing. She denied that Inkatha wanted women to stay in the home. W. Yengwa, another executive member, said the Women's Brigade had fought very strongly against the notorious restrictions placed on African women in Natal through the Natal Code and the Bantu Administration Act of 1927. She also claimed that the Women's Brigade had been aiding unions, through food boycotts (she mentioned the Fatti's and Moni's boycott of 1978) but was clearly unsure of her facts and finally said that Inkatha was not working with existing unions but starting its own. (This was in 1979.) (KCAV, 188.)

In 1974 W.S.P. Kanye, executive councillor for justice, introduced a motion in the KLA calling for the introduction of a select committee to investigate the legal disabilities of women under the Natal Code. Kanye was careful not to offend 'traditionalists', and admitted that there might be some members of the KLA who would be offended by the idea that women be given powers 'which they did not possess formerly', undoing 'that which belongs to the nation'. Buthelezi seconded the motion. The debate was notable for sexist remarks (KLAD, 4:64). The committee was to be chaired by S.Z. Conco. In 1975 an interim report was tabled (KLAD, 6:349), and later in the session presented by Conco (KLAD, 7:823-848), but no debate took place. Conco said that very few replies had been received to the thousand questionnaires sent out. He blamed this on illiteracy, obstructive officials, and social conservatism.

The final report, which was discussed in 1976, was only four pages long. Dr A.H. Zulu said that if the KLA was committed to freedom then they had to accept the report. He continued that the KLA had previously 'accepted the necessity for adjusting its laws, contrary to custom, if it should be found necessary to do so', referring, for example, to the 'un-Zulu' way in which the role of the king had been defined. He said that the inferior position to which women had been allocated had been 'according to Zulu custom', but that Secretary for Native Affairs Shepstone, in 19th-century Natal, had artifically frozen the position (KLAD, 9:536-538). The changes proposed would not affect the practice of lobolo (paying bridewealth). Conco said that a function of Inkatha would be to implement the recommendations, and made several calls for the total repeal of the Natal Code rather than just Section 27, which was the only part dealt with.

The Natal Code of Native Law, in this case, refers to the 1891 codification by the Natal Legislative Council of what they perceived to be 'traditional customary law', but that in many cases bore very little relation to pre-colonial practice. This was especially the case with regard to property and other rights of 'Zulu' women (cf Welsh, 1971:169). What codification also did was to impart 'a rigidity to customary law which it had not had in its traditional context' (Welsh, 1971:171). 'The social base of traditional law' was being constantly eroded through the demands of capitalism and the actions of the state, while the codified laws were inflexible and could not adapt to changing circumstances. African women, in particular, 'suffered a deterioration in status as a result of the Code' (Welsh, 1971:176).

Section 27, the only one the KLA decided to request the central government to repeal, dealt with the perpetual minority status in law of African women in Natal. Unless she was 'emancipated'

a Bantu female is deemed a perpetual minor . . . and has no independent powers save as to her own person . . .' She is always under the guardianship of a man . . . first under . . . her father, or, if he should die or become incapacitated, the head of the kraal concerned. When she marries, her husband is her guardian; and if she becomes divorced the guardianship reverts to her father . . . If she becomes widowed, the guardianship is the head of her husband's kraal (who may be her eldest son if he is a major in law) [Horell, 1968:3].

'Emancipation' could occur if an unmarried, widowed or divorced woman, by virtue of good character, education, thrifty habits, 'or any other good and sufficient reason', was freed by order of Bantu Commissioner's Court from the control of her guardian (Horrell, 1968:3).

A motion was accepted calling on the central government to repeal Section 27, and to amend Section 226 of the Criminal Procedure Act (56/1955), which would allow exemption from giving evidence against their husbands not only to women married under Christian rights but also to 'customary union' marriages (KLAD, 9:595-6). During that same session in 1976 the executive councillor for justice said women were to be employed at the same ranks and rates of pay as men in his department. Earlier the education councillor had turned down such a suggestion on the grounds of insufficient funds (the justice department decision would only affect 32 women at that time).

The Youth Brigade will be discussed in greater detail later (see pp.183-89), but some introductory remarks are appropriate here. The Youth Brigade dates back to 1976, but held its first conference only in 1978, when an eight-member committee under Musa Arnold Mkhize was elected. Mkhize came from Evaton in the Transvaal. He said that Inkatha had to be promoted at universities 'to counter the influence of the South African Students Organization (SASO)'* (Langner, 1983:153). Langner notes that from 1980 there have been moves to change the Youth Brigade into 'youth corps':

> For the sake of discipline the children were dressed in uniforms and time was devoted to marching and the singing and shouting of Inkatha songs and slogans. The children were also involved in community projects such as soil preservation and gardening, and Buthelezi foresaw a situation 'where young people who have left school are going to have to spend a year or so working for the community in the rural areas' . . . they would earn their keep and a 'more permanent group' would get 'a modest salary' from Inkatha *and the KwaZulu government* [Langner, 1983:154, emphasis added].

From this change came the Emandleni-Matleng youth camp. As early as 1974 Buthelezi had envisaged a labour contribution during a 'compulsory year . . . similar to the one year during which White youths are compelled to do military service' (KLAD, 5:141). The 'Youth Service Corps for Social Reconstruction' (YSC — the Emandleni-Matleng camp) was established in January 1982. After the 1980 schools boycotts, ruthlessly repressed by Inkatha members (Kane-Berman, 1982:156), Buthelezi called for 'well-disciplined and regimented impis in every Inkatha region' (SP, 22 Jun. 80). The Inkatha Institute drew up the curriculum for the YSC (McCaul, 1983:27).

'Development' is one of the mobilizing slogans employed by Inkatha and the KLA. A multitude of activities has been presented under the umbrella of 'development', from gardening to involvement in profit-making through bottle-stores. In a rousing speech to the national executive committee of the Youth Brigade (BS, 23 Nov. 80, quoted in Teague, 1983:68) Buthelezi not only referred to the semi-military role that the Youth Brigade (or rather a 'Youth Service Corps' in this case) was to play ('I can envisage a camp in our rolling countryside where 10 000 youth will be mustered, drilling, learning, teaching and being taught, disciplining themselves to become fashioned steel for the struggle'), but also grandiose development projects ('I can see units of the Youth Service Corps constructing dams, building bridges, salvaging drought-stricken soil, introducing forms of life-saving technology, building schools, conducting literacy classes . . .').

Teague commented that she would conclude that the YSC 'has essentially three aims':

---

*SASO was the first specifically 'black consciousness' organization to be formed, in 1969. It was banned by the state in 1977 (See Davies, et al, 1984:302-08).

Firstly, on an ideological level, it provides Inkatha with the opportunity to inculcate members of the Youth Brigade with a strong sense of loyalty and duty towards the 'Zulu nation' — and thereby Buthelezi and Inkatha. Secondly, it provides Inkatha with the means of substantiating Buthelezi's constant threat that Inkatha will 'pick up the gauntlet' thrown down by its enemies, imagined or otherwise. And thirdly, the 'social reconstruction' aspect — the training in rudimentary development skills — is part of the recognition by Inkatha that in order to retain and attract support, it needs to become more involved in 'bread and butter' issues in the community [1983:72].

The first two aspects of Youth Brigade and YSC activity will be discussed later. At this point it can be added that another important function of the Youth Brigade and YSC is an attempt to absorb at least some of the thousands of young people who annually leave school with not the slightest chance of a job, and who have formed such an important and volatile element in the civil war in South Africa since 1976. Professor Schlemmer (of the Inkatha Institute and the University of Natal) said in a TV interview that what was needed was a mass youth movement of the unemployed (*Midweek*, 16 Jan. 85), while the head of the Inkatha youth affairs section said in an interview that the Emandleni-Matleng camp arose out of the unemployment crisis in KwaZulu (McCaul, 1983:25).

As early as 1976, in a KLA debate, the executive councillor for community affairs admitted the problem of youth unemployment. Explaining a R700 000 item in his budget for youth camps, he said that

These are actually places where the youths, who cause a disturbance in the community, are placed . . . those youths who are undesirable or who are delinquents [KLAD, 9:318].

The existence of such large numbers of young people whose aspirations for jobs and security cannot be met under the present economic and political system in South Africa is of grave concern to those interests who would lose most through the destruction of the apartheid state and economy. Given its present role in South Africa and in the Natal region especially, it is cause for concern that the Inkatha movement should be attempting to mould these people into a political weapon.

In a briefing paper dealing with 'development' and Inkatha's role, secretary general Oscar Dhlomo spelt out very clearly what they had in mind. He and the Women's Brigade's Ms Mchunu were on a visit to Israel where they discussed the formation of a Youth Service Corps, a large-scale, 'para-military' project, with a camp 'for something like 10 000 trainees'. Dhlomo's document continued:

We need to discuss this [YSC] concept with people who have possibly been involved in military training camps and in small scale community-bound light industries and service industries.

. . . we would like to meet people who could offer guidance on:
1. The use of military trainees on community service programmes, rural agricultural work and work in building infrastructure for development.
2. The requirements of attaining self-sufficiency in military training camps . . .
5. The appropriate ratios of training to routine military exercises to leisure in training programmes . . .
6. The type and duration of specialized training and psychological preparation of leaders and officers in preparation for larger training camps . . . [Dhlomo, 1981:8]

The Youth Brigade was modelled on the Young Pioneers in Malawi and the Zambian Youth Service. Gibson Thula, then KwaZulu urban representative in the Transvaal, was sent to Zambia in 1976 to study the Youth Service there (Bernstein, 1977:135-6). Musa Mkhize visited Malawi on a similar trip (DN, 27 Mar. 80). Members were also being sent to the Coady Institute in Canada to give effect to the 'development' aspect of the Youth Brigade's activities — the Coady Institute also provided training for the setting up of the Inkatha Development Office (McCaul, 1983:21). With the record that the Malawian Young Pioneers have gained for being 'party thugs' and 'storm-troopers', this model could not have been less auspicious (McCaul, 1983:42).

In 1979, at the time of the Inkatha delegation to London to meet the ANC — the meeting that led to the dramatic break in relations — *Beeld* editor Ton Vosloo said that Afrikaners and Zulus should talk: '. . . If the Afrikaners and the Zulus, as the two biggest components in our patterns of people, could make a compact, the road ahead would be infinitely easier' (SE, 18 Nov. 79). These sentiments have been expressed by Buthelezi as well, and nowhere more clearly than during addresses to Afrikaans students; he has, for example, addressed the Afrikaanse Studentebond (ASB), an arch-conservative student organization. The 'compact' that Vosloo desired has been a de facto position in the contacts between the Inkatha Youth Brigade and the ASB. While the formal relationship between the two parent bodies (the National Party and Inkatha) has been very strained at times, the youth organizations have managed to cooperate in joint structures over the years. University of Stellenbosch Students Representative Council members and Inkatha members had discussions on several occasions before the links were formalized through the establishment of the South African Youth Foundation in 1981 — a 'think tank'. In 1980 ASB executive members visited Ulundi and invited Inkatha Youth Brigade leaders to their conference. In 1984 Youth Brigade organizer Ntwe Mafole received a standing ovation from ASB delegates at a meeting in Bloemfontein on South Africa's political future until the year 2000. During the same year, 1984, the Youth Brigade annual conference condemned NUSAS, Diakonia (the Durban-based ecumenical organization), and others and said that 'Inkatha's youth were aware that the struggle for liberation had been "long inhibited by white, coloured and Indian liberals who thought that they knew what was best for us"' (Survey, 1984:12). The ideological affinity and cooperation of the various youth groups, such as the recently formed Jeugkrag SA (Youth Power SA — 'aimed at countering radicalism from left and right') which was to hold a joint conference with Inkatha's Youth Brigade, no doubt facilitates other levels of contact between Inkatha leaders and Afrikaner leaders (political, cultural and economic).

Inkatha's membership

The membership increases by Inkatha have been nothing if not spectacular. After a ten-year period of existence (1975-1985) it neatly achieved the one-million member mark, or an average of 100 000 members per year:

1975 - formation
1976 - 30 000
1977 - 120 000
1978 - 175 000
1979 - 250 000
1980 - 300 000

1981 - not known
1982 - 411 000
1983 - 750 000
1984 - 900 000
1985 - 1 million

[figures McCaul, 1983:7; Survey, various; Inkatha conference reports. It must be stressed that these figures reflect a selection from contradictory claims].

Exaggerated and contradictory claims are made for membership totals and for composition. For example, in 1978 Chief Buthelezi claimed 150 000 members, but added that for every member there were between 30 and 50 sympathizers giving true support of between four and seven million people (Survey, 1978:28). Other examples are discussed below.

It is stating the obvious to say that the membership claims have to be treated with a measure of caution. First, 'spectacular' totals and 'phenomenal' growth are of tremendous importance to the movement and to those who support a central, national role for Inkatha and for what it stands for. The larger the organization, the more legitimacy for its claim to speak for 'the people'. What distinguishes Inkatha from other bantustan-based parties is that it claims a vast membership. This will ensure that it, and not any other claimants, can deliver the goods (non-violence, the last chance for peaceful negotiated change, free enterprise, stability, anti-socialism, etc.). Its 'constituency', that term favoured by Inkatha's leaders, distinguishes it from being another 'Muzorewa option' — a reference to the ill-fated attempt by the Rhodesian regime to find a credible black face to forestall a take-over by the liberation groups. Membership claims are, therefore, hardly ever subjected to any kind of scrutiny and critical assessment, but simply taken at face value.

Second, these figures are important in the struggle for popular support against other, antagonistic organizations. It is quite true that there has never been a mass movement in South Africa that has been able to claim a signed-up membership of a million. Most certainly the ANC had never been able to achieve this, even in its legal heyday. Lodge wrote that the peak during the 1940s was only some 5500; it was no more than 7000 in 1951, but then reached a high of 100 000 by the end of the Defiance Campaign in 1953. However, 'official membership figures do not accurately reflect the full extent of the ANC's influence' (Lodge, 1983:75). This is borne out today by the support reflected in attitude surveys, funeral attendance, the power of the ANC symbols within the present revolt in South Africa, and the state's own costly and time-consuming, if ineffective, attempts to counter the symbolism and focus that the ANC provides. The ANC has been operating illegally for 26 years, and membership and support are criminal offences. Even before it was banned the ANC was subject to intense state repression, while the Inkatha movement operates within state structures and with official approval. Comparing their membership figures is a spurious exercise.

The only contemporary comparison is with the United Democratic Front, which claims to be more representative than Inkatha, and is certainly a national organization in a way that Inkatha is not, but which is composed of affiliated organizations. The UDF's present centrally organized strength is very much affected by the state's repressive apparatuses. The Congress of South African Trade Unions (COSATU) represented at the time of its formation in November 1985 a paid-up membership of 400 000 workers, organized into a democratic and disciplined structure (Lewis and Randall, 1985; Carrim, 1986). The point to be made here is that Inkatha's massive claimed membership must reflect, for its supporters inside and outside the movement, not only an ability 'to deliver the goods', but also to deliver in opposition to counter-claims.

Third, these Inkatha-supplied figures represent joining figures (based on entry fee receipt numbers), rather than paid-up membership. Kane-Berman said, for example, that by the end of 1979 350 000 people had been enrolled and 'fully paid-up' (1982:155). However, by the end of 1980, despite a gain of 61 000 new members, there were only 187 000 paid-up members. In other words, only 36% of members had renewed membership. Inkatha views it differently though, and calculates membership on the basis of once a member always a member:

> . . . membership does not lapse with failure to pay the annual subscription and resignations . . . have been negligible. In Inkatha's view, 350 000 added to 61 000 would give a more accurate reflection of membership in 1980 [Kane-Berman, 1982:155].

Buthelezi, in a letter to all branches in 1979, wrote that only 5% of Inkatha members were paid-up. He attacked the 'thousands who, when I return from abroad or address meetings, mob me with shouts of "Buthelezi is Our Leader", and yet fail to pay their membership fees' (STb, 4 Nov. 79).

Despite all these qualifications, even from Inkatha's president and from such supporters as Kane-Berman, Buthelezi still speaks of having 'a paid-up membership of nearly one million' (this was in 1984; see BS, 29 Jun. 85:23). The frequent use of the term 'paid-up' may reflect Buthelezi's knowledge that only in that way can any organization judge the true commitment of membership to the aims that it stands for. A constitutional provision is, therefore, usually made for participation in leadership and decision-making only by members who are paid-up.

Fourth, methods of recruitment are also of relevance in a critical assessment of membership figures. Beyond those who find, in an unproblematic way, their aspirations, of whatever description, met within the organization, there are also those who are 'nudged' into membership. This euphemism is used by Schlemmer (1980:122) to describe the use of the 'sanctioning power of the KwaZulu administration'. With the overlap between Inkatha and the KLA a range of services become 'pressure points' to ensure membership, such as pensions, work-seekers' permits, houses, land and jobs.

It is not our intention to give a comprehensive picture of the 'nudges' that are employed. A few examples will suffice. In 1976 the executive councillor for works, Chief E.T. Xolo, reminded chiefs '. . . that today people may not as much as purchase land without producing their citizenship certificates, and there will come a time when Inkatha will become such an important organization, that people who are not members thereof will find themselves in the cold' (KLAD, 8:147). In 1978 residents in the Mafunze tribal authority near Pietermaritzburg said they were facing eviction by the acting chief unless they joined Inkatha. They listed the tax and other financial obligations they had:

> Each and every resident has to pay R3 in respect of (1) Entrance fee to the National Cultural Liberation Movement — Inkatha; (2) An annual subscription which is R2: (3) R3 for a tribal fund; (4) A R5 slaughter fee for a beast; (5) KwaZulu Government tax of R3; (6) Chief Gatsha Buthelezi emblem which is 75c; and (7) 50c to cut thatching grass [NW, 7 Dec. 78).

More recently Belinda and Simon Mfeka won an interdict restraining an Inkatha central committee member, Thomas Mandla Shabalala, from threatening or assaulting them in the Lindelani area where they live and where Shabalala has his base. In an affidavit they claimed that Shabalala had threatened them with death if they did not leave the area. Shabalala said they must be 'UDF' because they had not joined Inkatha and paid their dues:

> . . . R5 for Inkatha, R1,50 for the Inkatha Women's Brigade, R3 for UWUSA [United Workers Union of South Africa, formed by Inkatha], R2 for Inkatha building fund and R3 for Mr Shabalala's bodyguard fund [*Echo*, 29 May 86].

When the Natal African Teachers' Union (NATU) affiliated to Inkatha, the chair of an Inkatha branch in KwaMashu, Ewart Bhengu, responded to the 'advice' issued by the KwaZulu secretary of education, G.L. Steyn, that all teachers under KwaZulu should join Inkatha. He said that 'in his opinion teachers were not bound to become . . . members. Their membership was, however, vital as it would squash speculation that Inkatha was a Communist organization' (NM, 27 May 77).

Closer to the present we find that Buthelezi made it clear that organizational affiliation has a lot to do with employment in KwaZulu. He said that United Democratic Front (UDF) members were not welcome in the civil service as the organization 'did not compete in the market place of ideas that could be accepted or rejected on a democratic basis' (DN, 20 Dec. 85). Early in 1986 seven doctors employed at KwaZulu hospitals had their permanent employment turned down, despite a critical shortage of qualified medical personnel in the region. Health minister Dr Frank Mdlalose refused to tell them the reasons for the refusal. 'It is my prerogative whom I employ,' was his reply and he was also not willing to confirm or deny that political motives informed the decision. Four of the doctors said that they had refused to sign a pledge that they would not denigrate or criticize the KwaZulu government and its chief minister, while they were students at the (black) medical school in Durban. The pledge was required of all bursary holders. When their bursaries were held back they instituted legal proceedings and the bursaries were restored before the case came to court (DN, 31 Mar. 86; STb, 6 Apr. 86).

However, all these important qualifications notwithstanding, Inkatha does undoubtedly have a large following and to ignore this would be to misjudge the consequences that its existence will have on attempts to construct a post-apartheid South Africa. What can be said about this membership? Why are people attracted to the movement for reasons other than short-term gain, the necessity of allegiance to survive in a hostile environment, and other 'negative' reasons that might 'nudge' people into paying at least a joining fee?

The 'Zulu tradition'

It has been admitted by supporters of the movement that Inkatha over-whelmingly draws on the support of Zulu-speakers. In other words, most of the reasons for 'positive' identification with what the movement says it stands for have to be sought in the Natal region. Furthermore, it must be approached historically, because the reasons for which people joined in 1975 might very well not be the reasons for which they joined after the court decision in Inkatha's favour over the incorporation of Ingwavuma into Swaziland. This was a tremendous victory in the eyes of Inkatha, and was presented as a vindication of its policy of working within the system. It was said to have boosted membership considerably in 1982. Inkatha's figures show a membership leap of 400 000 in that one year, more than doubling it to 750 000.

On 18 June 1982 proclamations in the government gazette did away with the Legislative Assembly in the KaNgwane bantustan and removed the Ingwavuma district from the administrative control of the KLA, in preparation for moves to hand over these land areas, and the people in them, to the Swaziland state. It caused a national and international outcry. Inkatha and the KLA took a central part in opposing the state moves and ultimately won several court decisions against the technicalities of the proposed handover. Much has been written on these events and the reasons why the state should have taken such a politically dangerous step, from which it later had to withdraw (see, for example, DSG/SARS, 1982; 1984)

What concerns us here is the effect Inkatha's response to Ingwavuma had on the membership drive of the movement. The enormous increase in claimed membership is no doubt due to the massive publicity that Buthelezi, Inkatha, and the KLA received over the issue — most of it apparently positive. The publicity was given a boost with the successful court action by Inkatha. Legal action, however, removes an issue from rank-and-file level and places it in the hands of leaders and legal experts. The court action did boost Inkatha's membership, but it rested on crude doses of ethnic chauvinism. While the dispute was in progress it also allowed Inkatha to deploy its Youth Brigade in the district of Ingwavuma, and several accusations of intimidatory behaviour were made against them by the population of this remote part of Natal.

The propaganda battle was largely fought on the level of competition for the historical ethnic origins and allegiances of the people in question. This is understandable on a superficial level because of the way in which the state, with its own ethnic obsessions, chose to define the issue of incorporation — 'Swazis belong together', was how it was put. Buthelezi argued, for example, that 'Dingane was buried in the Ingwavuma district, adding weight to the correctness of KwaZulu control', and at the end of May (1982) he announced that a tombstone would be erected to commemorate this event 'to emphasize the Zulu presence' (DSG/SARS, 1982:10; KLAD, 6:379). In familiar fashion Buthelezi told the press conference that he would

> 'not be at all surprised' if fighting between Zulus and Swazis broke out in mine compounds, townships and hostels in and near South African urban areas [RDM, 25 Jun. 82].

He told the Inkatha conference that

> Zulus had the same right to exist as any other national group. It was insulting to talk down to them when they were the largest national group — bigger that the white group, the Swazis or the Sothos — even though they did not want national sovereignty as spelled out by Pretoria [DSG/SARS, 1982:15].

In 1975 Buthelezi was already suggesting that the border with Swaziland be patrolled by 'Zulus' trained by the South African Police (KLAD, 6:577). In a revealing comparison he referred to a Sotho-speaking group in KwaZulu:

> We are now placed in the same position as . . . when Chief Molefe held out; you know, in other words refused to conform to the Bantu Authorities Act and to become part and parcel of this Assembly because he aligns himself with the Basotho Qwaqwa [bantustan] in Witzieshoek [KLAD, 6:380].

In addition to supporting ethnic appeals, the incorporation issue also allowed Buthelezi to engage in threats of violence, going so far as to say that 'if we had guns we would resist with guns' (DSG/SARS, 1982:10).

The initial positive appeal of the Inkatha movement was to people who accepted a self-definition of being 'Zulus'. It was formed as a 'Zulu' movement, as was documented in Chapter 3. Much of the appeal was, therefore, to the consolidation of the 'Zulu nation'. For example, the first Inkatha secretary general, Professor S.M.E. Bengu, told a Labour Party conference at the end of 1977 that the Inkatha strategy was 'to organize the Africans of Zulu origin into a cultural unit, regaining whatever had been lost of their traditional values' (St, 28 Dec. 77). Jill Wentzel was told, in an interview with Inkatha's Dr Nyembezi, that what was said when recruiting people was 'you have a fine leader in Buthelezi. You must support him. You must work for the Zulu first and then attract all for the good of the community' (1977:7). In May 1976 Buthelezi envisaged that there could be several Inkathas, joining together 'in a national movement towards liberation', while at a 'local level [Inkatha] is bound to have a local ethnic flavour, which should enrich the all-embracing Black Inkatha when we meet at that level rather than be detrimental to it' (KLAD, 8:92). Karis (nd:B10) said this emphasis soon changed and the call became one for other Africans to join Inkatha. Formally this was the reason offered for the changes in the constitution in 1979, a factor that was given a great deal of publicity when Buthelezi was called in by Justice Minister Jimmy Kruger to be told Inkatha must remain Zulu.

Buthelezi's frequent references to his origins and legitimacy within a specifically Zulu tradition no doubt appeal to many people who have maintained links with the land and therefore, of necessity, with the system and ideological justification of chieftainship. The appeal to a 'Zulu tradition' is accompanied by memories of the warrior qualities of 'Zulu people', and the history of resistance to British occupation of Natal and to Boer settlement of this part of South Africa. The message is that this was a noble past that can be recalled, and striven for again, with pride. Such an ethnic nationalism will find ready acceptance by many in Natal, in view of the historical availability of the 'Zulu nation' as a mobilizing idea, nearly 25 years of implementation of NP policy specifically centred around the supposed continued existence of a 'Zulu nation', and the social collapse that had occurred in rural Natal, as it has in all other bantustan areas of South Africa. Not only had population density and land degradation made any but the most limited production an impossibility, but the conditions were further aggravated by the abolition of the labour tenant system on white farms, which forced some 300 000 African people mainly into the bantustans (SPP, vol 4, 1983:53; Maré, 1980:8-15). In the words of the 1932 Native Economic Commission, labour tenancy referred to 'the giving of services for a certain period in the year to the farmer by the Native and/or his family in return for the right to reside on the [white] farmer's land, to cultivate a portion of land, and to graze his stock on the farm'.

A 1972 report painted this picture of the ravages caused by the forced abolition of this system in favour of full-time wage labour by a reduced number of workers living on the farm or migrating as 'single' workers from the bantustans:

Scores of farm workers and their children, shunted away from the Weenen district into the bleak homeland settlements after the abolition of the labour tenant system, are starving in the Msinga district . . .

75

Once a progressive community, these people were pastoral peasant farmers and each had more than 200 goats. Now they are living in a rural slum [NM, 17 May 72].

Dr Anthony Barker wrote in 1974: 'Where I live at Nqutu [in KwaZulu], just as in a hundred other areas, the numbers of people are greatly increased, throwing out of balance the older equations of economic viability on a basis of subsistence agriculture. The homelands have become the nation's overcrowded back yards' (1974:1; also Clarke and Barker, 1974).

It was in this context of social disintegration, a process that started in the 19th century but was hastened by the NP government's bantustan policy and the concomitant forced removals, that Inkatha was formed. It offered, at least initially, elements of an historical pride through membership of an organization that had its roots in that history, a leader that was as firmly part of it, and that expressed itself in the rhetoric of 'cultural liberation'.

This is how journalist Louis du Buisson described 'KwaZulu 1982 — Buthelezi's Year' (*Pace*, Dec./Jan. 1983):

1982 also saw the Zulu monarch, King Goodwill Zwelithini, step more visibly into public life. For the first time in his ten-year reign, King Goodwill shared the political platform and the public limelight with Chief Gatsha Buthelezi. At the height of the Ingwavuma affair, he addressed mass meetings all over his kingdom, culminating in a massive Imbizo (meeting) at Nongoma attended by 20 000 Zulus.

Two days later the king was in Pretoria, discussing the Ingwavuma affair with the Prime Minister, Mr P.W. Botha, and members of his cabinet. He returned triumphantly having extracted from the Government an undertaking to reconsider the move after consultation with the Zulu people.

King Goodwill was greeted with cries of *Usutu* when he returned — a royal greeting which had faded with the decline of the Zulu monarchy after the defeat of King Cetshwayo a century ago, but which suddenly took a new meaning in the stormy days of Ingwavuma . . .

In the sudden surge of nationalism that followed the Ingwavuma affair the ranks of Inkatha swelled at an unprecedented rate . . . The Inkatha Youth Brigade in particular showed a phenomenal growth, with membership approaching 100 000.

It was, of course, the Youth Brigade that was mobilized to recruit members in the Ingwavuma area, and to counter any moves to secede. In light of such appeals to past glories, it should not come as any surprise that the Inkatha 'stormtroopers' and vigilante groups in townships should call themselves the 'amabutho' — the age-regiments formed under Shaka, primarily for military purposes, but also to form hunting parties or to engage in public works (Maylam, 1986:29).

It is revealing to note some of the other appearances of the king, since the ethnic revival of 1982, after having been kept constitutionally and politically on the periphery by Buthelezi during the first five years or so of the existence of KwaZulu. In 1986 King Goodwill made two well-publicized public appearances. At one he announced the meeting to launch UWUSA as a counter to COSATU and added his voice to the call for Zulu attendance, and the second was a Soweto Day 'Address to the Zulu Nation' at Nongoma. During the latter he called on the 'purging' of Zulu communities of the UDF, the ANC and COSATU (see Chapter 8). He also appealed for a restoration of 'Zuluness', to counter the 'alien values' that had entered 'the largest population group in the whole country' (GS, 16 Jun. 86).

The ANC tradition

Another tradition invoked by Inkatha that is readily available and has served to draw many into the organization is that of African National Congress, the longest existing African nationalist movement on the continent. This may seem contradictory in the light of the attack on movements including the ANC just quoted, but it should be noted that Inkatha leaders make a distinction between the ANC before it was banned in 1960 and the 'ANC Mission in Exile'. This will be discussed in greater detail later (see pp.136-49), but a few comments are needed on the ANC and Inkatha membership.

A fair amount of confusion must have existed in the minds of many Africans, and not only in Natal, about the relationship between the ANC and this new movement, formed by a person who frequently refers to his ANC membership, and even more frequently to the fact that he had been asked to participate in bantustan politics by ANC leaders, who places Inkatha within both a Zulu history and an ANC history, and whose movement uses the ANC colours and uniforms similar to those of ANC members. The fog of deliberate confusion has steadily cleared as the relationship has become more strained between the ANC 'Mission in Exile' (as Buthelezi without fail refers to the ANC) and Inkatha, and as Inkatha has been forced to give greater content to what it claims to represent within the ANC and where it differs from that organization.

It is not only Buthelezi who was once a member of the ANC. There have been and still are several people in Inkatha who once occupied positions within the ANC. Jordan Ngubane, friend and mentor of Buthelezi, was a founder member of the ANCYL but left the ANC 'because of his belief that it was increasingly susceptible to communist manipulation' (Lodge, 1983:87). Ngubane joined the Liberal Party and established links with the PAC (see, for example, WIP 12, 1980); H.J. Bhengu, an attorney and member of the Inkatha central committee, was on the ANC national executive committee (but a member of the Liberal Party after that); S.S. Lugongolo-Mtolo was ANC provincial treasurer in 1950-7, and in the 1970s served on an Inkatha CC sub-committee; H.S. Msimang was a founder member of the ANC in 1912 and then a member of Inkatha until his death in 1982; Bishop A.H. Zulu, another important influence on Buthelezi, was a member of the ANC from 1942 until it was banned, but has been prominent in KwaZulu bantustan and Inkatha politics for many years (see, for example, Deane, 1978; *The Nation*, various issues). Many other leading figures in Inkatha also played prominent roles within the ANC. Other former members of the ANC are, or were, involved in Inkatha because they perceived a link between the two organizations, at least in the form that allegiance to the ANC took in Natal. In a 1975 study Webster (1979:63) found that when workers were asked which leader, past or present, could 'improve the position of African workers', 44% said ANC president Albert Luthuli, with Buthelezi scoring next highest at 19%. Mandela was supported by 10% and Moses Mabhida 8%. Mabhida, the South African Communist Party secretary general who died in 1986, came from the Pietermaritzburg district.

There are several reasons why ANC members in Natal should also have been so prominent in Inkatha, other than changing political allegiances or any genuine belief that Inkatha was the ANC reincarnated. The ANC in Natal had, at various times, been marked both by conservatism and a separatist streak (similar to that found in white politics in the province). In the 1940s ANC president Xuma had to

77

rely 'heavily on [A.W.G. Champion] an embarrassingly conservative colleague in Natal affairs'. Champion was ousted by Chief Luthuli in 1951 as president of the ANC's Natal region (Walshe, 1970:394-5). This is not to argue that conservatism was always dominant.

The fact that chiefs and the Zulu king were drawn into ANC activity also brought with it fairly strong rural membership. Xuma, for example, had called on the Zulu paramount chief Mshiyeni ka Dinuzulu, to 'bring in his people' by blessing ANC recruitment. In trying to increase provincial autonomy in the 1940s, Champion had turned to chiefs in the province to contribute more towards ANC funds (Walshe, 1970:386,389).

Lodge wrote of ANC Natal leaders who were dissatisfied with the Umkhonto (the ANC military wing) regional command in the early 1960s, apparently because of the degree of autonomy the latter enjoyed. He said the problem seemed to have 'derived from the absence of any consultation by the ANC's national executive of lower echelons when Umkonto was established' (1983:237). Buthelezi subsequently played on this regional dissatisfaction through references to the undemocratic nature of the 'Mission in Exile', and the 'undemocratic' decision to enter into armed struggle (eg, BS, 29 Jun. 85:20; 29 Aug. 82:26).

Finally, for some the positive drawcard would be their agreement with the general political strategy and tactics advocated by the Inkatha leadership.

Inkatha's strategy and tactics

As recently as 1983, Inkatha secretary general Oscar Dhlomo published an article entitled 'The strategy of Inkatha and its critics' (Dhlomo, 1983; a mimeographed version dated April 1983 was also available). Dhlomo's presentation of the Inkatha strategy forms the basis of this initial discussion of what Inkatha offers its members as policy. He distinguishes between a 'strategy of survival' and an 'organizational strategy'.

Buthelezi justifies the *strategy for survival* with Mao Tse Tung's dictum: 'The basic principle of war is to preserve oneself and destroy the enemy' (Dhlomo, 1983:49), and that the wise general will let his soldiers die only 'at that moment when there is nothing else left for them to do'. This survivalist approach dictates that Inkatha *participates openly* in politics in South Africa, hiding nothing from the security police, quoting banned leaders and meeting with the ANC (at least until 1979). It also demands *constituency politics,* in which various interests (constituencies) such as workers, professionals, youth, are brought together under a 'basic common goal' (Dhlomo, 1983:51), this goal being 'the total liberation of black people in South Africa'. Each constituency 'at a particular point in time, is in a position to become effective in opposing any version of apartheid, provided the opposition is properly organized and appropriately conscientized' (1983:51).

In a slightly different context, the constituency has been called the many and varied 'bricks of black nationalism' — there are 'ethnic groups, there are tribes, there are trade unions, drama societies, black church groups, student organizations, cultural groups and many others' (Buthelezi, 1976, quoted Maré 1978). Buthelezi has since become more discriminating, giving pride of place within the wall of black unity to 'workers and peasants', but this all-encompassing approach has made Inkatha obsessed with controlling as many activities, organizations and funds as possible in its area of influence. The corollary is that any independent activity is perceived as threatening, to be treated with wariness or eliminated. Unity through Inkatha is the implication.

Dhlomo argued that constituency politics 'serves to increase the cost to the state in case it attempts to act against a liberation movement by way of either banning it or banning its leaders' (1983:52). The obvious truth in this statement has been commented on by many observers. But the element of Inkatha strategy that has served to protect the organization as much, if not more, is its participation in the KwaZulu bantustan, and the ultimately non-threatening nature of its demands. This aspect is discussed later in great detail.

The *organizational strategy* has several elements: the first is *black unity,* which, according to Dhlomo, is a unity that recognizes diversity and is based on a respect for 'the right of everyone to present his views to the masses and to attempt to establish a movement with aims and objectives in support of his views' (1983:52). In practice this is demonstrably sanctimonious rhetoric — the reality has been that only views that correspond with those propagated by Inkatha are tolerated. To support his contention, Dhlomo referred to the Black Unity Front (BUF) and South African Black Alliance (SABA), as well as informal contact with the ANC and black consciousness organizations during the 1970s. He said that Inkatha calls for black unity from a 'position of immense strength', and that any political solution in South Africa would have to include Inkatha.

Second, *the strategy of non-violence* is probably the most often repeated element of what Inkatha stands for. Dhlomo wrote that 'Inkatha's strategy of pursuing non-violence . . . is pragmatic . . .' and then listed the reasons why it had been adopted:

a. because violence has never been propagated by a movement operating inside the country, for which the example of the ANC is given. This argument rests firmly on Inkatha's view that the ANC is purely a 'Mission in Exile', and on its claims that the policy of armed struggle does not carry the support of the majority, or even a large number, of black people;

b. no country bordering South Africa is willing to make its territory available for bases from which to launch attacks. Logistically violence is, therefore, 'not feasible', as a secure base would be essential for effective armed struggle;

c. armed struggles have 'partly' contributed to the liberation of countries such as Mozambique, Angola and Zimbabwe, but these have been the exceptions on the African continent. This view equates independence with liberation, and, regardless of history, levels the experiences of a continent, both before and since independence;

d. South Africa is exceptional in that the white ruling population is larger and more entrenched than anywhere else in Africa ('a determined tribe'), oppressors who 'command the most lethal military machine and the most vibrant economy in the Southern hemisphere';

e. Inkatha cannot allow Africans to be 'lured' into a position where they will have to fight from weakness, being unarmed. In 1978 an interesting interchange took place over this issue. Buthelezi had been interviewed by the BBC, and said he understood why the ANC had turned to Moscow for aid, when the West would not help. He was then asked: 'If you had the tools would you become a revolutionary?'. Buthelezi replied that he would 'decide that when I have the tools. It's not a thing that we discuss hypothetically' (RDM, 16 Mar. 78). That statement would appear to make nonsense of much of what he usually says about non-violence, and Buthelezi was quick to correct this bit of bravado. In the English-language press he was reported to have said that he was speaking 'hypothetically . . . There is not the remotest possibility of that happening' (St, 16 Mar. 78). The Afrikaans press asked him whether by 'tools' he had meant weapons, to which he replied 'no', he was referring to 'development tools' (Bd, 17 Mar. 78);

f. Inkatha is convinced 'that there are effective non-violent means of crippling the South African government and that these are preferable to armed struggle' (Dhlomo, 1983:55). Dhlomo then referred to the 'soft underbelly' of the economy and worker and consumer power that could be used to force the South African government 'to capitulate'. This is what Buthelezi himself has referred to as 'active non-violence, whereby for instance we disrupt services, etc., and show disobedience' (KLAD, 5:84).

This aspect of the non-violent strategy is frequently advanced by Buthelezi and other Inkatha spokesmen. It is obviously necessary or Inkatha would have no arrows in its quiver to show how it means to bring the apartheid system down. However, a non-violent strategy is only valid with a regime as ruthlessly entrenched as the NP government if there is a simultaneous threat that it could change to violence. This has to be a threat so phrased that everybody knows what you are talking about, even if it is not directly stated. Buthelezi is a master of this kind of statement and seldom gets caught out as in the BBC interview mentioned. Some examples make this clear. In his presidential address to the 1979 Inkatha conference Buthelezi said: 'If the time ever came when I was forced at the point of a gun to take Transkeian-type independence, non-violence for me would cease to be noble' (NM, 2 Jul. 79); in 1983 Buthelezi warned that in the 'new political dispensation, I will be answerable almost exclusively to my black constituency in which there will be hardening attitudes and an ever increasing demand for the kind of politics in which I have not yet been involved' (*Letters*, St, 28 Mar. 83); in 1979 he told the Women's Brigade that Inkatha might have to turn to violence at some point as the ANC had done (RDM and St, 18 Dec. 79); and in 1980, speaking at the unveiling of King Cetshwayo's tombstone, Buthelezi told about 5000 applauding people that the 'Zulu people had to spill a lot of blood in defence of their heritage and their country and were prepared to do so again if necessary' (DN, 29 Sep. 80). Inkatha 'will review its attitude to violence at the end of this decade' was the message of an Inkatha position paper in 1983 (Inkatha, 1983).

The strategy to threaten is valid, argues Buthelezi, because he is both led by 'the people' and a leader of 'the people'. The use of worker and consumer power would remain a threat, he argued, until it became an 'articulation of what is in the hearts and minds of black people'. Added to that, according to Inkatha, is the need to mobilize a constituency, to 'have prepared the people for the hardships which are entailed in using these strategies' (STb, 6 Nov. 83). However, when Kane-Berman asked Buthelezi in an interview whether Inkatha was not powerful enough already 'to paralyse Durban by a strike', he replied: 'Of course. Definitely. One might say we should have a show of strength. But we must have an issue to hang it on, something that affects workers directly' (*Frontline*, Oct. 1980). The contradictions mount, because this does not square with Inkatha's frequent rejection of strike action, even around issues that affect workers directly, nor with the movement's response to worker stayaways. The strategy is the threat.

The tricameral constitution is one issue on which worker and consumer action has been threatened. Another was when Dr Piet Koornhof, then Minister of Co-operation and Development, said in 1981 that a cabinet committee was looking into means of stopping the 'swamping' of whites by black people in business and residential areas (NM, 30 Jul. 81); another is bringing whites to a conference table, and 'bringing whites to their knees'. Whatever the issue, Buthelezi and Inkatha have shown a consistency since at least 1973 in threatening worker and consumer action. Booysen, in her analysis of the content of Buthelezi speeches, commented that the theme of the use of this power for the achievement of political goals had increased since 1978 (1982:178).

Inkatha has allocated a supportive role within the strategy of worker and consumer mobilization to those Buthelezi calls 'the peasantry':

> When I think about use of worker power, I think about food production, so that when there are stay-aways people are not going to go under because they haven't got enough mealiemeal for porridge to eat. Yesterday I was talking to ordinary peasants about the importance of food production not just to fill their tummies but as part and parcel of the liberation struggle [Buthelezi in *Frontline* interview, October 1980].

This thinking has been voiced in Inkatha for a long time. Bernstein interviewed Dr Bengu, the first Inkatha secretary general, and was told that 'one of the aims and functions of the Inkatha Youth Brigade is to improve crop production methods "so that when we go on strike, we can eat"'. She commented that he 'repeated this phrase in two different contexts' (1977:152).

Over the years the Inkatha leaders have consistently rejected armed struggle for the members of the movement. At the same time, however, Buthelezi has been ambiguous towards the armed struggle option of the ANC. His initial response during most of the 1970s was that there were different ways of trying to reach the same goal and that while he was firmly committed to peaceful change it was a valid decision for the ANC to have taken the path of violence. He also expressed understanding of the factors that led to that decision. However, as Booysen's analysis of Buthelezi speeches has shown, he evaluated 'external' violence positively, especially between 1974 and 1976, but in 1979, when the break with the ANC occurred, this changed to a negative evaluation (1982:146). Addressing the Association for Public Justice in Iowa in 1979, he said: 'Those who take up arms while there are other alternatives embark on barbarism. The premature resorting to violence is expediency of the worst order' (DN, 27 Aug. 79). Yet in 1981 a general council resolution expressed understanding of the exiles who had been driven to violence, but totally opposed 'the senseless destruction of meagre facilities serving black areas such as railway lines and power substations, which result in hardship to blacks . . .' (St, 22 Jun. 81; Dhlomo, 1983:56).

Buthelezi, in an article on the referendum results, where threats were important again, warned that he had 'never discouraged those among them [black people] who wished to join either the PAC and the external mission of the African National Congress' (STb, 6 Nov. 83) — seemingly forgetting that four years earlier he had called on the Women's Brigade 'to do all in its power to see to it that young men did not go into exile . . .', as there was '. . . the wealth of human experiences and values that could be had by staying with the ordinary people in their suffering' (RDM and St, 18 Dec. 79).

Inkatha in the system

Along with non-violence and constituency politics Inkatha advocates participation in apartheid structures. 'We must not destroy the foundations of the post apartheid society we long for', hence the 'only option' was participation in the structures of bantustan South Africa, Buthelezi told the Convocation of the Black Washington Technical Institute (St, 9 Nov. 76). Canadian business people were told the previous year that, ironically, it was the instruments of apartheid that were used to revive 'voices within South Africa' (St, 6 Nov. 75).

In effect, this participation has given Buthelezi 'an unprecedented foothold in white society and an unparalleled organizational base in the rural and urban areas' (Bernstein, 1977:159). On the one hand participation is presented as part of the strategy *chosen* by Buthelezi in order to prevent KwaZulu being ruled by a National Party stooge, while on the other hand he had to be *forced* to accept the position of chief minister — 'much against his will' — by the people of KwaZulu (Dhlomo in *Post Natal*, 3-6 Feb. 82). Furthermore, he was *destined* to lead the Zulus and this had nothing to do with the apartheid policy, and yet participation is no more than a *strategy* for creating a 'liberated area from which I can engage in the liberation struggle on South African soil' (Buthelezi interviewed by Chris Freimond, RDM, 12 Aug. 80). By 1985 the strategy had paid off, according to Buthelezi:

> We have created a springboard from which we can go forth to conquer in ever widening circles [a reference to the cooperation between KwaZulu and Natal in provincial government — authors]. We have created for Black South Africa a liberated zone from whence we can mount our strategies and attacks on apartheid which are vital to the country as a whole [BS, 29 Jun. 85:6].

Probably his most revealing statement on the implications of this strategy was one he made to a group of visiting US Congressmen in 1981:

> Inkatha leaders believe that the institutional structure of South African society has to start changing soon. Underlying the institutional structure are structures of power and control.
>
> In order to understand these structures and influence them Inkatha cannot afford to be a marginal protest movement. Our policy is to become *institutionalized* ourselves so that we gain experience of power and that we become linked into the major structures in our society.
>
> We have shares in business, we participate on the Board of the KwaZulu Development Corporation and we are the cabinet of KwaZulu. This means that we are not as vulnerable as we might otherwise have been. We also have an ongoing interface with the Government. We are in control of whether or not Government policy succeeds or fails, at least for the group that the Government regards as KwaZulu citizens [emphasis original, quoted Sow, 11 Aug. 81].

An Inkatha document, apparently circulated within the movement, sets out the movement's 'viewpoints on change and liberation' (Inkatha, 1983). It is fascinating reading and worth referring to in some detail. In a section on 'how Inkatha sees the South African system' it describes that system as a 'massive military-industrial machine and [a] huge bureaucracy', the power of which makes 'simple strategies of protests and rebellion pathetically ineffective' (1983:2). Instead, it is 'in fact better to *increase* one's activity in the system and in so doing to increase the influence one has', rather than to 'pretend' to be outside 'as some black consciousness spokesmen try to do'. Through 'infiltration' on the economic and other fronts change will be brought about. Using an equilibrium model of society the document argues that:

> A system is most easily changed from the inside. This is because all parts of a system depend on one another, and if one part presses hard and effectively for change other parts have to allow that change [Inkatha, 1983:5].

This strategy gives content to at least two slogans: 'Through reform revolution becomes an evolutionary process' (1983:8), and 'Inkatha believes in the strategy of participatory democracy, that is, to infiltrate and influence the system to change' (1983:10).

But institutionalization, or infiltrating the system, is not only a strategy. It has consequences that affect, or even contradict, the reasons advanced or claims made for that strategy — such as to be a *liberation* movement. We go so far as to argue that institutionalization is what Inkatha leaders desire — not so much to change the system from within as to become part of it, because what Inkatha advocates in economic and political terms does not demand any fundamental change. As Anglo American's Gavin Relly said so succinctly in an interview when asked whether Anglo American supported Buthelezi: 'You can't expect us to run away from the single black leader who says exactly what we think' (NM, 10 May 86).

The following words used in the 'reprimand' meeting called by Minister Jimmy Kruger (see p.40) indicate what the Inkatha leaders want for themselves and their class interests:

Mr Kruger: You don't like the smallness of the cake, this is your trouble.
Chief Buthelezi: Why should we like . . .
Mr Kruger: You want the whole cake, Chief.
Chief Buthelezi: Not for me alone. I want us to share the whole cake, Mr Minister, all of us.
[Inkatha, nd:23].

In the next chapters the nature of that cake, as perceived by Inkatha leaders, will be discussed. Now we turn to Inkatha's institutionalized participation in the KwaZulu bantustan. The background has already been presented in Chapter 4.

The bantustans, whether 'independent' or 'self-governing', are essentially parts of South Africa. They may be separated on racial and ethnic terms and given a degree of administrative authority and budgetary control, but in terms of overall political direction, financial control and regional economic and labour systems, they are an integral part of apartheid South Africa. The best way to characterize them would be as branches of the state that created and maintains them. They are more than mere 'apparatuses of the central state', in the degree of autonomy and the complex multi-functional nature of their administrations (in contrast to, for example, the primarily singular function of the educational apparatus of the central state) — bantustans duplicate, in miniature, the functions of the central state.

The ZTA, formed in 1970, started off with an executive council (cabinet), composed of a chief executive officer, Buthelezi (who also held the portfolios of finance and economic development, and authority affairs), and executive councillors for justice (Chief S.O. Sithole), works (Chief E.T. Xolo), community development (B.I. Dladla), agriculture and forestry (W.S.P. Kanye), and for education and culture (J.A.W. Nxumalo) (Temkin, 1976:128).

By 1982 KwaZulu had reached stage two self-government (in 1977), and had had elections (in 1978). The cabinet now looked like this: the chief minister is still Buthelezi; he still controls the portfolios of authority affairs and finance and is also in charge of police (which had initially fallen under justice when transferred from the central state in 1980) and of the KwaZulu information service, handed to the KLA by the Department of Information in 1977 (KLAD, 10:71). The minister of justice is C.J. Mtetwa, also involved in the Natal African Chamber of Commerce (Inyanda) and chairman of the Msinga rural licensing board. The minister of education, Dr Oscar Dhlomo, is secretary general of Inkatha and a former lecturer at the University of Zululand. Dr Frank Mdlalose, the minister of the interior, was chairman of the Madadeni town council between 1972 and 1977, a branch president in the ANCYL (1950-53) and a medical doctor. The minister of works, Chief M.A. Ngcobo, director of Sukumani Development Company, has a sugar farm in the Ndwedwe district. Finally the minister of health and welfare, Dr D.R.B. Madide, another doctor, had also served as chairman of a licensing board (that of Hlabisa) (Deane, 1978; KLA, nd).

In other words, the KLA, like the nine other bantustans, has a civil service (with its own Public Service Commission), a police force, ministers and parliamentarians (who argue about salaries and travel and subsistence money), a capital and parliamentary buildings (the cost of which started at R8.3m but escalated rapidly), a budget, and obligations.

It also has a peripheral, yet important, role in reproducing South Africa as both racial and capitalist. Its various dependencies on the central state have already been mentioned. Its citizenry is defined by the central state, on at times spurious ethnic grounds. The majority of the parliamentarians are chiefs, legacies of a pre-capitalist past and/or the colonial power's need to resort to a system of indirect rule when the resources, both human and financial, were not available for direct administration and repression. The chiefs are non-elected members. Though the KLA voted in 1983 to increase the number of elected members from 55 to 65, they still form a minority in the 141 member assembly (Survey, 1983:347).

Inkatha, through its almost total overlap at the regional level with the KLA and its tasks, is caught in the duties and expectations that go with being a branch of the state in apartheid South Africa. Rhetorical denial of ultimate responsibility and attempts to distance the movement from certain consequences of this participation, both expected and unintended, mean very little to the people who suffer under the policy — for the victims it matters little if the beneficiaries applaud their cleverness in hoodwinking the central state through its own structures.

Let us look, first, at the extent and the manner of Inkatha's overlap with the KLA. As was seen in Chapter 4, the idea of reviving Inkatha was raised in the KLA, the constitution was circulated in the KLA for discussion and approval, and Inkatha was initially given a dominant role in relation to the KLA (Bernstein, 1977:128). Inkatha depends almost totally on the participation of chiefs for its own existence and growth, as does the KLA. Eighteen of the 26 regional authorities were present at the inaugural meeting of Inkatha (the regional authorities are also the basic unit of the KLA). Later in 1975 Buthelezi said 'the Zulus had "rooted" their Legislative Assembly "in the will of the people through Inkatha"' (Langner, 1983:24). Buthelezi felt that the formation of Inkatha would allow 'demonstrable constituencies' to give greater clout to the KLA — which he described as 'a Black entry point into the national political arena' (quoted Langner, 1983:24). Initially members of the KLA would automatically also have been members of Inkatha (see, for example, KLAD, 9:640-41). This constitutional provision, which in effect already placed Inkatha as the supreme body over the KLA, was changed in 1979 to read that members (of the KLA) 'who are members of the Movement' shall be national council members. Langner wrote that Inkatha has several sub-groups 'to act in advisory capacity in their respective fields and liaise with the relevant KwaZulu Government departments', and in this way make outside expertise available to the KLA (1983:91).

At present the KwaZulu cabinet members are also all members of the Inkatha CC, with several holding important positions. Dr Dhlomo is not only KwaZulu minister of education but also Inkatha secretary general; Buthelezi is chief minister of KwaZulu and president of Inkatha; Dr Frank Mdlalose is chairman of the Inkatha CC social and cultural sub-committee and KwaZulu minister of health and welfare.

There are other spinoffs that are beneficial to Inkatha: participation in the KLA means that a regular stream of news is made available to the press, especially in Natal, and hence regular contact is maintained with the organization's actual and potential members. The Zulu-language transmission of the SABC has played an important role in this regard, despite criticisms of bias made at times by Buthelezi. Participation makes funds available to the Inkatha movement, either directly (such as when the KLA voted to finance the expenses incurred by the Buthelezi Commission), or indirectly — who is to say what is KwaZulu business and what is Inkatha business for leaders? Participation makes 'pressure points' available through services controlled by the KLA, to 'nudge' people into membership of Inkatha. Participation means that opposition activity and membership recruitment can be made very difficult. For example, student and pupil mobilization into organizations such as the Congress of South African Students (COSAS, banned in 1985 by the central state) has been difficult in conditions where Inkatha has so frequently taken a strong and at times violent position against education protests. Teachers are often antagonistic or not in a position to show their sympathy because their salaries are paid by the KLA, and community 'parent' groups have been used to 'discipline' pupils. This is not to argue that KwaZulu schools have been free of protests, boycotts and demands. This is simply not true. Nor does it mean that the Inkatha Youth Brigade has a day-to-day organizational strength in the schools. On the contrary, the Youth Brigade is noticeable by its absence on this level, which might account for the involvement of outside groups to 'police' the schools during times of education unrest in Natal.

In 1982 the Inkatha publicity secretary for Imbali, a township outside Pietermaritzburg, warned church ministers to open their buildings to Inkatha meetings as they 'belong to the community'. He threatened that Imbali would soon fall under KwaZulu authority, and that then the ministers 'would have to contend with our Ulundi Government' (NW, 25 Mar. 82).

It did not come as a great surprise that Inkatha should have made a clean sweep of the KwaZulu elections held in 1978, emphasizing the overlap and inseparability of the movement and its political and administrative home. In a 38% poll they took all 55 elected seats in the KLA (as against 75 'traditional', non-elected members, the chiefs) (*Frontline*, 1, 1).

The central committee of Inkatha controls the selection of candidates to stand for the movement in 'Parliamentary and Local Government' elections. The wording of the constitution, that nobody 'shall be selected as a candidate . . . unless he or she is a member of the Movement', led to some confusion among potential participants (Langner, 1983:85). 'The word "selected" was confused with "elected" and served as a deterrent for a number of prospective candidates who construed it as an absolute disqualification for non-members of Inkatha'. It says much that it should be thought that Inkatha could make such rules. Buthelezi said the 'exclusive' clause in the Inkatha constitution meant only that Inkatha members would vote for Inkatha candidates.

These elections had been delayed for some time because of Buthelezi's and the

KLA's insistence that KwaZulu citizenship certificates be used for voter registration. Buthelezi argued that the use of reference books would open up opportunities for irregularities, that the pass book was a 'badge of oppression', that people who had not paid their tax (this would be reflected in their reference books) would not register (a noble concern that no longer applied when tax had to be paid to KwaZulu) (KLAD, 2:49). There appears to have been considerable resistance to the taking out of citizenship certificates, despite pleas and threats: '. . . we do envisage that the possession of a citizenship certificate will in future be essential to obtain all benefits that lie in the gift of the Government. Please do not force us to adopt such measures . . .', warned Buthelezi (KLAD, 4:41). He said it was mainly among 'educated Zulu' and in some hospitals that resistance was strong. The resistance was clearly much more widespread — Buthelezi expected 2mn voters, and yet only between 630 000 and 690 000 voters were registered (ST, 19 Feb. 78; KwaZulu Govt Diary, 1979:65). It is not clear whether voter registration remained tied to citizenship certificates, as Buthelezi so strongly insisted, because as early as 1976 he said that 'it does not seem possible that we will manage to do so [issue enough citizenship certificates] during this year, and it therefore seems sensible that we should expedite matters by making it possible for people to use their reference books to register as voters' (KLAD, 7:1054). This proposal by Buthelezi was apparently rejected (Survey, 1976:249).

The Inkatha movement not only won the elections, but also organized them. Buthelezi said as early as 1975 that all KLA members were Inkatha national council members, and 'it will be Inkatha Committees that will be charged with the duty of assisting the people in the conduction [sic] of these elections'. These committees would be set up where they did not yet exist (KLAD, 7:920-1). This role given to Inkatha in the elections that it was to fight was expanded on by Buthelezi when he objected to the electoral proclamation that a magistrate could appoint any member of his staff as 'registration officer' (the objection was that there were civil servants who were 'not neutral' — they had supported the Shaka's Spear opposition party). Buthelezi said: 'In KwaZulu we now have the National Liberation Movement, and as such, we have electoral committees in terms of the Constitution of Inkatha.' He argued that this should be made part of the electoral proclamation as the Inkatha constitution was accepted by the KLA (KLAD, 7:947). An amendment was accepted that registration officers could only be appointed after consultation with the central committee of Inkatha (KLAD, 7:949). The bantustans, as branches of the central state, mirror most of the functions and trappings of the power that created them, but in KwaZulu the expected separation of 'state' and 'party' does not exist, even while rhetorical allegiance is paid to democracy and the 'marketplace of ideas'.

Only between 26% and 50% of potential voters registered. This very wide discrepancy is due to widely different claims made at various times. Interior minister Madide claimed that 'just over 50 per cent of the eligible people within KwaZulu and about 12 per cent of those outside KwaZulu had registered' (Langner, 1983:163). Fewer than 40% of the people who had registered voted. It must be noted that Inkatha was unopposed in 12 of the 26 constituencies (townships were included under regional authorities for the purpose of the elections) which would further decrease the number of voters who could have participated. On the other hand, voters could vote for a slate of candidates — while votes cast equalled 46% of registered voters, this was far in excess of the number of *voters* who participated.

Schmahmann analysed the election results and commented on the suspect tactics used in some constituencies. She found that the percentage poll varied from 25.7% in Vulindlela to 52.5% in Hlanganani, that all 23 of the 'independent' candidates claimed to be members of Inkatha and loyal to Buthelezi, 'and all expressed confusion over the main issue of the election . . .' (1978:291). This would seem to signify that not all Inkatha members were willing to accept the strict internal discipline and the reasons for selection of specific candidates. In one constituency a candidate stood as an independent because official candidates were chosen only from regional executive members. This man withdrew after Inkatha harassment and threats, and claimed that had he known that the elections had nothing to do with local issues he would have viewed his initial candidature differently — 'This election was not based on issues or candidates. It was "for Buthelezi and his leadership of Inkatha"' (Schmahmann, 1978:296).

The intimidation of candidates appears to have been widespread. One independent said he could not understand it as Inkatha and Buthelezi enjoyed 'overwhelming Zulu support'. What Schmahmann wrote is of relevance to much of what has happened since 1978:

> If these reports are indicative of such a spirit encouraged by the movement, it is an indictment of its leadership;

and later:

> The danger is, of course, that should support for Buthelezi and his movement wane, the machinery with which he could maintain his dominant position, and the anti-democratic methods by which it could work, will have been established [1978:298].

But it was not only the candidates who were harassed. Schmahmann quotes a newspaper investigation which revealed that in Izingolweni considerable pressure was put on pensioners — frightened old people were arriving at the polls 'long after the elections were over. Inkatha registered a massive victory here' (1978:293).

It is not difficult to imagine the effect of having 'official' candidates, selected by a movement that had already declared itself to be synonymous not only with the 'Zulu nation' but also with the government of that 'nation', a movement whose agreement had to be sought on the appointment of election officials, and which organized the election. If any independent had managed to get elected, that would have marred the clean sweep made by Inkatha. In Clermont, with a population of 70 000-80 000 in 1978, Inkatha membership was 600. These members selected the 'official' candidates for whom half the 19 000 voters cast votes (Schmahmann, 1978:299). The Clermont township was in early 1986 vigorously campaigning to avoid incorporation into KwaZulu in terms of the state's consolidation proposals. Eight years of representation in the KLA have not convinced these 'citizens' that there is any value in becoming part of KwaZulu territory.

The 'official' candidates generally received seven times as many votes as independents. Langner concluded that the elections had shown a massive Inkatha win, but that only about '6 per cent of the eligible Zulu population cast a vote', while only 18.3% of voters went to polling stations outside KwaZulu (1983:166-7). These figures indicate that this was a typical bantustan election, with participation negligible where the influence of the authorities was not directly felt, and that those who were opposed to the system itself, rather than an opposition within it, did not bother to participate. Dr Dhlomo, of course, saw the whole exercise in a different light: the results had 'demonstrated in "actual practice", . . . that it was possible to thwart Pretoria's designs to make black people non-citizens in the land of their birth' (RDM, 15 Dec. 79).

In September 1983 KwaZulu's second elections were held, with much less publicity than the first time around. In only four of the 26 seats were there opponents to the Inkatha slate of candidates. The Inkatha candidates won all four contested seats.

The similarities far outweigh the differences between the KwaZulu/Inkatha elections and those held in other bantustans. A similar lack of enthusiasm characterizes all elections for ethnic government, and similar cases of intimidation, victimization and favouritism can be found. In practice, what Inkatha has done by making the KwaZulu bantustan elections such a test of its popularity is to deflect, in one more area, the actual and potential involvement of people in direct national politics of liberation.

Inkatha and the chiefs

The 1891 Natal Code stipulated that the Governor of the Colony, as 'Supreme Chief', could appoint chiefs and remove them, and that the chief 'in charge of a tribe or section of a tribe, is a minor deputy of the Supreme Chief . . .'. Daphne wrote that:

> As 'minor deputies' of an administration which was often hostile to the interests of the black people of Natal the chiefs were, by definition, no longer the representatives of the people. The power to appoint and to remove chiefs was taken out of the hands of the tribe although in fact the system of hereditary succession was allowed to operate provided it did not challenge the colonial government [1982:2].

After Union, frequent subsequent legislation dealing with the role of chiefs, most important the 1927 Native Administration Act and amendments, did little to change this position. Later the State President became the 'Supreme Chief' to reflect the Republican status of South Africa. Even the KwaZulu legislation dealing with the functions of chiefs followed the central state's allocation of roles and duties (see Appendix 4). Control is the predominant theme, with, 'almost as an afterthought', the stipulation 'that a chief should "generally seek to promote the interests of his tribe and of the region and actively support, and himself initiate measures, for the advancement of his people"' (Daphne, 1982:5; Maré, 1982a).

The 1978 elections reduced the total dependence on chiefs but it left them as the numerically dominant component within KwaZulu politics. Not all chiefs have been enamoured of the Buthelezi style of 'traditionalism' and, at various times, with some central government aid, they have rallied round the king or the symbol provided by the king as an executive figure. This could have been embarrassing during elections that were required to show a massive degree of solidarity. Both Schmahmann and Langner refer to a meeting held at Ulundi at the end of September 1977, ostensibly to 'explain the election role of chiefs', that the institution of chieftainship could last as long as it served the interests of the people, and their role in Inkatha (RDM, 1 Oct. 77). Most of the chiefs attended. The KwaZulu urban representative said chiefs had resisted being drawn into Inkatha because they believed the state's accusation that the movement would strip them of their power (Schmahmann, 1978:304), and that the meeting had been called to clarify the position. Buthelezi addressed this meeting, and denied the state's allegations that he was standing in the way of an 'envisaged rebirth of the Zulu nation', pointing out that he was a chief himself and that, 'being morally and pragmatically opposed to apartheid, he did not regard his vision of Black unity as militating against Zulu unity'. As for Inkatha, he warned that if chiefs did not involve themselves in the affairs of the movement it 'would be regarded as dereliction of duty and active involvement *against* Inkatha would be "of course much worse"'. He pointedly reminded them that Pretoria no longer controlled their 'fate as chiefs' which would be decided at Ulundi 'if necessary' (Langner, 1983:174). Langner said the meeting of chiefs had since become an annual event.

There is no doubt that Buthelezi 'believes' in the position of chieftainship and its validity in late 20th century society. He is extremely sensitive about his own chieftainship, and repeats claims for its legitimacy regularly to justify the authority due to him. It would be wrong to see his support of the role of chiefs as totally pragmatic or as Machiavellian. However, as has been argued, it is nonetheless a specific support of the role of chiefs in Zulu society, placing himself at the top, and one that demands allegiance to his position. In the KwaZulu Government Diary (1974:10) Buthelezi wrote that:

> We will preserve the traditional system of Chieftainship in KwaZulu and re-affirm our constitutional relationship with the Paramount Chief and will *build our future state* with due regard to our cultural heritage and traditions adapted and fructified by the ideals of Western civilization and democracy and modern scientific principles.

He said the KLA was not a 'mere transplant of Western democracy upon the Zulu nation', preferring 'to view it merely as a natural extension and development of traditional Zulu Culture and government' (KLA, nd:5).

To consolidate this reliance on chiefs a 'special section' was created in the department of the chief minister 'to accelerate the activation of tribal authorities and to train them in local government techniques' (KwaZulu Government Diary, 1981:39). So, 30 years after the Bantu Authorities Act had been passed, after many people had lost their lives in opposition to these structures, and after having claimed to have resisted them for years in KwaZulu, Buthelezi 'activated' them as a central element in local government.

Efforts have been made to make the chiefs more effective. An illuminating debate took place in the KLA in 1976 when certain amendments to the Natal Code were proposed, the most important being one to replace references to the State President as 'Supreme Chief' of all Africans with the 'Executive Council of KwaZulu'. It was submitted by the executive councillor for justice on the grounds that the requirements that decisions by chiefs be referred to the State President caused unnecessary delays. The example he gave — delays in deporting various kinds of 'disobedient people' — received support from several speakers during the debate. Councillor Conco said that 'we have already reached a solution in terms of which to end the riots and fighting and disorder', but that it was negated by administrative delays (KLAD, 8:40). Chief M. Ngcobo agreed that the delay in deportation was troublesome.

During the debate KLA members spoke of 'insolence', violent behaviour, 'hot headed disobedient people', and the need to maintain law and order. Some wanted the fines imposed by chiefs to be increased from R4 to a maximum of R100 (this was agreed after an initial amendment to increase the fine to R40 was rejected), to bring it in line with the 'value of a beast', which was the usual form in which the fine was paid. The central government gave permission to increase the fine to R200 (KLAD, 9:602). A revealing remark was made by A. Kholwa, who

89

said that increasing fines 'would not change the insolent behaviour which exists in the community because we normally find that people who are disobedient to their chiefs are the poor people', for whom corporal punishment might be necessary as they were not in a position to pay fines (KLAD, 8:45-46).

Later in the debate a chief proposed a motion that 'the advisability be considered of empowering the chiefs-in-council to eject undesirable persons and/ or families from their areas, and that a place be made available by KwaZulu for such ejected people' (KLAD, 8:243). Another chief added that the problem was due to the lack of employment, and he moved that the KwaZulu government be given the power to place people in employment without choice — 'In this way this problem of unemployment will diminish. Communists and house breakers can be given a separate place where they can be kept' (KLAD, 8:246-47). A year earlier the term 'communists' had been used for 'strangers' in a chief's area (KLAD, 7:778-80).)

In the 1976 session moves were made to 'strengthen the chiefs' criminal courts', but this had to await the next stage of administrative authority. An 'administrative guide' setting out procedures for greater effectiveness of the courts was accepted: '. . . it will become obvious now which chiefs are not using their power to the full in the maintenance of law and order in their areas', said Buthelezi (KLAD, 9:413).

It is clear that even, or especially, at the local level the KwaZulu authorities are not accepted as wholeheartedly as they like to make out. The references above indicate dissatisfaction; so does a remark in an article in the publication celebrating ten years of the existence of the KLA (KLA, nd:10) in which the author acknowledged that because of the standards of administration KwaZulu had set itself 'it has to work within the frustrations and the anger of the people'. There are many causes, other than high standards, of such frustrations and anger. The allowances for chiefs are based on the number of taxpayers in their areas and this has led to increased overcrowding in some areas, and anger has been directed at the tax collector for many years now (see, for example, Survey, 1959/60:108; KLAD, 1:12). Corruption and bribery accusations appear in newspaper reports and are even made in the KLA.

In 1975, during the period of massive social disruption in part due to the eviction of labour tenants from white-owned farms, chiefs were warned 'not to continue with the unlawful practice of receiving money or kind in return for the allocation of a site' (KLAD, 7:695). The chiefs were literally cashing in on the land hunger of displaced people. In 1978 Buthelezi attacked chiefs for 'fleecing' the people in that they were charging for sites, arable land and services such as pensions (DN, 11 Dec. 78). These practices have been confirmed by Zulu, in a paper based on research conducted in the early 1980s (nd:2-3). He wrote that 'nine out of every ten respondents who required a site on which to build a house had to make some monetary payment either to the chief or the local induna', and in some cases this payment became an annual 'rent'. In his sample 40% of the respondents had to pay for an induna to approve pension or disability grant applications. While gift exchanges had been a traditional practice, the obligation now fell on only the subjects:

It is common practice that chiefs 'demand' some contributions from their subjects. These may include collections towards the purchase of a new car, or a new building, a son's marriage, etc. [Zulu, nd:3].

In 1982 a newspaper report spoke of corruption in various tribal locations (settlements) falling under the Vulindlela Tribal Authority, involving workseeker permits (costing a R20 bribe), and pension applications needing a KwaZulu government stamp or tribal signature (NW, 22 Apr. 82).

Many other cases could be quoted to substantiate the argument that chiefs are often corrupt. Bekker, in his report for the Human Sciences Research Council, dealing with the role of chiefs, wrote that they were guilty in other areas: the most common fault mentioned by magistrates of all chiefs in their areas was that of favouritism; they did not know how far their powers went, and they continued to hold power after serving sentences for theft, arson, and assault. They were immediately biased against the accused or defendant (in a study covering a four-year period, the 551 cases tried by seven chiefs did not once favour the defendant). Bekker recommended that chiefs not be expected to fulfil judicial, administrative or legislative functions (undesirable in itself, but aggravated as chiefs had generally received no training in these functions) (Bekker, 1983:60-5). Nearly all of these points were confirmed by Zulu, who wrote of tribal authority members not being trained for their duties, and the absence of job descriptions. He concluded that the tribal authority system 'is more of an extension of the state apparatus than an organ representing the interests of the people' (nd:7), and that the system was inimical to rural development projects (nd:8; also Daphne, 1982:12).

Despite all these failures and illegalities, many of them admitted, Buthelezi has consistently argued that the chiefs are the 'base of government' in KwaZulu (eg KLAD, 6:412; 10:72). When he opened the Makhanya tribal authority headquarters and offices, Buthelezi told the gathering that:

> I respect Chieftainship as an indigenous African institution of the people. In KwaZulu it is the very basis of our administration.

However, he warned that the institution had to keep pace with the 20th century (BS, 3 Sep. 83).

It is not only the chiefs that are criticized and opposed. KwaZulu's civil service has similarly fallen far short of expectations of public duty and nation building, and not necessarily because they have not always given their undivided allegiance to Buthelezi, the KLA, and therefore, by implication, to the 'black cause', as Buthelezi defines it (see KLAD, 7:821 & 899).

In 1972 Buthelezi threatened breathalyser tests for civil servants (DN, 26 Oct. 72). By 1978 the tests were in use (DN, 17 May 78). Drunkenness on duty and complaints from, for example, pensioners about their treatment at the hands of drunken officials have been referred to in many instances (eg KLAD, 5:297; Schmahmann, 1978:230). Bribery is common (KLAD, 1:23 & 44), and was said to encourage lawbreakers (KLAD, 4:313). Minister of justice Mtetwa warned that 'bribery traps' would be set (DN, 16 May 78). Losses from fraud and theft were said to be in the region of 10% (R92m) of the 1975 budget (DN, 8 Nov. 75). In a 1978 fraud case staff of the department of works stole R21 545, while in the same year the KwaZulu government's principal accountant revealed that over three years there had been 30 proven cases of theft and fraud, involving R150 000 (NW, 18 Nov. 78). The auditor general's report for the 1980/81 financial year mentioned R117 000 stolen in 96 cases of theft with KwaZulu officials 'known to have been involved in at least 43 of these cases' (NM, 27 Apr. 82).

Many reports have detailed inefficiency, due to lack of funds, lack of training and staff shortages, in the departments of works, education, justice, health and welfare. The KLA does not have a vigorous opposition that would undoubtedly have unearthed many further cases. Inefficiencies in the supply of materials and services increases the drastic plight of the 'citizens' of this bantustan as of the other nine, while pension problems have received a measure of publicity, in part because the Black Sash monitors this area (see references below, and Maré, 1981).

The bantustan policy inevitably produces such corruption, bribery, theft, and inefficiency, but the point is that in KwaZulu the responsible party is a 'national liberation movement' with international recognition and probably an increasingly central role to play in 'reform politics' in South Africa in the near future. The implications of this for short- and medium-term political, social and economic change need to be discussed, as well as the personality of Inkatha's leader, the obsession with status, and the material benefits accruing to participants in the KwaZulu bantustan. These issues are relevant to political recognition, status and partnerships, and to economic development schemes and funding.

Paying for what they are worth

The salaries paid to KLA members, to chiefs, and primarily to Buthelezi, were one of the first issues raised in the debates of the newly constituted KLA in 1972. On p.7 of the first volume of the debates Buthelezi mentioned his salary (R4500 per annum) and compared it with that of the Prime Minister. He said B.J. Vorster was then receiving R24 000 plus R3000 house allowance plus R4500 tax free allowance — 'I mention these figures just to show the Assembly the necessity of finding additional sources of Revenue, if the Republican Government is prepared to assist only to the extent of enabling us to get a Kaffir wage structure . . .' (KLAD, 1:7). This provided the cue for some noble sentiments, with one member suggesting that the R7000 that was proposed as a reasonable compromise salary for Buthelezi be found even if it meant that 'we, as Members here, starved rather than our "Boys" who are doing the work for us should starve' (KLAD, 1:17).

In 1973 salaries were once again prominent, with pages of debate devoted to the issue. Buthelezi referred to the sacrifices he was making, travelling over bad roads, etc, and now called on the central government to pay for the bantustan system they had created:

> I do not think it would be good enough for me to accept a Kaffir Prime Minister's salary . . . That was not the intention of separate development . . . We were promised separate dignity, separate freedom. We are now begging you for the separate dignity and the separate freedom . . . Please dish out [KLAD, 3:86].

He did include the rest of the KLA in his plea. With ironical foresight, considering his subsequent roving ambassadorial role and the role that Inkatha later played in the unrest in Natal, Buthelezi said the amount needed to increase salaries should be taken from the Defence or Information Department votes in the central parliament — it would do more good if it was paid to him.

To justify the increases reference was also made in the debate to the salaries paid to Transkeian ministers and the members of the Coloured Representative Council (CRC), and to the fact that Zulus were the largest ethnic group, 'larger than even the Whites'. Buthelezi said 'we are doing the job now', and should not have to wait until a later stage in constitutional development ('. . . because in the eyes of the Zulus, as far as my responsibilities are concerned, I am the Prime Minister of the Zulu people'). There was also a request for an increase in the subsistence allowance for executive councillors because 'when we . . . travel in connection with our duties it is expected of us to maintain a dignified standard, which becomes our position and status . . .' (KLAD, 3:211).

In 1975 Buthelezi and the KLA took offence at a *Natal Mercury* article on the KLA salaries which revealed that KLA members received R3000 per annum, cabinet members R9300, while Buthelezi got R11 400 and a R1200 non-taxable allowance. Once more the R3000 more per annum that was paid to Chief Kaiser Matanzima, chief minister of the Transkei, offended KLA members (KLAD, 5:158-9 & 184). Special allowances for Buthelezi and the king were called for, for such needs as when Buthelezi held a 'prayer breakfast' and needed a suite in the luxury hotel where it was held (KLAD, 5:257-8). Buthelezi said that '. . . if the Paramount Chief is visiting or travelling in his official capacity . . . then as future Head of State or the Head of the Zulu nation, it is right that this Government should provide transport for him', but that it would not include paying 'for his private cars, because the King has a fleet of cars which are his private ones' (KLAD, 5:258). Buthelezi queried the higher salaries in the Transkei (why should the 'Zulu people deserve less than the Transkei?') and said that in his case 'exposure, . . . as far as the international scene is concerned, for me personally is much more than that of any other Homeland Leader' (KLAD, 5:282).

However, a request from the KwaZulu civil servants for pay increases received short shrift with reminders that they had to make sacrifices and that if they did not like it they could leave — 'Then we will get the kind of people who will be prepared to make sacrifices, because I [Buthelezi] have reason to believe that I make sacrifices myself in doing the job I am doing' (KLAD, 5:312). The executive councillor for community affairs supported Buthelezi and reminded civil servants that '. . . we are not obliged to take any instructions from our own employees' (KLAD, 5:316). Small wonder that corruption is widespread and that many civil servants appear to have little spontaneous loyalty to KwaZulu and Inkatha (see also KLAD, 6:670).

That was not the last time salaries were to be discussed. The KLA showed greater understanding for the plight of the chiefs (who, after all are the majority in that assembly) than for civil servants, calling for 'substantial salaries' to make the chiefs the richest people in their areas, as it should be (KLAD, 8:69). It was felt that the chiefs should be rewarded because they were of royal blood (some of them), because they ensured that people paid taxes, because the fines that were supposed to provide their income were too small and frequently not paid, and because:

Over and above all this work, the chief also has a duty towards the Government — he has to be on the look-out for the infiltration of Communists and he must report to the Government if he has the slightest suspicion that a person may be a Communist [KLAD, 8:69].

'It is a known fact,' said Chief Sithole, executive councillor for agriculture and forestry, 'that Communists always try to approach the poor people first.' (KLAD, 8:77).

Despite his obsessive concern with status, Buthelezi attacks those in the 'homeland' structures who 'accept the gold-gloss paint on the chains that shackle us as people' (BS, 7 Aug. 76):

I think, as Blacks, our struggle for liberation should be related to the struggle of the ordinary man in the street . . . We must always relate our earnings, even if we feel that what we are earning is not what we are worth, to those of the ordinary Black man [KLAD, 6:670].

In 1975 the 'ordinary Black man' in industry was earning less than R30 per week in Durban (Survey, 1976:277). According to Schlemmer and Muil, attempts elsewhere in Africa to restrict parliamentary salaries (eg in Tanzania) would be inappropriate in KwaZulu because to create 'a pocket of socialism in a wider capitalist society would risk alienating those who feel their skills could be more adequately rewarded in White areas', but this has a hollow ring (1975:116). The civil servants were told to buckle down (a 'pocket of socialism' for some) while Buthelezi and the KLA voted higher salaries for themselves. He demanded credit, at the same time, for putting his 'work and service to [his] people first', despite the fact that he could be 'living in clover' overseas on the salaries attached to jobs he claimed to have been offered there (KLAD, 5:312). In 1974, during a clash with his former councillor for community affairs, B.I. Dladla, the issue arose of the new house Buthelezi's tribe was building for him. His biographer comments:

Buthelezi should perhaps have said something more about the new house in terms of status for himself, his tribe and his nation. After all, R76 000 may be a considerable sum of money by comparison with what was spent on most houses in KwaZulu but it is paltry when related to, say, executive standards in Johannesburg [Temkin, 1976:234].*

Status and the messianic element that often appears in Buthelezi's personal role both appear in the salary issue. One of the 'independents' who stood in the 1978 elections in KwaZulu told Schmahmann (1978:299) that he had been motivated as a 'believing Christian' to oppose 'a "worship" of Buthelezi which he believed is becoming widespread'. Not only does Buthelezi often refer to his own Christianity (several times to find common ground with NP politicians such as during the interview with Jimmy Kruger in 1977), but he is referred to and refers to himself in Biblical imagery. In 1975 when he was re-elected chief executive councillor he used the image of the temptation of Jesus by the Devil (in this case a temptation through political power) (KLAD, 7:887-8). The Labour Party's defection from Buthelezi's South African Black Alliance (SABA) to the greener grass of tri-cameralism reminded Buthelezi of 'Peter's vehement declarations that he would not deny Christ . . . There seems to be a parallel' (quoted RDM, 21 May 83). Y. Chinsamy, leader of the Reform Party and member of SABA, called Buthelezi 'our saviour'. When Teague asked Buthelezi why his leadership seemed to inspire either hero worship or mistrust, he replied: 'You could also ask what it was about Jesus Christ or Mahatma Ghandi' (Teague, 1983:11).

Buthelezi's sensitivity is also well known. In denying reports that he had lost his temper at a press conference in the USA, he said that all he had done was to 'discipline' the reporter (St, 16 Sep. 82 and 26 Oct. 82). Langner wrote in his conclusion that:

Should the Government decide on a detente strategy, the style of negotiation of the parties might pose another obstacle. Buthelezi, although desirous to negotiate and

---

*'It is now [1975] proposed that houses costing some R950 should be provided [for middle-class Africans], with interior doors to bedrooms, a pantry, shelves in the kitchen, and [where facilities were available] an indoor bathroom with a water closet and a small bath, and a sink in the kitchen' (Survey, 1975:84).

consider alternatives, has acquired a reputation of having a low level of tolerance towards opposition to his ideals, especially those he regards as non-negotiable [1983:281].

Bernstein admitted that he is 'extremely sensitive to criticism of any sort' (1977:141). The number and tone of the letters Buthelezi writes to the press, responding to attacks both real and imagined, offers further evidence of this, as does the content of many of his speeches.

This chapter has examined Inkatha's structure and analysed some of the claims made by Inkatha. It has been argued that the movement and the bantustan overlap to the extent that they have become inseparable, and that this is a burden of responsibility that Inkatha's leaders will always have to carry. Even in the case of something as odious as the state's forced removals policy, the Surplus People Project study found that Inkatha's denial of involvement or even knowledge of planned removals was an indictment of the lack of power of bantustan governments (vol 4, 1983:8). The report goes further and argues on the basis of case studies that when Inkatha does intervene it removes any initiative from the communities themselves, as had been the case with the struggle over the planned incorporation of Ingwavuma into Swaziland. There have also been cases where deals have been made between KwaZulu and the central state without the participation of the communities involved (SPP, vol 4, 1983:10). However, there have been cases where Inkatha leaders at a local level have played a positive role in representing the wishes of their communities.

The capital of KwaZulu, Ulundi, is a showpiece of the state's policy of fragmentation of the South African population. With the KLA and administration buildings costing more than R10m, with its own airport, etc, it gives more than strategic content to Buthelezi's claims of regional administration. These are more properly symbols of the integration of Inkatha into state structures than the ambushes of a 'liberated area'. Inkatha, in its own words, is part of the system and has chosen to be so. At the same time the movement's leaders and the KLA do control the branch of the state they occupy (within certain broad parameters), and the degree of its autonomy should not be underestimated. It is within this autonomous space that Buthelezi, because of his wider ambitions and the strength of a mass movement behind him, becomes at times a recalcitrant part of the system. But, even this recalcitrance is probably of greater value to the central state in the long term than the often submissive attitude of some of the other bantustan leaders.

6. 'A Pinch of African Communalism'

Working class interests are increasingly a part of the political as well as the economic struggle in South Africa. There are competing claims to true representation of workers' interests, and this is now an essential part of several ideologies and political platforms. Trade union claims to representation initially arose in the general unions with their close links to the communities in which their members live, but increasingly they have become part of all progressive worker organizations. As Webster commented, 'by establishing independent working class organizations, the emerging unions have created the embryo of a working class politics in South Africa' (1984:86). More recently it was noted that 'there is now clear evidence that all emergent unions not only accept that they have a political role to play, but are willing to act accordingly' (Lewis and Randall, 1985:84).

Political bodies also lay claim to worker representation, with the 'socialist Azania' call from the National Forum affiliates, and the 'socialist Freedom Charter' of the United Democratic Front and its affiliates. As early as 1976 the youth in revolt came to realize the importance of linking their struggles with those of their parents in the townships and the factories. The African National Congress confirmed the 'special role' of the working class in the struggle for 'liberation and socialism' at its 1969 Morogoro consultative conference (Davies et al, 1984:289), and again at the 1985 Kabwe conference (Barrell, 1985:12). Inkatha, too, appropriates for itself the voice of the 'will of the peasants and workers', and now lays exclusive claim to this representation. How does Inkatha justify its claims to have something to offer both capitalism and the working class?

This chapter examines Inkatha's economic policy and its direct involvement in economic practice, either on behalf of capital or through its own enterprises. Worker membership cannot be equated with the representation of worker interests. Inkatha might well have large numbers of (predominantly Zulu-speaking) workers, both employed and unemployed, as members, but it represents the interests of capital. The debate on worker interests and representation has taken a new turn with the formation of the Inkatha union, the United Workers Union of South Africa (UWUSA).

Inkatha's economic policy

There has been little change over the years in the policy Inkatha leaders have advocated in the economic sphere. This is not because economic policy takes a back seat in the voluminous pronouncements of Chief Buthelezi and others. On the contrary, they have been at pains to take issue in this field and to defend the Inkatha approach. But does this policy present a coherent economic structure for a future South Africa?

The consistency in Inkatha's approach to the economy lies in its favourable perception of capitalism, or the 'free enterprise system'. Initially Buthelezi suggested that the supposed excesses of capitalism in South Africa could best be curtailed through the introduction of some (unspecified) 'socialist' elements and diluted through the addition of 'African communalism'. If the South African economic and social system is frequently characterized by its radical critics as 'racial capitalism', then what Buthelezi is suggesting is that non-racial, or multi-racial, capitalism is not only a possible but a desirable alternative.

In the eyes of the class interests dominant in Inkatha the fault with the economic system is that it does not offer the same 'benefits' to all, but is discriminatory on racial grounds. In the words of Inkatha secretary general Oscar Dhlomo, 'I believe what Inkatha would like to see happening is the overhaul of the free enterprise system aimed at ensuring that black people have equal access and that they derive equal benefit from the system' (FM interview, 17 Sep. 82). Abolition of discrimination against all 'black' people (probably meaning African in this case) would mean, for example, worker participation in the 'free enterprise system', as this would allow the benefits of the system, equal to those 'enjoyed by the white man', to be shared through trade unions. Traders are singled out in glowing terms — 'Each occasion when a black manages to be in a position to establish any business is an auspicious occasion, not only for himself, but also for the entire black community . . . [striking] a blow for us in the liberation struggle now being waged by blacks,' said Buthelezi in 1977. He listed 'at least equal pay for professionals' in a 1978 interview with the *New York Times* as one of three government actions that would convince him that 'it was prepared for genuine change' (the other two were 'free and compulsory education' and the abolition of the migrant labour system). The long debates in the KLA over salaries would perhaps be part of the same struggle for equal rewards. Finally, regional sharing has to occur in South Africa: 'white South Africa is morally bound to channel our share of wealth' to such areas as KwaZulu (quoted in Maré, 1978:302).

That this 'sharing' is strictly within the bounds of the capitalist system became clear when Gibson Thula, one time publicity secretary of Inkatha who left this position to enter the township liquor trade, suggested that if Inkatha participated in government the mining industry would be nationalized. He was rapidly contradicted by Buthelezi, who used the occasion to re-affirm his belief in capitalism and said that if Inkatha were to wield state power he 'would never allow a situation where whites — or blacks — were deprived of the fruits of the sweat of their brows'. He suggested, though, that after 'liberation' capitalism would probably have to be 'diluted' with 'African communalism' (ST, 3 Sep. 78).

In the same manner, Buthelezi has repeatedly assured the beneficiaries of the capitalist system that Inkatha's first secretary general, Professor S.M.E. Bengu, had got it all wrong when he advocated a more radical sharing order in South Africa. Professor Bengu gave a series of lectures entitled 'Cultural liberation:

principles and practices' at the University of Natal in 1977. He told his audience that:

> In our economic policy we state unequivocally that the wealth of this country has to be shared by all the inhabitants . . .

Buthelezi could have supported this, but Bengu went on to suggest how this should take place:

> The capitalist system which concentrates all effort at the creation of wealth as if this were an end in itself has to go. With our communalistic traditional background we cannot stand to see the economic resources being tapped by only a few capitalists who exploit the majority of Africans who live in abject poverty. Inkatha strives for the promotion of African patterns of thought and the achievement of African Humanism otherwise commonly known in Nguni languages as Ubuntu and Sotho languages as Botho [lecture 4, 1977:5].

As it turned out Bengu was the one to go, in a cloud of accusation and rumour. While Buthelezi strongly affirms his and Inkatha's allegiance to Ubuntu-Botho, this is couched more in sentiment than in the more concrete economic policy suggested by Bengu.

As with Buthelezi's non-violence rhetoric, he has often presented capitalism as something he might give up at some future date if he was not given a share of the proceeds. This tactic is best illustrated in his message to the business community before their 1981 meeting with P.W. Botha. He rejected socialism and declared himself a 'willing recruit for free enterprise now', but warned that 'my people' might not want him to hold to this course for much longer:

> As President of Inkatha, I preside over people who are dominantly workers and peasants. These members have what one can perhaps call middle-class tendencies.
>
> They want better jobs; they want houses; they want progress in their standard of living and they want their children to live in a far better world.

He warned the business leaders that they could not 'go it alone' with the government, not even if they took 'the black middle class' with them:

> I would not dream of crossing a bridge into the future if I had to leave the workers, the peasants and the destitute shanty-town dwellers behind me. You would do so at your peril. More, you do so at our peril [ST, 8 Nov. 81. This statement was widely reported in the English and Afrikaans press; also see RDM, 1 Mar. 79, for a similar statement, this time addressed to a computer programmers' graduation ceremony].

The point Buthelezi was making was that the business community had better help him to meet the 'middle-class tendencies' of Inkatha members. 'My utility lies in my following,' he told the SABC-TV 'Eyeline' programme (16 May 85). That following will not always go along simply through ideological appeal, or pressure to ensure membership, but will require major political advances and material improvements.

The Ubuntu-Botho, or African humanism, concept does not appear to serve as the basis of an economic policy for the Inkatha movement, though as a slogan it serves to 'dilute' Buthelezi's otherwise uncritical acceptance of capitalism as a system. Indeed, Inkatha has not 'yet seen fit to propose a political or economic blueprint for the future', said Buthelezi. He claimed that all black South African organizations lacked an economic policy (ST interview, 19 Oct. 80).

Langner suggested that what informs Buthelezi's suggestions for economic change is the reasoning that 'people won't burn down buildings in which they have a stake . . .' (1983:161). It is noteworthy that the tripartite company plan was presented as for 'the people', giving everybody a potential share in the wealth created. Tri-partite companies, or tripcos, were instituted in the mid-1970s to allow 'white' capital into the bantustans. The three parties were the Bantu Investment Corporation, the bantustan authority and the business concern. Initially the idea was that shares would increasingly be held by bantustan citizens.

In 1977 Bengu still referred to the reinstitution of 'African communalism' instead of the exploitation of capitalism. Buthelezi himself frequently called for 'a pinch of African communalism' to flavour 'unbridled' capitalism. Such language has become less and less part of the rhetoric of the Inkatha president. While the suggestion that capitalism should be 'bridled' has remained, he no longer offers even such a nebulous concept as 'African communalism' as the solution. Four years ago Buthelezi told a conference at Yale University on US business in South Africa that 'much of the suffering in South Africa could be traced to irresponsible capitalism, white economic greed and businesses that are immune to the pleas of black people' (RDM, 23 Sep. 82). In 1985 he told a rally at Ulundi that while academic debate takes place around the relative merits of socialism and capitalism, '. . . when all is said and done . . . the free enterprise system remains the most powerful system man has devised which is capable of fostering sustained growth' (CC, 1, 1985:13). Predictably, Booysen found, in her analysis of the relative evaluation of issues and concepts in Buthelezi's speeches, that 'communism' is perceived 'strongly negatively' (Booysen, 1982:144). For example, in 1984 Buthelezi told a Stellenbosch University audience that there were two lunatic fringes in South Africa: the one accepting apartheid while the other was 'seeking to establish a socialist/communist state which would be ruled by a powerful authoritarian, dominantly Black government' (BS, 6 Aug. 84:4). In contrast to this unproblematic linking of 'socialism' with 'authoritarianism', Buthelezi has claimed, equally unproblematically, that the 'free enterprise system goes hand in hand with democratic government . . .' (BS, 10 Jan. 85:8).

It is not at all clear, in the face of overwhelming evidence to the contrary, how Schlemmer could write the following on the 'economic ideology' of Inkatha:

> There is a welcome absence of the superficial Marxist sloganeering which one encounters elsewhere in southern Africa, but nonetheless the analysis tends toward the *one-party state socialist model* [emphasis added, 1980: 113];

or how Dhlomo could say (1983:2) that 'Inkatha's advocacy of an economic system which takes the best out of the free enterprise system and the best out of socialism is born out of a study of the functioning of the economic system in capitalist and socialist states'.

More typical is the approach to economic matters that Buthelezi conveyed to a meeting of the Swiss-South Africa Association, that 'South African blacks had suffered so much under the oppression of racism that they did not wish to exchange it for the totalitarianism of a marxist military state' (NM, 15 Oct. 85).

If there should be any doubt of the value Inkatha places on the capitalist system, it is soon dispelled by the stand Inkatha takes on foreign investment and its potential role in bringing about political change and improving the economic situation of African people. Proponents of disinvestment, or of ending loans to the state, or of sanctions in a number of fields, argue that foreign investment and contacts with the apartheid regime prop up the system of racial oppression and/or economic exploitation. Inkatha, however, not only denies this view but sees investment in South Africa as 'a strategy for liberation' (CC, 1, 1985:3). In other words, not only will workers suffer through the withdrawal of foreign funds, but they will benefit in the struggle for liberation through the continuation of investment. Inkatha also denies that economic pressure is legitimate non-violent pressure to apply to the South African state, and to capital in South Africa, to bring about change.

Buthelezi has placed himself firmly in the camp of the most conservative foreign governments on the issue of investment in South Africa. He praised the role played by British Prime Minister Margaret Thatcher at the 1985 Commonwealth Conference in staving off and diluting the mandatory sanctions that had been proposed by some of the delegates and supported by most. He has said that the Reagan government had gone beyond 'the radical rhetoric which has emanated from some[US] Administrations', and expressed the thanks of 'we Blacks' for the concrete help 'we receive from time to time from the US' (CC, 1, 1985:18). Buthelezi has always had close relations with the US consulate in Durban, notably with the previous Consul-General, Harry Geisel, who spoke of his close relationship with the Chief. Geisel, on his departure from Durban, was praised by the city's mayor 'for his role in helping to build bridges between the city and KwaZulu' (NM, 24 Jul. 85).

When the Natal townships were in flames, Buthelezi was in Israel on a ten-day trip 'to meet Israeli leaders, to visit holy sites and inspect agricultural developments in once-barren areas'. While there he also confirmed his support for an arms embargo but not for economic sanctions (NM, 12 Aug. 85). On his return he placed his visit in a political perspective: to forestall criticism for visiting yet another conservative government, he told a dinner of the Natal Jewry and the Natal Zionist Council that the 'ANC mission in exile sit easily with Yasser Arafat and they feel at home in Cuba, Moscow and Hanoi, and campaign constantly for the rejection of Israel'. He said the 'international propaganda campaign against Israel was distorted' (NM, 27 Sep. 85).

There is no doubt that his close contact with governments and business outside South Africa is related in the short-term to the disinvestment/sanctions campaign, and in the long-term to the political and economic future these interests would like to see in South Africa. Thatcher's meeting with both Buthelezi and Helen Suzman in August 1985 was interpreted as an attempt to rally support for her rejection of economic sanctions, while across the Atlantic Buthelezi is feted for his political and economic conservatism.

Inkatha's opposition to economic pressure against South Africa is based on a few simple arguments: first, that such measures are (or will be) ineffective, a view directly contradicted by the simultaneously held position that sanctions will ruin South Africa and leave a destroyed economy for a future black government to take over; second, that they will hurt black South Africans much more than they will whites or the state; third, that such measures have never been supported by Inkatha members or African people in general.

Parallel to the view that sanctions would not be effective in bringing about reform in South Africa is the argument that investment allows foreign companies to play a positive role for change in the country. 'Reform is the inevitable consequence of economic progress in our country,' Buthelezi said in Durban (DN, 1 Oct. 85). The enormous foreign investment during the 1960s and simultaneous repression of all opposition, including the banning of the ANC and the PAC and many individuals, makes nonsense of this claim. The degree of 'reform' that has occurred in South Africa since the late 1970s is the result of the social and economic crisis in the country, in part brought about through South Africa's integration into a world economy through foreign investment, and by the tremendous popular and working class pressure exerted since 1973. Buthelezi's devaluation of this pressure is an indication of the extent to which it has been out of his control, or in fact actively opposed by Inkatha.

While he opposes withdrawal of capital, the cessation of further investment and loans and a total or selective trade boycott, Buthelezi has said that investors have a responsibility to bring about change. He has argued that they can achieve this through setting certain standards within their employment practices (by adhering to the so-called Codes of Conduct drawn up by the Reverend Leon Sullivan for US investors and by the European Economic Community), and by calling on the state to introduce reforms. As early as 1972 Buthelezi involved himself in suggesting a role for foreign companies when he served with Dr Beyers Naude (later general secretary of the SACC), Professor Lawrence Schlemmer of the University of Natal (later part-time director of the Inkatha Institute), and Professor Hudson Ntsanwisi, chief minister of the Gazankulu bantustan, on a panel investigating the employment practices of the Phalabora Mining Company and the Rio Tinto Zinc Corporation (see Buthelezi et al, 1973).

Aspects of the panel's report are still relevant today. First, it sees labour as a 'vital partner' in business, a perception that continues to inform Buthelezi's approach. Second, management has a 'responsibility' to promote 'development' within South Africa, and this will aid a change process — in Buthelezi's words in the report opposing withdrawal: 'The question of whether it will be a peaceful denouement or a violent confrontation can be dictated by the extent to which we are or are not assisted right now to stand on our two feet as blacks' (1973:66). Third, the groups within South Africa which oppose investment were presented as a small minority and they were doing so 'as a tactical consideration rather than a long-term strategy' (1973:70). Examples of such groups were the (coloured) Labour Party (now part of the tri-cameral incorporation) and 'some black student groups' who were said to have sided with the 'hitherto highly respected . . . WCC'.

It is 13 years since the authors of the report wrote:

> The panel has provided reasons as to why it regards a *strategy of constructive engagement* in South Africa combined with action according to the Code [suggested by the authors], rather than a strategy of withdrawal, as responsible and suitable for private enterprise inside and outside the country. It is convinced that such a strategy, if implemented on a wide scale, and complemented by other evolutionary changes in society, goes a long way towards evolutionary development . . . of more equal participation of all race groups in the economic, social and political sphere, and the achievement of at least a human standard of living [Buthelezi et al, 1973:133].

During these 13 years unemployment has rocketed, a concerted assault has been launched on the value of wages paid to the black working class, tens of thousands of African people have been relocated under the apartheid policy, and there are no signs that the government is willing to move away from its policy of ethnic fragmentation, to mention but a few issues. Yet Lawrence Schlemmer could recently say to an Institute of Personnel Management seminar that those who believed that economic pressure would bring about social change 'seldom understood the inherent mechanical slowness of constitutional reform' (ZO, 7

Jun. 85). Buthelezi delivers the same message as in 1973, but now with the advantage of being feted by certain international interests. During one year, 1985, the BBC, NBC, Voice of America, and the SABC broadcast his views supporting foreign investment; he spoke at a Business International conference with the then Minister for Cooperation and Development, Gerrit Viljoen, in London, at the University of California, in New York (again with Minister Viljoen), and on many other occasions.

However, business invests to make profits and not to bring about social change. For a long time South Africa, through the policy of apartheid and the repression that is part and parcel of that policy, was a most lucrative place to invest in: in 1965 the rate of return on British investment in the country (12.1%) was the highest for any country in which Britain had substantial investment; in 1974 90% of US manufacturing firms' profits in Africa came from South Africa (First, 1972; Seidman and Seidman, 1977).

Foreign investors have no inherent motivation to pay higher wages, advance black people, provide money for housing and education or use labour-intensive techniques. If any of these are profitable or will ensure profitability in the short or long term then they will be undertaken. It is with this awareness that the 'codes of conduct' were drawn up — to apply some pressure to make the face of foreign capital in South Africa appear slightly more acceptable, and to stall the pressures that were mounting during the 1970s. The Inkatha leadership jumped on this bandwagon and started announcing that thousands of worker members would monitor the codes (for example at a South African Black Alliance meeting in Chatsworth in mid-1978 (see Schmahmann, 1978:412)). Buthelezi said the codes were the 'visible stirring of conscience as far as the business community was concerned' (NM, 12 Sep. 80). In 1979 he said the principles of the Sullivan Code were 'the basis of *constructive engagement*' (emphasis added); he said Inkatha had asked its 250 000 members to help in the 'meaningful monitoring' of the codes and the organization would visit some of the corporations (Buthelezi, 1979:70).

Like many of the initiatives Inkatha announces with such publicity, the monitoring of the codes seems to have produced very little public information, if indeed it continues at all. Bernard Simon, writing in 1984, commented that the codes evoked a 'clear lack of enthusiasm among those [who] . . . are meant to benefit most, namely black workers and their families'. He mentioned that 29 signatories of the Sullivan Code had 'refused to contribute to the costs of the . . . monitoring agencies', and that the main criticism of the codes had been that 'companies have spent the bulk of their time and money on showy bricks-and-mortar projects which look good in corporate publicity brochures, but are not necessarily near the top of blacks' list of priorities' (1984/5:96). Black advancement in the signatory companies, other than into their industrial relations and personnel and community affairs departments, is one of the areas that has shown very little improvement.

A study of the reports submitted by 107 companies to the British government concluded with a stinging attack on 'tricks and distortions' to hide low wages and to avoid recognition agreements with trade unions, and on a general disregard of the EEC Code. Seven companies were said to be paying 'starvation wages', including BTR whose Sarmcol plant in Howick has now been locked in a struggle with the Metal and Allied Workers Union for years (see LMG, 1985; and *International Labour Reports*, Sep.-Oct. 1985). In KwaZulu itself the Canadian Bata company has an atrocious labour policy, as does the US-owned Tidwell

Housing company operating at Ezakheni outside Ladysmith. In 1985 Tidwell Housing paid a minimum starting wage of R25 per week (see, for example, FM, 9 Sep. 85; NW, 29 May 85).

Despite the mediocre record of the codes and of Inkatha's monitoring, the KwaZulu government is currently drawing up its own code to govern employment practices in the bantustan! This follows an anomalous situation where the incomplete withdrawal of South African labour legislation in KwaZulu had allowed loopholes for employers to exploit workers even more than is the case in the bantustans generally. KwaZulu has recently corrected this state of affairs — but by fully adopting the labour legislation applicable in South Africa (see for example, Lewis and Randall, 1985:65).

Chief Buthelezi has assured investors in the bantustan that the proposed KwaZulu code of conduct 'is not a device to corner anyone' (FM, 9 Sep. 85). The questionnaire on which the 'Code of Employment Practice for KwaZulu' is to be based was sent out during 1985 by Professor Schlemmer, through the Centre for Applied Social Sciences. A covering letter says the code was commissioned by the KwaZulu Finance and Investment Corporation (KFC).

In 1976 Buthelezi and Dr Beyers Naude, then director of the Christian Institute, issued a fairly mild statement that if foreign investment was there to benefit the central economy and an elite, then it was 'devoid of all morality' (KLAD, 8:122). This was interpreted, at least by the press, to be a call for disinvestment, allowing Chief Kaiser Matanzima, chief minister of the Transkei, to launch an attack, in language remarkably similar to that usually employed by Buthelezi, on 'two well-fed, well-dressed and well-paid individuals who were preaching the virtues of mass unemployment' (RDM, 7 May 76). Buthelezi responded in a surprisingly placatory tone, saying that his position had been misinterpreted.

The central aspects of Buthelezi's (and hence Inkatha's) position on foreign investment can be summarized as follows: first, it is supported on the spurious grounds, for which, to our knowledge, no evidence has ever been presented, that foreign investment creates jobs, or creates more jobs than would have been provided through local investment and national capital growth. This position has been questioned in several local case studies on the effects of South Africa's dependence on international capital and technology (for example, Brown, 1975; Nattrass and Brown, 1977; Maré, 1982).

Second, it is argued that foreign investment can lead to the development of the 'ghetto states' as Buthelezi referred to the bantustans (Buthelezi, 1972:17-18; STb, 2 Apr. 79). The record of foreign companies operating in the ultra-low wage zones of the bantustans makes nonsense of this claim. While foreign companies offer very little other than badly paid employment, Buthelezi has offered them much more: in 1982 he assured 50 leading US investors on a 'fact-finding mission' to South Africa that they would be safe from 'nationalization in KwaZulu' (NM, 16 Feb. 82), and would find 'stability' in an area where 'the free enterprise system can flourish' (Buthelezi, 1980:5).

Third, it is argued that 'blacks, by queueing for employment, were voting for investment' (Post, 16 Jun. 78). Further 'proof' offered in support of investment is the verbal acceptance of his stance at his meetings, and attitude surveys, specifically the one undertaken for the US State Department by Schlemmer (see Schlemmer, 1984). Attitude surveys have taken the place of demands for debate. During open debate sufficient information can be presented by opposing parties to allow the participants in decision making to choose between a more complex range of options than the simplified choices of attitude surveys (see New York Correspondent, 1985).

The legality of voicing support for disinvestment is seriously in doubt, and under the semi-permanent state of emergency in South Africa it would appear to be a clear offence. It is absurd to interpret the lack of dissenting voices at political meetings of one's own supporters, on an issue that is put in misleading and over-simplified form, as the views of 'tens of thousands, maybe even millions' (Buthelezi interviewed for SABC-TV by Cliff Saunders, 3 Mar. 85), or of 'the black people of South Africa [and] the people of southern Africa' (NM, 9 May 84).

Alec Erwin, FOSATU (now COSATU) education officer, argued, in a debate with Professor Lawrence Schlemmer, that the South African economy was already in such bad shape, with people 'suffering on a massive scale . . . hungry, unemployed, very angry and bitter', that the vast majority supported *any* pressure that would topple the present government (NM, 4 Sep. 85). In a meeting with ILO officials, Buthelezi warned, in what could be seen as an indirect attack on the union position, that trade unions should apply pressure 'as trade unions' and not as 'adjuncts of political parties or tools of ideology' (DN, 8 Oct. 85). What he was saying, in effect, was that trade unions should not take up positions that differed from the Inkatha interpretation of what workers wanted.*

The Inkatha position on investment makes Buthelezi a most desirable ally of foreign capital, of the South African state, and of the conservative governments of South Africa's major trading and investment partners. Buthelezi's frequent appearances on SABC-TV, favourable mention in the propagandist 'Comment' editorial on SABC radio and extensive news and editorial coverage in the commercial press (both English and Afrikaans) in South Africa, is not only due to the role perceived for Inkatha in the reform process, but is directly linked to the increasing intensity of the disinvestment campaign against the country. Law and Order Minister Louis le Grange expressed this as follows:

> I have been looking at the relevance of the problems between organizations — with quite some interest. If I can just elaborate on one particular issue. Take the question of investments, not only in KwaZulu but also in South Africa as a whole. Because Inkatha has experience as a governing body, they know what it means to provide employment for their people. They know what it means to feed the people, to look after their well-being. Chief Gatsha Buthelezi and his government are responsible for the well-being of their people, they know what it entails. The ANC and the UDF don't seem to be

---

* In a recent study of the various attitude surveys relating to investment, researcher Mark Orkin argued that the reason two apparently contradictory sets of results relating to support for disinvestment should have been found among Africans by Schlemmer (1984) and by the London *Sunday Times* (Godwin and Lipsey, 1985), was that the questions were dichotomous. They posed 'the matter . . . in an "either-or" fashion' (Orkin, 1986:5). His own study conceived disinvestment 'as a three-way rather than a two-way issue', and 'also gave the most typical motivation for each position, and an indication of the tendencies which supported it' (1986:7). This was done because 'we wanted our survey to approximate to democratic political choice'. Orkin found that 'on an adequately discerning conception of the issue [of disinvestment], it emerges that nearly three-quarters of urban black South Africans actually favour some or other form of disinvestment' (1986:3). It was also found that 'in answering "which one leader or organization would you like to represent you, in solving [your] problems or grievances"', 31% supported Mandela and the ANC, 16% Bishop Tutu, 14% the UDF and radical groups, and only 8% Chief Buthelezi and Inkatha (1986:35).

bothered about that. They propagate disinvestment irrespective of the results for their own people . . . [Le Grange, 1984:31].

Buthelezi's simplistic presentation of the effects of investment and disinvestment also influences his perception of the southern African region. In an interview he said the 'pacts that have been made between Mozambique and South Africa, which are dictated by sheer economics', served to convince him of the need for investment to 'lay the foundations for stability' (ST, 2 Apr. 79). He ignored the fact that regional links with South Africa as the dominant and exploitative partner have arisen precisely out of the investment pattern that has developed historically in southern Africa (see, for example, Seidman and Seidman, 1977; Seidman and Seidman Makgetla, 1980; Saul, 1985). Nor does he acknowledge that most southern African leaders have supported sanctions.

The other (contradictory) argument is that investment both ensures peaceful change ('. . . if my people have nothing to lose but their skins then the prospects for peaceful change become less and less' (ST interview referred to above, 2 Apr. 79)), and creates the anger that is so necessary to Buthelezi's presentation of himself as the last moderate who can produce a disciplined following. He said this anger does not come from the working class but from an 'emerging middle class' benefiting from 'job advancement and in-company training' and being promoted to managerial and supervisory positions, and encountering the restrictions of apartheid (NM, 12 Jun. 85).

He does not see all boycotts as bad. He favours an arms embargo and argues that 'ordinary black South Africans encourage cultural and sports boycotts' and that these boycotts have 'actually achieved results', though he objects to sport being used as a political weapon (NM, 19 Apr. 85).

Inkatha and capital/Inkatha capitalism

There are two broad areas in which Inkatha has become structurally involved (rather than ideologically or for propaganda purposes) in the capitalist system, and this involvement makes the movement not only a supporter but an active participant in exploitation. First, there is the involvement of capital in KwaZulu and with certain people in KwaZulu; and second, there is Inkatha's direct participation in and initiation of projects. As it would be difficult to separate these two aspects in practice they are dealt with together.

An examination of the rhetoric of the leadership, of Inkatha's involvement in 'reform' (such as through the Buthelezi Commission), and of the personal and cultural links between business leaders and Inkatha leaders, shows the multiple connections that have been established with large-scale (monopoly) capital and with the political bodies and pressure group that represent these interests, such as the Progressive Federal Party (PFP) and the Urban Foundation (UF).

The Inkatha leadership has shaped the ideological position of the movement in such a way that opposition to the class exploitative nature of South African society is neutralized. This has been achieved through a populist appeal that denies any differences amongst the supposedly uniformly oppressed African population, through outspoken and militant support for capitalism (defined as potentially harmonious and to the benefit of all) and through a commitment to 'the system' and to reform from within. At the same time, however, the class specific economic actions and ideological bias of the movement have brought it into conflict with working class and community interests, and will increasingly do so. It has advanced the interests of sections of the petty bourgeoisie (specifically some traders) and of the remnants of the pre-colonial authority structures (the chiefs).

Inkatha has, until now, been largely unsuccessful in attracting the bantustan bureaucracy and professionals and intellectuals. The clashes over salaries (see p.93), when civil servants tried to follow the example set by members of the KLA, gave an early indication that the bantustan government did not have the undivided allegiance of this group. Early in 1986 Buthelezi felt it necessary to warn civil servants that if they belonged to the UDF they would be dismissed. It is possible that one of the effects of an administrative, and possible legislative, amalgamation of Natal and KwaZulu would be to create conditions that would allow for the incorporation of this part of the petty bourgeoisie: higher career opportunities would be opened up, salaries would be adjusted, a new ethic of careerism and ambition might become possible in a combined civil service. Professional positions and intellectual activities would no longer carry the stigma of racially separate and inferior bantustan origins. But until then most of this group will probably remain on the fence, between the UDF and Inkatha.

Inkatha has been more successful in attracting and advancing the interests of the trading and small scale industrial interests of Zulu-speakers, or of sections of this group, through making money available for 'development' and for expansion of existing or future commercial interests.*

Buthelezi has said 'white South Africa' should invest in KwaZulu as a moral duty. However, realizing that not many businesses would invest for moral reasons, he added that profitability was a major concern (Temkin, 1976:191). He said investment would be welcomed because in this way 'development' could be achieved in KwaZulu, and 'free enterprise [is] an effective vehicle for development' (Buthelezi, 1980:4). Further, such investment would be 'absolutely vital, if we are going to stand on our own as a State' (KLAD, 4:130); investment would also create employment. He suggested that investors be given 'growth point concessions' to set up businesses in the townships around Durban as this was where the 'rural' population was increasingly to be found, 'competing for jobs that simply do not exist' (FM, 2 May 80).

It was with full knowledge of the appeal that cheap, controlled labour holds for investors that Buthelezi's advertisement offering 'problem-free labour resources' appeared not only in the commercial press, but also in the KwaZulu government-approved *KwaZulu Government Diary* in 1974 — the year after strikes had rocked Natal. On the one hand Buthelezi was eager to incorporate the mass action by the workers into his threats of the potential power of the African people; on the other he promised to discipline the working class and stressed in the advertising campaign (sponsored by the Trust Bank) that sanctions would hurt black people (Survey, 1973: 186-87). 'Profits comparable to those in White areas' is what Buthelezi stands for (Schmahmann, 1978:169), but once again he wants the best of both worlds: support for investment and high profits, and at the same time a concern for the effects of investment. Schmahmann refers to his objection 'in principle' to border industries, although 'while Zulus were not exploited the

---

*In 1978/79 the KwaZulu Development Corporation (KDC) granted loans worth R3.9m to entrepreneurs: of 97 loans granted, 34 went to general dealers, 19 to bottle store operators, and 12 to butcheries (Survey, 1980:440). By 1984 the KDC had financed nearly 900 businesses to the value of R32.7m (Survey, 1984:602).

KwaZulu Government would maintain cordial relations with them' (1978:164) — he is concerned about the low wages paid in these industrial areas that the KwaZulu government 'is powerless to influence' (1978:166).

Early on in the existence of the KLA Buthelezi must have realized that his promises to bring 'development' to the impoverished, over-crowded area that he had chosen as his launching pad would come to naught unless he was able to provide at least some jobs there — even at low wages. Sensitive to the possibility that his calls for foreign investment in KwaZulu would be construed as support for the apartheid system, he asked that the bantustans be allowed to raise their own loans independently of central state agencies. The Bantu Laws Amendment Act of 1973 empowered the bantustans to raise public loans directly, although the approval of the Minister of Bantu Administration and Development was still necessary (Schmahmann, 1978:132-3; Horrell, 1978:53).

However, the launching of the tripartite companies (tripcos) scheme gave shape to the purposefully vague notion of 'development' that has been such a rallying cry with the Inkatha leadership. The close cooperation between major business interests in the region and the creation of Inkatha's own investment arm, Khulani Holdings, show Inkatha's class interests in the 1980s. The existence of and their participation in the KwaZulu bantustan had indirectly benefited certain economic interests during the early years, but it was only in the mid-1970s, at the time of Inkatha's formation, that a more direct involvement with capital came about, through the establishment of tripcos.

The first agreement was signed in Pretoria on 26 July 1976 between the KLA, the Bantu Investment Corporation (BIC), and individual businesses such as Greatermans (representing the retailers Checkers), and Sasko Milling (Umlazi Bakery). The signing ceremony was both a victory for Buthelezi and the first concrete tie between large-scale business and a bantustan petty bourgeoisie (and nascent bourgeoisie). It followed a long and bitter battle against the South African Information Department and the Bureau of State Security, who tried to foment conflict and fashion an alternative leadership to Buthelezi out of 'traditionalist' and conservative elements mobilized round the king. Significantly, opposition to the tripco deals included a further element: sections of the trading petty bourgeoisie, who sought to protect their ethnically safeguarded interests.

Tripcos were a way in which 'white' (retail) capital could enter the ethnic stockades that the bantustans were meant to be for African entrepreneurs. A large part of the income of migrant workers was never remitted, but some of it was nevertheless finding its way back to be spent in African-owned stores; more important, the increase in commuter labour from the KwaZulu townships on the outskirts of the Durban-Pinetown, Pietermaritzburg, Ladysmith, Newcastle, and Richards Bay/Empangeni industrial areas in Natal, meant that these people were also spending money outside the areas where large-scale capital operated — hence the business interest in tripcos. The other beneficiaries would be those among the bantustan petty bourgeoisie with links to the KLA. The BIC, the third party, would ultimately sell its shares to the planned, and since established, KwaZulu Development Corporation (KDC, now the KwaZulu Finance and Investment Corporation, the KFC), which has come under the direct control of the KLA (and hence Inkatha).

Opposition to the tripcos came from traders who were threatened by the expansion of the distributive networks of the large retail and food-producing firms which accounted for most of the 'white' capital entering the agreements. The opposition African traders were predominantly, but not exclusively, located in the townships close to industrial areas, exactly the areas which would attract large retailers as these were the largest concentrated markets, rather than those served by small rural trading stores. The exceptions were traders who had already been helped by the BIC or by 'white' capital. Here the name Winnington Sabelo emerges for the first time — a person who has since made a name for himself with his fanatical allegiance to the gist if not the specifics of Inkatha policy (see pp.203-04). Sabelo's name was linked to the original idea of tripcos through the 'favourable impression made on African traders when Checkers helped an Umlazi businessman [Sabelo] set up his own supermarket' (NM, 20 May 75). Sabelo had also had the help of the other party to the tripco alliance in the form of an enormous R187 000 loan from the BIC early in 1974 to build a shopping centre — 'to bring West Street [Durban's main shopping street] to Umlazi township' (quoted Maré, 1978: 305). Ironically, what appears to be the current trend is for the few people in Umlazi who are in a position to benefit from the abolition of racial restrictions in some central business districts to set up shop in West Street itself.

These beneficiaries of the tripco links were in the minority and politically unsure in the townships at that stage, in the mid-1970s. The more common traders' position was probably that articulated by B.I. Dladla, first councillor for community affairs in KwaZulu, a trader himself, but one with bad experience of the BIC (see, for example, KLAD, 3:50-54). Even before the possibility of tripcos these traders had spoken of the need for KwaZulu to purchase all shops 'owned by Non-Bantu in KwaZulu' and to lease these to Zulus (KLAD, 3:50). A policy statement in the KLA in 1973 'firmly rejected any policy . . . which would have the tendency and/or ultimate result that the wealth, resources and commercial opportunities of KwaZulu would no longer be reserved and developed exclusively for us' (KLAD, 3:169). Dladla added that Zulu wealth was being taken by 'other nations' (referring specifically to the operations of the BIC in KwaZulu) (KLAD, 3:182).

The lines were clearly drawn: on the one side were the beneficiaries of KwaZulu policies, who were also the beneficiaries of the BIC's loans, and who were starting to establish links with white-owned capital, as well as individual African traders who hoped to benefit from these various avenues through their support for the politically powerful controllers of the KLA and later of Inkatha. On the other side were opponents of the BIC (because of the selective basis of its loans, or because of unfavourable experiences once loans had been taken) and opponents of 'non-Zulus' whom the barriers of the bantustan policy had failed to keep out. Fearing new threats from 'outsiders', they opposed tripcos.

The opponents searched desperately for political allies against the total control held by Buthelezi and Inkatha over the structures, policies and favours of the bantustan authority. The symbol that suited all the various parties to the opposition alliance was the king. He suited the central state, which had years earlier anticipated an executive role for him in Zulu politics, only to be deprived of this conservative influence by Buthelezi who managed to consign him to a constitutional periphery. He suited traditionalists, who saw in the king, and not in the prime minister, Buthelezi, the true leader of the Zulu nation. And he suited the traders, who could not by themselves take control of political processes and structures, formed around the chiefs, that were necessary for capital accumulation. Buthelezi perceptively commented in 1975 in the thick of the tripco conflict, 'I would like to ask the honourable members [of the KLA] . . . not to pretend that they love the King more than we do, merely because they want the support and the prestige of the King to support their stand on the concept of the tripartite companies . . .' (KLAD, 7:1017).*

Supporters of the tripcos knew that the future lay not in the limited though real benefits for the trading class in the protective measures of apartheid, but in a closer alliance with established capital. The financial editor of the *Sunday Tribune* neatly explained why the distributors of commodities were interested:

> Homeland trading is the obvious plum for the large chains, particularly Checkers, which is having to seek new trading areas in the face of the Pick 'n Pay and OK hypermarket developments. Checkers submitted a series of proposals to KwaZulu . . . [including that] no similar venture unless wholly owned by Africans, be allowed to operate near Checkers' KwaZulu outlets for 10 years [3 Aug. 75].

Buthelezi then used the power that the opponents of the tripcos had made unsuccessful attempts to capture. He had the principle of tripcos accepted by both Inkatha and the KLA (see KLAD, 7:973; NM, 6 Aug. 75). He challenged the power of Inyanda (the Natal and Zululand African Chamber of Commerce), representing some 400 of the 1600 traders and focus for the opposition to tripcos, by calling a meeting of traders. This set the style of calling public meetings of supporters to endorse policy that is then presented as reflecting the wishes of all. It could not fail as the meeting, held at Ulundi, was most convenient to rurally-based traders (those who had least to lose from tripcos) (Maré, 1978:309). Inyanda fell into line and with official approval had about 2000 active members by the end of the decade (Du Plessis, 1981:41).

Initially the plan was to phase out 'white' capital over time, but by 1980 this had been dropped, though Africans were still buying shares in tripcos (R71 000 worth in 1980) (DN, 6 Jun. 81). *The Developer* (journal of the KDC) wrote in December 1982 that more than 1300 people had bought shares to the value of approximately R500 000. The article also showed that private companies had invested very little, relying instead on the money advanced and facilities provided by the KDC: white entrepreneurs had spent R2.6m in share capital while the KDC had spent R2.3m in shares, R2m in loans to entrepreneurs and had a further R15m invested in buildings (also see DN, 6 Jun. 81).

---

*An example of how the alliance worked was in the formation in 1975 of the Inala Party (named after one of the king's regiments). Chief Mhlabunzima Maphumulo said the party was formed out of the dissatisfaction of the king, members of the royal family and businessmen with Inkatha and Buthelezi's leadership — especially with the break with the 1928 Inkata. They also objected to tripcos, the lack of democracy within Inkatha, and the initial compulsory patronage of the movement by chiefs (Langner, 1983:169). It was because of the Inala Party that the first special meeting of the Inkatha national council was called in 1976, to be followed by a sitting of the KLA which led to the withdrawal of the king from politics, and a decision by the national council that there was no need for political parties because 'we are still in bondage'. Maphumulo was charged with 'misconduct in terms . . . of the KwaZulu Act on Chiefs and Headmen' of 1974 (Langner, 1983:169). The main charge levelled against him by people who had ostensibly rejected the bantustan system was that he had taken part in the activities of an organization 'of which the aims were the unconstitutional overthrow of the [KwaZulu] government'. Maphumulo was found not guilty on this charge but guilty of involving the king in politics (Langner, 1983:169). Years later, in 1983, Chief Maphumulo was assaulted by Inkatha youths outside the KLA buildings, for not joining Inkatha. Buthelezi, who had seen the incident, along with the KwaZulu police and a massive crowd, condemned the assault but added that 'whoever challenged him challenged the people, who would deal with them' (Survey, 1983:53 and 347).

A recent case indicates that while the political battle may have been won, the directness with which certain economic interests are being advanced through the KwaZulu authority and its financial wing is creating tensions, if not enemies. Buthelezi was again full of praise for the tripco scheme when he opened a R1.5m bakery in Edendale township outside Pietermaritzburg. The bakery was a venture between the KDC and Premier Milling, a giant food chain, and was claimed to be the biggest in Natal, with the potential of producing 17m loaves a year (*Developer*, Dec. 83). The KwaZulu authorities had a vested interest in seeing that potential realized. In May 1984 it was revealed that traders were complaining that the bread from Edendale Bakery was cold in the morning and that consumers were dissatisfied (*Echo*, 17 May. 84). They suggested a boycott of the bread if the situation was not rectified, and added that bread from a competitor had never been cold. In November 1984 Albany Bakery, apparently in competition with the tripco Edendale Bakery, announced that it had been sent a letter by the KDC telling it to withdraw from supplying bread to the Vulindlela district (where Edendale is located). In denying the Albany claim KDC director M. Spies showed how decisions affecting the consumers of Edendale were now taken in the boardrooms of monopoly companies:

> The decision that Albany Bakers should withdraw from supplying bread in the Vulindlela district was made jointly by the Premier Group and Tiger Oats and National Milling. Tiger Oats is the holding company of Albany Bakery [*Echo*, 15 Nov 84].

Inyanda, representing small traders (those most directly affected by consumer dissatisfaction), was brought into the conflict, as were 'some black people who bought shares' in the tripco — 'they are not happy about the bad image of the Edendale loaf'. At the opening of the bakery Buthelezi had proudly announced that 1000 shares had been bought. In May 1985 the press announced that the bread had improved.

In the year that the tripcos were first being formed and opposed, 1975, the central government announced that it was to phase out the often criticized Bantu Investment Corporation (BIC) and would instead establish development corporations for each of the bantustans 'in accordance with the Government's policy to involve the African people in increasing measure in the development of their homelands' (Survey, 1975:148). Four of the ten directors of each regional corporation would be nominated by the bantustan itself. These nominees could not be executive councillors, and preferably not legislative assembly members. Buthelezi criticized the new direction, in that it would not be controlled directly enough by the bantustans, and that bantustan cabinet ministers could not serve on the boards.

The KDC was formed in April 1978. All four African members were also members of the KLA (Survey, 1978:305). The KDC was 'regarded as the economic arm of the KwaZulu government' (Langner, 1983:159). Since 1981 the chairman of the KDC board has been Dr A.H. Zulu (ex-bishop, speaker of the KLA, and longtime friend of Buthelezi). The KDC has become even more closely integrated into the bantustan structure, as Buthelezi had desired in 1976.

In 1984 the KDC took control of the industrial development functions in KwaZulu previously in the hands of the national development body, the Corporation for Economic Development (CED, formerly the BIC). The CED then disbanded and its remaining functions were taken over by the Development Bank of Southern Africa (DBSA). The KwaZulu government, rather than the

CED, then became the shareholder in the KDC (*Developer*, Sep. 83). The KDC took over R191m worth of assets from the CED, while the KDC's own assets were R145m (*Developer*, Oct. 84). Also in 1984 it was announced that the KLA would pass legislation to make the KDC the 'development agency' of KwaZulu. The KwaZulu government would henceforth appoint directors.

The greater involvement of the KwaZulu authorities in profit-making ventures as well as strictly development work is one result of the incorporation of the KDC (now the KFC). The KwaZulu Shoe Company provides one example of the implications. This was a joint venture between the KDC, through shares previously held by the CED, and the Bermuda-based holding company of he Canadian Bata company, Western Industrial and Trading Company (WITCO). The venture employs 439 people and it was reported (*Developer*, Nov. 84) that the company 'lays claims to a deep social commitment, believing in taking work to the people rather than opting to establish manufacturing units exclusively in the more densely populated urban areas'. What this glowing report on 'development' neglected to say under its headline of 'KwaZulu Shoe Factory Helping to Give Poverty the Boot in Remote Area' was anything of the company's past. In 1982 there had been a strike by about 700 workers over the dismissal of a woman worker and the non-recognition of the trade union, the National Union of Textile Workers (NUTW). Some workers were being paid R14 per week, which indicates why the company had established itself in such an out of the way place as Loskop in the Natal midlands: the industrial council for the leather industry (a wage regulating body) said that as the KwaZulu Shoe Company was situated 'outside of South Africa', it was not covered by minimum wage regulations. KwaZulu minister of the interior Dr Frank Mdlalose agreed to send his department's 'labour officer', Z.S. Khanyile, to mediate, after a meeting with the management. The strike was broken after more than a month because of Khanyile's involvement, said the NUTW (see, for example, St, 16 Apr. 82). A union statement issued after the workers had returned alleged that:

> The decision follows the complete failure of the KwaZulu appointed Mr Khanyile to mediate in the dispute. The bitter frustration and disappointment with Mr Khanyile reached a climax when it became known that Mr Khanyile had been to the factory secretly and had formed his own committee amongst the strike breakers. [He] claims to have mediated between that committee and the company, thereby fully satisfying himself that the workers' claims were unfounded, their grievances false and the union completely unrepresentative [also see Cooper, 1984:180-83].

The KDC became the KwaZulu Finance and Investment Corporation (KFC) in 1984. Shareholding and responsibility were transferred to the KwaZulu government (Survey, 1984:616). Buthelezi announced that directors would be appointed by himself and that shares in the KFC would be made available to the private sector, 'as part of a broad plan to encourage its involvement in the development of KwaZulu' (Survey, 1984:616).

There were no surprises when Buthelezi announced the first board of directors of the KFC: chair, Bishop Alphaeus Zulu; deputy chair, Dr Anson Lloyd, prominent in the sugar industry; executive director, Dr Marius Spies, previously of the KDC; directors, Tony Johns, secretary of works in the KwaZulu government; R.B. Lobban, senior partner in an auditor's firm; W.T.V Luthuli; M. September, businessman and KLA member; S.J. Mhlungu; and Professor Lawrence Schlemmer, director of the Centre for Applied Social Sciences, University of Natal, and first director of the Inkatha Institute.

The KFC acquired the industrial estates of Isithebe, Ezakheni (near Ladysmith), and Madadeni (close to Newcastle), previously controlled by the CED (STb, 5 Dec. 84). These are all notorious low-wage areas, given further protection through the inadequate wage legislation applying in KwaZulu (see A. Lawyer, 1983:72-74). The KwaZulu government does have the power to legislate on labour matters, yet in 1984 labour lawyer Richard Lyster said that "'a free for all" situation had been created in KwaZulu by the lack of basic conditions of employment' (NM, 20 Jan. 84); it was reported that clothing industry machinists in Isithebe were earning 45% less than for equivalent work outside KwaZulu.

The KDC also took over from the CED eight branches of the KwaZulu Savings Bank, later changed to Ithala ('a safe place') Savings Bank, which had 18 500 operative savings accounts. The possibility of establishing the Zalabisa Savings Account, to run as a building society in KwaZulu, was also raised at the time (*Developer*, 12, 1984; Survey, 1984:602).

It has not only been through the KDC/KFC that KwaZulu, and hence Inkatha, have become involved in capitalism. More directly Inkatha and Inyanda (the Natal and Zululand African Chamber of Commerce) have established Khulani Holdings, as though to prove through this joint venture that their old conflicts over tripcos have now been resolved, or at least swept under the carpet. Khulani is committed to profits, but this word does not often feature in Inkatha rhetoric, which describes it in terms of 'building common bridges and developing communications through the free enterprise system' (ST, 22 Aug. 82). Khulani is said to allow 'small black shareholders an opportunity to invest in the free enterprise system, and we are showing them it can work for them', according to S.J. (Johnny) Mhlungu, managing director of Khulani, director of the KFC, KLA member, Inkatha central committee member, member of the Mashonangashoni regional authority (which Buthelezi heads), and a member of the regional board of Barclays Bank (DN, 9 Apr. 86).

Khulani Holdings was registered late in 1979 with 660 shareholders, an issued share capital of R500 000 and loans from the KDC (ST, 22 Aug. 82). Its first subsidiary, Khulani-Brown Wholesalers, was incorporated on 11 February 1980, with 51% of shares held by Khulani. The remainder belong to W.G. Brown, a subsidiary of Tiger Oats. By 1986 Khulani-Brown had 'four large wholesale stores with a turnover of R36m a year' and the ability to operate in 'white areas' (adding another dimension to the tripcos which brought 'white' capital into the bantustans) (ST, 5 Jan. 86). Khulani is also involved in retail, property, and bookselling (see diagram). Khulani Booksellers has a large turnover due to its sales to the KwaZulu government (Charney, 1983:38).

The directors of Khulani in 1983, other than Mhlungu, were S.Z. Conco, senior Inkatha member, KLA member and on the executive of the newly established Inkatha union UWUSA; M.Z. Khumalo, Buthelezi's personal assistant, administrative secretary of Inkatha and a businessman; A.P.E. Mkhwanazi, secretary of the KwaZulu department of economic affairs; R.D. Sishi, Inkatha member, businessman and mayor of Mpumalanga township; W.T. Luthuli, businessman and cane farmer, member of Inkatha and the KLA; M.A. Nzuza, businessman, member of Inkatha and the KLA; and G.J. van den Berg, then finance officer with the KDC (Charney, 1983:38). This list clearly indicates the total overlap between Inkatha, the KLA and Khulani Holdings, and includes Inyanda, existing African business interests, large-scale 'white' capital and the KDC/KFC.

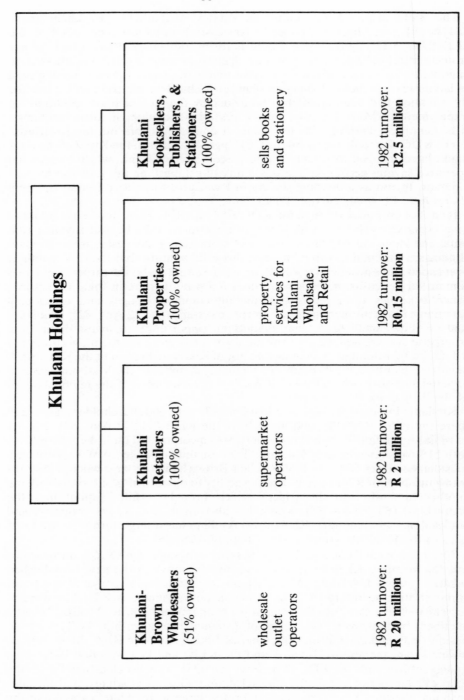

from *Management* (June 1983)

Through its holdings Khulani expands these overlaps. For example, when in 1982 it entered into an agreement (although Mhlungu subsequently said that it had only taken an option to buy) with the Summerley family trust (the Magnum group), and the Rupert family trust (under Johan Rupert, son of tobacco millionaire Dr Anton Rupert), it considerably expanded its alliances. It did likewise when it formed Khulani Insurance Brokers in 1985 with Bowring Barclays and Associates (SA), in turn owned by Anglo American, Barclays and March & McLennan. Directors were P.J. (Peter) Davidson, a director of the ill-fated Executive Hotel in Umlazi,* along with Mhlungu, M.Z. Khumalo, Khulani director (mentioned above), W.T.V. Luthuli, director of Khulani and the KFC (mentioned above), and A.P.E. Mkhwanazi, Khulani director (mentioned above).

The parallels with the way Afrikaner capital had mobilized on an ethnic basis to take political power and boost the interests of a distinctive ethnic fraction of capital, has not escaped commentators on Khulani. Reporter David Meades wrote (Bd, 21 Sep. 82) that it was significant that Johan Rupert should play a central role in the establishment, with Khulani, of Magnum National Life Assurance. His father, Anton, had been one of the prime movers in the economic consolidation of specifically Afrikaner capital (but has since, along with many similar Afrikaner economic giants, become integrated into monopoly capitalism generally). It was also through insurance (SANLAM) that Afrikaner savings were mobilized. As O'Meara wrote, in words that have to be adapted only in part to apply to what Inkatha claims to be doing:

> The Santam/Sanlam group aimed to pool the money resources of all Afrikaans-speakers in a central fund, there to be converted into productive capital [1983:99].

Two of the biggest differences are that Khulani will not mobilize money coming from the farming sector, as was the case with Afrikaner ethnic mobilization, and that it has already entered into alliance with monopoly capital, from a position of individual weakness but collective political strength.

Khulani will also provide employment for African managers and other professionals. When plans to move the Khulani head office to Durban from its original site in Ulundi were first mooted, the reason given was that professionals were not prepared to move to the geographical and cultural isolation of the KwaZulu capital. Both Charney (1983) and Roger Smith (writing in STb, 5 Dec. 84) argued that it is political power that Inkatha is after, through Khulani. The other side of the coin, that political power is an essential part of a successful accumulation strategy, is even more important. Charney wrote:

> It [Khulani] will also provide tangible benefits to Inkatha's power base among its policy-holders and employees, much as the Afrikaner Economic Movement did for that of the National Party in the 1940s.
>
> For power is ultimately the name of the game. If the Nationalists hadn't won the 1948 election, Sanlam would probably still be one of the smaller insurance companies instead of a financial and industrial powerhouse. Mhlungu, too, is aware that Blacks need political power if they are to secure a firm foothold among the corporate giants,

---

*The Executive Hotel in Umlazi became known as a place where Inkatha planning was undertaken. In 1985 it was target of a bomb attack. In 1986 it was announced that the Ulundi Trading Company (UTC, chaired by S.J. Mhlungu) had declined to take up an offer to buy the hotel from the KFC. UTC had been leasing the hotel since 1981. 'Unfavourable trading conditions' were said to be the reason for closing the hotel (DN, 17 Feb. 86; NM, 18 Feb. 86).

and regards the aid of a possible future Inkatha government as an essential part of long-term strategy [1983:38].

At the fourth annual general meeting of Khulani Holdings Buthelezi himself drew attention to the example of the 'Afrikaner route to power' [STb, 5 Dec. 84].

If the general role of the bantustan branches of the central state is to ensure the social conditions for profitable production, then KwaZulu and Inkatha have added to that the task of direct profit making. Both these roles would tend to bring Inkatha into conflict with working class organizations.

KwaZulu, Inkatha and the labour movement

The formation of the Congress of South African Trade Unions (COSATU) in November 1985 brought the strained relations between the Inkatha movement and the working class and its organizations to a head. Even in the choice of slogan for the COSATU launch mass rally — 'Workers unite, One federation, One country' — there was both a commitment to a specific direction and an implicit criticism of the politics of fragmentation of which the bantustans are a part and in which Buthelezi participates.

COSATU has brought together 400 000 paid up workers, with a signed up membership far in excess of this (Lewis and Randall, 1985:84-5). It has also taken a confident political stance from the time of its launch. However unintentionally, it has shifted the historical base of the 1970s unions away from Natal. COSATU's political stance is well illustrated by the issues raised by its president, Elijah Barayi, in his inaugural speech and subsequent statements, and by general secretary Jay Naidoo. They committed COSATU to work towards socialism and to campaign (including the use of civil disobedience) for the abolition of passes; they addressed political events and threatened the non-payment of rents and taxes if 'the political order in this country does not change soon' (NM, 9 Dec. 85). 'There is no longer going to be any difference between the black person on the shop floor and the black person in his political life,' said Barayi (DN, 2 Dec. 85; SALB, 1986:43-68). Little wonder that hundreds of trade unionists and members were amongst the detainees of June-July 1986 and subsequently.

The shift of COSATU's political 'centre of gravity' away from Natal means a wider representation of workers, and their leaders will be less hesitant in responding to moves by Inkatha that are perceived as contrary to workers' interests than was the case with the primarily Natal-based unions, or unions with a regional autonomy. It will also mean less sensitivity to regional peculiarities.

Inkatha lost no time in attacking COSATU — such a strong body, democratically organized on a national basis, with stated political aims could not but come into conflict with Inkatha's strategies and goals. COSATU had to be a threat to an organization that claims to be all of these things but whose claims ring increasingly hollow. Inkatha's leadership cannot allow any challenge to its claims of representing every section of the African population of Natal and even of South Africa — if you represent 'the people' you represent everybody. But 'the people' is a fragile construct, especially along the fault lines of class.

During the week leading up to COSATU's formation Buthelezi said that its aim was not to oppose Pretoria but to challenge Inkatha. Barayi replied Inkatha had not even been mentioned at meetings preceding the formation and accused

Buthelezi of just being scared (NM, 2 Dec. 85). The essence of Buthelezi's accusation was that COSATU was a 'front for the ANC'. He mentioned a fear of being assassinated and called on Inkatha members 'to be vigilant and to let me know what their observations are' (NM, 5 Dec. 85).

Buthelezi's long-time friend and political ally, Norman Middleton, Natal coordinator of the Council of Unions of South Africa (CUSA), issued a statement on behalf of CUSA and the Azanian Congress of Trade Unions (AZACTU) that these unions would not be joining COSATU because COSATU represented the interests of a white minority, implying that nearly 500 000 black workers had been duped. This assertion shows many similaries with Buthelezi's arguments, though Buthelezi's accusations of political manipulation in the past have been directed at non-Africans — both Indians and whites — rather than non-blacks.

Currently, the two major areas of conflict appear to be that COSATU is 'political', and that Barayi has called for sanctions. 'Political' in this case means being against the bantustan policy and those who are working within it. Specifically, COSATU had expressed solidarity with the residents of Hambanathi and Lamontville in Natal in their struggle against incorporation into KwaZulu. Inkatha secretary general Dhlomo, neglecting to mention that it was Buthelezi who had first attacked COSATU, accused COSATU of having been hostile to Inkatha from the outset. He continued with the threat that Inkatha might have to set up its own trade union — 'mobiliz[ing] the full strength of Inkatha's workers to find alternative means of negotiating for worker rights if any particular trade union abandons this prime responsibility in favour of playing a party political role' (STb, 8 Dec. 85). It is difficult to believe that Dhlomo was not aware of the irony in his threat when he was himself speaking on behalf of a 'political party'.

Barayi raised the sanctions/disinvestment issue in his inaugural address in Durban on 1 December 1985 when he attacked bantustan leaders who spent money travelling the world advocating continued investment when that money could have been spent on alleviating poverty at home, such as by paying pensions. This was a reference to the inability of the KwaZulu administration to pay pensions to all those entitled to them within its area of jurisdiction. Buthelezi responded with a call on the COSATU leaders to resign from their jobs so that, operating as 'ANC surrogates', they could 'taste' what they were advocating. He said 'seven million Zulus' had not given him a mandate to call for sanctions (DN, 3 Dec. 85).

In the arena of working class organization and demands, as in many other areas. Buthelezi and Inkatha have shown a fair measure of consistency over the years. This consistency has drawn changing responses from working class organizations and activists in the process of gathering strength after the vicious state repression of labour and political movements in the 1960s. Initially, during the first stirrings in the early 1970s of what was to become the independent union movement, Buthelezi and some other bantustan figures were seen as potentially useful allies in wresting organizational leeway from the state. For example, the Institute for Industrial Education (IIE), in their study of the 1973 strikes in Durban, recommended that 'homeland governments' could, amongst other things, recognize branches of the trade unions in their areas of administration, press for the recognition of trade unions with employers and apply pressure on foreign firms to improve living conditions, publicize the fact that trade unions for African workers were not illegal, 'and should give support to the formation of such unions' (IIE, 1974:189-190).

The first half of the 1970s was a time of turmoil in industrial relations in South Africa, especially in Natal. Errol Drummond, director of the Steel and Engineering Industries Federation of South Africa (SEIFSA), speaking for the majority of employers, said in 1974: 'In this industry there will be no — and you can underline no — negotiations with African trade unions' (Survey, 1974:317). Drummond was speaking with confidence in the belief that the state would not be forced to yield to working class demands. Several right-wing white unions and federations also opposed the idea of trade unions for African workers.

Even before the landmark strikes in 1973 that involved more than 100 000 workers in Natal there had been several events that had boosted the collective strength of the working class in the province. For example, in February 1972 the bus drivers in the Hammarsdale industrial border area dormitory township of Mpumalanga went on strike. Strikes affecting commuter transport are always, by their very nature, high profile affairs, affecting most workers in the area concerned. In October 1972 Durban dockworkers stopped work in demand for more pay (they were reportedly earning R8.40 per week). Some of the workers involved called on Buthelezi to intervene in the dispute, but he did not respond (Survey, 1972:326). The workers involved were migrants and therefore easily dependent on a 'traditional' authority figure such as Buthelezi. His failure to respond to these early requests did not augur well. Schmahmann (1978:192) wrote:

> The first contacts between KwaZulu and the Black urban labour movement occurred in Durban in October 1972, and were not auspicious. Buthelezi's non-intervention in negotiations between the striking stevedores and their employers evoked widespread disappointment [see also Schlemmer and Muil, 1975:128].

It was not only the stevedores who received low wages. The South African economy as a whole has always been characterized by low wage employment and the early 1970s were no exception. As the IIE (1974:84) commented:

> Low wages, increasing cost of living, increased transport costs and lack of adequate bargaining machinery created the underlying grievance climate which made the [1973] strikes possible. But none of these factors are peculiar to Durban. Wages for African workers vary throughout the country, but they vary only between low and very low. [Survey, 1972:325-8].

It was, however, in Durban that the massive wave of strikes took place during the first half of 1973. The first KwaZulu intervention occurred right at the start of the strikes, and was largely in keeping with previous requests for involvement. Hostel dwellers, migrant workers at Coronation Brick and Tile Company, had been visited by King Goodwill during 1972. The 2000 workers were left with the impression, from this other 'traditional' authority figure, that they could expect their wages to be increased in 1973. When this had not happened by 9 January they brought the plant to a standstill, demanding an increase of R11 per week (which would have brought their wages up to R20 per week). King Goodwill then talked the reluctant workers back to work with a further promise that he would negotiate on their behalf. An authority that had nothing directly to do with the industrial arena had intervened in a labour dispute.

The king's involvement brought both 'traditional' and bantustan politics generally squarely into the labour struggle, confirming a confusion that still exists in Natal. First, Goodwill's second promise to negotiate was accepted by the

BILLY PADDOCK

Symbols of 'Zulu identity', Shaka Day celebrations, Umlazi 1985. Left: Buthelezi denounces the ANC. Right: Buthelezi and King Goodwill dance with the amabutho warriors.

Above *The king's bodyguards with his new Mercedes Benz (registration 'Zulu King 1')*
Below *Buthelezi in traditional dress.*

BILLY PADDOCK

May Day 1986 Above: *Buthelezi arrives at the Uwusa launch in a suitably marked helicopter.* Below: *Security forces patrol outside the rally. Chiefs had been instructed to bus people to the stadium.*

BILLY PADDOCK

The Uwusa launch was an opportunity for attacks: on the 750,000-strong union federation, COSATU (above) and (below) on Bishop Tutu and the campaign for sanctions.

BILLY PADDOCK

workers only after the king's representative, Prince Sithela Zulu, pointed out to them 'that if they would not trust his [the king's] word, this would "lower his dignity"' (IIE, 1974:12). The apartheid policy, with its separation of African areas from places of employment and its maintenance of distorted authority structures in the homelands, has allowed a greater influence of non-capitalist political control than would be expected in a similar industrialized setting elsewhere. In Natal the distortion of authority has been aggravated through the continuation of the monarchy. The existence of the Zulu royal house has given conservative interests a useful lever in attempting to control the working class, as was the case with King Solomon in the 1920s and 1930s. In a repeat performance King Goodwill is now being used to bolster the Inkatha-initiated United Workers Union of South Africa (UWUSA — see below, p.133).

Second, the clash between Buthelezi and the king during the tripco issue of the mid-1970s had an effect in the industrial arena. Buthelezi also referred to the dignity of the king in this conflict, but for a different purpose: he told Goodwill to stay out of controversial issues as his involvement would impair the status of the constitutional position that had been allocated to him the previous year. Buthelezi told the KLA that bad things had happened in Zulu history when kings had not listened to their 'prime ministers' (KLAD, 2:40). The king backed down. Thus, instead of meeting the Coronation Brick and Tile Company directors to represent the workers' case, he attended the opening of the KLA session.

It was not so much the 'dignity' of the king that concerned Buthelezi as his fear of alternative bases of power that could challenge his still-uncertain position in KwaZulu and later in national politics. The working class appeared to offer one such base for alternatives to KwaZulu bantustan politics, and later to Inkatha, or within Inkatha. Buthelezi has consistently called for the formation of trade unions, but unions of a specific ilk.

The KwaZulu leadership gained a credibility in the labour field within the relative political and economic vacuum of the early 1970s, whether due to the absence of working class organizations (trade unions or a political party), the brief dominance of liberal reformists in political activity at this period in Natal or a belief that bantustan politics (and later Inkatha) might offer the possibility of advancing progressive struggle. It was probably a combination of these and other factors, such as a need to protect the trade unions that were being formed. The official economic climate was very hostile, and many employers also preferred direct repression to institutionalized conflict. The value of a 'patron' who had seemingly built up some immunity from state action through participation in the bantustan policy would have had its attractions. Whatever the causes, the effect was a fudging of the lines of division between working class activity and bantustan politics, lines that are now very much clearer, more than a decade later.

For many Buthelezi represented the only option of resistance to apartheid — at least in the short term, although there was doubt about his choosing to work within the bantustan structures. Some felt this could prevent him from playing an otherwise useful role. Even the South African Students' Organization (SASO), the most prominent of the black consciousness organizations, displayed a certain ambiguity when it came to Buthelezi (and even Matanzima, at this time). For example, 'Frank Talk', in a column entitled 'I write what I like' in a 1972 edition of the SASO *Newsletter*, condemned the 'system' of the bantustans but continued:

> What is most painful is that Matanzima and Buthelezi are perhaps more than anybody else acutely aware of the limitations surrounding them. It may also be true that they are

extremely dedicated to the upliftment of Black people and perhaps to their liberation. Many times they have manifested a fighting spirit characterizing true courage and determination. But if you want to fight your enemy you do not accept from him the unloaded of his two guns and then challenge him to a dual [sic] [1972:20].

The wages commissions that existed on most of the English-language campuses in South Africa in the 1970s had their origin at the Durban and Pietermaritzburg campuses of the University of Natal. Drawing on student involvement and university resources, they produced news-sheets, publicized wage determination hearings amongst workers and presented evidence at these hearings, and researched working conditions (such as the well-publicized investigation into the wattle industry in Natal with its large foreign capital involvement). A large part of the groundwork for the formation of worker organizations in Natal, and some other regions, came from the wages commissions. The importance of the publicity they gave Buthelezi should not be underestimated. For example, the second issue of *Abasebenzi* (April 1973), a newsletter produced for workers in the western Cape by the wages commission at the University of Cape Town, devoted its first page to a message from Buthelezi under a heading (in translation) 'Words of encouragement to workers from Chief Minister of KwaZulu Legislative Assembly — M. Gatsha Buthelezi'. The message contained such 'encouragement' as a reminder that B.J. Vorster (then Prime Minister) had promised that no victimization would take place for participation in the state-promoted works committees offered as an alternative to trade unions for Africans, a call for worker unity, and two references to 'peaceful' resolution of problems.

In a subsequent issue of *Abasebenzi* (June 1974) B.I. Dladla, KwaZulu executive councillor for community affairs, is quoted as attacking TUCSA 'parallel unions' (a reference to the racially separate unionism then advocated by this conservative trade union body, the Trade Union Council of South Africa). Dladla is described as a member of the KwaZulu cabinet and a 'champion of [workers'] causes' in Natal.

It was, however, not only student organizations such as the wages commissions which, consciously or not, shaped a certain image for the KwaZulu leadership during this period. More directly, their support and involvement, in their official capacity, was thought to be of value by such bodies as the Institute for Industrial Education (the IIE) and the Trade Union Advisory and Co-ordinating Council (TUACC). The former was formed in Durban in 1973 to offer courses in trade unionism under the guidance of unionists and academics, with Ruskin College in Oxford serving as an external examining body. Buthelezi accepted the IIE's invitation to serve as the honorary 'Chancellor' of the Institute (SALB, 1974:54). Members of the IIE working committee at this time were Foszia Fisher (chair), Eddie Webster (vice-chair), David Hemson (treasurer), and Omar Badsha (member). A steering committee that had preceded this working group brought together people from trade unions (eg Norman Middleton and David Hemson), the Wages Commission, Young Christian Workers, the SAIRR, KwaZulu government, academics (Lawrence Schlemmer), and the Central Administration Services (Harriet Bolton).

The TUACC arose out of the need to coordinate the activities of the first trade unions formed in Natal. Early in 1972 a General Factory Workers Benefit Fund was formed in Durban. In April 1973 the Metal and Allied Workers Union (MAWU) and the Transport and General Workers Union (TGWU) were formed. In October 1973 the TUACC brought together MAWU, the National Union of Textile Workers, the Chemical Workers Industrial Union, and TGWU. Bonner (1979:7) wrote rather vaguely that 'TUACC's constitution, which initially allowed a place for B. Dladla, a KwaZulu Government representative, was overhauled again [?] early in 1974 in response to the bannings of trade union officials earlier that year, which made the consolidation of existing unions all the more urgent . . .'. Bonner argued that the constitutional change was also necessitated by Dladla's involvement in a textile strike early in 1974, aiding the union 'and so highlighted the need for a worker controlled coordinating body which could liaise with other organizations' (1979:7). Hemson (1978:24) wrote more directly that TUACC 'was initially developed in cooperation with the KwaZulu Government when Barney Dladla, the Minister [sic] of Community Affairs, gave support to the strike movement. After vigorous protest from employers in Natal, Dladla was removed from this post, and the connection [of KwaZulu] with the trade union movement is now non-existent.'

Details aside, the point is that it was felt necessary and appropriate that a representative of the KwaZulu authority (Dladla) should serve on the TUACC, and that employers should at that stage have protested so strongly. It is of interest to note that Dladla had welcomed the news of the initial strike at Coronation Brick and Tile in 1973 with the words that his 'heart was filled with joy', and that striking 'is our only strong weapon of defeating the Whites who are after our energy' (KLAD, 2:44).

The fairly brief formal relationship between the fledgling union movement and the KwaZulu authorities was troubled, mainly due to Buthelezi's conflict with Dladla, who was probably the strongest alternative leader within the constituency to which they both appealed. For example, the editors of the *South African Labour Bulletin* (SALB), with close links to the labour movement, felt called upon to comment on this clash, in which labour matters became an issue in bantustan politics (see SALB, 1974a:3). Some anti-Buthelezi politicians attempted to use the real worker support for Dladla, although its true extent might not have been very clear, to attack Buthelezi. There were rumours that Dladla was to be involved in a 'Labour Party' to oppose Buthelezi, and that 'trade unions' were supporting Dladla. Dladla was certainly active in appearing at strike scenes, much more so than Buthelezi. In March 1973, for example, Dladla was delegated to meet with management and with workers after KwaZulu authorities were called on to intervene in a strike at the Alusaf refinery in Richards Bay in northern Natal (IIE, 1974:118-20). Dladla supported worker demands for higher wages and said KwaZulu would prevent the recruitment of labour if the matter was not resolved to the satisfaction of the workers. The central state intervened by despatching soldiers to keep the plant going. The clash between KwaZulu and management and the state ended when the workers accepted an offer of R2 extra per week.

Dladla's stand (supported at this stage by Buthelezi) was deplored by business. The Natal (and Federated) Chamber of Industries asked the central state to halt interference in labour matters by the bantustans. This call was supported by the Trade Union Council of South Africa, which used the opportunity to foment suspicion between Buthelezi and Dladla, accusing Dladla of being '. . . a sectional Black Power politician . . . basically trying to find any issue which will gain him the senior position in KwaZulu politics, that of Chief Executive Councillor'(Survey, 1974:320-21).

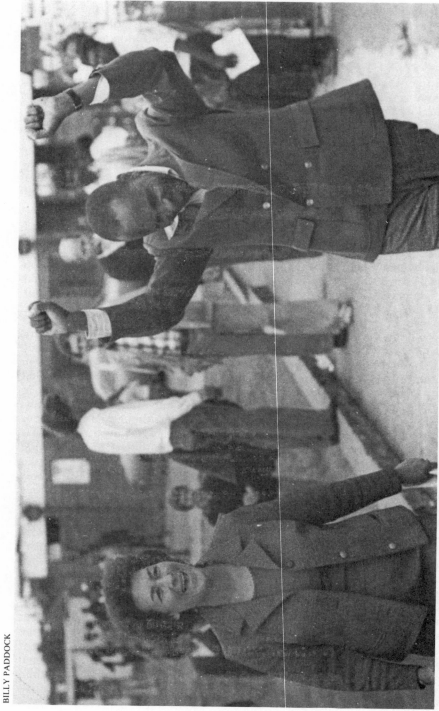

The late Barney Dladla with Harriet Bolton of the Tucsa-affiliated Natal Clothing Workers Union, on his way to a protest meeting after the banning of four Natal trade unionists in 1974. Dladla, a member of the KwaZulu executive council, was expelled when he clashed with Buthelezi over his union activities.

In January 1974 Dladla led a march by some 5000 workers in the New Germany industrial complex to the main mill of the notoriously exploitative Frame (textile) Group, following a strike that started with 1200 workers in the Frame Pinetex Mill and rapidly spread to other textile plants. The workers were told the results of negotiations that had been in progress and were addressed in the nearby Clermont stadium by Dladla and trade unionist Halton Cheadle. Soon after this Dladla was one of the main speakers at a meeting protesting at the banning by the central state of Cheadle, David Hemson and other Natal trade unionists (see Survey, 1974:328; Bernstein, 1977:111). Bernstein claimed that Dladla's involvement was with the full knowledge and support of the KwaZulu authorities (ie Buthelezi) and of the workers, but action during that year (1974) against Dladla must throw considerable doubt on this claim, at least as far as the KwaZulu authorities are concerned. Other commentors (Butler et al, 1977:59) wrote that Dladla 'negotiated on the strikers' behalf without consulting or waiting to receive instructions from Buthelezi's cabinet'.

The ambiguity of the role the KwaZulu authorities were to play in labour matters was demonstrated by the way Dladla was treated, and also, at this early date, by the conflicting demands of bantustan 'development' and worker interests. Schlemmer and Muil captured this ambiguity when they claimed at one point that Buthelezi fully supported Dladla (1975:129) but added later in a footnote that Dladla's powers had been curbed in mid-1974 (1975:134). Responsibility for 'Zulu labour affairs' was shifted to Solomon Ngobese, the KwaZulu urban representative. Ngobese was mayor of Umlazi 'and a former oil company employee' — hardly the ideal qualifications of a labour spokesman (Butler et al, 1977:67).

Dladla probably offered the last chance of a self-consciously pro-worker political direction from the KwaZulu authorities, and later the Inkatha movement — not that Dladla was an unambiguous spokesman for worker interests. He probably represented a faction of the bantustan petty bourgeoisie sufficiently disenchanted with the restrictions imposed by the apartheid system to have sought a social base other than capital to advance their interests, and he might have found that the working class demanded a fuller allegiance than he was willing to give. A reporter commented at the time (ST, 19 May 74):

> The possibility of a rift between the thousands of Zulus employed in South African industry, on the one hand, and the rest of the Zulus on the other is one of the most serious aspects of the two-man clash.

During 1974 Buthelezi went so far as to condemn strikes, 'presumably taking into account the effect of strikes on business confidence and willingness to invest' (Schlemmer and Muil, 1975:114). It was during 1974 and 1975 that Buthelezi and other bantustan leaders lent themselves to a state-sponsored advertising campaign for investment. Full page advertisements appeared in such publications as *The Economist*, *The Times*, *New York Times* and *Washington Post* with Buthelezi, for example, being quoted: 'Make no mistake, we're not the only people you help when you start your factory in our country. First and foremost, you'll be helping yourself' (Butler et al, 1977:98).

Buthelezi's position on strikes illustrates the emptiness of so many of his threats. He used the mass strikes of 1973 as an example of what the withdrawal of labour by the African working class could achieve: 'I appeal to White South Africa not to force us by her attitude to disrupt the economy of our Country. Because this is what is going to happen Sir, if we continue to live in this state where we have nothing to lose except our skins' (KLAD, 3:174).

In contrast to Buthelezi's vague threats, Dladla suggested a practical way of implementing liaison between the working class and KwaZulu. He proposed a 'Super Committee' of works committees to negotiate 'in the absence of trade unions' (this was in May 1973), which 'should at all times be in contact with the KwaZulu Government' (KLAD, 3:190).

The next year Dladla told the KLA of some of the contacts he and others had been engaged in on behalf of the KwaZulu government. He attended the formation of the Metal and Allied Workers Union, while J.A.W. Nxumalo, executive councillor for education and culture, was present at the formation of the IIE. Dladla had been invited to address the inaugural meeting of the National Union of Textile Workers, and there had been several requests to intervene in labour disputes. 'At times like these the KwaZulu Government has to consider the fate of its citizens very urgently,' Dladla said (KLAD, 4:153-54; see also Dladla, 1978). It was soon after this report to the KLA by Dladla that a fellow member, S.Z. Conco, launched an attack on him. From the transcript it is not clear what the issue was, but Conco accused Dladla of talking about violence (KLAD, 4:158). Conco later became chief whip in the KLA, a director of Khulani holdings and executive member of UWUSA, the Inkatha trade union. Dladla, on the other hand was removed from the KwaZulu cabinet late in 1974, and died of a lung complaint a few years later.

From this time on the most frequent KwaZulu interventions in worker affairs were vague threats to withdraw labour. In 1975 after Buthelezi's near-annual pilgrimage to Soweto, he threatened withdrawal of labour 'from industry and commerce if the Government did not respond favourably to demands made by homeland leaders' (St, 10 Feb. 75). This threat was made in response to the negative reception Prime Minister Vorster had given a 'summit' meeting of central government and bantustan leaders in Cape Town the previous September, when a request for a federal scheme, greater consolidation, home-ownership, and the abolition of influx control were discussed.

These repeated threats to use 'worker and consumer power' would seem to contradict the grandiose long-term strategy of the Inkatha 'viewpoints' document (Inkatha, 1983), which argued that:

> For strikes to be used as successful strategy for liberation, rather than for specific grievances which form a part of an industrial system, they have to be well *co-ordinated and disciplined*, and occur on an extremely *broad basis*. Isolated strikes for political purposes only hurt individuals in the end, and may well weaken the black labour movement. Much organizational work still has to be done before strikes can become a useful political tool . . . [1983:6].

The apparent contradiction disappears if we remember that threats are an integral part of Inkatha strategy.

In 1979, the year the Wiehahn Commission recommended trade union rights for African workers, Buthelezi made renewed approaches to unions to coordinate activities, but very much under Inkatha's dominance. With a confidence belied by subsequent events he warned that 'nobody would be able to call a successful strike of any magnitude in the Transvaal or Natal without the movement's involvement' (RDM, 4 Aug. 79).

A month later Inkatha secretary general Oscar Dhlomo welcomed the extension of union rights to migrant workers and commuters. These workers had at first been excluded from proposed legislation to give effect to the Wiehahn Commission's recommendations. Dhlomo said that 'what Inkatha had been striving for had now been won' (RDM, 26 Sep. 79). In apparent contrast the Transkeian authorities argued that what might be a 'progressive move' in the rest of South Africa 'would be detrimental to Transkeian national interest' (RDM, 11 Oct. 79). With current moves by Inkatha in the labour field these two positions, of KwaZulu and the Transkei in 1979, are not as far apart as they would appear to be on the surface.

Buthelezi views the labour movement with as much suspicion as he does any organization or political position that falls outside Inkatha's all-encompassing representational claims: while unions remain firmly within the area of legitimate work-related activity they are to be tolerated and even supported at times, but any class political demands or involvement is to be stamped on, if these are not initiated by Inkatha.

In October 1979 Buthelezi had a meeting with Manpower Utilization Minister Fanie Botha, who tried to get an assurance from Buthelezi that he would not involve himself in labour matters, as the state and business had previously sought following the 1973 strikes. Buthelezi refused to give this assurance and in a central committee document he reiterated his position that Inkatha might have to mobilize the 'economic muscle' of the working class 'to minimize bloodshed' (DN, 17 Oct. 79). When Buthelezi spoke at the launch of a Federation of South African Trade Unions (FOSATU, which in 1985 became part of the new federation COSATU) shop stewards council at Richards Bay he threatened the power of 'Inkatha . . . a powerhouse of potential activity, which, if combined with trade union interests, could upset many of the little applecarts which South African Cabinet Ministers trundle around our country' (St, 30 Mar. 81).

However, Inkatha argues that unions and unionists are not to have independent political aims and connections. A central committee resolution in 1981 accused 'white activists' of exploiting African workers 'for their own political ends' and acting as 'mere surrogates of certain exiles'. The resolution made it clear that unionists in Durban and Pietermaritzburg were included (RDM, 16 Feb. 81). Yet Inkatha claims that it is legitimate to involve workers and trade unions in its own politics.

In his 1979 policy speech Buthelezi said that while he had 'been extremely reluctant to allow Inkatha to trespass on the legitimate domains of trade unions', the movement could not 'stand by and watch as one of the most potentially effective forces for peaceful change lie under-utilized' (KLAD, 15:57; also 18:101 and 103; 24:1315). In 1980 KwaZulu interior minister Dr F. Mdlalose grandly claimed the recognition of African trade unions recommended by the Wiehahn Commission as a 'victory for our movement'. He continued:

When the hon. the Chief Minister speaks for labour unions amongst blacks, it must be remembered that he is speaking for all Blacks in Southern Africa. It must be remembered that migrant workers come from both within and from outside the Republic. I repeat, when the Chief Minister speaks, he speaks for all the Blacks in Southern Africa [KLAD, 18:154].

When KLA member A.M. Dlamini replied to the chief minister's policy speech in 1984 (KLAD, 32:204), he said trade unions affiliated to the UDF would have been much better off under 'proper and well organized organizations'. He continued:

> I remember very well that our Chief Minister was very much concerned about these trade unions and he felt that it would be a good thing if these unions were affiliated to Inkatha, and had Mr. Fanie Botha [South African Minister of Manpower until 1983] not refused, these trade unions would have been under Inkatha at this moment in time.

In 1982 Buthelezi was joint recipient, with trade unionist Dr Neil Aggett, who had died while in security police detention, of the American Federation of Labor/ Congress of Industrial Organizations (AFL-CIO) George Meany Human Rights Award. There must be a strong suspicion that the award was given to Aggett posthumously to make the award to Buthelezi slightly more palatable in the international labour context. Buthelezi, on receiving this award from an organization with a dubious record in the advancement of independent worker interests, launched an attack on both the right-wing Trade Union Council of South Africa (TUCSA) and the South African Congress of Trade Unions (SACTU) — according to Buthelezi 'two poles in the South African trade union movement which would not stand the test of time' (RDM, 20 Oct. 82). SACTU, the exiled labour movement that had been a member of the Congress Alliance in the 1950s, celebrated 30 years of existence in 1985. The applause its message of support received at the COSATU launch in Durban late in 1985 showed that SACTU still has at least a symbolic relevance in South Africa.

To summarize the first aspect of Inkatha's position on working class political unionism, Inkatha desperately needed political unionism, but with the politics of Inkatha and nobody else. Even during periods when there was no apparent conflict between Inkatha and the new unions in Natal, Inkatha leaders still spoke with envy about the power of the organized working class and defended the future right of the movement to enter the labour field, for political ends, and/or to draw trade unions into Inkatha structures.

The second aspect of the Inkatha position on the working class is that the relationship between capital and labour is seen as one of harmony, potential or actual. Within this relationship Inkatha sees its role as 'a channel for communication between workers and management' (RDM, 16 Feb. 81). In February 1982 KwaZulu's chief labour officer spoke at the official opening of FOSATU's northern Natal branch. After sketching the functions of trade unions in very economistic terms, he continued that the KwaZulu government supported trade unionism 'because it is committed to the free enterprise system, under which every worker through his trade union may decide and negotiate under what conditions his labour and skills are offered'. With the formation of trade unions a 'harmonious relationship will be guaranteed by the cooperation of industrialists and trade unionists'. He continued that trade unions must 'train' members in negotiations, otherwise strikes would 'never cease to occur', while employers were advised to 'train' workers 'on what to expect in an ideal trade union that will perfectly suit their requirements' (Khanyile, 1982:88).

At this level Inkatha *does* support trade unionism, as an essential part of industrial relations machinery. There were undoubtedly benefits for the fledgling trade unions in the first half of the 1970s from this support, however qualified and at times reluctantly given. It was also in line with the IIE's 1974 recommendations (see above, p.117). Furthermore, a careful examination of the movement's involvement in labour shows that certain officials have been less cautious about taking a stance in support of unions or workers. As late as 1980, for example, Inkatha called a meeting in Edendale outside Pietermaritzburg where Bishop Zulu and Professor Sibusiso Nyembezi called on workers to join unions and attacked strike breakers (*Echo*, 4 Dec. 80). There might, however, be specific reasons for Inkaktha's support in these cases, reasons that might not hold for the movement in general, where support given to workers is strictly within the 'partnership' between labour and management. As Buthelezi said on a visit to Mondi Paper Mill: 'There will be no real victory in the struggle for liberation unless it is a victory that Blacks and Whites achieve together; a victory that workers and management achieve together . . .' (BS, 8 Jan. 86:1). In the same talk he more than once used the term 'partnership' for the relation between workers and management.

The third aspect is that Inkatha is engaged in campaigns to subvert unions and attack unionists, in what it would define to be the interests of the liberation of black people in South Africa. The fact that the Inkatha constitution makes provision for the representation of trade unions affiliated to the movement within its national council would seem to contradict this claim, but this formal representation is not seen in terms of advancing the class interests of the working class, but simply as a link with another important social grouping within the broad scope of Inkatha's populist mobilization. Furthermore, 'six representatives elected by the members of Trade Unions' are a small minority in a national council composed of, among others, members of Inkatha's central committee, 'members of a Legislative Assembly who are members of the Movement' (in effect all the KLA members), and 'ten representatives of the Security forces, once we are in a position to have them' (1979 amended constitution, chapter VI, 29(1)).

Up to the present only one union has affiliated to Inkatha, and, as it turned out, that has hardly been to Inkatha's credit. The union is the National Sugar Refining and Allied Industries Employees Union (NSRAIEU), which decided to join Inkatha in May 1984. At the time it claimed a membership of 25 000 in industries such as building, steel and sugar (where it had its origin in management-created liaison committees at the sugar mills). General secretary Selby Nsibande claimed that the union would be the 'labour wing of Inkatha', while Buthelezi promised the union a seat on the central committee and said that there would not be interference in each other's affairs, 'but together we can stand shoulder to shoulder and march into the future to dominate over racism and the politics of apartheid'. Nsibande said the union had joined because many of its members were also Inkatha members and NSRAIEU supported Inkatha's anti-disinvestment stand (see McCaul, 1984). The union has recently been in the news again. At the end of 1985 Nsibande was interdicted from acting as union general secretary and from having anything to do with union finances. In a lengthy court case Nsibande did not deny buying a R75 000 Daimler motor car or spending about R17 000 on his house. He merely denied that these were unauthorized expenditures from union funds — which left the NSRAIEU with a mere R45 in its account (eg, NM, 10 Aug. 85; 14 Feb. 86). Nsibande was found guilty of defrauding his union and sentenced to six years' imprisonment. He has appealed (IRDATA, 6, 5, 1987).

Although Nsibande and NSRAIEU were welcomed in Inkatha, other unions have not had an easy time in KwaZulu — not surprising since the bantustans are notorious low wage areas which thrive on the disorganization of all opposition, including workers. KwaZulu is not the most extreme bantustan in this, probably because the Inkatha movement has a large worker membership in KwaZulu and

Natal. However, active anti-union activity from within KwaZulu and Inkatha has taken place and increased in intensity over the years. At present a campaign is being waged against COSATU trade unionists in the townships of Ladysmith, Newcastle, Empangeni and Richards Bay. Affidavits alleging Inkatha members' complicity in the campaign have been lodged with lawyers in Durban and released by COSATU (see Chapter 8).

Actions against worker organizations date back several years. In 1976, circular 5, ref S2/1/1, signed by the Director of Works at Ulundi (W.A. van der Merwe), had this to say:

Trade unions
1. It has come to my notice that trade unions are interfering more and more with the workers of this Department. While there can be no objections to kwaZulu workers joining trade unions, it must be stressed that trade unions are *not* recognized by the kwaZulu Government and that, therefore they have absolutely no official standing as far as the workers of kwaZulu are concerned.
2. The conditions of service of any employee of the kwaZulu Government Service are as determined in the kwaZulu Public Service Act (Act 7 of 1975) and the Staff Regulations promulgated in terms thereof. Lines of communications are firmly established at all levels and trade unions do not form part of such lines of communication.
3. Kindly inform all workers that any submission to the Executive Councillor for Works and this Department on their behalf by trade unions will, in future, be ignored. Workers must, at all times, follow the official lines of communication.

Five years later, in 1981, the South African Allied Workers Union (SAAWU) accused the KwaZulu department of works of stalling meetings on the wage grievances of workers in its employ, some of whom were being paid as little as R3.29 per day. Other workers complained of being kept on in a 'temporary' capacity for as long as five years. The reply to a letter from SAAWU's Isaac Ngcobo to the KwaZulu minister of works referred him to the department's then director Tony Johns, who refused to meet SAAWU or worker delegates (NM, 4 May 81).

In an interview with organizers of the National Iron, Steel, Metal and Allied Workers Union (NISMAWU) in 1982 the unionists said the KwaZulu department of works 'has also tried to intimidate our members' (as had the central state). Workers were taken to a police station by a senior foreman of the department, and a worker member was fined after refusing to resign from the union. The organizers commented:

The KwaZulu government does try to control progressive trade unions, but in a very much more refined way than the Ciskei government in its dealings with Saawu.

Recently, the KwaZulu Minister of the Interior, Dr Mdlalose, made a press statement to the effect that some unions are actually misleading KwaZulu employees. He stressed that the KwaZulu government is in favour of trade unions. That's why Chief Buthelezi has been awarded that award by AFL-CIO [see p.126], because of his involvement with the workers. But the employees of the KwaZulu government are not allowed to join trade unions. They have to belong to staff associations [SALB, 1983:73].

In 1983, the year after Buthelezi was given the George Meany award, he presented an 'aide memoire' to Irving Brown of the AFL-CIO for discussion in

Geneva (reproduced SALB, 9, 4, 1984). This document was basically a request for funds 'to support a person and provide for the costs he or she will incur as we search for wisdom . . . .' The wisdom would be searched for through the Inkatha Institute, who would employ such a person in a senior capacity to devise ways of 'establishing a working relationship between Inkatha and the trade union movement'. That relationship would preferably be through 'having union interests represented on [Inkatha's] Central Committee', and it was projected that 'in due course trade unions will reciprocate and establish the possibilities for Inkatha's presence in their decision-making bodies'. This would be necessary, argued the document, because of the 'very important role' that unions had to play 'in the struggle for liberation', which demanded that workers 'cannot continue indefinitely to confine labour action to legitimate disputes with management in the work situation'. Inkatha, because of its dominantly worker membership, could not stand aside on the issue 'of what it can do for its workers'.

This document does not reflect any change in approach to trade unionism: it simply initiates plans to bring unions closer to the kind of politics advocated by Inkatha. The leadership that was responsible for this document has also been responsible for attacks on 'party political trade unionism', for accusations that unionists are simply the tools of the ANC, and for active opposition to working class action outside the factory, such as boycotts.

It must be borne in mind to whom this document was directed and from whom the funds were being requested. The AFL-CIO is a central element in the Reagan administration's policy of 'constructive engagement' with South Africa — this phrase was already part of Buthelezi's language in the early 1970s. Chester Crocker, Assistant Secretary of State for Africa, told the University of Kansas: 'We have initiated training programs in cooperation with the AFL-CIO, for black South African trade unionists to which the US government will contribute over one million dollars this year and the next' (St, 3 Dec. 83). Such programmes had been on the AFL/CIO cards with the KwaZulu bantustan leadership no less than ten years earlier. In 1973 the same Irving Brown had said that:

> We are ready [to train black unionists] if KwaZulu is ready. Whether they are able to invite us or not is basically the question of whether they actually have independence under the homelands policy . . . We have good contacts in South Africa and we have talked about how assistance in the training field could be arranged [Survey, 1973:272].

It would appear that whereas the South African government took some years to realize Buthelezi's potential for fragmenting resistance politics, the US State Department showed much greater foresight. Buthelezi first visited the US in 1963; in 1965 he could not take up a US government leadership grant for a two-month expenses paid trip, because the South African government had confiscated his passport (Temkin, 1976:91; 131).

The George Meany award from the AFL-CIO to Chief Buthelezi, hardly a spokesman for working class demands, nor for the independent trade union movement in South Africa, makes more sense in terms of accusations made by the Australian Broadcasting Corporation in a programme late in 1983, that 'the CIA, through the . . . [AFL-CIO] is assisting the South African Government in a deliberate programme to undermine the independent trade unions in South Africa' (STb, 2 Oct. 83). UWUSA, only weeks after its launch, approached the AFL-CIO and its operations in the region through the African American Labour Centre (AALC) for 'large-scale assistance' (WM, 9-15 May 86).

S.Z. Conco, now in his capacity as an executive member of UWUSA, also confirmed that the union had approached Israeli and West German sources for money. In 1985 it had been revealed that the NSRAIEU, the Inkatha-affiliated union, had 'become recipients (along with the Black Allied Workers Union) of large amounts of aid from Israel' (IRDATA, 1985:15). The editors of IRDATA, an industrial relations journal, commented that the 'choice of these two slightly eccentric unions appears to stem from an Israeli belief that they are somehow closely linked to Gatsha Buthelezi's Inkatha movement which the Jewish state clearly feels is deserving of its support' (1985:15). The close links exist with the NSRAIEU, but BAWU and the Council of Unions of South Africa (CUSA) were singled out by interior minister Dr D. Madide in his 1984/5 policy speech as unions who made 'full use of the services of [his] office . . . for advice whenever they encounter problems in their negotiations with the employers'. BAWU, established within the black consciousness tradition, has 'recently been making pro-Inkatha noises' (FM, 24 Jan. 86). It has opposed disinvestment, but, rather out of character, has condemned the formation of trade unions by political organizations, a pointed reference just before the launching of Inkatha's United Workers Union of South Africa (UWUSA).

The last clash between Inkatha and FOSATU, before the federation was taken up in the larger COSATU, was led by petty bourgeoisie trading interests in Inkatha. From the composition of the first UWUSA executive it is clear that similar 'Zulu' business interests dominate the new union.

The clash had its origin in the consumer boycotts that had been organized with much success on a regional basis in support of both local and national demands such as 'troops out of the townships' and the ending of the state of emergency. In the eastern Cape the boycott crippled many businesses, and the tactic was also employed elsewhere (see Obery and Jochelson, 1985). In Natal a one-day stayaway in Pietermaritzburg on 18 July 1985 in support of the Sarmcol strikers was a massive success, and was followed by a call for a consumer boycott to start on 15 August 1985 in support of the strikers (see LMG, 1985). Late in August the Natal region of FOSATU decided to participate in a national FOSATU-supported consumer boycott from 2 September. which had the approval and participation of other unions involved in the unity talks that led to the formation of COSATU at the end of November. This wider boycott demanded the lifting of the state of emergency, the freeing of detainees, troops and police out of the townships, etc (NW, 29 Aug. 85).

The Sarmcol strike-related boycott had, in the meantime, led to a 60% fall-off in African custom in Pietermaritzburg (NW, 31 Aug. 85). FOSATU's Alec Erwin said a boycott of white-owned shops was called because whites had a 'greater ability to force the Government to bring about reforms'. The first countermoves by the large retail outlets came when Pick 'n Pay urged black traders 'not to cash in on the boycott of white-owned businesses' (STbH, 1 Sep. 85). A week into the boycott, traders admitted that the effect was being felt in Pinetown, Hammarsdale (an industrial area between Durban and Pietermaritzburg), and in and around Pietermaritzburg, although in Durban the boycott did not seem to have taken.

However, late in September, after a meeting with FOSATU, Inyanda (the Natal and Zululand African Chamber of Commerce) 'declared war' on the trade union federation, and called on all KwaZulu 'citizens' to crush the boycott in Pietermaritzburg. Inyanda president P.G. Gumede said that the 'war' on Alec Erwin and 'his men' was to 'prove to the world our claim that this region is unique'. He added that as Buthelezi had come out against the boycott, continuing it would be an open challenge to the Inkatha leader (DN, 24 Sep. 85). Probably in part because of the escalation of the Pietermaritzburg boycott into a 'war', it was decided to call it off.

The links that had been established by certain trading interests with white-owned commercial undertakings had been paying off, for both sides. In the Durban townships, where the violence of early August had left many shops in ruins, the Durban Chamber of Commerce came to the aid of the affected shopkeepers. Inyanda could not be seen to support a boycott of the very people who were aiding them, or with whom they were in partnership, even though the boycott would have helped African traders who were still operating. The strong condemnation of the boycott indicated that pro-Inkatha traders who had established links with large-scale capital were by now in firm control of Inyanda policy. The interests which had been against tripcos ten years earlier had no voice this time around — or they would have cashed in on shopping diverted from white-owned stores during the boycott.

It was in this climate of confrontation between African traders and Inkatha on one side and the FOSATU unions in Natal on the other, that increasingly frequent mention was made of Inkatha unionism. Nothing came of the appointment of a labour researcher in the Inkatha Institute for which funding had been requested from the AFL/CIO, but Inkatha approached an industrial/personnel relations firm to advise on labour matters in 1985. It appears that events somewhat outstripped any recommendations from this firm as a week after the launch of COSATU Dhlomo announced that Inkatha 'could form its own trade union', and that the NSRAIEU could form the nucleus of such a union (STb, 8 Dec. 85).

Buthelezi continued with the tactics of challenge, throwing down another gauntlet to COSATU in his speech at Mondi Paper Mill (BS, 8 Jan. 86) — 'we *as Inkatha* will if necessary enter the field of labour relations' (emphasis added). Before the end of January it was formally announced that a union was to be formed, favouring foreign investment and capitalism. The moving force at this stage was said to be an ex-FOSATU shop steward, Philemon Gumede, who is also a community councillor in the Esikhaweni township outside Empangeni and chair of the local Inkatha branch. Several attacks have been made on COSATU trade unionists in this township, including the wounding of Metal and Allied Workers Union president Jeffrey Vilane.

COSATU warned against the recognition of 'sweetheart' unions by employers, and also deplored the violence against its members. Buthelezi replied that while Inkatha had 'never threatened anyone with violence, . . . no self-respecting Inkatha member will tolerate all the insults that Cosatu has hurled at the president of Inkatha . . .' (DN, 10 Feb. 86).

Gumede was coy about his role prior to the formation of UWUSA, referring enquiries to the 'parents of the new baby' (as he told researchers in April 1986), namely S.Z. Conco, KLA member, company director and Inkatha CC member in charge of labour. In the preparations for the May Day launch of the new union even the king was released from the strictures of his political role to call on Zulus to attend the launch.

For COSATU members nationally May Day was a celebration of international labour solidarity. For Inkatha it was a cynical choice of symbol to attack progressive unionism and to make a statement in support of local and foreign capital and the political line and personality of Chief Gatsha Buthelezi.

In accordance with the by now thoroughly discredited argument that economic growth, that is, high rates of profit and foreign investment, will lead to the dismantling of apartheid, Conco told a press conference in Johannesburg that 'UWUSA believes that economics holds the key to political reform in South Africa and that the country's history has proved this beyond doubt.' He did not offer any evidence for this highly debatable proposition. He also claimed, probably with an eye on BAWU and CUSA, that '. . . there is every indication that several major unions will affiliate to UWUSA after the union is officially launched on May 1' (Conco, 1986:4).

The language of commodities and the marketplace is to be found in UWUSA as it has been in the speeches of Chief Buthelezi. In an interview Conco told Mark Bennett: '. . . we think, as a marketing man would say, we think our product is good. If the product is good, the facilities are there and if we don't have the expertise we will have to buy the expertise. It may be a bit expensive for us' (Bennett interview, 1986). The expertise that Conco was referring to was the aid that he claimed was forthcoming from the USA — '. . . after 1 May we have arranged with trade unions of United States to send some of their people to do the training here to help organize us'. It appeared that quite a lot of help would be needed because while UWUSA had 'set up a managerial structure' in preparation for the launch, they had had to 'retain the services of consultants to help us, both in the matter of industrial relations and public relations and we are just now organizing a legal team to train our negotiators — shop steward training — we are importing people from the United States and Europe to come here and try to organize shop stewards'.

UWUSA certainly did have a 'managerial structure' after its launch. The first executive looks like this:

President — P.S. Ndlovu (personnel manager with the giant Tongaat-Hulett sugar group and initiator of the NSRAIEU, the union that had affiliated to Inkatha)

General Secretary — S. Z. Conco (KwaZulu businessman, director of Khulani Holdings, member of the KLA, member of Inkatha's labour affairs committee)

Vice-president — P. Msomi (Johannesburg-based township superintendent)

Treasurer — P. Davidson (Umlazi hotelier, director of Khulani Insurance Brokers, with other business interests such as in building)

National Organizer — M.P. Gumede (ex-Paper Wood and Allied Workers Union shop steward, town councillor in Esikhaweni)

Executive members — P. Malunga (Pietermaritzburg businessman)

G. Hadebe (law student, former Tongaat-Hulett personnel officer)

M.V. Hlatswayo (Newcastle businessman)

Majela (East Rand township superintendent)

D.J. Mtiyane (former PWAWU president and regional FOSATU chairman for northern Natal)

A glance at this list will show that worker interests are under-represented, — but then UWUSA had clearly stated that it was a union of capital.

Inkatha had made the May Day rally a test of strength from early in the new year. Having accused COSATU of using 'classic marxist strategy', Inkatha then challenged the Congress 'to a mass rally' (eg DN, 14 Feb. 86). This planned rally was being boasted about in the USA even before it became public knowledge in South Africa with a figure of 100 000 mentioned as the expected attendance.

The Inkatha campaign to get people to the UWUSA rally at Kings Park cost a large amount of money. Early in March a full-page advertisement appeared in the Zulu-language newspaper *Ilanga* to publicize the meeting. Buses were hired, and it was claimed that Inkatha 'had laid on 17 trains to bring people from all parts of the country . . . to its rally' (NM, 1 May 86). Chief Buthelezi flew to the rally in a helicopter displaying the name of the new union on its sides. The stadium was hired from the Natal Rugby Football Union through Rowley Arenstein, himself reported to have been prominent in the moves that led to the formation of UWUSA (WM, 9-15 May 86; 23-29 May 86).

There were probably as many reasons why some 70 000 people should have attended at least the first part of the UWUSA launch (not much publicity was given in the commercial press to the mass exodus of people during Buthelezi's speech) as there are explanations for Inkatha's membership. They were there partly because of the pressures of 'traditional' authority — chiefs were instructed to fill buses (provided without charge) and to get the people to Kings Park. The king launched once again into politics after his long Buthelezi-enforced absence with a call on those who opposed disinvestment to attend the rally; he also attacked COSATU president Elijah Barayi, and pointed out that he was a Ciskeian (NM, 21 Jan. 86). Even Nelson Mandela was used with a pamphlet distributed in the townships around Durban claiming that he would have attended the Kings Park rally if he had been free to do so.

However, many people were also there because they supported the Inkatha movement. Until the launch of UWUSA a dual allegiance was possible in Natal, with both the political line of Inkatha and the advantages obtained through membership of the strong FOSATU-affiliated unions. It will now take time for the limitations of the management-oriented and inexperienced UWUSA leadership to show themselves and for workers to decide where their interests are best served. The Inkatha union launch was not a worker rally in the sense that COSATU's nation-wide May Day rallies and its highly successful stayaway were a celebration of working class solidarity. It was a conservative gathering to counteract the strength of the working class, it enjoyed the support of the state and of the bantustan, and it was attended by representatives of regional capital.

More important than the nature of Inkatha's support, however, is the fact that it, and before that the capitalist aspirations that were being articulated through the KLA, had become involved with large-scale 'white' business in the region. The sortie into worker organization only makes sense if seen within a broader mobilization under a populist appeal. This appeal, while denying differences amongst the black population, is nonetheless geared to serve the overall interests of capital and to discipline the working class away from action that might jeopardize capitalism. Neatly contained within a non-antagonistic wrapping of 'free enterprise', 'growth and development' and 'investment', Buthelezi and Inkatha hope to offer UWUSA to those in contemporary South Africa who advocate reform instead of radical change.

7. The Politics of Pragmatism and Populism

In the political sphere Buthelezi (as chief minister of KwaZulu, president of the Inkatha movement and chairman of the South African Black Alliance) and Inkatha have achieved a prominence that must be the envy of many others in their quest for media acclaim. This prominence, based on the desirability of his participation in national negotiations to forestall more radical claims, has in large part been of the media's making. It has also been the result of his populist leadership and the reception he has received from international politicians, overwhelmingly of a conservative bent (Reagan, Thatcher, Kohl, to name but a few), and from internal white political parties and politicians, ranging from the NP to the PFP. At the same time he has clashed verbally (while members of his organization have resorted to violence) with most of those in opposition to the state and its policies. In fact the most remarkable aspect of Buthelezi's and Inkatha's actions in the political arena has been their cordial relations with individuals and organizations structurally involved within, or supportive of, apartheid and the state, and their antagonism towards those who oppose apartheid from outside those structures. The list of the latter is long, and includes student organizations, church groups, political parties, trade unions, civic associations and international pressure groups.

This chapter examines apparent contradictions in an organization that claims to be a 'liberation movement'. It is clear that a central plank in the Inkatha strategy is participation in 'the system', or 'infiltration of the system' as Inkatha describes it. Its goal is a greater share in 'the system' and not its fundamental transformation. Thus opposition groups challenge not only the Inkatha strategy of change from within, but also Inkatha itself as part of the economic and political structure of South Africa.

Another important reason for the apparent ambiguity of Inkatha's choice of political allies and opponents lies in its populist claim to represent the interests and aspirations of 'the people' or of 'black people'. Such a claim loses much of its potency in competition with other organizations that have an equivalent or larger support base.

Inkatha itself is not exempt from the effects of these tensions. A large part of its support comes from those who perceive it as a true 'liberation' movement. To these supporters it has to present itself as separate from the 'system' it is supposed to be liberating them from. After all, it is only in the extent of its support, in the size of its organized constituency, that its influence will be felt, even within the 'system'. So Inkatha threatens but hardly ever takes action against the state, offers itself for participation and then often withdraws, deals with individuals within the 'system' or through intermediaries while apparently rejecting the structures and organizations of apartheid, and draws on the symbols of resistance while rejecting their implications.

These various points are most clearly illustrated by Inkatha's changing relationship to the African National Congress, because of the potency of the revolutionary symbols offered by the ANC, and its historical continuity. Writing about the ANC from within South Africa presents insurmountable obstacles. The organization is banned and cannot be quoted without ministerial permission, its publications cannot be possessed, and it is an offence to advance its aims and objectives. Thus the focus must be largely on Inkatha's attitude to the ANC, and on what Inkatha claims the ANC is doing and saying. For example, at the beginning of 1986 Buthelezi released the text, and later a photocopy, of a note of thanks from Nelson Mandela, the jailed ANC leader, written in appreciation of Buthelezi's sympathy during Mandela's recent illness. There is no way of verifying the context within which this note was written, nor of assessing Mandela's feelings about the use being made of this personal note. This is the problem with many Inkatha claims about communications and events, and what transpires at meetings with the ANC. Hopefully the other side of the story will also be written.

This chapter also examines Inkatha's relationship to other organizations, as well as Inkatha's initiatives in the political sphere, such as suggesting a federal option through the Buthelezi Commission, and demanding a national convention to resolve the country's political stalemate.

Inkatha and the African National Congress

To understand the Inkatha leadership's attitude to the African National Congress, it is necessary to understand the central position the ANC has occupied, and still occupies, in the history of resistance to white domination, discrimination, oppression and racism in South Africa, a position due in no small part to the ANC's 74-year history of struggling against a minority regime that has been supported by the ex-colonial powers and the USA.

In effect this means that no opposition political movement in the country can ignore the symbols of resistance created through the ANC. These can be as direct as the name, the colours, the Freedom Charter, or they can be as complex as the pride that carries young South Africans across the borders for military training to pit themselves against the armed might of the South African state. In a 'treason trial' involving residents of rural KwaZulu, four of these resistance fighters claimed they were not bound by the rules of the court. They demanded prisoner-of-war status as soldiers in the war being waged in the country, soldiers of a movement that has been illegal in South African for 25 years. Indeed, a powerful array of symbols and ideas are provided by the ANC.

While all internal resistance groups must respond to these symbols, their response can be straightforward, such as total rejection or uncritical acceptance, or it can be complex and selective as in the case of Inkatha. It is necessary to unravel this complexity somewhat to make sense of it, and to extend the analysis to Inkatha's responses to the formation and political and ideological positions of other organizations.

To start with the obvious: Inkatha is not the ANC 'reincarnated' in South Africa after 15 years of being banned. It might seem obvious, yet Inkatha has been perceived and presented at times as just that — the above-ground ANC. It has selected from the history and the symbols of the ANC, adopting some, because of the credibility granted to these symbols through the ANC's history of opposition and struggle, and rejecting others, because it has to present a more acceptable option to members and to other organizations, governments and economic interests, than the underground ANC and its political agenda.

Basically, Inkatha claims a continuity with the ANC, if not always in organizational structure then at least in political direction. Inkatha secretary general Oscar Dhlomo put it this way: '. . . after 1960 when two major black liberation movements were banned . . . no significant political activity took place in South Africa for almost a decade or more . . . Inkatha was founded in response to the political vacuum that had been created when the African National Congress and Pan Africanist Congress were banned' (Swart interview, 1984). Dhlomo said in the same interview that 'Inkatha was founded on the principles of the founding fathers of the ANC. Now we mean the ANC before it was banned in 1960'. While wanting to place itself within the heritage of the ANC, Inkatha is careful to distinguish between the 'founding fathers', and the 'Mission in Exile'. Writing in the glossy *Leadership SA*, Dhlomo explained that:

> In Inkatha circles the so-called ANC is officially referred to as the 'External Mission of the ANC'. This is so because according to recorded history the external mission of the ANC in the person of the current caretaker of that movement, Mr Oliver Tambo, was sent overseas by the last constitutionally elected President of the ANC, the late Chief Albert Luthuli, to drum up support for the liberation struggle of black people inside South Africa. There was never any intention that the external mission of the ANC would eventually develop a completely autonomous movement that would be free to decide on any liberatory strategies that would implicate millions of black people inside the country, without first consulting them.
>
> Chief Buthelezi always refers to the external mission of the ANC as the proverbial 'tail that wags the dog' [1984:47].

The contradictory nature of so much of what Inkatha claims to stand for in its public pronouncements holds here as well. While clearly separating the pre-1960, or specifically the 'founding fathers' of the ANC, from the contemporary movement, and identifying Inkatha with the former, Inkatha also says that 'there are no genuine differences between Inkatha and the external mission of the ANC' other than strategic ones, of which the role of violence is the most important (Dhlomo, 1984:47). The 'common goal' line has been less frequently used since 1979. The approach, if indeed it has been consciously worked out, seems to be that through the confusion of the Inkatha movement's stance on the ANC it will get the benefit of the doubt from some people, in the absence of a direct ANC presence.

Ironically, for a movement that is itself trying to escape the implications of its first 'Zulu' and bantustan constitution, the 'mission in exile' criticism of the ANC seems to be constitutionalism run rampant. This criticism also ignores history: the nature of the ANC's struggle changed drastically with its banning and the repression of its members and leaders during the early 1960s so its strategies have changed. While these strategies can be criticized, it would seem inappropriate to make the same demands of an organization operating underground as of an organization participating in state administration as Inkatha does. The ANC has maintained a continuity of underground or exiled leadership and ironically, Buthelezi has helped to maintain an awareness of that continuity through his regular visits to ANC leaders until 1979, and his equally frequent attacks on the organization since then.

According to Inkatha's thesis of an 'illegal' or 'unconstitutional' ANC, great store is placed on the mantle of leadership handed on by Luthuli as the 'last constitutionally elected President of the ANC' and it is not surprising that Buthelezi has made much of his links with Luthuli, both while he was alive and in his memory, and with Luthuli's wife, Nokukhanya. In 1972 Buthelezi delivered the opening speech at the unveiling of the memorial stone to Albert Luthuli in a church in Groutville where Luthuli had lived and died. In January 1975 Buthelezi visited President Tolbert of Liberia, a month before Prime Minister John Vorster did the same in his Buthelezi-supported 'detente' policy with conservative African states. Buthelezi told Tolbert that he had accompanied Mrs Luthuli to Maseru to receive the OAU Albert Luthuli award and had been asked by Mrs Luthuli to express thanks on her behalf (KLAD, 5:80). Temkin noted that there had been tension between Buthelezi and ANC members in Maseru and it had been doubtful whether Buthelezi would even be allowed to speak, making the occasion more problematic than Buthelezi suggested to Tolbert (1976:300).

In 1976, on his way back from Japan, where his wife Irene had launched a ship, Buthelezi stopped off in Nairobi, where he met Picton Mbatha, who at the time 'represent[ed] us there in certain matters'. Mbatha has since broken with Buthelezi over his pro-investment stance. He had been a member of the Luthuli Memorial Foundation (LMF). In his report on this trip Buthelezi told the KLA that he and Dr Zulu were to leave for Swaziland the next day to attend an LMF meeting to discuss ways of raising money; Buthelezi was attending even though it appears that he was not a member of the LMF. This fund was mentioned again by Buthelezi in 1980 when he said that he had set it up in memory of Chief Luthuli but that the ANC's Oliver Tambo and Alfred Nzo had cut off scholarship funds from it because it was a Zulu institution with bantustan links. It appears that this fund was set up in London but that Buthelezi had established the South African side (BS, 10 Oct. 80).

The attack on Buthelezi in 1982 by Albertinah Luthuli, daughter of the ANC president, in which she accused Buthelezi of being a traitor to the ideals of her father and of 'allegedly manipulating her mother to enable Buthelezi to hold a rival memorial service for Chief Luthuli' (St, 4 Jan. 83), caused him to threaten to reveal correspondence with Pretoria attempting to arrange her return. Buthelezi, against the evidence, said he had never needed Chief Luthuli as a 'political prop'. He claimed credit for speaking on the same platform as members of the 'External Mission of the ANC' in Maseru, neglecting to add that this had not been welcomed by the ANC.

In 1983, possibly because of this attack on Buthelezi's interpretation of his links with Chief Luthuli, an Inkatha document was circulated (it is not clear to whom) with a brief section on the 'history of the relationship between Inkatha and the ANC'. More directly than anywhere else the claim is made that 'In a symbolic meeting between Chief Luthuli and the Hon. Chief M.G. Buthelezi in the 1960's, the heritage of the leadership of the liberation struggle was passed on to the Hon. Chief Buthelezi' (Inkatha, 1983:12). The document continues with the statement that Inkatha 'is as much a descendent [sic] of the old ANC as the present external mission' [1983:13]. Buthelezi's personal history and his brief membership of the

ANC Youth League (ANCYL) are offered as support for these claims, while claims to have operated with the approval or on the advice of ANC figures such as Sisulu, Mandela and Tambo, as well as Luthuli, all add to Buthelezi's stature as a national personality; these credentials are also made to work in the opposite direction, with ANC approval cited for his decisions to enter the chieftainship or bantustan politics.

Buthelezi usually gets away with these claims without any real challenges, but in 1979 he made a speech in Soweto in which he quoted Mandela in justifying the Inkatha position that 'selective participation' in state institutions was justified 'where it thwarted fulfilment of apartheid' (RDM, 14 Nov. 79; BS, 21 Feb. 79). When it was pointed out to Buthelezi that the article he had quoted had been written in 1958, prior to Mandela's imprisonment, with the primary purpose of justifying 'participation by coloured voters in the election of coloured representatives to Parliament in the 1958 general election', and did not argue for participation in any of the Bantu Authorities structures, he denied having said that Mandela had made the statement in jail. Furthermore, he said 'that [the Bantu Authorities Act] is a matter on which you can quibble on semantics with Mr Mandela himself. I was merely conveying to the [Soweto] meeting what had come to me through some of the emissaries who had been in contact with executives of the ANC'. He said that he was 'not prepared to talk for him [Mandela]'. However, that is what he had been doing, and few people were in a position to 'quibble on semantics' with the jailed Nelson Mandela.

Most people in South Africa only heard one side of the meetings that have taken place between Inkatha leaders and the ANC over the years, a case in point being the 1979 meeting in London that appears to have been the turning point in the relationship between the two movements. Inkatha and the KLA leaders repeatedly referred to these meetings. However, the eight ANC members who were expelled from the ANC in 1975 and subsequently called themselves the 'ANC of SA (African Nationalists)' gave as one of the causes of their dissatisfaction Tambo's 'weak leadership' that had allowed Buthelezi to present contact with the ANC as endorsement by the ANC.

Claims of contact have been regularly made over the years. In 1974 during the Buthelezi-Dladla clash, Buthelezi read a letter in the KLA from Oliver Tambo to himself. Tambo apparently said Buthelezi had left him with a useful bundle of clippings (KLAD, 4:211). In 1976 Buthelezi told the Inkatha general conference that it was necessary to maintain contact with the ANC and that he had had contact with both the ANC and the PAC. Gibson Thula told the court in a case over claims arising from damages suffered during the 1976 unrest that 'one of his [Thula's] duties was to keep in touch with the ANC, PAC and people in exile' (he claimed that all these organizations had been taken by surprise by events in 1976) (St, 16 Feb. 82). In 1983 Buthelezi suggested a 'marriage of convenience' between Inkatha, the ANC and the PAC to respond to the referendum results. The ANC and the PAC rejected this plan and called on Buthelezi to 'stop participating in enemy institutions' (STb, 6 Nov. 83). Yet at the same time Buthelezi claimed that the PAC and ANC had requested a meeting with Inkatha central commttee and KLA cabinet members, and that the meeting had taken place (St, 7 Nov. 83). In 1984 Buthelezi went even further when he told journalist Graham Watts in an interview during the Inkatha conference that he was still in touch with the ANC — 'I would not say I brief Mr Tambo . . . but I brief some of his colleagues'. He repeated the claim that Inkatha was 'the largest representative of the ANC tradition as propounded by the founding fathers of the national liberation struggle' (SE, 1 Jul. 84). The 'briefing' argument had also been advanced by Dhlomo when he said that Inkatha maintained contact with the ANC not to gain credibility but for the benefit of the ANC, as Inkatha was 'in total contact with the oppressed masses in South Africa' (1983:53-54).

Another factor in Inkatha's claim to continuity with the pre-1960 ANC is the number of people who had been members of the ANC and are (or were) now in Inkatha. This is the way in which Buthelezi put it in 1983:

> Many thousands of Inkatha members were active members of the ANC while it existed in this country . . . We only have an ANC mission abroad and an ANC sentiment in the country. Much of that sentiment is in fact found in Inkatha. . . . Until the mission in exile is free to return home and to appeal to the people for support, they must necessarily be living a mythological existence based on sentiments of yesteryear. Were ANC what the myth makes them to be, Inkatha would never have developed the largest Black constituency that this country has ever seen [Teague interview, 1983a:5-6].

Buthelezi seems to be arguing here — and it would fit the actual position — that some ex-ANC members see the 'sentiment' of the 'founding fathers' and aspects of the pre-1960 ANC in Inkatha and that is why they have joined. However, he goes on to say that these are the true sentiments, for if the 'mission in exile' expressed the true sentiments then people would not have joined Inkatha in such numbers.

Bernstein made a similar comment:

> Many of the people occupying top leadership positions . . . were involved in the ANC's 1952 Defiance Campaign and they reflect the firm commitment to the non-violent, non-racial tradition at the core of the ANC opposition to white rule [1977:159].

It was S.Z. Conco, a prominent figure in KwaZulu and Inkatha politics, who proposed Buthelezi for another term of office as chief executive councillor of KwaZulu in 1975. Buthelezi expressed his appreciation and said he was 'deeply moved' as Conco had 'once worked as a clerk to Dr. Pixley ka Isaka Seme, who was married to King Dinuzulu's first daughter, the founder of the African National Congress . . .' He continued that he saw this as a challenge not to betray the ideals of Seme and the founders of the ANC. He said that he (Buthelezi) had written letters for Seme, who had lost an eye, while he was a matriculation student at Adams College (KLAD, 7:889).

The idea of 'dual membership' and adherence to the ideals of the pre-1960 ANC was given an interesting twist by Oscar Dhlomo in an article on the relationship between Africans (Inkatha) and Indians (*Post Natal*, 3-6 Feb. 82). He said Inkatha was working for a national convention 'where even the members of the ANC will particate in the drawing up of a constitution acceptable to the majority of the citizens of South Africa'. However, 'we will demand that they either cooperate with Inkatha or call a national conference of the ANC to elect authentic office bearers on South African soil. As former members of the ANC we will put forth our own candidates in these elections. If they fail to do any [sic] of these two things, then we will allow the black people of South Africa to pass judgement on them.'

Inkatha has also adopted the ANC tradition in outward signs associated either directly with the ANC or with radical opposition to apartheid and economic exploitation in South Africa. Clenched fists shoot up at Inkatha rallies, in line with its claims to be a liberation movement, while khaki uniforms give the correct degree of regimentation.

The colours chosen by Inkatha for itself are those used by the ANC when it operated legally in South Africa. They are also the colours of flags that have draped coffins during hundreds of funerals in South Africa since the ANC was banned. They are in cloth, wool and beadwork worn by many who interpret the past and the present in a radically different way from Inkatha's version. When Buthelezi was asked why the ANC colours had been chosen he replied: 'Are they ANC colours? I didn't know that. I regarded them as the colours of the black people of South Africa and the ANC is an extension of the people' (quoted McCaul, 1983:12). A year later, in 1980, Buthelezi replied to a similar question: 'Why don't you rephrase your question and say: "Is there any reason why KwaZulu and Inkatha recognize Nkosi Sikelela Morena Boloka as the national anthem as the ANC recognizes them?"' (quoted MCaul, 1983:12). Gibson Thula called the choice of colours 'a coincidence', which it was not. Buthelezi again: 'We in KwaZulu were the first organization since the days of the ANC to show the national colours of the black people of this country' (in an interview with Patrick Laurence, RDM, 26 Apr. 78).

While Inkatha has seen fit to appropriate much of the ANC's symbolism of resistance, there are many symbols it rejects — the negative side of Inkatha's view of the ANC. As might be expected, this arises out of the distinction Inkatha draws between the 'ANC' and the 'ANC mission in exile'. The negative aspects most frequently mentioned are the areas in which Inkatha claims for itself a positive rating. The ANC ('mission in exile') is characterized as being undemocratic, especially in terms of the election of leaders, in presenting itself as 'sole representative' of the African people, and in the way the decision to engage in armed struggle was taken. Most of these characteristics, according to the Inkatha view, arise out of the ANC's lack of a constituency. Some of these points have already been dealt with above, especially the division of the ANC into an internal (organizationally extinct) and an external wing said to be characterized by a small elite that is out of touch and manipulated by Moscow and non-Africans. Inkatha's Youth Brigade referred to the ANC as 'just a consortium of political miscreants thriving on sheer political pipe-dreams' (St, 30 Aug. 83). Buthelezi said 'those in exile are removed from the ordinary people and are unable to determine what the people want. They have to assess the situation from newspaper reports and guess the people's wishes' (Chris Freimond interview, RDM, 12 Aug. 80).

The way Inkatha has used the ANC tradition of resistance and its interpretation has changed with the times. The first period, from the formation of the ANC in 1912 until 1960, when it was banned, is presented as fairly unproblematic and coherent, although it is still given a specific content, such as the prominence of Zulu participation, stress on conservative elements, stress on the democratic practice of the ANC, selection of certain figures such as Dube, Seme, Luthuli, for special mention within the ANC tradition and therefore the exclusion of others, and mention of certain figures (Mandela, Sisulu) mainly for their alleged advice to Buthelezi to enter bantustan politics.

Two other areas dealt with in a specific manner are the ANC Youth League and the Freedom Charter. The Youth League features prominently because of Buthelezi's brief membership, and hardly at all in any other context. It is notable that no reference has been found that draws links between the ANCYL and the Inkatha Youth Brigade, as might have been expected. The Freedom Charter is not accepted by Inkatha, being replaced by Inkatha's 'Statement of Belief'. This document, presented to the KLA in 1977, has been described by Dhlomo as 'an attempt by Inkatha to describe an ideal state it would establish if it came to power. The same can be said of the Freedom Charter to which the External Mission of the ANC subscribes'.

It is not clear why the Freedom Charter, drawn up during the ANC's legal and 'democratic' period, should be rejected by Inkatha and left to the 'external mission' and internal opposition groupings. In an interview in 1984 Dhlomo described the Freedom Charter as 'an outstanding document and historical document of the oppressed, wherein they state what type of socio-political order they would like to see in the country'. However, he added that it should not be 'rammed down the throats of the people . . . who might have their own freedom charters', and 'I don't want anyone to force me and tell me now that this is my political bible' (Swart interview, 1984). Although Inkatha rejects the Freedom Charter, the movement's Statement of Belief is nevertheless linked to the ANC tradition. In an article in 1982, Dhlomo wrote that 'Our Statement of Belief is clear proof of this [that Inkatha subscribes to the political principles as enunciated by the founding-fathers of the ANC]. This is the ANC that operated in South Africa from 1912 to 1960' (*Post Natal*, 3-6 Feb. 82).

To return to the political chronology, the second period is that from 1960 to 1979/80, when Inkatha maintained links with the 'mission in exile' without ever granting it the status of being a continuation of the 'true' ANC of the 'founding fathers'. Instead, 'according to recorded history', it was a mission sent by Luthuli 'to drum up external support for the liberation struggle of black people inside South Africa' (Dhlomo, 1984:47). It was said to be out of touch and in need of Inkatha and Buthelezi as its internal 'political thermometers'. South Africans were told the relationship was cordial, with Tambo approving the role Buthelezi was playing inside the country. The ANC 'mission in exile' was often presented as simply having a different strategy towards the same political goals as Inkatha.

However, the cloak of cordiality hid suspicions. Buthelezi expressed his concern to Minister of Police Jimmy Kruger about 'infiltration' by the ANC (Inkatha, nd:34-35). He said there was not much that could be done to prevent it in an organization as large as Inkatha. In 1979 Buthelezi warned the general conference against attempts to 'undermine the movement from within' (NM, 2 Jul. 79). In 1980 he warned the central committee that he would 'not tolerate the emergence of more Dr Sibusiso Bengus in our midst' (Bengu had been Inkatha's first secretary general. He was expelled from the movement in 1979 (Survey, 1979:40)). He added that 'black South Africans who feel compelled by their hearts to become involved in underground work owe it to the struggle to leave us and to cross our borders and seek refuge amidst our brothers in exile' (BS, 18 Jul. 80:8).

The third period is that from 1979/80 to 1983. The turning point was a meeting between Inkatha and the ANC held in London late in 1979. There had been regular and apparently cordial meetings before 1979, although tensions had also surfaced. In 1977, for example, Buthelezi commented on attacks made on him by saying that when an 'authentic voice rises internally' it did not fit the plans of the exiles: 'They are after all dependent on overseas financial support — and I am not' (*Deurbraak*, 1977).

The 1979 meeting came at a crucial time for both movements. Many of the supporters of the black consciousness philosophy in South Africa had left the country after their organizations were banned late in 1977. They attempted to set up a 'third force' (between the ANC and the PAC) in exile, to be known as the Black Consciousness Movement of South Africa (BCMSA). Inkatha would not have featured in these plans because of their strong stand against collaboration with state structures. Buthelezi claimed, whether with any accuracy is not clear, that through Tsietsi Mashinini, SASO member and president of the Soweto Students' Representative Council during the 1976 scholars' revolt, who had fled into exile, 'certain African states and the CIA' had attempted 'to create what they called a third force between ANC and PAC' (BS, 21 Oct. 79:29). Lodge wrote that the 'third force' had tried to get the financial patronage of European social democrats, but that the ANC, while initially maintaining a diplomatically correct relationship, stepped in during 1978 and established itself as an arbiter on funding requests (1983:342-3).

Lodge dated a 'determined effort by the ANC to gain for itself "sole legitimate representative" status' from this time, the late 1970s. However, this had been a sore point with Inkatha even earlier, just as the similar status accorded SWAPO in Namibia by the United Nations had been an irritation to the South African state and the Namibian 'internal' parties. In 1977 the *Daily Nation* in Nairobi quoted Buthelezi as criticizing the 'selective recognition of political movements' such as that accorded the ANC and the PAC by many African countries. He soon denied that he had questioned recognition of the two movements, but reiterated that 'selective recognition' in the 'whole Southern African situation' had to be looked at (RDM, 30 Aug. 77). In 1982 Buthelezi approved recognition of the ANC and the PAC by the United Nations, but added that division was created by the 'acceptance of their claim to be the sole voice' of black people (Sow, 24 Sep. 82). In 1983, during a lunch talk in the USA, he repeated this criticism and called for the 'total and immediate recognition for the authenticity and credibility of Inkatha' (RDM, 2 Feb. 83). A year later the publication of the KwaZulu Bureau of Communication argued that although the ANC was 'accredited' it had 'proved to be the most ineffective' of the world's liberation forces (*Clarion Call/ Inhlabamkosi*, 1, 11, 1984:11).

Even before the 1979 London meeting there were inevitably tensions between the two organizations. Inkatha could not allow the ANC to be presented as the 'sole' or even the senior body representing the political aspirations of the dominated people of South Africa, but at the same time it had until then not been willing or able to abandon the credibility it gained by maintaining links with the ANC.

The high-powered delegation that went to London (other than Buthelezi its 17 members included secretary general Dhlomo, Dr Madide, publicity secretary Thula and J.T. Zulu, the KwaZulu urban representative in Durban) inspired a great deal of public speculation. Some commentators linked the trip to a public denial by Soweto leader Dr Ntatho Motlana that Buthelezi could have any ANC links as the ANC would not 'collaborate with traitors' (St, 2 Nov. 79). Buthelezi devoted much of his subsequent Soweto meeting to Motlana's attack, starting his speech with a vivid description of the formation meeting of the ANC in 1912 by Mary Benson (Benson, 1963), moving on to affirm his own place in the history of the organization, and then viciously attacking Motlana. Buthelezi said he felt 'a spasm of anguish in my heart for having to undress Dr Motlana in public', to which he had devoted 15 pages of his speech, concluding: 'What creates revulsion in me doing what I have done today, is that after shaking up the political skunk which Motlana is, this leaves my own hands stinking' (BS, 21 Oct. 79:23).

The *Sunday Express* (4 Nov. 79) saw the London meeting as a slight for the BCMSA, while a 'special correspondent' in London wrote in the *Sunday Post* that it was an attempt by Inkatha to gain through the ANC the 'national credibility' that it would not otherwise have (SP, 11 Nov. 79). The same article played the meeting down, saying that Tambo 'keeps an open door' and that therefore no special importance should be attached to the meeting — although Inkatha had played it up with photographs, tape recorders, and reporters. The article quoted an ANC official as saying that 'He [Buthelezi] seems to think the ANC is an external wing of Inkatha'. Nicholas Ashford, writing in *The Times*, supported the idea that it was a public relations exercise by Inkatha. Back in South Africa Oscar Dhlomo told a Transvaal Inkatha meeting in April 1980 that during the meeting 'the president of the ANC himself in his address openly praised the role that Chief Buthelezi and Inkatha have played inside the country in keeping political activity alive'.

Several articles said that it was not Inkatha but its constituency that was important to the ANC. For example, Lodge argued that:

> With the development in South Africa of legal mass organizations with a Congress orientation, the solidly middle-class respectability of the Tambo leadership has an important function in ensuring that internal support for the ANC remains as widely based as possible [1983: 343].

Before the meeting Buthelezi himself had commented that the ANC would not attack him politically: '. . . which I think is good political wisdom. I don't think that if I were in their position I would want to disenchant an organization with 200 000 members' (STb, 2 Apr. 79).

Suzanne Vos, at the time a journalist and now Inkatha's 'Editorial Consultant' as Suzanne Griffin, wrote that Buthelezi, in a memorandum to Richard Luce, the British Under-Secretary of State for Africa, had presented the argument that:

> If the future is to be stable it is vital that a central and dominating force begins to regulate black opposition to apartheid.
> The vehicles for this dominant force are Inkatha and the African National Congress.

Buthelezi spoke of bringing the two organizations together in a 'united force' (ST, 4 Nov. 79). Just before the Inkatha delegation left for London, Buthelezi responded to an attack on him by Police Minister Louis le Grange by saying that the Minister should actually have welcomed the consultation with the ANC which Buthelezi claimed was occurring on a monthly basis. He said Inkatha could play a conciliatory role between the state and the ANC (Survey, 1979:43).

By July 1980 any hope Inkatha might have had of getting political mileage out of the meeting had faded, perhaps partly because of the way it had been handled and the subsequent pressure put on Tambo by ANC members who were less concerned about diplomatic relations with Inkatha. Buthelezi told Inkatha's general conference in Ulundi that month that 'the ANC had not responded to Inkatha's demands for "public recognition for the legitimacy of Inkatha"' (Langner, 1983:195). In his 1980 address to the Inkatha central committee Buthelezi seemed to have accepted that bridges had been burned. He said that 'each challenge they [the ANC] issue is issued to millions of my followers', and that the 'harsh realities of the South African situation will endorse them into political oblivion'. He added that 'when one thinks soberly about the ANC's position, the emergence of Inkatha must be seen as the people's challenge to the deviation of ANC's leadership' (BS, 18 Jul. 80:3). By now Inkatha was claiming a membership of 300 000 and could hardly be seen to accept a slight from the ANC — which Inkatha had criticized precisely because it was said to lack any organized constituency. At the same time, it was its membership that had allowed Inkatha to make the demands that had brought about the cooling of its relations with the ANC.

Some four years later Buthelezi had changed the Inkatha version of what had happened in London. Patrick Laurence wrote that Buthelezi 'said recently' that:

[The] 'External Mission' had hoped . . . to co-opt Inkatha and use it to further ANC objectives. When it failed, it turned on Inkatha, he contended. . . . 'I think they wanted us to be a surrogate of theirs, which we couldn't be because of the nature of our strategy. Thereafter they launched attacks on us. They believe their image as sole and authentic spokesmen for Black people is challenged by Inkatha' [1984:271].

It appears from recent documentation that Buthelezi's version of the ANC's past objectives, if not its subsequent political direction, is essentially correct. The ANC admitted at its Second National Consultative Conference in Zambia in 1985 that it had erred in its relationship with Buthelezi. Because of the need to establish a presence in the bantustans it was decided at the ANC's 1969 Morogoro Conference to maintain contact with certain bantustan-based politicians such as Paramount Chief Sabata Dalindyebo (who fled the Matanzima regime in the Transkei in 1980, openly associated with the ANC, and died in exile in 1986) and with Buthelezi. The ANC confirmed that Buthelezi had entered bantustan politics after consultation with the ANC, while Inkatha had originated from an agreement to form 'a mass democratic organization' in KwaZulu. However, Inkatha had become a personal power base for Buthelezi, in part because of the antipathy of certain ANC members to working within bantustan structures and their consequent refusal to give direction to Inkatha. It must be remembered that by this time, in 1975, people had had several years of experience of the limitations of 'working within the system'. Buthelezi, as argued above, presented Inkatha as the ANC revived, until the 1979 meeting, which the ANC had agreed to, on condition that it be secret and confidential. The ANC Conference agreed that 'in a way he [Buthelezi] is our fault'.

Late in 1985 it was reported that Inkatha was again proposing 'peace talks' with the ANC. However, early in January 1986 Oliver Tambo gave a press conference in Lusaka, which was allowed to be published in South Africa, in which he said that 'There is nothing at the moment which indicates that the rift is going to be mended'. Patrick Laurence commented that the 'thrust of his reply was to project the ANC as a force capable of unifying blacks in the struggle against apartheid without the support of Buthelezi'. Tambo continued:

We accept that Chief Gatsha Buthelezi as the Chief Minister of KwaZulu has a position of authority, can tell people where to go because he has been given authority by the [Pretoria] regime . . .

But we do not accept that our people in that part of South Africa [KwaZulu] have turned their eyes away from the struggle.

We do not accept they don't support the ANC . . . We do not accept that they agree with these ravings [by Buthelezi] against the ANC, rantings against the ANC (WM, 17-23 Jan. 86).

Buthelezi, in response, mustered all the familiar arguments discussed above: that the ANC could not claim sole representation, that it tolerated no opposition, that it is undemocratic, etc.

Other than Inkatha's apparent attempts at reconciliation and their rejection by the ANC, Inkatha's recent relations with the ANC have been strained at best and intensely hostile most of the time. Accusations have included the South African state's own line that the ANC is controlled by the South African Communist Party. Buthelezi has chosen the strangest places to attack the ANC, probably to present himself as a moderate where he would get publicity for it. For example late in 1980 he addressed the 'Club 100', 'a racially mixed organization of women active in society' in Cape Town, and said the ANC wished to 'reduce [him] to size politically' (DN, 6 Nov. 80). Despite these attacks he has held on to his 'brotherhood and comradeship over three decades' with Mandela (RDM, 15 Sep. 80). The break with the ANC but his inability to break with the legitimacy that it lends him has led to some strange contortions, such as when he condemned the South African Defence Force raid on ANC houses in Mozambique in January 1981 (the Matola raid), but qualified this by saying that it 'serves "to give the ANC in Maputo a credibility which they do not deserve"' (RDM, 28 Apr. 81). Two months later at the Inkatha congress Buthelezi read from a letter 'from a high-ranking ANC official', allegedly thanking him for condemning the raid (St, 25 Jun. 81).

The ANC's non-participation in the Buthelezi Commission during this period was another sore point. KwaZulu minister of justice C.J. Mtetwa, in referring to the rejection by the ANC, said it amounted to denigration of Buthelezi, and added that 'most of the ANC members who went across the borders had later been involved in political violence or other crimes' (DN, 13 May 82). This period saw Inkatha condemnation of ANC sabotage attacks rather than the previous expression of understanding for alternative strategies (this was probably an acknowledgement that the ANC had considerably stepped up this campaign). Buthelezi told a KwaMashu audience in 1980 that the ANC's successful attack on the SASOL fuel complex forced him 'a half-step' out of his diplomatic silence on these issues. He then accused the ANC of attempting 'to establish itself on the lunatic fringes of our society' (RDM, 9 Jun. 80).

In 1981 the seventh national conference of Inkatha 'expressed itself as totally opposed to the recent "senseless destruction of railway lines and power stations"' (NM, 22 Jun. 81). In a 1982 statement to the KLA which received very wide coverage, Dr Frank Mdlalose said there had been at least three incidents of black against black violence in KwaZulu and that nobody was safe from the ANC (DN, 12 May 82). In mid-1985 Buthelezi was cheered when he told the Lebowa Legislative Assembly that the ANC had no mandate from the black community for their policy of violence (St, 30 Jun. 83). The rejection not only of armed struggle as a strategy option, but also the condemnation of individual acts has continued since then with regularity (for example, in 1984 the bomb that exploded on the Victoria Embankment in Durban killing three civilians, and the attack on the Mobil oil refinery, also in Durban).

Buthelezi, and other KwaZulu politicians, have frequently referred to assassination plots against him by, among others, the ANC. Langner wrote that during the decade of the 1970s 'Buthelezi made revelations about threats against his life on at least eight occasions. The alleged threats came from, for instance, the ANC, White farmers, and the [Zulu] Royal Family' (1983:181).

Buthelezi commented in 1979, 'If I were to be assassinated nobody would know who killed me, because the whole affair would be so complex' (DN, 6 Jun. 79). Dhlomo, however, was inaccurate when he wrote in a letter that the 'Chief has never accused the ANC mission in exile of plotting to assassinate him' (Sow, 27 Jan. 82). In 1980 Buthelezi had told the Inkatha central committee of a broadcast monitored by the South African security police 'in which the ANC said they would kill him', and he accused the ANC of promoting a civil war against African people (STb, 20 Jul. 80). The *Sunday Times* of the same day reported that Brigadier Coetzee (now Commissioner of Police) had confirmed the threat and promised to protect Buthelezi. The following week the threat had been denied by Tambo, and a report said Coetzee had denied 'speaking of an explicit death threat'; Buthelezi said the South African Police could only protect him with the permission of the KwaZulu police (RDM, 21 Jul. 80). The scene for all this had probably been set by a revelation to a 'hushed' KLA by Dr Frank Mdlalose that he had been told five years earlier (1975) in a bar in Manzini, Swaziland, by an ANC member called Albert Dhlomo that Buthelezi would be killed because of his role in the Newcastle bus boycott (NM, 31 May 80; KLAD, 20:912).

This was neither the first nor the last time Buthelezi has been willing to use security police evidence to substantiate his speculations. In 1984, a year in which many sabotage attacks were launched in Natal, Buthelezi joined Professor Schlemmer in suggesting that the ANC was concentrating on this region to draw support from Inkatha. He said that Tambo had 'declared war on KwaZulu', and he 'pointed to evidence by Brigadier Herman Stadler, of the South African Security Police in the Pietermaritzburg treason trial . . . [in which Stadler said that] political targets of the ANC included "anybody who worked within the so-called system, like members of the KwaZulu Government"' (DN, 24 May, 84).

The fourth period of the Inkatha-ANC relationship was heralded by the formation of the United Democratic Front (UDF) on 20 August 1983, when 1000 delegates representing nearly 600 organizations met near Cape Town. The formation of the UDF posed the first true internal organizational threat to Inkatha. It challenged Inkatha from a number of directions, all questioning Inkatha's claims to legitimacy in 'the struggle'.

First, although it was a 'front' and, therefore, had affiliated rather than individual membership, the UDF had an undeniable constituency, weak in some areas but very strong in others. One of the first comments Buthelezi made on the UDF was that it was '"two or three steps away from the daily lives of the ordinary people" and "in real danger of becoming only a paper organization"' (Survey, 1983:53). This denied the UDF's claim to represent people, to have a membership at all. Second, the UDF was national to an extent that the Inkatha movement could never claim to be, and it also brought together, from the very start, all races in South Africa's divided society. This was something Inkatha had attempted through its South African Black Alliance, of which there was very little left by this time. Third, the UDF had self-consciously drawn on the same tradition in the ANC as Inkatha had done, and had done so with greater legitimacy. The UDF accepted and vigorously promoted the Freedom Charter and it elected patrons and office bearers who could successfully lay claim to that tradition, such as Nelson Mandela, Archie Gumede, Albertina Sisulu, and Oscar Mpetha.

How could Inkatha respond to this aspect of the UDF threat? With the simplicity of the obvious: Inkatha gave the UDF away to the 'mission in exile' and continued to claim for itself the 'true' tradition of the ANC 'founding fathers'. In 1984, with relations between the two totally antagonistic after the University of Zululand killings on 29 October 1983, Buthelezi said it was 'cowardly of the UDF to deny connections with the ANC, when the two bodies "were the same"'

(Survey, 1984:13), and in June of that year he 'claimed that because the ANC was unable to use Inkatha as an internally-based surrogate, it had set up the UDF in order to destroy Inkatha'. He said the UDF was trying to create 'no-go' areas for him in Natal (Survey, 1984:13). This term, and the idea that pockets of so' activity that do not fall under Inkatha threaten its existence, has been used several times by the movement's leaders. This can be explained partly by the appeal of Inkatha's claim that it represents 'the people' or 'the black people of South Africa', or variations on this theme — ie, an all-encompassing claim. Even a limited rejection of the Inkatha position, in the constituency that Inkatha has claimed for itself, casts doubt on the total appeal.

To try to unravel who made which accusation first, the UDF or Inkatha, and which pamphlet and event preceded which accusation, would be a most difficult task. However, a clash between the two was inevitable following the political history of the 1970s and the changes that had occurred in resistance to apartheid. The immediate, if not the longer-term, initiative had slipped from those who were caught in the politics of resistance from within the structures of apartheid, whether the bantustans, the CRC, or, more recently, the tri-cameral parliament. The focus of struggle had moved into the hands of those who throw stones, who stay out of schools and universities and away from the workplace and shopping centres, who blow up power stations and oil refineries and set off car bombs, who work towards making the country ungovernable and setting up alternative structures of government, rather than participating in government and repression.

While Buthelezi and Inkatha had talked of different strategies towards the same goal, of black unity, of understanding the legitimate grievances of workers and students, that apparent tolerance was sorely tested when workers and students took action that put their situation beyond Inkatha's control, when the strategy of violence escalated to what is in many parts of South Africa today a civil war controlled by an army of occupation. In contrast to its early tolerance towards activities other than those it had initiated itself, Inkatha increasingly condemned just about every action of resistance out of hand as ill-timed, badly organized, done without Inkatha's cooperation, against the interests of the participants, etc. In such a climate of condemnation it is little wonder that local Inkatha personalities should take it upon themselves to respond with violence to school boycotts, student protests, worker organization, community organization and, at times, attacks on Inkatha members and their property since Inkatha had been equated with KwaZulu and hence with the 'system'.

The basis of his attacks on the UDF and its affiliates, at least in Buthelezi's view, is that they are linked to, or a front for, the ANC 'mission in exile', formed in response to the threat to the 'mission in exile' posed by Inkatha, the 'largest constituency which our country has ever seen'. An issue of *Clarion Call/ Inhlabamkosi* (1, 11, 1984:15-17) reproduced correspondence between the UDF's Archie Gumede and Buthelezi in which Buthelezi stated that Inkatha did not need the UDF, but that on the contrary Inkatha 'would have been prepared to carry them as a burden to protect them from themselves and somehow manage to give them a role in the struggle for liberation'. Gumede accused Buthelezi of echoing the police in accusing the UDF of being a front for the ANC, to which Buthelezi responded that the security police did not need him (Buthelezi) to tell them 'what Mr Gumede is doing'. Buthelezi continued: 'In itself [the UDF] is not significant, but as a vehicle being used by the ANC's Mission in exile, it cannot be ignored . . .' On 6 October 1984 both main SABC-TV newscasts featured Buthelezi on his return from West Germany, where he had participated in a TV debate on the new constitution. All the SABC used, or all Buthelezi said, was that he was not at all surprised by Law and Order Minister Le Grange's attack on the UDF as an ANC front. He said he had read praise for the UDF every month in *Sechaba*, and that the UDF had also been praised by the ANC at a conference in New Delhi.

In 1985 a treason trial, involving several UDF leaders, was in progress in Pietermaritzburg, with the state alleging that ANC leader Oliver Tambo had called for the formation of the UDF. However, Inkatha had already 'convicted' the UDF. King Goodwill, speaking at a Shaka Day celebration, said township residents knew 'beyond any doubt' that the UDF was 'in cahoots' with the ANC (NW, 30 Sep. 85); while Buthelezi claimed that the UDF was encouraged in its attacks on Inkatha by the ANC (NW, 21 Oct. 85). Ironically, during October, seven Inkatha members, including a member of the Women's Brigade central committee, were found guilty of burning and stoning property (buildings and a car) belonging to UDF supporters in Hambanathi. They were sentenced to prison terms and canings (DN, 9 Oct. 85). The court found that Joint Rent Action Committee (JORAC) members had first attacked Inkatha members' houses, but that the action by some 300 Inkatha supporters was illegal.

By December 1985 Buthelezi had escalated his rhetoric and was telling the Youth Brigade that UDF members were receiving training and weapons from the ANC in order to 'maim, kill and incinerate our people in their houses' (DN, 10 Dec. 85). In December, 12 of the UDF leaders accused in the Pietermaritzburg trial were found not guilty and discharged.

Probably the most that Inkatha can hope for in saving its relationship with the ANC tradition and with the 'mission in exile' is that the latter should split into 'nationalist' and 'socialist' wings. In April 1986 a National Party MP called for those in the ANC who reject 'communism' to enter into dialogue with the state on resolving the crisis in South Africa (R, 13 Apr. 86). *Rapport* suggested that an attempt be made to drive a wedge between the 'nationalists' and the 'marxists'. More recently P.W. Botha has made similar calls. The very origin of calls for defectors from the ANC to participate in state-sponsored negotiations has already doomed any credibility such individuals might have should they ever emerge. Probably these people would have to be 'laundered' through the Inkatha movement. Buthelezi's continued allegiance to the political symbolism of Nelson Mandela, the jailed ANC leader, has left the door open for an alliance with elements of the ANC. Buthelezi has most strongly denied charges that he was not willing to participate in steps to have Mandela released, and has argued that his method of private approaches to the state have more chance of success (see, for example, KLAD, 8:94-95). During a 1976 session of the KLA Buthelezi strongly rebuked a member, Paul Sibeko, who had been caught up in a mood of general criticism of the ANC and argued that while he had been an ANC member in 1928 this did not make 'Xhosas' such as Mandela and Sisulu 'our leaders here in Zululand . . . The only gods in Zulu politics that I know would without doubt be King Shaka and Dingiswayo . . .' (KLAD, 8:161-62).

Inkatha and black consciousness

Booysen found in her study of the value Buthelezi attaches to certain concepts and personalities in his speeches that he was consistently negative towards the BPC, SASO and other black consciousness organizations (1982:127). This does not mean he has been antagonistic to the idea of 'black consciousness'. On the contrary, at least during the period that black consciousness was a powerful mobilizing factor, central to African extra-parliamentary political organization, Buthelezi frequently referred to it. However, as with several other mobilizing ideas, Buthelezi and Inkatha gave it a specific interpretation that was then contrasted with that advanced by the black consciousness organizations.

To take an example: at a seminar on 'Whither Black Political Thought?' held at the University of Zululand (Ngoye) in August 1983, Dr Dhlomo's address (disrupted by chanting students) discussed Inkatha's aims and objectives, including the aim 'to help promote and encourage the development of the black people spiritually, economically, educationally and politically' (1983a:2). This is not that far removed from SASO's Black Students' Manifesto and its call for a commitment to 'the assertion, manifestation and development of a sense of awareness politically, socially and economically among the Black Community' (SASO *Newsletter*, 5, 2). Dhlomo, though, argued that the 'greatest challenge facing black political movements in South Africa is not the mere enunciation of lofty principles and ideals', which could be undertaken by:

> any literate person . . . after reading a few books on political theory. What is desperately needed is the translation of these political ideals and principles into actual practice in the form of tangible political action programmes that the masses of our people will understand, adopt and use as tools in the struggle for liberation.

This was the basis of Inkatha's rejection of the political line of the black consciousness organizations — that they were composed of 'a bunch of elitists who seem to thrive on rhetoric, opportunism and drawing-room politics', as Buthelezi put it to the Inkatha general council meeting in 1976 (NM, 10 Jul. 76). The date is important, for the relationship between Buthelezi and black consciousness organizations and individuals had been cordial before the formation of Inkatha in 1975. Buthelezi had been invited to the opening of the 1971 SASO conference, at the suggestion of Curnick Ndamse, Transkei's minister of roads and works, who delivered the opening address. In April of that year Buthelezi spoke at the Edendale conference which led to the formation of the Black People's Convention, along with unionist Drake Koka and SASO's Steve Biko (Gastrow, 1985:197; Bernstein, 1977:76; Khoapa, 1973:8).

When Buthelezi was summoned by Justice Minister Jimmy Kruger in 1977 to account for his opening of Inkatha to 'non-Zulus', he still defended the black consciousness ideology against the Minister's attack as a 'very healthy thing' (Inkatha, nd(1977?):26). Later that year 17 organizations were banned, most of them falling under the banner of black consciousness. Buthelezi expressed his regret at the banning but added that the action taken against them 'did not give them added patriotism' (*Argus*, 14 Nov. 77). It seemed that what Gerhart had predicted, that Buthelezi 'may be able to use the eclipse of some of his "outside-the-system" rivals to make a new bid for mass support', was coming true (1978:314). At the same time there was probably some regret that the bannings had not affected Inkatha — a martyred Inkatha would certainly have claimed 'added patriotism'. As recently as 1985 secretary general Dhlomo told the Inkatha conference that the movement had expected a banning order in 1977 (Inkatha, 1985). That it had not been banned could, however, be interpreted as showing the

Slogans at Inkatha's 1986 Soweto Day rally attack the school boycott, the ANC and Archbishop Tutu.

BILLY PADDOCK

Above: Former Communist lawyer Rowley Arenstein receives special thanks for his support.
Below: Inkatha Youth Brigade members form a bodyguard for Buthelezi as he arrives at the 1986 Soweto Day rally. The T-shirts promote a paramilitary training camp.

Alliances traditional and modernizing. Above: *Chief Buthelezi comes down to dance with the* amabutho *at the 1986 May Day celebrations.* Below: *in 1979 with Frederick Van Zyl Slabbert, then national leader of the PFP (left), and Ray Swart, PFP leader in Natal.*

BILLY PADDOCK

Above: *Buthelezi receives an honorary degree at the University of the Witwatersrand from Chancellor Harry Oppenheimer of Anglo American.* Below: *University of Zululand graduation ceremony 1983. From left: Buthelezi (chancellor), Prof. Nic Wiehahn (then chair of the university council) Chris Saunders (chair, Tongaat-Hulett group).*

BILLY PADDOCK

guarded approval of the state for what was, despite its rhetoric, an ethnic organization.

The reasons for Inkatha's open and at times vicious attacks on the black consciousness position dating from the mid-1970s lie partly in church politics with the demise of the Christian Institute (also banned in 1977) and the rise of the South African Council of Churches, developments that affected fund-raising and international support. Another reason was the student revolt of 1976 and after — the 'black consciousness' ideology was becoming a popular expression and not just the elitism Buthelezi had been so scornful of. From now on Buthelezi was careful to distinguish between *disciplined* constituency politics, contained within Inkatha, and the mass politics that was clearly beyond his control.

When Buthelezi returned in triumph from the Arnold Bergstraesser Institute conference in West Germany in 1978, with his 'democratic' support confirmed by an Institute attitude survey, he issued a warning to the black consciousness supporters. 'These people [supporters of the black consciousness ideology] are on the warpath . . . we will be faced with a hard choice: Either destroy these elements or face black civil war' (RDM, 26 Jun. 78). This strong language — a message to those who continued to support the line taken by the banned organizations and to Inkatha's own members — was repeated by Oscar Dhlomo when he told the Youth Brigade that the 'black liberation struggle could not make any significant impact unless the black consciousness movement was eliminated from the political scene . . .' (RDM, 15 Dec. 79). Dennis Madide (KwaZulu minister and chairman of the Inkatha sub-committee on political, constitutional and foreign affairs) also asked in a letter to *Sunday Post* (10 Feb. 80) for the black consciousness movement to be 'eliminated from the political scene'.

AZAPO was formed in 1979 to continue promotion of the black consciousness philosophy. In 1983, the organization's vice-president Saths Cooper, SASO activist and prisoner under the Terrorism Act, was appointed convenor of the planned National Forum (NF), a 'blacks-only organization linking various groups united to oppose the 1984 Constitution' (Gastrow, 1985:63). Cooper drew a racist attack from Buthelezi when he said that '"No one from the oppressor or collaborationist ranks will be present, so that excludes groups like Inkatha and the community councils"' (St, 14 Apr. 83). A 'furious' Buthelezi responded that Inkatha had no wish to be part of the NF, and assured Cooper and 'any of his cronies' that he would ensure that nothing would happen to them:

> But I must warn that even I cannot guarantee that nearly three-quarters of a million of our Inkatha members will continue indefinitely to react to these insults from spokesmen of other race groups in terms of our philosophy of peaceful negotiation and non-violence.

Direct and indirect racism and racial stereotyping has reared its head in KwaZulu and Inkatha politics at various times. In 1974 Chief Sithole told the KLA that Indians had not been repatriated after the NP came into power because they went to Pretoria 'with their bags full of money' (KLAD, 4:361). Criticism of 'other race groups' attempting to do 'the political thinking for Africans' has been voiced several times, such as when Buthelezi attacked Dr Farouk Meer of the Natal Indian Congress (NIC), arguing that there is 'an African level [of fighting apartheid] whose dynamics can only be grasped by Africans', and that 'Africans resent being seen just as a mass of brown, that must be guided by brains of other race groups' (NM, 7 Oct. 77). If criticism of a political position is answered in racial terms then it cannot but be inflammatory in the South African context.

The 1949 'Indian Riots' (see Webster, 1977) are a point of reference in the anti-Indian rhetoric of Inkatha and its leaders. In 1949 the racial tensions born of social inequality and competition, especially between whites and Indians, flared up after an incident in which an African boy was slapped by an Indian shopkeeper. Altogether 142 people died, most of them Africans (87), while more than a thousand were injured. In 1976 the KLA attacked Fatima Meer, NIC activist and Natal University academic, for her friendship with ANC leader Nelson Mandela's wife Winnie. Mrs Mandela was warned by KwaZulu executive councillor for community affairs, W.S.P. Kanye, that though she might have been too young to remember the 1949 riots, and although at the time they were caused by different factors, '. . . it would appear from the manner in which she goes about things is likely to provoke a similar situation' (sic) (KLAD, 8:153). Later in 1976 Fatima Meer was again the subject under discussion in the KLA, and now Chief Sithole (executive councillor for agriculture and forestry) reminded his audience that 'when the Congress [ANC] was composed only of Africans, there were no problems, but that the trouble started when different nations were allowed to join. We must be wary of these Indians because they want to use us as their tools, as a ladder for them to reach their goals' (KLAD, 9:558). S.Z. Conco repeated the warning, with another reference to the 1949 riots. The debate then really warmed up with references to economic exploitation by Indians, and to non-Zulus (Winnie Mandela and a 'Mrs Phamula' who had criticized the KLA). Buthelezi was away in Japan at the time, but it emerged in the debate that he had wanted the issue of Fatima Meer discussed. The acting chief minister, J.A.W. Nxumalo, and one other representative tried to cool the debate down somewhat, but to no avail.

In 1983 Buthelezi, no doubt smarting from the Labour Party decision to participate in the tri-cameral parliament, causing the effective break-up of his SABA, warned Indians not to rush into accepting the new constitutional proposals: '"We have seen racial outbursts in this country and we know what mob anger can do"' (ST, 9 Jan. 83). This statement somewhat damaged his claim made seven months earlier that he had never used the 1949 riots to threaten Indians.

The hand of friendship has been reached out at times. The forming of SABA and the involvement of the Reform Party was one such occasion, and the various local level meetings with interest groups in Natal and KwaZulu, as well as donations that have been made by Indian religious groups, no doubt serve to lessen the effect of the racial threats and stereotyping — at least for those in Inkatha who wish to acknowledge the examples of peaceful co-existence. But such overtures do little to override the general climate created by racist remarks from prominent leaders in Inkatha and the KLA. The effects of this type of 'indirect instigation', frequently used by Inkatha, are of course impossible to measure.

Inkatha and the PAC

Buthelezi does not often refer to the PAC. In 1976 he accused them of planning his assassination (KLAD, 8:96), but the best known incident concerned the treatment he received at the funeral of the banned PAC leader, Robert Sobukwe. Buthelezi had been a student at Fort Hare with Sobukwe and for many years there appears to have been a cordial relationship. According to Karis (nd:B15) this changed: Sobukwe warned against Buthelezi's 'political tribalism' through the Inkatha movement, and considered him the 'greatest enemy of African freedom'.

Whatever the case, the arrival of Buthelezi, as well as the Transkei 'ambassador to South Africa', and Sonny Leon and Alan Hendrickse of the Labour Party, at the funeral in Graaff Reinet in 1978 was enough to incite the crowd, many of them wearing the colours of the BPC. Buthelezi was spat at; he commented that the event reminded him of 'the Crucifixion of my Lord'. Bishop Desmond Tutu advised him to leave — 'Reluctantly, and close to tears, the proud prince turned to go' (STb, 12 Mar. 78). In the rush to get to his car a Buthelezi 'bodyguard', Simon Dumakude, opened fire and wounded three youths, including an 11 year old boy (STb, 12 Mar. 78; RDM, 14 Mar. 78). Buthelezi had allegedly been asked to speak at the funeral by Sobukwe's brother and by ex-PAC members Nana Mahomo and A.B. Ngcobo from London (e.g. ST, 19 Mar. 78). It is not clear whether anything happened to the Buthelezi 'aide' who shot the children, but three youths were found guilty in the Graaff Reinet court of throwing stones at the chief (*Post*, 24 May. 78). It took a long time for the dust to settle, with fresh accusations and denials daily, and a person said to have been prominent at the funeral was threatened by Transvaal Inkatha members who said they would show him how his type would be dealt with in Natal (RDM, 22 Mar. 78).

The Committee of Ten

The Committee of Ten (CoT) was formed in Soweto in 1977 during the collapse of the discredited Urban Bantu Council (UBC) local government system in the township. The UBCs were local-level advisory bodies that were seen as collaborative and drew great township resentment during the generalized unrest arising from the student revolt in 1976. When the state tried to introduce massive rent increases in Soweto early in 1977, the UBC became a focus for attack and one by one its members were forced to resign. The CoT was elected at a meeting attended by 61 'Soweto Notables', members of black consciousness organizations, the Black Parents' Association (that had its roots in the events of 1976) and others. It was headed by Dr Nthatho Motlana, one time member of the ANCYL and a medical doctor in Soweto (Lodge, 1983:353-4).

The CoT wanted municipal autonomy for Soweto, freehold land tenure, and a large upgrading plan, hardly revolutionary demands outside the context of the mid-1970s, but conceded to by the state in such piecemeal fashion as to satisfy none of the escalating demands during the rest of the decade. The snail's pace of reform meant that the community council system that replaced the UBCs also lacked credibility and never achieved more than derisory levels of electoral support, a fate shared by the recently introduced Black Local Authorities (BLAs) (Survey, various years).

In the late 1970s Buthelezi had linked possible participation in the community council elections in Soweto with Dr Motlana's release from detention. Motlana, along with other CoT members, had been detained by the state at the time the 17 organizations were banned in October 1977. Five 'of the more conservative members' were released early in 1978, and Inkatha, while not officially participating, did not actively campaign against the community council elections in Soweto either (Lodge, 1983: 354). However, shortly before the 1979 Inkatha meeting with the ANC, and after Buthelezi's claims that he and the ANC were in regular contact, Motlana questioned whether the ANC would ever meet with a 'traitor' like Buthelezi (see above, p.143). Dhlomo told a Soweto meeting that Inkatha would 'employ harsh measures' if Motlana continued with his 'vilification'. He called Motlana an 'opportunist', having ridden on the backs of schoolchildren during the 1976 unrest, and having benefited through Inkatha since (DN, 25 Oct. 79). Dhlomo threatened organizations that gave Motlana a platform, specifically the 'Indian community of Lenasia' where Motlana had made his 'traitor' speech. In 1980 Motlana apologized for his remark (STb, 13 Apr. 80) and, though initially reluctant, Buthelezi seems to have accepted the apology (RDM, 28 Apr. 80).

However, a man mistaken for Motlana, who had been due to address an Anti-SAIC meeting in Durban in October 1979, was tarred and feathered by people who included prominent Inkatha members.* Among them was Winnington Sabelo, the Umlazi businessman who achieved further notoriety during events in the townships around Durban in August 1985. Inkatha secretary general Dhlomo said, in terms that have become even more familiar since then in attempts to distance the 'formal' from the 'informal' Inkatha, that while the group 'could have included people who incidentally are Inkatha members, . . . it would be unfair to hold the Inkatha movement responsible for the actions of individuals'. When Buthelezi was asked whether he was not afraid to enter Soweto after the incident, he replied that he 'came from a people which doesn't know fear — as you would know if you read your history' (STb, 21 Oct. 79).**

In 1979 the Soweto Civic Association was formed, the forerunner of many such bodies nationally. Inkatha saw the SCA as an attempt by the CoT to give form to its conflict with Inkatha. Gibson Thula, Inkatha publicity secretary, said the SCA was not a threat as the '"majority of people in Soweto are Zulu and we have their support"' (ST, 23 Sep. 79). The conflict between the CoT and Inkatha centred mainly around participation in or boycotting of community council elections, with each criticizing the other. Inkatha was probably correct in concentrating on the lack of a constituency of the CoT, which was in any case composed of a variety of people with views ranging from moderate to radical. Motlana criticized the 'Marxist terms' used by some 'academics and exiles' at the launch of the SCA. CoT member Percy Qoboza, a newspaper editor, allegedly accompanied Inkatha, bantustan and community council representatives in a delegation to the USA in 1979 (RDM, 16 Jun. 80), while the CoT's initial demands for an alternative administration for Soweto were mildly reformist by the standards of the demands being made today (see Lodge, 1983:355).

Inkatha and state institutions

Perhaps because Inkatha is so centrally and inextricably involved in that basic structure of apartheid South Africa, the bantustan, Buthelezi has been cautious of indiscriminate involvement in other, lesser state institutions. This does not mean

---

*The South African Indian Council was a state-created body for the administration of Indian people. It had been an appointed body for most of its existence. Anti-SAIC was formed to oppose limited elections for the SAIC, which subsequently became the equally discredited House of Delegates for Indians in the new tricameral parliament in South Africa. The Anti-SAIC campaign also influenced the formation of the UDF.

**This must have been what Oscar Dhlomo was referring to when he said that despite Buthelezi's commitment to non-violence, it was the chief's 'popularity and Zulu military background [which] made him the only leader who could mount an effective armed struggle in South Africa' (Survey, 983:13). However, Buthelezi's realism will no doubt convince him that military leadership and a successful armed struggle depend on more than the attributes conferred by ancestry, no matter how illustrious.

that participation has been excluded in principle, which would have been difficult while staffing the KLA and administering the bantustan region. Professor Schlemmer, as director of the Inkatha Institute, said one of the functions of the institute would be to pinpoint 'those government created institutions for blacks which could promote the interests of blacks without facilitating the system of apartheid' (Survey, 1980:51). In 1970, when the ZTA was formed and Buthelezi elected first executive councillor, the institute was not there to decide whether participation in the bantustan would 'facilitate the system of apartheid'.

Schlemmer's comment on the function of the Inkatha Institute came shortly after Buthelezi had told a public audience in the Transvaal that he supported the 'idea of dialogue through government-created councils', that these could be used in the 'black liberation struggle' by joining them to the South African Black Alliance (SABA) (Survey, 1980:51). This speech and Inkatha's attitude towards participation in the 1970s confused everybody, including the local Inkatha bodies and officials in the Transvaal. Commitment to participation, denials and qualifications followed each other rapidly. In the confusion the discredited Soweto 'mayor', David Thebehali, appeared in Inkatha uniform and proclaimed that Soweto was Inkatha and Inkatha was Soweto.

The community councils, now in the process of being replaced by black local authorities, were state-created structures for governing black townships outside the bantustan areas. Buthelezi saw them as structures that could be utilized to draw people into Inkatha (on this system of local government, see Grest and Hughes, 1983; 1984; and on Inkatha's involvement, McCaul, 1983). In October 1981 he told a meeting of the Urban Councils Association of South Africa (UCASA), that an Inkatha Institute survey had shown that two-thirds of Soweto voters would support community council candidates if those serving were to change them into 'bodies which will really represent Africans and will gain improvements' (Langner, 1983:214). Participation by Inkatha was therefore being considered in order to rectify the imbalance in the number of Inkatha branches in rural (KwaZulu) as against urban areas. Inkatha control over the resources that community councils had a say in allocating would have given the movement similar 'pressure points' to those it had already gained through its participation in KwaZulu (this argument has also been advanced by Bloch, 1982; Frankel, 1980; McCaul, 1983).

Whatever the reasons, and despite the ambiguity of its position towards the councils, Inkatha has never participated formally in the Transvaal. One reason could be that the attitude surveys by which Inkatha and its advisers set so much store have painted a picture of questionable support for the movement outside Natal and rural areas, and of even less credibility for community councils.

In Natal, however, Inkatha has participated freely, dominating community councils in the townships outside KwaZulu as well as township government within KwaZulu. This involvement has been anything but trouble-free, as is to be expected when finances are insufficient for services residents have been promised or might expect from local government institutions. McCaul quotes S.K. Ngobese, mayor of Umlazi, as saying that 'support for Inkatha in Umlazi had dropped seriously after 1977 because of cleavages in Inkatha ranks and because Inkatha's promises of patronage were not fulfilled' (1983:32). McCaul mentions that in KwaMashu, after its incorporation into KwaZulu in 1977, this pattern appears to have been repeated, with the council forced to increase rents because of financial difficulties.

It is not clear, and it is probably not meant to be clear, how participation in local government in Natal squares with the Inkatha position that there be no participation at this level 'while [it is] regarded as a substitute for democratic involvement at central Government level' (RDM, 26 Sep. 83). In the 1980s, with the new constitution bringing resistance to a head, three Inkatha members were 'excommunicated' in the Transvaal because they had 'flouted the organization's policy [sic] by partaking in the community council elections' (Sow, 29 Nov. 83). Nonetheless, Buthelezi has remained unwilling to condemn participation in the community councils (ie call for a boycott), or to give an undertaking that Inkatha would not participate unless clear conditions were met — such as guaranteed sources of finance.

Judging from press reports, the Inkatha attitude towards the regional advisory committees proposed by Dr Piet Koornhof, Minister of Co-operation and Development, in 1979 was as confused as that towards the community councils outside Natal. These committees were to be composed of invited individuals and were to advise the Special Cabinet Committee on Urban Blacks on the future of Africans outside the bantustans (Survey, 1979:386). The regional committees were proposed before Inkatha's constitutional initiative through the Buthelezi Commission took off in May 1980. Inkatha's lack of direction may have been due to the absence of a clear alternative to the state's own fumblings over the rights of Africans not accounted for by the bantustans. Gibson Thula, then Inkatha's strategies chair, accepted an invitation to participate, but was immediately criticized by Msuthu Madlala, member of the Inkatha central committee and member of the KLA from Soweto (Survey, 1979:44). Buthelezi was now in a difficult position; he chose to side with Thula and against the non-participation line advanced in Inkatha by Madlala and by such figures as Bishop Tutu and Nthatho Motlana outside the organization. Buthelezi argued, as he had done with participation in the KwaZulu bantustan structures, that Thula's presence 'would block the implementation of apartheid and prevent sellouts from misleading the people further' (Survey, 1979:44). Madlala resigned from Inkatha in October 1979, having refused to apologize to Thula for his public criticism (a constitutional sin in Inkatha). Dr Nyembezi, another Inkatha central committee member, had served on the Durban-Pietermaritzburg regional advisory committee but resigned in 1979 because of the futility of involvement. In an interview he said he had been invited to serve in his personal capacity, and was asked to make decisions for which he had received no mandate (KCAV, 156, 190).

In 1983 Buthelezi accepted the criticisms voiced by opponents of these ill-fated committees, apparently on the grounds that they were to give evidence to the Special Cabinet Committee, and he felt the hands of the latter body were tied by Government policy (STb, 13 Nov. 83). It is not clear why it should have taken Buthelezi four years to reach this conclusion when the position had been stated from the outset.

More recently Buthelezi has waxed hot and cold over participation in a proposed 'national statutory council' (NSC). At the end of January 1986 President Botha announced on the 'black' television services that, after consultation, he was to institute a body which he would chair that would allow Africans to present positions on their constitutional future. This was to be the NSC. A few days later Buthelezi addressed the ninth annual Investment Conference in Johannesburg and told his audience that he would consider participating in the NSC if there was an agenda, and if the deliberations were open to the public (NM, 5 Feb. 86). He gradually added further conditions to his participation. In mid-February he asked that the tricameral parliament first be scrapped, and that the Group Areas and Population Registration Acts be abolished. By March he had added the release of Nelson Mandela and the unbanning of political organizations. When he delivered his policy speech in the KLA late in March he reminded Botha that the NSC would not work without KwaZulu and Inkatha, but that the President should not see him as a 'regional political black boy'. He warned Botha that he was not there '"to carry his political bags. He either accepts me as a man, a leader and an indispensable force in the politics of change or he sinks on his own"' (NM, 21 Feb. 86).

There will no doubt be many more overtures and qualified rejections as Buthelezi walks the tightrope towards participation in state engineered national politics. On the one hand the politics of participation and 'infiltration' means that he cannot stay away for too long, and on the other he cannot be seen to be too keen or willing to compromise on too many principles. On some state initiatives Buthelezi has vacillated less. One such scheme was the creation of a 'constellation of southern African states'. A P.W. Botha pet project, this was to be a kind of confederation that would allow some re-integration of the bantustans, along with southern African countries, without having to admit defeat on the policy of 'separate development'. Buthelezi turned this grandiose scheme down.

Inkatha's own initiatives

Inkatha has not simply reacted to state initiatives. It has also undertaken some of its own activities to influence national politics.

Several of the issues for which Inkatha has claimed credit have been dealt with in the discussion of strategy and tactics, or have been implicit in the organization's position generally, but a few activities need to be singled out because of their importance to Inkatha and for what we can learn about the movement through them.

The South African Black Alliance (SABA)

The first hint of contact between Inkatha and other political groupings in South Africa, other than the bantustan allies, came in 1975 when Buthelezi mentioned in the KLA that he had been in contact with some coloured people from Zululand. This was a delegation led by Reginald Apollos, on their way to a Labour Party (LP) conference (the 'coloured' political party that took part in elections to the state-created Coloured Persons Representative Council — the CRC — but boycotted it once elected). It was suggested that a Zululand Coloured People's Committee be formed which would help Africans and work with Inkatha (KLAD, 7:679).

In October 1976 leaders of all bantustans except for the Transkei met Prime Minister Vorster to discuss a range of issues. It was for these leaders a most frustrating meeting. Immediately afterwards Buthelezi, Professor Ntsanwisi (Gazankulu), Dr Phatudi (Lebowa) and several other community and political leaders met to form a Black Unity Front (BUF). Inkatha central committee member Dr S.M. Nyembezi chaired the steering committee, which planned to bring together a cross-section of black organizations, bridge the urban-rural 'gap' and establish a disciplined community and black leadership (Survey, 1976:28).

Rather grandly it was envisaged that the BUF 'should be a united Black front with which the OAU, for instance, could liaise' (Langner, 1983:207). Wentzel wrote that Dr Nyembezi reassured whites about the intentions of the BUF, stating that 'we don't want communism; that is certain' (1977:6). It appears that the BUF did little during its brief existence other than to show confidence in its own importance. During February 1977 it held a conference in Lebowa where the aim of 'national unity' was proclaimed, and in April Dr Nyembezi announced that the BUF 'had set itself a five-year target for majority rule in South Africa' (Survey, 1977:37).

By December of 1977, however, Buthelezi was having talks with Yellan S. Chinsamy, which added fuel to the rumours of an alliance of the Reform Party (which Chinsamy led), the Labour Party and Inkatha (STb, 11 Dec. 77). The Reform Party (RP) had been formed after it was announced that the state-created South African Indian Council (SAIC) was to become fully elected, and that an inter-Cabinet council was to be formed involving the SAIC, CRC, and the white parliament — a forerunner to the tricameral parliament. In 1978 the RP had a reported membership of 3000 (FM, 17 Mar. 78). Despite its lack of size it became a partner of Inkatha and the LP in the South African Black Alliance (SABA), which was formed in Ulundi on 11 January 1978 after Inkatha secretary general Professor S.M.E. Bengu had suggested at an LP conference in December 1977 that the organizations join forces. The Gazankulu bantustan's Ntsanwisi reacted coolly, while Mopeli of the Qwa-Qwa bantustan gushed enthusiasm at first. In the euphoria, similar to that surrounding the formation of the BUF, contradictory statements were made about white membership and about a proposed national convention that was said to be SABA's initial goal. After its first meeting in Cape Town Buthelezi said Vorster would have to talk to SABA as Ian Smith had been forced to talk to black leaders in Rhodesia, a reference to the ill-fated attempt to involve Bishop Muzorewa, Ndabaningi Sithole and Chief Chirau in a long-term 'internal settlement'. Buthelezi said 'he did not want to "talk big" but he believed SABA could well be the group with which Mr Vorster would have to negotiate' (RDM, 14 Mar. 78). This was an ironical statement as P.W. Botha did finally negotiate with individuals and a party (the LP) from the SABA, but only after they had left the organisation, making the term 'Alliance' something of a misnomer.

SABA's first public meeting had to be cut short by the LP's Allan Hendrickse because of disruption by young people. The Natal Indian Congress rejected suggestions that it would join SABA; it was in any case mobilizing opposition to the proposed SAIC elections through the body that would become Anti-SAIC. Mopeli's Dikwankwetla party and the Inyandza movement of KaNgwane (under Enos Mabuza) had joined by mid-1978, but the former remained inactive and left in 1981.

SABA announced that it would monitor codes of conduct, that it would work towards a national convention, and that it would call a Southern African Treaty Conference. The potential for tension was clear as the LP had decided, at the conference that accepted the idea of SABA, to support 'the decision of Chief Gatsha Buthelezi . . . to campaign for economic sanctions and pressures against South Africa' (St, 3 Jan. 78). This had been LP policy but had certainly never been part of Buthelezi's strategy except for his meek statement with Beyers Naude referred to above (see p. 104).

The Afrikaans-language press responded to SABA by playing on possible coloured fears of racial domination by Africans in an attempt to keep the LP out. It must be remembered that SABA was formed shortly after the parliamentary elections for whites in which the water was first tested for an ethnically and racially fragmented parliament for whites, coloured people and Indians. Partners for the tricameral system had to be found among the ethnic categories who were to constitute it. An alternative formulation and political alliance through SABA could thwart the state, and had to be broken. The term 'imperialism' was used frequently, and *Die Vaderland* even said the formation of SABA was the first step towards a 'Zulu-dominated unitary state' (13 Jan. 78).

The next tension point also came from within the Labour Party, this time in a hint from Sonny Leon, one of its leaders, that coloured people might participate in the new constitution, as Buthelezi had participated in KwaZulu. Buthelezi denied any analogy, claiming that his role pre-dated the 'homeland' system by 16 years (RDM, 1 Sep. 78). There were fervent declarations in repudiation of Leon by several LP leaders that the party would not abandon their African fellow citizens over the coming years. Allan Hendrickse told a SABA prayer meeting in KwaMashu in 1980: 'Coloureds and Africans have found each other and were going to stay together . . . "No amount of buying us off will succeed"' (NM, 9 Jun. 80). However, there were also reports of dissatisfaction in the LP from left and right about the alliance with Inkatha — either because of Inkatha's antagonism to school boycotts and the disinvestment campaign or because the alliance would jeopardize LP involvement in central politics under the new constitution.

The Reform Party had similar problems and probably only remained in SABA because it was not strong enough to hold any political claim outside an alliance. It suffered from the same political dilettantism and opportunism as the LP. For example, J.N. Reddy, Baldeo Dookie and Amichand Rajbansi, who later participated in the House of Delegates of the tricameral parliament, had been members of the RP, and hence linked to Inkatha. SABA meetings have been overwhelmingly attended by Africans, after an initial enthusiasm among some coloured people in the western Cape. The fact that the Inyandza movement in KaNgwane, the only equivalent of Inkatha in South Africa and itself arising out of the 'homeland' structure, has been the only participant with a level of political consistency and reasonable support, probably says as much as anything about Inkatha's isolation and the limits to Buthelezi's political attraction in South Africa. Even in the political sphere where he might have expected to have success, in bantustan politics, *another* largely ethnic movement is not attractive, and might be downright threatening to people whose own power relies on an exclusive ethnic definition. Ironically, the only groups who are not threatened are white political bodies such as the PFP and NP.

Because of SABA's composition it was forced to reject participation in the national 'reform' process, which excluded Africans at that stage, because participation would have sidelined Buthelezi, the most prominent member, in an arena in which he wanted to participate. At the same time, however, it had to decry the Anti-SAIC campaign. Buthelezi told the KLA in 1979 that while he did not want to interfere in 'Indian politics' he did feel it was his 'duty' to issue a warning to the growing Anti-SAIC campaign (*Post*, 7 Jun. 79). He argued that the campaign also constituted an attack on SABA and, altogether inappropriately, he placed his Alliance in the tradition of the Congress Alliance of the 1950s, in which the ANC, the Congress of Democrats, the Coloured People's Congress, the South African Indian Congress, and the South African Congress of Trade Unions had served. SABA, in which all participants were involved in state structures, was in this sense far removed from the Congress Alliance tradition. The RP was at one stage the only obvious party to contest the elections for the South African Indian Council, and Chinsamy used the new legitimacy and power that he had gained through being associated with the Inkatha movement to repeat the general warning to boycotters. It must be remembered that an alliance of Indian and Zulu ethnic politics makes sense to the extent that numerically they dominate the Natal region.

SABA's Transvaal rally and conference in 1979, at which the Anti-SAIC campaign was attacked, was attended by several RP personalities, including J.N. Reddy and S. Abram-Mayet (participants a few years later in the House of Delegates). Buthelezi welcomed Reddy and said he was impressed with his political contribution. If we remember that the assault on the person mistaken for Ntatho Motlana occurred at an Anti-SAIC meeting, and that the Anti-SAIC campaign and political grouping was a forerunner of the UDF, it becomes clear why Inkatha greeted the UDF with hostility when it was formed four years later. The elections for the South African Indian Council, postponed to 1981, should have been a warning to Inkatha in its strategy of supporting discredited bodies. The poll was in almost all places less than 20%. The Reform Party won one of the 40 seats (Survey, 1981:20).

In 1980 SABA was still confident enough of its strength to say that its members were to prepare 'for a mass conference of regional and branch units as a preliminary step towards the calling of a national convention in South Africa' (St, 21 Jan. 80). Buthelezi said SABA was 'representing the real black solidarity which is crucial, and which will be decisive in the liberation struggle' (RDM, 24 Dec. 80). Dhlomo, with more optimism than accuracy, had spoken of SABA as 'one of the most powerful black political alliances ever to be witnessed in South Africa . . . The enormous power wielded by the [SABA] keeps on increasing each year as more political groupings join in large numbers' (1979:19).

In 1981 SABA found a new area of joint opposition (other than Republic Day celebrations, which were in any case not an issue for the vast majority of black people in South Africa), namely opposition to the President's Council (PC) that was to draw up a refinement of the constitutional proposals Prime Minister Vorster had been working on. Allan Hendrickse said LP members, as well as other SABA allies, would defy subpoenas to give evidence before the President's Council (St, 24 Sep. 81).

A few months later, early in 1982, things were a lot less clear for the politics of opportunism that characterizes the loyal resisters in state institutions. In October Hendrickse still told the SABA prayer meeting in Soweto that the Alliance 'is moving in a direction where the black man's dreams will become a reality'. But the writing was on the wall, and a month later LP participation under the new constitution was being discussed openly. It was admitted that without a platform from which to function the LP would probably die. The CRC, in which it had participated in order to prevent it from working, was dissolved in 1980 by the state (see John Battersby in RDM, 29 Dec. 82). The LP was in a quandary as the CRC had served as its paradoxical platform (in the same way that the SAIC had for the RP and the KwaZulu bantustan does for Inkatha). The LP and some of the ex-SAIC politicians may also have been taken in by a survey undertaken by Professor Schlemmer which showed that 47% of Indians and 37% of coloured people were willing to give the new constitution a chance (see columnist 'Gus Adams' in R, 22 Aug. 82).

The fact that the LP conference early in 1983 decided to accept participation in the tricameral constitution ran completely counter to Buthelezi's rejection of such a strategy and his increasing threats against Indians and coloured people if they should vote. His sensitivity to criticism did not allow him to spare others, such as Minister Chris Heunis, who was told to go and see a psychiatrist and called a 'clown in the cabinet', Botha's 'blue-eyed boy' and a 'tin god', and Law and Order Minister Louis le Grange, who had warned Buthelezi about his threats to Indian and coloured participants and drawn attention to Buthelezi's own participation in state institutions (eg RDM, 16 Oct. 82).

The LP conference, held in Eshowe in northern Natal — 'Inkatha territory' — was opened by Buthelezi. Bishop Zulu, of the KLA, prominent Inkatha member and now chaiman of the KFC, started the proceedings with prayer after Buthelezi had led in what was described as an 'impi'. This 'show of strength' was preceded by drum majorettes and the singing of 'We Shall Overcome'. Buthelezi's speech asked that Indians and coloureds should not become 'second class enemies' of Africans and that the LP and other SABA members establish a 'group of experts' to formulate a joint response to the new constitution. All to no avail, however.

What became clear at the conference was that Buthelezi and the LP had different ideas as to what was meant by the term 'black'. Buthelezi has always used it to refer predominantly to African people, whereas the black consciousness organizations had deliberately expanded it to include all people not part of the white oppressing group in South Africa. The state, in a clever move several years ago, changed the official terminology to allocate 'black' to the African population. When the LP voted to enter parliament they justified it in terms of gaining a foothold for a *section* of the black population from which the interests of *all* black people could be advanced. David Curry said, for example, 'We are adding to the liberation struggle in the long run by making black people more powerful so they can crush the system' (St, 5 Jan. 83).

An angry Buthelezi said the new constitution was becoming a federation of Indians, coloureds and whites against blacks (Africans). The remains of SABA (without the LP, despite Hendrickse's statement that he felt participation need not affect the LP's SABA membership) met at Currie's Fountain in Durban in February. In defiance of a magisterial ban on the meeting about 8000 people attended. Hendrickse had said at a meeting in the Cape that he did not need Buthelezi to tell him what he had to do, and that it must have been Norman Middleton, Natal trade unionist and a founder member of the LP, who had placed Buthelezi under the false impression that the LP would not enter parliament (Middleton had resigned from the LP after the Eshowe conference) (EPH, 26 Jan. 83).

The LP was expelled and a depleted SABA entered this historic year, 1983. It was announced that a township organization in Mamelodi, outside Pretoria, the Vulamehlo Vukani Peoples' (sic) Party under Bennet Ndlazi, might apply for membership (RDM, 26 Apr. 83), but nothing further was heard of this. Buthelezi went on another trip to the USA where, among other tactics, he placed a large advertisement in the *Wall Street Journal* in which he called upon 'progressive forces in the East and West' to help in the resistance to the new constitution, and hence to his old allies the LP (Bd, 4 Feb. 83). This advertisement also appeared in British newspapers while Buthelezi was there meeting such people as Cranley Onslow (Minister of the Foreign Office responsible for southern Africa), David

Owen (SDP-Liberal Alliance), and Denis Healey (Labour shadow Foreign Secretary).

The LP resigned from SABA in April, claiming that they had not been told of their expulsion, and lost no opportunity during the year to point to Buthelezi's inconsistency in condemning their participation, while approving of his own in KwaZulu and that of the RP in the old SAIC. Buthelezi entered the white voters' referendum fray on the side of the PFP in advocating rejection of P.W. Botha's ethnic constitution, while commentators asked whether his threats to coloured people, Indians, and whites were not having more success in driving people into the 'yes' camp than in giving people hope in the long-term future under Inkatha with a 'no' vote.

In the oblique style that Buthelezi has made his own when threatening something that he claims he is not actually threatening, he warned white voters that strikes 'would break out in Natal if most whites voted "yes"', but assured them that 'I'm just mentioning something that might happen. We are mature enough to stage successful stay-aways to show our feelings' (RDM, 26 Sep. 83). He campaigned country-wide but whites voted in favour of the constitution and if strikes broke out in response they had little to do with Inkatha.

Buthelezi had made frequent threats to 'existing good relations' between Indians and Africans (eg STb, 18 Sep. 83; *Ilanga*, 23 Sep. 83), and re-evaluated his position on sanctions and violence. P.W. Botha took him at his word and told the Cape congress of the NP that his own 'experience in public life taught him those who talked about violence seldom did it' (St, 27 Sep. 83). The Natal-based *Sunday Tribune* commented after the referendum that the threats of violence and then the killing of five students at the University of Zululand, in which Inkatha was centrally involved, on the weekend before the referendum, had caused many whites to vote in rejection of the Inkatha tactics (6 Nov. 83; also St, 12 Nov. 83). The highest vote in favour of the new constitution was in Natal and the Border region of the eastern Cape.

Not only had the threats of violence backfired, but approaches made by KwaZulu politicians to the discredited and repressive Matanzima administration in the Transkei to re-awaken the federation idea as a counter to the tricameral parliament, hardly advanced the Inkatha position; nor did the suggestion of a 'marriage of convenience' made to the ANC and PAC in a speech in the KwaZulu parliament, which was quickly rejected.

In 1984 Buthelezi committed 'Black South Africa' to the 'common task of rendering the new constitution unworkable' (Sow, 28 Mar. 84). Much time was spent in reviving the Buthelezi Commission Report (see below), and he visited Britain where he saw MPs and the business community, including Lonrho's Tiny Rowlands, and addressed the Wilton Park Conference on 'Federal and Confederal Futures for South Africa'. Buthelezi suggested a feasibility study, of which nothing more was heard, on how best to 'isolate' those elected to the Indian House of Delegates.

During 1985 very little was written or said about SABA. A meeting did take place between Inkatha and the LP but Buthelezi strongly denied that this could be seen as evidence of a relaxation in the conflict. Ironically, the LP has in many ways moved closer to Inkatha since it became a part of the state. The LP position on schools boycotts, the UDF, the ANC and foreign investment is at present similar to those held by Inkatha, probably as a result of its own less qualified participation in state structures than when it was a member of SABA and engaged in boycotting the CRC.

What had SABA achieved? Its initial grandiose claims — a national convention, majority rule in a few years, forcing the state to the conference table — came to nothing. Nor were the high hopes realized that it was a rejection of the state's ethnic fragmentation policy. Allan Boesak, in a perceptive commentary on SABA immediately after it was formed (*Deurbraak*, Apr. 78) wrote that he was sceptical about the basis of the alliance — there was too little ground for unity and a wide appeal. Furthermore, Inkatha was too much Buthelezi — 'With Inkatha chief Buthelezi gave in to the temptation to link a political movement to a personal cult (such as that around Peron in Argentina)'. Finally, he said SABA was an organization whose members would never leave government institutions if called upon to do so.

In retrospect the harm SABA did to Inkatha and its politics of 'black unity' probably outweighed anything gained from Alliance activities. Dr Dhlomo claimed SABA had brought back 'inter-ethnic' politics after the banning of the ANC (Bd, 26 Apr. 83), but the various black consciousness organizations achieved this with much greater success, because people were united around a positive political position rather than the vague and opportunist opposition to apartheid that characterized the participants in SABA. Dhlomo also claimed that SABA had organized opposition to the handing over of KaNgwane and Ingwavuma to Swaziland by the state, but this had involved two members of the Alliance (Inkatha and Inyandza) and a non-member (the PFP), and the most successful action was fought out in courts of law and not in the arena of mass politics. Finally, Dhlomo referred to successful boycotts of white bread after a price increase, and of Fatti's and Moni's products after a strike at the company. The latter involved many other organizations, especially trade unions, who could legitimately claim the credit for the boycott. This does not leave much of a positive evaluation of the Alliance after its early exaggerated claims and five years of existence. However, in 1986, with only the Reform Party (if it still exists beyond a leader) as a clear member, Buthelezi continues to head his speeches with the title of 'Chairman, the South African Black Alliance'.

Inyandza, the movement of KaNgwane leader Enos Mabuza, also suffered under the tongue of Buthelezi after Mabuza had met with the ANC. In a speech in the KLA Buthelezi warned Mabuza that he had associated himself and his movement with those whose motivation was the destruction of Buthelezi and Inkatha. He accused Mabuza of having 'capitulated to the forces of darkness', and asked whether Mabuza had 'made up his mind to side with the ANC Mission in Exile and, like them, declare war on me and Inkatha?' (BS, 14 Apr. 86):

> Because if he has, the world must know that this is his choice. The implications of such a decision will be far-reaching and of great significance. Events which will inevitably result from such a move will go down in history. And they will do so because we are talking here about life and death.

The Buthelezi Commission

The Buthelezi Commission (BC) and its report involved interests, such as Natal-based industry and agriculture, that either could not afford to be associated with the state's constitutional initiatives, or believed these initiatives did not promise the long-term stability essential to profits and 'development' in the region. The BC chose Natal-KwaZulu as the area for its investigation and recommendations but did not exclude — in fact it hoped for and suggested — national relevance.

The BC was formed in the climate of political change and ferment that characterized the last years of Vorster's government, the 'Information Department scandal', and the first years of P.W. Botha's initiatives for increased concentration of power and constitutional 'reform'. To a large extent resistance politics was still concentrated in the schools. In 1979 the Schlebusch Commission had been appointed to examine the introduction of a new constitution for South Africa. Inkatha submitted recommendations to the Commission (Inkatha, 1979) and presented a series of 'non-negotiables': for example, that 'South Africa is one state and should remain as such', but that 'regionality without ethnicity' would be acceptable if the existing 'homelands' were to be consolidated, given regional responsibility and provincial status; that ethnic realities should not be the basis for political rights (ie one citizenship, nationality, passport, economy, etc), and that discriminatory laws should be repealed as a first step; it also included a bill of rights. A reading of this document makes it clear how much easier P.W. Botha, with his rhetorical commitment to implementing many of these demands, has made it for Buthelezi to be a participant in state-initiated moves.

However, by May 1980 there was less pressure to co-opt Inkatha and Schlebusch recommended that a President's Council be established that would exclude Africans, and that a Black Advisory Council (BAC) would compensate for this exclusion. Inkatha rejected this sop and the Council never took off. 1980 was also the year, it must be remembered, in which Buthelezi made his strongest argument for participation in local state structures such as community councils, but at the national level Inkatha was playing for stakes that were too high to jeopardize through participation in an advisory body to a President's Council which was racially exclusive (of Africans).

The establishment of the BC was preceded by the formation and report of the Lombard Commission (LC) in which Professor Jan Lombard and three other Afrikaner intellectuals deliberated on an 'Alternative to the Consolidation of KwaZulu' (Lombard, nd). Professor Lombard was himself a member of the state's Central Consolidation Committee. The LC was formed at the request of Natal business, notably the South African Sugar Association (SASA), which would be affected by any consolidation plans. Consolidation would either affect production directly, if more actual or potential sugar growing land was to be brought into KwaZulu, or indirectly, in terms of the continued administrative separation of Natal and KwaZulu. Lombard had said Natal lent itself to an 'eie-soortige' (unique) solution because of the relative ethnic homogeneity (of Africans) in the region, the adherence by the three main political parties in Natal/KwaZulu to a recognition of plurality, a commitment to free enterprise, and federalism (R, 27 Apr. 80; RDM, 2 Aug. 80).

In the late 1970s and the early 1980s there had been a series of papers, theses and reports on an approach to South Africa's political ills that would take as a starting point 'economic realities' and not further ethnic division. These included Lombard Commission member Professor du Pisani's PhD thesis 'Streeksekonomiese Beleid in die RSA', a Mercabank report published by the University of Pretoria's Bureau of Economic Planning and Analysis, the Lombard Commission Report, the BC Report, and the proposals submitted by business to the Carlton and Good Hope Conferences (for a discussion of some of these developments and their implications, see Cobbett, et al, 1985). When the LC Report was leaked in July 1980 it was rejected by the NP in Natal on the basis that a single political authority for the region was not desirable (the report had suggested three regions — 'mixed' metropolitan, white rural, and KwaZulu — which would come together in one authority). It was welcomed by SASA in that it provided 'constructive alternatives' to the consolidation of KwaZulu and did not have adverse economic implications for the sugar industry — hardly surprising as that was its brief (St, 6 Aug. 80). Lombard and other commentators stressed that this was not a plan for secession, but rather a vision that could be extended to the rest of South Africa. The same insistence on national replication was to be the case with the BC Report and with the 1986 Natal-KwaZulu 'Option'. *The Star* editorialized on the LC Report under the heading 'Forget Politics and Think Economics' (1 Aug. 80). The PFP's Van Zyl Slabbert used language that would become a catchword of the BC Report and the Natal-KwaZulu moves when he asked the government not to reject the report submitted by Lombard and his team out of hand, as Natal could be a 'political laboratory' for the rest of the country (SE, 3 Aug. 80). Chris Saunders, prominent Natal industrialist, sugar industry leader and co-director with Lombard of Standard Bank, said the Lombard Commission had arisen out of a suggestion by Dr Piet Koornhof, then Minister of Co-operation and Development, that alternative plans to the state's much criticized consolidation proposals be submitted. Saunders denied a 'Natal plan', but did ask for political flexibility. It was suggested that he had asked 'his friend' Buthelezi to apply 'Black pressure' through the subsequent Buthelezi Commission, as business had done directly through the Lombard Commission and its proposals (Martin Schneider in RDM, 9 Aug. 80; see also Southall, 1982:3-4).

The BC was established through an Inkatha central committee decision in March 1980, in a province 'in which experimentation on racial harmony and power-sharing [could] start', as Buthelezi put it (DN, 31 Mar. 80). In April Buthelezi announced the establishment of the BC to the KLA, which would fund the Commission and its secretariat the Inkatha Institute (DN, 23 Mar. 80).

The Buthelezi Commission invited representatives of various interest groups, under the chairmanship of Natal University's Professor Deneys Schreiner, to deliberate on the region. The Inkatha Institute, formed in July under Professor Lawrence Schlemmer, functioned as a secretariat, undertaking and commissioning research for the BC. The BC started formal deliberations in October 1980. It was composed of 46 members and alternate members; a third of the membership was from the business world and a quarter from universities. Noticeable by their absence were representatives of the ANC and the NP, although both had been invited. Also absent were representatives of extra-parliamentary opposition organizations, although 11 commissioners represented white, African, coloured and Indian political parties which operated through state structures. Nine people were drawn from the professions or non-academic professional organizations and there were two religious personalities. Trade unionists were not represented. Despite this skewed representation of interests, and the non-participation of many interests, Inkatha has referred to the BC's deliberations as an 'example of the type of National Convention envisaged by Inkatha' (*Inkatha*, 1983:14).

Professor Schlemmer said the BC investigation would give content to P.W. Botha's 'constellation of states' idea (ST, 27 Apr. 80) (see above, p.157). He continued: 'The rational conservative thing to do is look intelligently for a plan that is going to create the greatest stability for the future. I think this lies with

Chief Buthelezi's proposals.' He felt that while conservatives were likely to consider the BC proposals they would be rejected by the 'radical left'. It turned out that intially they were rejected by both. The Natal Provincial Council (NPC) and the party that dominated it, the New Republic Party (NRP), welcomed the formation of the BC and so did the PFP, which had helped to get it started. The NP said the BC's terms of reference went beyond the area of Buthelezi's jurisdiction (ie KwaZulu) and would not take part, although Dr Koornhof took a relatively mild line, reprimanding a NP backbencher who had attacked Inkatha, reminding him that Inkatha had acted against school boycotters and bus boycotts and that Natal had been trouble free in 1976 (St, 9 May, 80). In September, however, P.W. Botha finally rejected NP participation in the BC.

When the BC got off the ground the Natal-based *Sunday Tribune* greeted it with the headline 'IT'S ON! Black and White Elite Launch the Push for Peace' (2 Nov. 80). The launch was attended by the US consul general in Durban, the sole diplomatic representative. Extensive publicity was given to the BC during its deliberations in 1981, both because of the close contacts Buthelezi personally had built up with a sympathetic press, and because the participants and supporters of the Commission had ready access to publicity. Buthelezi regularly assured people that this was a 'black initiative' (probably to give it greater credibility). Schlemmer said that 'many overseas' leaders considered the BC 'the most important development in South Africa today', while the chief, in character, warned of possible violence if the report should not be accepted. Professor Giliomee (1982) said violence would come from the ANC if the BC recommendations were not accepted, while sections of the Afrikaans-language press pressed for a sympathetic hearing from the state for the BC deliberations.

To prepare the way for the major compromise away from majority rule that the BC report would contain, Buthelezi said before its release that 'Black majority rule . . . would probably lead to civil war between blacks and whites' (St, 4 Feb. 82). When the New Republic Party refused to sign the main report Buthelezi threatened to withdraw from the Joint Consultative Committee that had been established in 1975 between the Natal administration and that of KwaZulu, and to end negotiations to extend the areas of joint activity between the provincial and bantustan authorities. He went overboard, using such terms as 'dinosaurs', 'jackals' and 'scavengers' to describe the NRP (this might also have encouraged the support Natal's conservative white voters gave the 'yes' option in the constitutional referendum at the end of 1983). Dr Dhlomo warned of youth violence if the report should be rejected. However, the Minister of Finance and NP leader in Natal, Owen Horwood, rejected the BC report, but Professor Schreiner suggested the government be given a year to reconsider.

The report (*The Requirements for Stability and Development in KwaZulu and Natal*) compromised on the issue of majority rule in a unitary state, and for political reasons this was presented as a change in Buthelezi's standpoint. However, this 'compromise' had been there for at least seven years. In the mid-1970s Buthelezi had said: 'We see the autonomy of such a state [of KwaZulu] as a unit in one federal multi-national state of South Africa. This is a compromise solution and an interim measure, before we can expect a one-man-one-vote situation which is an ultimate inevitability' (quoted Temkin, 1976:336). Dr Dhlomo suggested that government rejection of the BC report did not really matter to Inkatha's following as there 'is no question of a liberation movement losing credibility if the oppressor rejects demands for the liberation of the masses' (*Voice*, 12 Mar. 82).

The BC proposals were widely publicized, not only by the participants, but also by a range of academics who had been directly and indirectly linked with the report, by newspapers, and by the PFP, which held joint meetings with Inkatha on the issue. The *Graphic* (28 May, 82), a newspaper directed mainly at Natal Indian people, pointed out that while whites and Africans were catered for in the BC report, Indians, who outnumber whites in the province, had received minimal attention — a remarkable omission, since Inkatha had set so much store by the South African Black Alliance.

Later in the year the KLA accepted the BC report, while stating that it did not abandon its ideal of '"universal suffrage and open democracy"' (STb, 5 Dec. 82). The BC report recommended geographically based federalism and a system of consociationalism, not necessarily based on race or ethnic definitions, which would take groups as the starting point and then bring the leadership of these groups together.

The report's analysis of the economic sphere was largely directed towards acknowledging the clear interdependence of the region, and most attention has been directed to its political recommendations, which took as their starting point this 'economic interdependence', and the view that South Africa is a complex 'plural society'. From here, accepting that KwaZulu-Natal needed a single democratic government to avoid conflict (or rather to create stability), to cut costs, and to improve administrative efficiency, it recommended that the region should have a form of consociational government (for a critical essay on the 'thought processes' behind the BC report, see Pretorius, 1981).

Consociationalism is geared to achieving elite consensus and to engineering mass acceptance. Southall (1982:23) noted that consociationalism 'by emphasizing coalition between segmental elites (rather than mass based rule), . . . seeks to manage the problem of pacifying the economically disprivileged populace'. Even arch-conservatives such as Professor Samuel Huntington (1982:10) have admitted to the anti-democratic nature of consociationalism:

> What the theorists have labelled 'consociational democracy' is . . . nothing of the sort; it is more appropriately designated 'consociational oligarchy' . . . In essence it is an elite conspiracy to restrain political competition within and among communal groups. In many societies, this may be desirable, but that does not make it democratic.

Huntington argued that consociationalists accept that the system will only work if:

> two conditions are met: a) a high degree of trust and cooperation exists among the elites of the different groups; and b) each elite effectively controls its followers (1982:10).

Neither the BC nor the KwaZulu-Natal 'Indaba' (conference) can remotely be presented as having either a democratic mandate or any accountability to constituencies. Furthermore, and especially with the BC, there was not even a pretence that many of the participants represented any but their own immediate class interests, or an ideological class position.*

---

*See Buthelezi Commission Report (nd (1982)) and SAIRR (1982) for the recommendations. See Southall (1983) and Pretorius (1981 (sic)) for analyses, and Prinsloo (1984) for a discussion of corporatism and consociationalism as aspects of the same process of restructuring the state and the economy in contemporary South Africa.

National Convention

The Buthelezi Commission deliberations were presented as a type of national convention, and as such accurately reflected the interests that would dominate such a convention if Inkatha had its way. The idea of a national convention had its origins in KwaZulu politics, predating the formation of Inkatha by several years, having been a plank in the Buthelezi political platform from at least the early 1970s. Langner (1983:46) wrote that Buthelezi first appealed for a national convention in 1971, a call that was predictably rejected by Bantu Affairs Minister M.C. Botha, because the NP 'knew "precisely what path and course to take for the future"'. Shortly after Inkatha was formed Buthelezi repeated his call for a convention 'in order to get Black consensus on the burning issues of the day at this crucial time in the history of Southern Africa' (KLAD, 8:94). This was a repeat of a call for 'a series of national conventions' made in Soweto two months earlier (RDM, 15 Mar. 76). A resolution at the Inkatha conference in 1976, after the Soweto uprising, called on the *government* to call a national convention, which would also involve SASO and the Black People's Convention. The BPC rejected the call because it was issued through the press, and demanded that Buthelezi first leave bantustan politics and change Inkatha's constitution, which at that stage was still an exclusively Zulu document (STb, 18 Jul. 76; 25 Jul. 76).

In 1978 Buthelezi, speaking in the KLA, called on the United Nations secretary general to call a 'peace conference', and later in the year a call was made on the new prime minister, P.W. Botha, to call a conference of the leaders of the various race groups. During that year Dhlomo returned from West Germany with the mandate conferred on Inkatha and Buthelezi by the Bergstraesser Institute's attitude survey (Survey, 1978:27-8; and above, p.151), and said a national convention could only be held after a meeting between Buthelezi and P.W. Botha, 'to formulate a basis for discussion'. He said Buthelezi should be the leader to negotiate this as he was the most popular political figure in South Africa (Cit, 21 Sep. 78).

Between 1978 and 1980 there were regular calls for a national convention from Inkatha leaders, with demands that political prisoners be released and exiles allowed to return to participate in the convention. In 1980 two developments gave it greater impetus. Following the Mugabe victory in Zimbabwe and a *Sunday Post* initiated petition calling for the release of Nelson Mandela, so that a convention could take place, a Release Mandela Campaign was started with the support of a wide range of organizations including Inkatha, Diakonia, COSAS, AZAPO, etc, but was rejected out of hand by the NP government (Survey, 1980:242-3).

The second development was revealed when it was leaked that several people from a range of organizations had been meeting in the Transvaal for a couple of years under the auspices of the Black Sash, particularly of Joyce Harris, then president of the Black Sash. They included the PFP, Inkatha, the Labour Party, the Reform Party, Actstop (a Johannesburg anti-Group Areas Act grouping which subsequently denied involvement), and Bishop Desmond Tutu (RDM, 30 Dec. 80). It seems that the intention had been to extend invitations to a larger spectrum, including AZAPO and the CoT. Joyce Harris denied that plans for a national convention had been drawn up, but confirmed that constitutional options were being examined (STb, 21 Jun. 81).

The flame of a national convention has been kept alive, without its proponents doing much to clarify what they mean by such a convention. In 1983 the Transkei's minister of justice said that a 'national convention of black leaders to demand participation in South Africa's political future will be called within a fortnight'. This call was said to follow a February meeting between Buthelezi and the Transkei's Kaizer Matanzima in which they had committed themselves to black unity (EPH, 21 Apr. 83). SABA was also a central element in plans to call a national convention (see Langner, 1983:211;and above).

In 1984 the National Forum rejected calls for a national convention as 'a "ruling class strategy" intended to entrench power in the hands of the "racist capitalist regime and their puppets"' (Survey, 1984:16), but Inkatha once more supported the idea. In 1985 Inkatha and the PFP launched yet another attempt to give organizational form to moves for convening such a meeting: the National Convention Movement (NCM).

By now, however, the political climate, at least on a national level, had changed to such an extent that by the end of October 1985 J. Browde, chairman of the NCM, announced that Dr Dhlomo of Inkatha and the PFP representatives had withdrawn from the steering committee, '"because confusion had arisen in the minds of the public concerning the role in the movement of the PFP and Inkatha"' (NW, 30 Oct. 85). In January 1986 there was speculation that the ANC would organize an alternative alliance to counter Inkatha. The NCM's Browde, as well as previous leader of the opposition PFP, Van Zyl Slabbert, have acknowledged that while Inkatha is linked to a 'convention alliance' there is little chance of the ANC — or any of the internal radical groupings, including organized labour — joining it. This does not mean they would not participate in a convention at a future date, but that Inkatha is not seen as part of a real thrust for change in South Africa. It would be very difficult for the NCM ever to escape its origins in the PFP and Inkatha.

If any indication was needed that 'centre of the road politics committed to negotiation and peaceful change' (BS, 14 Apr. 86:6) can be an unwanted fellow-traveller in national political initiatives, the snub by the National Convention Movement provided it. Meanwhile, however, Inkatha was launching another initiative in Natal, less ambitious but more certain — the 'Indaba'. Before discussing this further some additional background is necessary.

Federation

As with his calls for a national convention, Buthelezi has proposed the idea of a federation for many years. In a similar way to his compromise on universal adult franchise, opting instead for a consociational system or group representation through leadership elites, a unitary state has been postponed in favour of a federal structure for South Africa. It would have been difficult, if not impossible, for Buthelezi, with his ideological and material commitment to regional administration and development and his belief in a politicized cultural pluralism, to have argued for a strongly centralized system of government. A federal system would favour Inkatha's present position of regional strength and national weakness, and provide probably the most likely route for Buthelezi's inclusion in national 'reform' politics. Inkatha defends the federal option on the basis that it is practical politics during a transitional phase in which white people would become accustomed to shared power.

Buthelezi says he has been talking about federation since 1973 but the clearest early exposition of his views was in 1974 when he delivered the Hoernlè Memorial Lecture to the South African Institute of Race Relations (BS, 16 Jan. 74; also 11 Aug. 74; Survey, 1974:50). Just before this lecture Buthelezi had met with Harry Schwarz, then Transvaal leader of the United Party (later to become the New Republic Party), and they issued a statement that became known as the 'Mahlabatini Declaration'. This document committed the two signatories to a federation and the safeguarding of the 'identity and culture of the various groups constituting the people of South Africa' (Survey, 1974:3; ST, 6 Jan. 74; KLAD, 4:139).

While there are some ambiguous exceptions, Buthelezi has most often linked the federal idea to ethnicity, if not race. In the Hoernlè Lecture, for example, he proposed three types of states: some in which African ethnic interests predominate, some where white interests predominate, and 'multi-national' states (Langner, 1983:43). Buthelezi repeated this proposal in the KLA, adding that the government should be pleased that he had accepted the reality of the 'homelands' within his federation (KLAD, 4:133). A later speech was filled with references to 'multi-nationalism' within a single economy, with a single passport and free internal movement:

> It means that KwaZulu will be one of the units of this multi-national state and that we will still have the Paramount Chief as the head of the KwaZulu state, but then representatives of KwaZulu will also meet in the Federal Parliament in which members from all other states, from Transkei and certain White states, will meet and decide on the future of all people of this country (KLAD, 5:83).

In 1976 Buthelezi said he had the support of both the KLA and Inkatha in his federal offer.

In the Inkatha proposals to the Schlebusch Commission in 1979 (see above, p.164) the idea of provincial status for the bantustans was repeated ('provided the areas were "effectively" consolidated') (Langner, 1983:269). In 1983 Buthelezi wrote to the *Sunday Times* that a federal compromise could safeguard racial interests (16 Jan. 83). Karis commented that with his 1974 proposals Buthelezi 'placed himself near the right end of the political spectrum' (nd:B5). Subsequent proposals have tended to confirm this.

The other aspect of Buthelezi's federal proposal is that it is a necessary compromise. In May 1984 Buthelezi told the 265th Wilton Park Conference in Britain that:

> As a market place politician my own constitutional thinking is dominated by assessments of what is politically practical rather than by what is theoretically ideal. Whatever the future holds, I believe it holds out either a unitary state with universal adult franchise as an end product of an armed revolt, or a federal system of government as the end product of the politics of negotiation . . . I believe that existing levels of interdependence between race groups make it realistic to hope that through consociational government we could establish a future federation of South African states which would preserve that which would be lost in an armed revolution [BS, 8 May 84:2; 7-8].

It is worth noting that in the Wilton Park speech Buthelezi linked his federal ideas with the consociationalism proposed in the BC report, quoting from the report. These ideas informed the KwaZulu-Natal Indaba in progress in Durban in the first half of 1986.

The KwaZulu-Natal Indaba

A mixed bag of organizations was invited to the Indaba — 37 initially, then more after nine of those originally invited had refused. There appears to be no real pattern to the invitations: certain organizations could not but have refused and this must have been known to the organizers, Dr Dhlomo of Inkatha and Frank Martin of the now abolished Natal Provincial Council. However, nine of the participating organizations had taken part in the Buthelezi Commission, and another four had taken part under a different name. In other words, 13 groups had already endorsed the BC proposals.

Eight of the participating bodies represented business, while seven were from local and second tier government — not surprising as these groups, especially the business groups, and their political representatives, of whom there were eight, had been the major forces behind previous attempts at formulating regional or federal options, such as the Lombard Commission, the Buthelezi Commission, and the many structures of administrative cooperation that already exist between the province and KwaZulu. Thus, in the Indaba, in true consociational style with decisions being reached between elites in secrecy, the same interests that have dominated Natal economically and politically for decades were again trying to resolve the national crisis of profitability (accumulation) and stability or governability (reproduction) at a regional level.

As some commentators have written:

> The closed doors, the pre-selection of participants, many of whom are not responsible to a constituency, and the unstated agenda do not augur well for a democratic future for Natal [Beall, et al, 1986:46].

It is notable that, although the emergency has taken its toll of individuals and organizations in South Africa through state action, the participants in the Indaba have been left remarkably unscathed, while the only meetings that have been allowed within the region, ostensibly to oppose state policy, have been those addressed by Buthelezi and the Zulu king. It is an ironical replay of the 1920s Inkata that sugar interests, the African petty bourgeoisie in Inkatha and Zulu ethnicity are coming together again. Already there is talk of a political party to join together the various interests that have been involved in the Indaba. The model being offered is that of the Democratic Turnhalle Alliance (DTA) in Namibia. Following previous claims that SABA would force Vorster to the conference table in the same way Ian Smith had met Muzorewa, Chirau and Sithole, the Turnhalle conference was once again a singularly inappropriate choice for a 'liberation' movement, though it revealed the shallowness of Inkatha's analysis. The Turnhalle conference was an attempt by Vorster to stabilize Namibia in the wake of independence in the Portuguese territories, at the same time that Rhodesia was trying its hand at the facade of multi-racialism with Muzorewa. The Turnhalle conference, in September 1975, had been described as 'a motley gathering of largely South African-selected tribal delegates', and gave rise to the Democratic Turnhalle Alliance (CIIR, 1986:19-20). This is where the Indaba and Inkatha found their historical precedents.

Inkatha and white politics

The most striking aspect of Buthelezi's and the Inkatha leadership's contact with

171

white political parties and personalities is its contrast with their clashes with most black and non-racial opposition groups.

The 'Mahlabatini Declaration' signed by Buthelezi and Harry Schwarz (see above, p.170) contained five 'principles' of peaceful change: material and educational advancement, consultation in constitutional planning, a federal system and the safeguarding of cultures through a bill of rights (KLAD, 4:139; ST, 6 Jan. 74). Harry Schwarz was then in the United Party (UP), which has since become the New Republic Party (NRP). Schwarz later led a breakaway party which later joined with the Progressive Party to become the PFP. For many years Buthelezi has had close contact with the PFP and its forerunners, especially with the Natal members of this party of big business. In mid-1976 he called for a 'shadow' body to consist of the Progressive Reform Party (PRP, now the PFP), the UP and Inkatha (St, 4 Dec. 76; Langner, 1983:218). This was presented as defiance of the Improper Interference Act which prohibited joint political action between races, and which has now been withdrawn.

In 1977 Inkatha issued a memorandum entitled 'People's Movement for Radical Peaceful Change', to form the basis of discussion with the PRP. Its 17 points were said to be in line with PRP thinking except for the last point which went further in its advocacy of 'the greatest possible redistribution of wealth commensurate with maximizing the productivity of commerce, trade and industry whether state or privately owned' (RDM, 14 Jan. 77). Despite its title this document was far from radical, except in its expressed belief in a non-racialist future for South Africa. From then on the contact between the PRP/PFP and Inkatha increased until it was formalized with a standing steering committee formed in 1980 (Langner, 1983:220; NM, 20 Nov. 80). This was a confirmation of repeated assurances that the two parties agreed on most matters of principle (for example, RDM, 21 Aug. 78; ST, 24 Aug. 78). Hackland has commented that from the PFP's side:

> . . . the party was forced to rely almost exclusively on its contact with Inkatha, the personal political vehicle of M.G. Buthelezi, to demonstrate the compatibility of its policies with black aspirations: a fact that Buthelezi was not slow to point out to the party [1982:23].

Their agreement is not surprising since the 'class agency' Inkatha has consolidated in 1970s and 1980s South Africa is similar to the role the PFP has fulfilled. Possibly the suggested 'Natal Alliance' will allow the organizational linking of the two political bodies on a regional basis.

Inkatha, with its politics of realism, has maintained contact with the National Party, since it is after all the governing party in the country. Initially, during the 1950s, 1960s and early 1970s, the state would have preferred a more pliable bantustan leader in the numerically dominant 'Zulu' territory, but by 1978 they had come round sufficiently to hold formal discussions. In November that year an Inkatha 'think tank' met Dr Gerrit Viljoen, rector of the Rand Afrikaanse Universiteit, chairman of the Broederbond and now Minister of Education and Development Aid, and other prominent NP members (RDM, 10 Nov. 78). Buthelezi suggested in an interview early the next year that the Broederbond was now meeting Inkatha because it had become a force to be reckoned with (interview Dick Usher, STb, 2 Apr. 79).

Since then there have been many contacts, both formal and informal. Buthelezi has addressed students at Afrikaans campuses, while the youth alliances between the Inkatha Youth Brigade and conservative Afrikaner youth bodies have been mentioned (see above, p.70). Even the Unification Church (the Moonies), through the International Cultural Foundation and the Professors World Peace Academy, has been instrumental in arranging contact between Inkatha leaders and NP academics and politicians. In 1981 a meeting in Greece brought together 22 South Africans 'from a wide range of political backgrounds', including Inkatha representatives, the Rev. Allan Hendrickse of the Labour Party, and NP figures such as MP Dr Stoffel van der Merwe (eg St, 1 Jun. 81). The Moonie connection probably works through the South African state.

Against his fairly cordial relations with the NP in recent years and his close contact with parliamentary white opposition politics over a long time, there are the vitriolic attacks Buthelezi has directed against whites who criticize him or his movement from a left-wing perspective. For some reason he has reserved the term 'liberal' for them, such as in his verbal attacks on then NUSAS president Andew Boraine in 1980 and on former Witwatersrand University Students Representative Council president Sammy Adelman in 1981.

Selling Inkatha

While this book largely deals with the content of what Inkatha 'sells' to a regional, national and international audience (Buthelezi's political 'marketplace'), it is important to draw attention to the manner in which it is done. The most effective salesman for the movement is without doubt Chief Gatsha Buthelezi himself. He appears to relish publicity and is well aware of the power of mass media. Events are frequently staged for the benefit of local and international television and the press, such as the 'protests' outside the home of the US consul general in Durban in favour of continued investment, and during Senator Edward Kennedy's visit to Durban, the welcoming parties when Buthelezi returns home from overseas, and the UWUSA launch on May Day 1986, to name but a few. Chief Buthelezi has drawn most of Inkatha's public image to himself — he is the one who is interviewed, who is photographed in an impressive range of dress and headgear, and who is given 'human interest' magazine coverage. It has never been possible to think of the Inkatha movement without central reference to Buthelezi. He personifies Inkatha in a unique fashion; his central position is unchallenged.

This central position arises out of several factors. There is his 'traditional' role in Zulu society, his unbroken leadership in the politics of the bantustan, and his presidency of Inkatha, a position practically reserved for him in the constitution. These historical and structural factors, combined with his personality, have made him the 'voice of the people'. The only other person in Inkatha making a significant number of speeches at present is secretary general Oscar Dhlomo.

If we take Buthelezi's speeches from the years 1984 and 1985 (of which we have 163 on catalogue) we find, as is to be expected, that the largest number of speeches were addressed to Inkatha members (22), but the others show a remarkable awareness of the value of foreign business and political contact.

The table over says nothing about the content of the speeches. While such an analysis has not been undertaken for the purposes of this book (see Booysen, 1982, for such a study), a distinction can be drawn between speeches obviously given with the knowledge that they would be reported, and those given to Inkatha's rural constituency. The latter are important because of the illiteracy among many of Inkatha's members; the spoken word, directly heard, has a

overseas meetings with business	7
local meetings with foreign business	9
overseas meetings with politicians	10*
local meetings with foreign politicians	15
other overseas (eg universities)	13
meetings with local business	14
local politicians and national politics	12
KwaZulu and regional politics	16
Inkatha (eg conferences, Brigades)	22
media representatives	3
religious	7
local trade unions (Inkatha's first affiliated union)	1
Afrikaans universities	4**
English universities	2
Zulu history (mostly Shaka Day celebrations)	6
other	22

greater impact on them. Inkatha meetings in rural areas, therefore, have all the paraphernalia of marches, uniforms, songs, banners and flags, and food (an important drawcard where many people are starving).

The media-orientated speeches are more important for the wider distribution of their content than for their immediate purpose. The immediate delivery is a formality, and the content frequently has little reference to that moment and the event it claims to be addressing. Copies of speeches are distributed to the press with great efficiency, or published (see Buthelezi, 1979a), or partially reprinted in one of the KwaZulu or Inkatha glossy publications. These are at present *Clarion Call* and *Umxoxi*, both published by the Bureau of Communications, Department of the Chief Minister. The Bureau is KwaZulu's own 'information department' and is yet another benefit to Inkatha of its near total overlap with the KLA.

The two publications above are not Inkatha's first ventures in the media field (in the past it published directly and not through the KLA). In 1973 Buthelezi told the KLA that the publication of *The Black Voice* had been delayed as he would like to launch it personally — 'although it is not a publication of the KwaZulu Government it has our blessing' (KLAD, 3:256). In 1974 'The Voice of the Black People' was still being spoken about, this time by B.I. Dladla who told the KLA that a fundraising document had been drawn up by Buthelezi after a 1972 trip to Germany, in consultation with 'German editors of the paper which was going to be published here in KwaZulu under the name: "The Voice of the Black People"'. Dladla said he was not sure whether the money had been raised (KLAD, 5:46). Nothing appears to have come of this publication.

At the end of 1976 *The Nation* was launched, a mostly English-language monthly newspaper with a distribution that ranged from 25 000 to 40 000. It was hoped that it would become a weekly by the end of January 1977, and ultimately a daily, but it remained a monthly until late in 1978. This newspaper was said to be

---

*These include three memoranda, to President Reagan, Prime Minister Thatcher, and Israeli foreign minister Shamir, respectively.

**These include an address to the Annual Conference of the Centre for Investigation into Revolutionary Activities.

the 'culmination of years of struggle by KwaZulu leader Chief Gatsha Buthelezi to establish a newspaper that would "express black aspirations within the struggle for black liberation"'. The publishing company, Isizwe-Sechaba under the managing directorship of Walter Felgate, was reported to be owned by Inkatha (FM, 6 Jul. 79). However, at the time of formation it was denied that it was to be a mouthpiece for Inkatha (DN, 7 Dec. 76).

Felgate, with his long-standing contact with Buthelezi and a business background said to have included working for Rio Tinto mining corporation, apparently wanted to keep fairly close control over the content of the paper. After several consecutive issues had been banned by the state Felgate decided to move the Transvaal-based editorial staff to Durban, to make it a Zulu-language newspaper, and to confine it to the region. The editor, Gavin Robson, and senior editorial staff were not Zulu-speakers (Langner, 1983:90). Robson and seven reporters were fired. They argued that this move and the language change would reinforce the government's policy of 'tribal separatism' (FM, 6 Jul. 79). Felgate in turn argued that the move was made to consolidate in one area (it would facilitate distribution and the advertising the paper carried was mainly from small traders). *

In 1980 it was announced that *The Nation* was to cease publication. KwaZulu government information officer, the former exile Jordan Ngubane (see WIP, 1980), said it was due to 'a combination of factors', but other sources said the problem was financial. The latter reason had been given some support by fund-raising activities in Holland. Apparently, after a visit there by Buthelezi, a small action group was started and at the end of 1978 an advertisement was placed by the 'Newspaper for Black South Africa Work Group' in three major Dutch dailies, by the group's secretary S. Moll. The advertisements called for R25 000 to employ a journalist for *The Nation*. When asked why Buthelezi's name had not appeared in the advertisement Moll said there was no need as *The Nation* was independent and, more to the point, 'Gatsha Buthelezi's name would have a negative effect, because many people in Holland regard him as a sell-out of some kind' (RDM, 28 Dec. 78).

It was not only *The Nation* that suffered at the hands of the state in the mid-1970s. In 1976 the security police seized copies of the *Inkatha Bulletin*, printed by Zenith Press, of which Felgate was a director. Buthelezi took the matter up with Minister of Police Kruger after being informed by Felgate of the seizure (RDM, 25 Sep. 76, 27 Sep. 76; Schmahmann, 1978: 386).

The major English-language commercial newspapers, and more recently also the Afrikaans press, have given Inkatha and Buthelezi a disproportionate amount of coverage in terms of the range of political organizations and political positions that exist in South Africa. This has not only been in news coverage but also editorial discussion. It should be clear why this has been the case, with Buthelezi representing the conservative, non-violent, pro-capitalist, anti-disinvestment, compromising and pragmatic position that would coincide with the pressure of monopoly capital for a move towards non-racial capitalism. The appeal of the Inkatha position to newspaper interests has meant that what is often sycophantic journalism has been published while, on the other hand, material critical of the movement has been suppressed, consciously or less directly. In 1985 tensions created by a pro-Inkatha slant led to a 'sit-in strike' by several journalists

---

*Other editors included Buthelezi, Gibson Thula, L. Hodnett, G.R. Simpson, and Oscar Dhlomo.

employed by the Zulu-language *Ilanga* newspaper. They were protesting the 'newspaper's bias towards the Inkatha movement' (NM, 9 Dec. 85). *Ilanga*, along with all major Natal papers, is controlled by the Argus company's Natal Newspapers. The journalists said they feared for their lives because of the paper's bias — 'residents wanted to assault Ilanga journalists who went into townships, because they believed the journalists supported Inkatha', a representative of the strikers said. They claimed that all 'stories critical of Inkatha were discarded' (NM, 9 Dec. 85).*

With the amount of press coverage he receives it is little wonder that Buthelezi has received several 'Newsmaker of the Year' awards, such as that awarded by the Pretoria Press Club early in 1986. In 1985 he was the *Financial Mail's* 'Man of the Year'. This weekly commented on the award:

> History . . . is made by individuals. And the question is: who can deliver SA to a new era of conciliation and relative harmony? (We use the adjective 'relative' advisedly; it would be naive to believe that anything short of a smoking ruin would satisfy many of those now fomenting violence. They will have to be put down) . . .
> One name comes easily to mind . . . and it is that of Chief Mangosuthu Buthelezi . . . a man of compromise . . . he eschews violence . . . against disinvestment . . . against consumer boycotts . . . an unabashed free marketeer [6 Dec. 85].

With a certain irony the same issue of the *Financial Mail* reported a Human Sciences Research Council study that was to be released in that week, which found that Buthelezi received 'a surprisingly low 2.4%' of support as the person Africans would want to lead the country.

It is not only in the commercial press that Inkatha and Buthelezi are feted. While there is no doubt that the state and its mouthpiece, the SABC (radio and television), were initially very hostile to the Inkatha movement, that has changed dramatically over the last 18 months or so. In 1974 the SABC's 'character assassination' of Buthelezi was condemned in the KLA. Ten years later the same Cliff Saunders who had been the guilty party then was guiding Buthelezi and others in an attack on the ANC on the SABC-TV 'News Focus' programme. This is one of many such programmes in which Buthelezi's views are now given, if not always complete approval, then at least necessary toleration.

'Inkatha' is taught at school level in KwaZulu (see elsewhere for a fuller discussion), while a film — *The Power is Ours* — is shown to hundreds of thousands of children through the educational system in the bantustan, a comprehensive publicity exercise.

Inkatha undertakes propaganda and publicity directly through the 'elections, publicity and strategy' committee of the central committee and through the Bureau of Information in the (KwaZulu) chief minister's office. However, in 1979 the central committee also established the Inkatha Institute (Langner, 1983:87). It appears that the institute only took off in 1980 when its first director, Professor Lawrence Schlemmer, took a year's sabbatical from his post as director of the Centre for Applied Social Sciences at the University of Natal (FM, 1 Aug. 80). In

---

*Ironically, the same comment has been made by the far right South Africa First Campaign in a smear pamphlet entitled 'Buthelezi and Inkatha: the truth exposed' (Willmer, nd), which claimed that 'Much of the prominence Inkatha enjoys can be ascribed to the unstinting, servile and uncritical coverage given to Inkatha by the Argus/SAAN press'. However, Buthelezi has recently taken to suing these newspaper groups for some of the comment and reporting their newspapers have carried.

a reply to press questions about the formation of the institute, Professor Schlemmer reaffirmed the Inkatha policy of 'becoming institutionalized as an imperative force for the political change within the system'. The Inkatha Institute, which was fully operational by July 1980, was to help Inkatha become more relevant 'in the planning for peace'. In pursuit of the goal of 'becoming fully part of the political and social order', Inkatha had published its own newspaper (a reference to the ill-fated *The Nation*), had invested in 'business interests in various sectors', and had 'added a new subject to the black school curriculum in Natal' (Inkatha Institute, 1980).

The Inkatha Institute set itself the task of, inter alia, formulating a 'black response' (sic) to critical issues of debate (the present director is also a white, Peter Mansfield, a member of the PFP and a city councillor in Durban). It would provide information and do research, seeking 'constructive ways' of co-operating in development projects with private enterprise and state bodies at various levels. It would also create publicity material for Inkatha, to be disseminated through publications, conferences, the media, etc. The institute has set itself a clear path in the politics of contemporary South Africa: '. . . the institute would strengthen Inkatha's ability to pose alternatives to strategies employed by other black groups which lead to the growth of a violent revolutionary consciousness' (Survey, 1980:51). We have seen that in the eyes of the Inkatha leadership this would include just about every black or non-racial opposition group in South Africa.

After an initial stint in offices in poorer areas of Durban, the Inkatha Institute now shares an arcade with the supreme court in central Durban and occupies large and technologically well-equipped offices. It receives acknowledged funding from the department of the chief minister of KwaZulu, the Konrad Adenauer Foundation and the Urban Foundation (Inkatha, 1985:19). It has a staff of about 15 people.

One of the tasks of the institute has been to counter 'negative propaganda against Inkatha by some exile groups in parts of Europe' (Langner, 1983:89). A large part of this task is already fulfilled by the many overseas trips and addresses by Chief Buthelezi and other Inkatha functionaries. As Dhlomo told the Inkatha conference in 1985:

> Owing to financial constraints we are still unable to establish more information offices in London, Bonn and the USA. Nevertheless it is clear to us that our continued presence in the international political scene is becoming more and more important. Consequently, the Movement will have to devise financial means whereby the President will be enabled to travel more frequently overseas to put our case. I personally feel that we must aim at sending the President overseas at least six times a year. Our struggle is a just and noble one, and it is up to us to sell it to the international community as aggressively as possible [Inkatha, 1985: 9].

These trips have been going on for a long time.* In 1975, for example, Buthelezi told the KLA about a trip to Liberia, following an invitation by President Tolbert and his meeting with officials in Accra on the way back (KLAD, 5:79). Later in the session he read eight letters he had written to African leaders; in a newpaper column he was writing at the time he told his readers he had already visited

---

*His trips were mentioned in the Terrorism Act trial of Harry Gwala and nine others in Pietermaritzburg in 1976, when an alleged South African Congress of Trade Unions (SACTU) organizer told the court that it was felt necessary to form ANC cells because Buthelezi was '"occupying his mind with overseas matters"' (RDM, 8 Sep. 76).

Zambia, Tanzania, Kenya, Liberia, Ethiopia, Swaziland, Lesotho and Ghana (NM, 10 Mar. 75). This was the period of 'detente', a policy of Prime Minister Vorster's of which Buthelezi approved; he probably wanted to make the point that he was an important element in its success. Also in 1975 he told the KLA he had been invited to Canada to address the Synod of the Anglican Church there. He hoped that expenses for himself, his wife and an aide would be borne by the Canadian church but he assured the KLA that 'Although I am going under the Flag of the Church . . . I am in fact going there to perform these duties on behalf of KwaZulu' (KLAD, 7:966-7). The regular 'prayer breakfasts' Buthelezi holds fill a similar dual function.

On a visit to the USA in 1979 Buthelezi was reported to have spoken to the Foreign Policy Association, the World Affairs Council, a Christian political conference of the Association for Public Justice, State Department officials, the Phelps Stoke Foundation, Howard University, to have promoted a book of his speeches edited by the Rev Leonard Sullivan, to have given a *New York Times* interview and to have appeared on a national talk show hosted by Tom Snyder.

Inkatha has had the idea of establishing overseas missions for a long time, but especially since its break with the ANC in 1979 (DN, 20 Oct. 80). In 1980 the central committee was considering appointing a roving ambassador and it was speculated that Jordan Ngubane, with his range of foreign contacts gained in his years in exile, would fill the post (DN, 4 Jun. 80). This did not happen. In the same year Buthelezi told European audiences that Inkatha was to set up offices in Europe and the USA (ST, 19 Oct. 80). Inkatha's Dr Mdlalose said the movement was 'in an outward mood, we are marching ahead', and threatened to take aid from 'the East' (on Inkatha's own terms) as the West 'is not concerned with our welfare' (STb, 27 Jul. 80; Munger Africana Library Notes, 1980).

In 1983 Langner wrote that Inkatha had an 'information representative' in Washington DC — Dr Lorna Hahn. She was said to be assisted by retired senator Vance Hartke 'who bears the title of American Legal Counsel for Inkatha', and Professor Albert Blaustein of Rutgers University Law School, 'who is Inkatha's Advisor on Constitutional Affairs' (1983:90). Hahn's formal relationship with Inkatha was claimed to have been of short duration, but it was said she continued to introduce Buthelezi during his trips to the USA (personal communication, Inkatha Institute, 1984).

In 1982 Buthelezi attempted to raise money from the Konrad Adenauer Foundation for the establishment of a 'permanent Inkatha office in the West German capital' (NM, 31 Mar. 82). The West German connection through the Konrad Adenauer Foundation and the Christian Democratic Union (CDU), and earlier through the Arnold Bergstraesser Institute, needs fuller investigation because it has existed for so long. In 1986 the ruling CDU publicly announced its full support for Inkatha, calling Buthelezi 'the most important leader of the blacks in South Africa'. The CDU called for a negotiated transition to majority rule in South Africa and said that 'revolutionary marxist groups could not be the guarantors of peaceful change . . .' (NM, 22 Feb. 86).*

The Arnold Bergstraesser Institute (ABI) attitude surveys from 1974 to 1977, released at a conference in Freiburg in 1978, set the tone for many subsequent

---

*West German investment in South Africa is very large — direct investment was said to be DM 6m in 1976, while roughly 300 companies have South African subsidiaries. Their profits 'are protected if returned to West Germany because of a double taxation treaty signed with Pretoria in 1973, which was retroactive in 1965' (Schultz and Hansen, 1984).

surveys to determine attitudes of Africans to political leaders and change. These studies have become a surrogate democracy, with battles fought on academic platforms instead of at public meetings and with public participation. The ABI study gave Buthelezi considerable prominence. The *Sunday Times* wrote in an editorial:

> This week Chief Buthelezi, armed with the authoritative research of German academics which placed him ahead of all others as a leader of blacks . . ., stepped on to the national political stage to confront the man who is equally dominant in his leadership of whites. . . This week he made his move. He was no longer merely a Zulu chieftain. He and Mr Vorster, said Chief Buthelezi, were the two individuals most intimately involved in the country's political struggle. . . But we offer this admonition to Chief Buthelezi: Serious debate has scant hope of success if the language used lacks temperance . . . [7 Jul. 78].

(Also see Duncan, 1978, and the response by Dhlomo, 1979).

The one European city where an Inkatha office has been established is Amsterdam, from which the prolific publicist Reina Steenwijk operates (see Steenwijk, 1984). It was reported that, because of the Dutch government's policy of not granting visas to bantustan officials (unless on holiday or visiting relatives), Buthelezi travels to Holland as president of Inkatha and not as chief minister of KwaZulu (SABC Radio Today, 5 Nov. 84).

These examples show that the Inkatha movement has a wide-ranging involvement in selling itself both nationally and internationally. Inkatha is welcomed overseas by conservative groups in the main, and provided with a number of platforms for publicizing itself. Locally Inkatha has had an overwhelmingly sympathetic press, careful in the extreme not to offend Buthelezi and to publicize his views even when these fairly directly contradict Inkatha's actions on the ground.

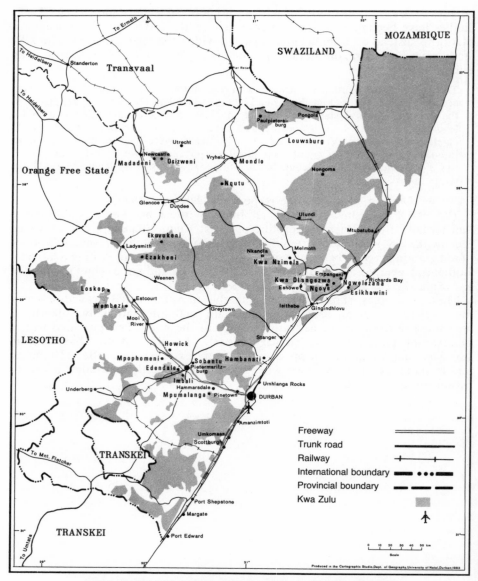

POLITICAL MAP OF NATAL PROVINCE
indicating KwaZulu boundaries,
towns and major African townships

8. Picking up the Gauntlet

.I think it is time for Inkatha to establish training camps where branches and regions are schooled in the employment of anger in an orderly fashion. We need to be able to control riots. We need to be able to conduct meetings in the midst of chaos which other people try to create. We need to tone up our muscles so that the dove of peace sits easily on the spear. I think we need to create well-disciplined and regimented Impis in every Inkatha region which can be called out for the protection of that which is so sacred to Inkatha and black South Africa* [BS, 20 Jun. 80].

In many ways activities at the provincial, bantustan and local level prescribe Inkatha's stance at the national and international level. However, it is in local politics that Buthelezi's international pronouncements are most obviously belied. The international rhetoric of non-violence is frequently not borne out by Inkatha practice at the local level.

The scale of violence in Durban's townships since August 1985, coinciding with the height of the general unrest in South Africa, has obscured a continuity with previous unrest in the region over the past ten years. While much of the impetus towards unrest stems from social and economic conditions, it is also necessary to explain the nature of some of the local political forces at work in Durban and other parts of Natal and KwaZulu.

Amongst precursors of the violence that erupted in August 1985 are several points of simmering contention in the relations between the KwaZulu Legislative Assembly and Inkatha, and the black people of Natal. For a decade Inkatha and the KLA have met opposition in implementing the obligations vested in them by the central state, such as policing, taxing, collecting rent and maintaining the structures of rural control (the chiefs). Almost by definition, collaboration with the apparatus of the central state in providing services such as education, health and welfare, housing and transport, means that the KLA and Inkatha do not have the means to tackle the political and economic frustrations of an impoverished and powerless people. When it comes to delivering the goods in terms of services, the KwaZulu government is as impoverished; when it must fulfil its obligations to its 'constituents', it is relatively powerless to protect them from the depredations of

---

* An 'impi' is an armed force. The term 'amabutho' is used more specifically: 'One of the fundamental elements of northern Nguni society, the homestead, continued to operate as a productive unit under Shaka's rule. But its productive capacity was to some extent gained by the enforced service of young males in age-regiments (amabutho). The homesteads would be deprived of the labour of these men for the length of their amabutho service. Which could last up to twenty years. The primary function of the amabutho, which were commanded by izinduna, was military, but they also served the state in other ways, forming hunting parties or labour-gangs for public works' (Maylam, 1986:29). Buthelezi has used the term 'amabutho' to refer to the youth attending the Emandleni-Matleng camp (see below), eg 'The 50 amabutho arrived at the end of January 1984 to start a period of training in basic community agriculture. . .' (BS, 27 Nov. 84:6).

apartheid, or to resist the true role of a bantustan government. In this it is no different from other bantustan branches of the central state.

Education for nationhood

In the mid-1970s, shortly after Inkatha's formation, education and schools were early testing grounds of the political integrity of the burgeoning movement. The politicization of educational problems in Natal must be seen in the context of South Africa in the period which led to the Soweto uprising of 1976, when the appalling quality, and outright lack, of education for black people became a symbol of wider political frustrations.

The most visible and maintained popular opposition to the South African government in the past 10 years has been that of schoolchildren and students. It is not surprising that black schools are so important an arena of opposition. The education available to black people is in itself inferior, and the inequality of education and opportunity between blacks and whites in South Africa in a time of recession and high unemployment has emphasized the sheer lack of opportunity for black youth generally, and African youth in particular. In the face of repression, schools and other educational institutions have provided a rallying place for opposition and a relatively organized constituency for mobilizing and directing dissent.

Early in its existence, Inkatha recognized the importance of youth, particularly schoolchildren, as a constituency to be captured and defended against more radical ideologies and political movements. The schools themselves provided Inkatha with a convenient site of mobilization. The school syllabus in KwaZulu also offered a potential vehicle for indoctrination. Hence an early initiative of the KwaZulu Legislative Assembly was to assert control over education in KwaZulu.

In South Africa the education system is divided along racial lines. The intentionally inferior education the government offers Africans is referred to colloquially, and derisively, as 'Bantu Education'. In 1978 Oscar Dhlomo brought a motion to the KLA to repeal the Bantu Education Act. The wresting of KwaZulu schools from the control of Bantu Education was portrayed as a liberatory act, a demonstration of the KLA's commitment to oppose government alongside the countrywide protests against Bantu Education that rocked South Africa in 1976 and 1977. Talking about disturbances in KwaZulu schools in 1979, Oscar Dhlomo said:

> . . . I haven't found any evidence of unrest relating to political factors . . . The pupils in Soweto were substantially revolting against the system of Bantu Education . . . we no longer have that system in KwaZulu . . . we did away with the act . . . and replaced it with our own act . . . And secondly, our schools are not built by the Department of Education and Training, so they cannot be said to be symbols of oppression, as the Soweto kids used to say of their schools [KCAV, 158-166].

Dhlomo neglected to confront the fact that changing the Act had not changed the poor content of Bantu Education. On the contrary, the quality of education in KwaZulu, judged by the conventional criteria of exam results, facilities, teacher training and pupil/teacher ratios, is probably poorer than that provided by the central government Department of Education and Training in the townships outside KwaZulu (see, for instance, Bot, 1985; DN, 18 Feb. 86; STb, 9 Jun. 85; DN, 19 Jul. 85). But control over education in KwaZulu had allowed the KLA and

BILLY PADDOCK

The 'KwaNatal' proposals would share power in Natal between Buthelezi and the white establishment.

BILLY PADDOCK

US links: Buthelezi on a US visit meets representatives of IBM, Goodyear, Envirotech International, General Motors, 3M, Mobil Oil and Union Carbide.

BILLY PADDOCK

Inkatha impis march at the head of Buthelezi's cavalcade at the 1984 Shaka Day celebrations in Lamontville — with Lamontville community leader Sibiya at the head. Most residents fled.

Prince Gideon Zulu (in black cap to right of van, above) leads impis on the rampage in Umlazi during the 1985 Shaka Day rally while the police look on.

BILLY PADDOCK

Inkatha to introduce an ideological thrust in KwaZulu's schools.

In 1976, when KwaZulu education was still controlled by the central government, the Department of Education and Training (DET) gave permission for education personnel to become Inkatha members as long as this did not interfere with their duties. This was followed in 1977 by a circular from the DET which told circuit inspectors to allow school principals to hold Inkatha Youth Brigade meetings in schools (Langner, 1083:175). Buthelezi said the DET had made these concessions because there was proof that Inkatha had kept unrest out of KwaZulu schools (DN, 10 May 78). In 1978, after the repeal of the Bantu Education Act, Oscar Dhlomo, as the new minister of education and culture, warned that teachers who remained 'outside the ambit of Inkatha' would be 'suspect' and might not be 'entrusted with the future of our children'. He said his new department would investigate which schools had neglected the formation of Inkatha Youth Brigade ·branches, and those which had would have to explain themselves 'convincingly' (NM, 12 May 78).

Inkatha established the Inkatha Youth Brigade in 1976 for the stated purpose of playing 'the vanguard role of upholding and consolidating the gains of the movement'. Schools were the main areas of recruitment, though 'youth' was broadly defined as 'those people who are accepted by the youth population as youth'. It has been argued that Inkatha's portrayal of itself as the internal wing of the liberation movement with the Youth Brigade as its radical spur has been an important factor in attracting young people to the brigades (Teague, 1983:18-23).

In the face of growing militancy Inkatha has needed to placate its youth membership on the issue of armed struggle by emphasizing that non-violence is a strategic rather than a moral choice. In 1978 Buthelezi told trainees at a youth leadership course:

> Even though Inkatha understands the impatience of the youth and the fact that others had no option but to choose the armed struggle, the movement believes that constituency politics and the mobilization of the people will bring about change . . . I have a duty to warn you as our youth to be careful, and to make a distinction between real bravery and foolish bravado. We all admire and praise our brothers and sisters who have died in jail . . . But we have to admit that we have achieved very little by their supreme sacrifice [BS, 27 Jun.78].

The Youth Brigade's path is strictly controlled and guided by Inkatha's leadership. Far from being Inkatha's vanguard it appears to play a supportive, rearguard, and increasingly militaristic role in carrying out the directives of Inkatha leadership. In 1978, though, Buthelezi may have had reason to worry about more radical tendencies in the Youth Brigade. In August that year three members of the Youth Brigade were expelled. One newspaper said the expulsions followed the discovery of a conspiracy aimed at undermining Buthelezi's integrity during the Youth Leadership Training Course mentioned above. Also implicated in the conspiracy was Professor Sibusiso Bengu, secretary general of Inkatha and an important ideologue in the movement's early years. Bengu was dismissed from his post as secretary general, and amongst the reasons given for his dismissal was the accusation that he was leading youth against Buthelezi (NW, 20 Oct.78).

Bengu was popular with students because he had shown sympathy for their educational grievances and probably also because his political ideas and sympathies did not follow the direction Inkatha was taking. He was not dismissive of other political movements or groupings that had considerable appeal to young people at the time. He said Buthelezi had accused him of supporting the Black People's Convention, and his response was: 'What I said and will continue to say is that Inkatha is not working against BPC or other liberation groups.' Bengu seems to have been the last idealistic heretic in Inkatha's central committee and in some ways his dismissal signalled a growing intransigence in Inkatha's ideology and the muzzling of youthful dissent. At the second Inkatha Youth Congress in 1979, after Bengu's departure, the Youth Brigade charged all young members of Inkatha to prevent disturbances and to secure sound human relationships in schools.

Once the KLA had captured KwaZulu's educational terrain, Inkatha moved to capture hearts and minds both through promoting the formation of Youth Brigade branches in schools and through institution of the Inkatha syllabus in 1979. This was a compulsory hour per week throughout primary and secondary schooling to sell the philosophy of 'Ubunto-Botho', variously described as 'the mixing of African communalism with free enterprise' and 'the fusion of traditional African and Westminster models' (FM, 11 May 79; Teague, 1983:21). Dhlomo said it should be regarded as 'a basic step to train youth for nationhood, service, devotion and commitment' (Langner, 1983:176).

When asked, in 1979, whether KwaZulu was developing an educational system specific to regional needs, Dhlomo said that while on a general level the school syllabus was not changed, two attempts were being made to move away from the deficiencies of Bantu Education. One was to foster the growth of technical education, which had been discouraged on the grounds that technical jobs had been a white preserve. The other was to introduce 'a subject that sort of builds up the self-image of our pupils . . . a reaction against the teachings of Bantu Education'. He said this subject, called 'good citizenship', would be based on 'the teachings of Inkatha, self-reliance, self-esteem, and so on . . .' (KCAV, 158-166).

Buthelezi has compared the Inkatha syllabus with 'civics' taught in other countries:

> The only political teaching done in schools is the impartial representation of the political influence, for instance, that had brought about the state of affairs that exist in any country together with the political or government structure of a country . . . It has never been considered wise to introduce politics as such into schools . . . [KLAD. 6:529].

He stressed that the Inkatha syllabus dealt with all liberation movements: 'with the ANC, the PAC, with black leaders in the history of South Africa. It is not indoctrination in any sense' (Buthelezi interviewed by Joe Thloloe, Post, 17 Mar. 80). David Msomi, Inkatha's regional organizer in Natal, was probably more accurate about the syllabus's intent when he explained that people are taught how the political vacuum left by the banning of the PAC and the ANC was filled by the emergence of Inkatha and how it became 'the black voice, the expression of the aspirations of the people who were politically poor, and how they enrich themselves through Inkatha' (quoted in Teague, 1983:22).

There are inconsistencies in some of the claims made about membership of the Youth Brigade and the number of branches that have been established (Teague, 1983:23). For instance, in 1981, Lawrence Schlemmer said a recruiting drive in secondary schools had resulted in an increase in membership that meant Youth Brigade membership was 29% of Inkatha's total membership (Survey, 1981:26). In 1980, however, the Youth Brigade had claimed a membership of 120 000, giving it 40% of Inkatha's total membership (Survey, 1980:48), which would suggest either a drop in Youth Brigade membership between 1980 and 1981 or a dramatic increase in Women's Brigade or general membership. Taking other figures into account, though, there clearly has been a dramatic rise in Youth Brigade membership since the introduction of the Inkatha syllabus. What is more pertinent is that the increase in Youth Brigade membership does not appear to have increased its ability to fulfil its mandate of preventing 'disturbances' in schools.

In 1977, Buthelezi told a rally in Umlazi, 'Our Zulu youth has shown consistent responsibility. They did not burn down our schools which we built ourselves and by which we raise ourselves' (DN, 14 Mar. 77). The relative quiescence of Natal schools during the nationwide school unrest in 1976 and 1977 has been attributed by some to Inkatha's 'restraining influence', for which Inkatha was happy to take credit. The years between 1976 and the KwaMashu school boycott in 1980 were not unmarked by conflict, but Inkatha tended to explain student protests in this period as being the work of manipulators, particularly the BPC and Soweto students, and underplayed student grievances about overcrowding, lack of facilities, and various unpopular school regulations (Teague, 1983:32).

In 1980, a well-supported schools boycott in KwaMashu began to erode the myth of Inkatha's ability to channel youthful anger within the allotted boundaries of Youth Brigade activity. When KwaMashu pupils joined the country-wide boycott at the end of April 1980, the initial response of Buthelezi and Inkatha was one of guarded sympathy for the 'Indian and Coloured' protests against unequal education, while KwaMashu children were urged to return to school. By the middle of May, with no sign of KwaMashu children obeying Inkatha's instructions, Buthelezi turned against the Indian community and 'non-Zulu' agitators. He said the boycotts were orchestrated by people at the University of Durban-Westville and at the Medical School of Natal University, which attracts black students from all over the country. Just as Soweto students had been blamed for school unrest in Natal during the 1970s, in 1980 the boycotts were variously deemed by Inkatha to be the work of 'Xhosa' lawyers, 'foreign representatives', 'political opportunists', and trade-union leaders (KwaZulu Government Diary, 1981; Teague, 1983:36; DN, 15 Dec. 80).

By the middle of May it was clear that Inkatha had assumed the task, performed elsewhere in the country by the police and government, of forcing children to return to school and punishing those that didn't. Riot squad police patrolled the streets of KwaMashu in significant numbers but Inkatha was as immediate an opponent of the boycotters, both ideologically and in its employment of force and violence. On one occasion the riot squad police intervened to prevent an Inkatha impi armed with knobkerries (clubs), spears and knives from marching on a group of about 500 pupils (RDM, 19 May 80).

Inkatha seemed even more determined to stop the boycotts when there was evidence of strong support for scholars from parents and other members of the community (see WIP, 1980b:31; and 33-34). On 12 May a meeting of about 1000 parents elected a parents' committee to support boycotting pupils. By this time the boycott encompassed all KwaMashu schools and had spread to five schools in Umlazi. At a rally in KwaMashu on 18 May Buthelezi told the crowd:

> Evil political forces thought that they could attack Inkatha by mobilizing children. There is a total onslaught against Inkatha . . . We can identify the political riff-raff . . . We will shake them and drive them out from our midst, and if they are not careful they may find that they run risks in what they do, one of which may be having their skulls

cracked, as none of us can predict what form the anger they raise takes [BS, 18 May 80].

Considerable attention was given by the press and the judiciary to Inkatha's willingness to employ force against schoolchildren during the 1980 school boycotts in KwaMashu. In response to criticism by the ANC, Buthelezi said he had not called on impis to smash the boycott. He added:

There was *destruction of black property* and use of violence to which we reacted by calling out *parents and other members of the public* [emphasis added] [NM, 2 Jul. 80].

Replying to a critical article in the *Rand Daily Mail*, Buthelezi wrote:

There is no black person who can condone the inadequacies which black children suffer from as far as the South African Educational system is concerned. When coloured children followed by Indian children launched the boycotts I perfectly understood . . . when black children did so in sympathy later on, I also appreciated this . . . But just then the school boycotts were being used by certain exiles and their surrogates in South Africa *to denigrate me. It was this to which I was opposed* [emphasis added] [RDM, 15 Jan. 81].

Buthelezi's responses to accusations of violence by Inkatha supporters are quoted at length here because they illustrate some recurring trends in Inkatha's mode of justifying violence and distancing itself from liability. First, there is the suggestion that black property is sacrosanct and that its destruction deserves righteous retaliation. Second, Inkatha vigilantes are described as 'parents and other members of the public' as though their actions were simply the predictable and legitimate responses of orderly citizens faced by naughty schoolchildren. Third, opposition is deemed to be engineered by outsiders. Finally, the boycotts are portrayed as an attack on Buthelezi, and therefore, more than ever, deserving of retaliation.

Buthelezi had good reason to feel sensitive about student activism in May and June 1980. While KwaMashu and Umlazi schoolchildren stood firm in their boycott despite sustained harassment by the police and Inkatha, students at the Ngoye campus of the University of Zululand were demonstrating that Inkatha held as little appeal for them as for the boycotting scholars. Inkatha's attempt to break the school boycott in KwaMashu is likely to have contributed to student restiveness at Ngoye. In addition there was a five-year history of tension between students and Inkatha and Buthelezi. Students had long been vocal in their criticism of Buthelezi as a government puppet and Inkatha as a bantustan movement (see Teague, 1983;46-51).

At a meeting in the middle of May, students adopted a resolution calling on Buthelezi to keep Inkatha supporters from wearing their uniform at the graduation ceremony and for 'traditional warriors armed with sticks' to be kept off campus. Buthelezi's response was one that was becoming predictable. He claimed that student actions were masterminded from outside — in this instance he held Dr Sibusiso Bengu responsible. This was followed on the day of the graduation ceremony by the arrival of impis 'in a massive show of force' while students had earlier been dispersed by police with dogs and tear gas (STb, 15 May 80; ST, 25 May 80).

After the ceremony, the president of the Ngoye SRC, Reggie Hadebe, and several other students were beaten by Inkatha supporters. So angered was Buthelezi by the opposition of students in the heartland of his KwaZulu that he suggested Ngoye was dispensable if the students didn't toe the Inkatha line:

> . . . If I find a conflict between Inkatha's aims and objectives and our means of implementing those objectives on the one hand and the activity encouraged or perhaps even tolerated by an institution such as the University of Zululand . . . then I will question the authenticity of that university in our midst. I will have no hesitation in setting about the establishment of a true university of the people of KwaZulu if the current state of affairs continues [Presidential address in *Inkatha*, June 1980:16].

In a way Buthelezi *did* set up a new kind of post-secondary education. This is the Youth Service Corps. In response to the Youth Brigade's failure to assert control over scholar and student opposition in 1980, Inkatha agreed at its National Conference of that year to set up a Youth Service Corps along paramilitary lines. In June 1980 Buthelezi told the Inkatha annual conference:

> It is quite clear to me that our teachers have failed to inculcate in our youth the right attitude to our struggle. They have failed to elicit from the youth that sense of commitment which adds to our total strength in unity . . . Our communities must produce more viable parent/teacher associations. Our branches have failed to tackle this most important aspect of liberation . . . in the matter of education we are failing [BS, 20 Jan. 80].

There is little evidence of the Youth Brigade's presence in the 1980 school boycott. Teague suggests that since the boycott, at its height, was one hundred percent effective, it seems likely that Youth Brigade members supported, or at least sympathized with the boycott, and that this came as a shock to the Inkatha leadership (Teague, 1983:44). Buthelezi's call for more viable parent/teacher associations also suggests the failure of Women's Brigade branches in fulfilling their brief of playing 'an instructive role' in the 'upbringing of the children towards the objectives of the movement'. In October 1980, responding perhaps to Buthelezi's chastisement, the Women's Brigade reaffirmed total opposition to school boycotts and called on members to use 'any means at their disposal' to prevent them (NW, 17 Oct. 80).

In contrast to Inkatha's failure to demonstrate unity of intent and action between youth and parents, the solidarity between the boycotting children and their parents in KwaMashu was impressive while it lasted and it may have played a part in developing Inkatha's sensitivity about accusations of 'ageism' dominating the movement. Steve Biko hinted at an important dilemma for Inkatha when he said:

> Gatsha is supported by oldies, for good reasons, since Gatsha protects the stability that the older persons need. We do not look upon the solution to injustice as an expectation but a duty. Here lies the dilemma of the old: between duty and bread [Teague, 1983:19].

Inkatha tackles this claim in a number of ways. The introduction of Youth Brigades and the Inkatha syllabus were both initiatives to extend Inkatha's hold on young people. In 1983 Buthelezi said:

> Inkatha is responsive to the demands of youth and youth in Inkatha is responsive to the demands of adults. There is in Inkatha no formal clash between the Youth Brigade and adult membership [interview with Buthelezi by Teague, 1983].

In 1984 he added that unlike the Congress of South African Students (COSAS), Inkatha youth were the 'masters of their own political destiny' and that there was 'no rift between the generations in Inkatha' (Survey, 984:11, 12).

However, the Brigades and the syllabus have not been sufficient to capture the imagination of an increasingly politicized youth, especially, or most visibly, those in the urban areas of Natal. Hence, in recent years, Inkatha has had to develop further strategies for enticing youthful imagination and commitment. These strategies are evident in Inkatha's insistence that there is no generation gap and in the promotion of an ideology of family life, as proposed in Dhlomo's report to the Inkatha Conference in June 1985 (*Inkatha*, 1985:23-25). A social and cultural sub-committee of Inkatha under the chairmanship of Dr F.T. Mdlalose 'seeks to influence the Black Community away from deviant socio-cultural practices and towards more African socio-cultural ways of life' (*Inkatha*, 1985:23). The committee wished to restore 'African socio-cultural' values in such matters as 'pre-marital pregnancies', 'family planning' and the 'roles of various members in family life'. The programme on 'protocol, courtesy and chivalry' was convened by S.D. Ngcobo and regular meetings were held between the sub-committee and the SABC in 'an endeavour to set up socially acceptable programmes on radio and TV' (*Inkatha*, 1985:24, 25).

At a more practical level Inkatha concentrated, after the 1980 boycotts, on the development of its Youth Service Corps. To an extent the Youth Service Corps relied on Youth Brigades structures. At an address to the Youth Brigade Conference in 1982, Buthelezi said the training schemes envisaged for the Youth Service Corps would be based on the structures of the Youth Brigade which would be formed into 'companies' belonging to a 'regiment' for a particular area. The formation of the Youth Service Corps suggested that Inkatha realized it needed a readily trained and mobilized force to carry out its threats to pick up the 'gauntlet' thrown down by its opposition. In July 1980, in a paper presented for discussion to Inkatha's Central Committee, it was said:

> We will not brook black divisive forces and the disruption of our programmes . . . a para-military development is also necessary from the point of view of providing us with protective mechanisms which safeguard those things we erect in the national interest. When we build schools . . . we must see to it that those schools serve the function for which they are intended. *When we set about improving the calibre of our education, we must do so with a widespread discipline that brooks no interference* [emphasis added] [*Inkatha*, 1980:2].

The KwaZulu education department remains structurally and financially dependent on the very inadequate planning and budget of the central government. It seems probable that the KLA's inability, under the circumstances, to improve education or employment opportunities, or to mediate student grievances, has informed Inkatha's rationale for para-military developments. In 1982 Buthelezi mentioned the Youth Service Corps' role in harnessing the energies of young people with a bleak future by providing an alternative to formal education or employment:

> There are many who will not be fortunate enough to remain at school or go to university after they have completed their schooling. They will be victims of apartheid in circumstances beyond their control . . . For them we must have a special place. This place is the Emandleni-Matleng camp development [BS, 21 Aug. 82].

While it is often underplayed by Inkatha, the para-military thrust of the Youth Service Corps has been well documented (Teague, 1983:67-75; Central Committee Resolution, Ulundi, 19 Jul. 80). Langner suggested that Inkatha had decided to move into a 'paramilitary phase', in reaction to 'the snubbing by the ANC', in 1979 (Langner, 1983:154). It seems likely that an important purpose of this militarism has been to placate youthful radicalism and frustration with Inkatha's non-violent strategies.

There are many constructive aspects to the Youth Service Corps programme, especially where it involves rural development and disaster relief (Teague, 1983:68-74). Its paramilitary nature has been dwelt on here because it is relevant to Inkatha's strategies for confronting opposition. The extent to which the Youth Service Corps and the Youth Brigade have channelled the frustrations of urban youth will be explored in the discussion below of Inkatha's moves to capture and defend the urban terrain.

'Making geographical gains': the townships

In Natal, not only the country-wide dynamic of migrant and commuting workers links towns and townships to rural bantustans: the townships themselves are, in most cases, within the ambit of a bantustan administration, the KwaZulu Legislative Assembly.

In the townships surrounding the urban areas of Natal there appear to be differences in the way residents of KwaZulu townships and those of townships in the 'prescribed' white areas have responded to the problems of township life. Gwala suggests that relatively low rents in the KwaZulu townships of Umlazi and KwaMashu have meant that rent increases have not been an issue for community protest as they have been in the Port Natal Development Board (PNDB) townships, those of Lamontville and Hambanathi in particular (Gwala, 1985). This does not mean that rents have not been a problem for the KwaZulu administration. There were rent boycotts, and considerable friction between residents and Inkatha, in Mondlo in 1980 (WIP, 1980c:28-29).

Schoolchildren have also sometimes responded differently to national boycott calls or to conditions in schools in KwaZulu and PNDB townships, and this no doubt has something to do with the actual differences between schools under the KwaZulu Department of Education and Culture and those under the central government's Department of Education and Training.

However, there has not been enough detailed research to make generalizations about the way material or political conditions translate into different responses in KwaZulu and PNDB townships. The following discussion of Inkatha's response to its urban opposition in Natal will tend to focus on particular incidents that have led to conflict between Inkatha and township residents. Particular campaigns and incidents may shed light on broader trends of political response but the purpose of their selection here is to demonstrate patterns in Inkatha's behaviour. Incidents have been chosen that demonstrate the predictability, over time, of Inkatha's response to opposition and to counter the myth that Inkatha supporters' vigorous and violent ousting of township opposition since 1985 has somehow been a temporary aberration beyond the bounds of the Inkatha leadership's sanction.

In its early years much of Inkatha's intolerance of dissent was visible in its responses to scholars and students, though these were not necessarily the most important clashes in its defence of its dual role of policing and servicing the KwaZulu population. Bus boycotts in the townships of Madadeni and Osizweni outside Newcastle in 1975 revealed considerable friction between the boycotters and Inkatha leaders, particularly Dr Frank Mdlalose, now KwaZulu minister of

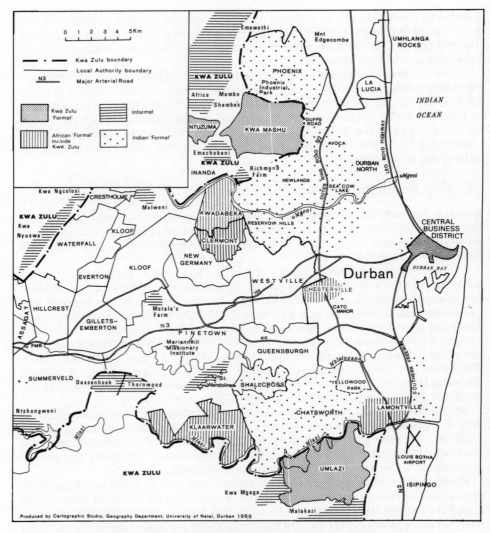

DURBAN METROPOLITAN REGION
showing townships and informal settlements

health and welfare, and suggested 'the contradictory position that KLA and Inkatha leaders find themselves in because of the financial stake that the bantustan authorities have in . . . bus transport, and productive and redistributive enterprises' (WIP, 1980c:52).

Protests in township schools, especially those around Durban and Pietermaritzburg, may be the best publicized because the media have easier access to them. Likewise more is generally known about township conflicts than about rural ones. But there are other reasons why it is likely that the encounter between Inkatha and its opponents has been most volatile in the urban areas of Natal. Apart from obvious problems generated by the appalling conditions of urban life for blacks, many of the townships and informal settlements are at the periphery of the KLA and Inkatha's political and ideological map and more available to other influences. Certainly, if Ulundi is the centre of KwaZulu, the major urban areas are geographically at its peripheries, and the geographical and administrative map has similarities with the organizational structure of Inkatha. The movement's highly centralized leadership is both a 'strength' in that a co-ordinated policy, a 'single' face, is presented, and a weakness when local officials and aspirant leaders set up fairly independent fiefdoms under the broad banner of Inkatha.

In 1979, when community council elections were held in Lamontville (part of the Ningizimu Town Council comprising Chesterville and the S.J. Smith and Glebe hostels) and Hambanathi — two of the townships administered by the Port Natal Administrative Board (now the PNDB) — some residents believed that if people with a commitment to solving township-dwellers' problems were elected, they might find ways to relieve some of the problems that beset the PNDB townships. Township residents were concerned about a desperate shortage of housing, poor services, almost no maintenance of roads or housing and very few recreational facilities. These problems, coupled with political frustration and powerlessness, were on the table when the community councils came into operation in 1979.

In the Transvaal, despite confusion about its stance, Inkatha has maintained a non-participatory line as far as community councils are concerned (see Chapter 7, above). In Natal, Inkatha members participated freely and, on the whole, dominated community councils. For a brief period the councils in Lamontville and Hambanathi tinkered with this pattern. Two councillors, Harrison Dube in Lamontville and Ian Mkhize in Hambanathi, were at first optimistic about working within township structures but this gave way to a realization of the councils' structural and financial impotence and to total rejection of the council system by the two councillors and significant numbers of supporters. Both Dube and Mkhize set about trying to involve their communities in the issues that had been discussed behind closed doors by the old advisory boards.

The Hambanathi council developed a level of popular credibility through its representations to Dr Piet Koornhof, then Minister of Co-operation and Development, to prevent the threatened removal of African people from Hambanathi. In addition various improvements were made to township facilities and 300 new houses were built. These were the only houses built in any PNDB township in the past 24 years.

In Lamontville Dube began calling public meetings to gauge the popular response to various issues, but this created tensions between himself and other councillors. By the time the PNDB announced major rent increases on 7 October

1982, hostilities between Dube and other councillors were serious (Challenor, 1984:55). Even though the Ningizimu Community Council rejected rent rises they were powerless to do much about them. Dube was the most articulate councillor opposing increases. He also took a leading role in a bus boycott that was an important focus of community mobilization. The Durban Transport Management Board increased bus fares by 12.5% on 1 December 1982. A one-day boycott on that day planned by a Joint Commuters Committee represented in six townships, lasted over a month in Lamontville.

In April 1983 rent action committees from most of the PNDB townships in Durban affiliated to form the Joint Action Committee (JORAC). A petition signed by 2000 Lamontville residents was sent to the PNDB and to Koornhof listing the following problems:

a) high unemployment because of the recession,
b) considerable financial hardship resulting from the bus fare increase,
c) dissatisfaction with the lack of maintenance of houses, streets and sidewalks and the shortage of community facilities (Challenor, 1984:72).

Harrison Dube was murdered on 12 April 1983 and this precipitated three months of violent unrest in Lamontville and polarized opposition between JORAC, of which Dube had been a leader, and the community council. JORAC supporters saw the murder as being politically motivated, and it appeared they had good reason since 'Moonlight' Gasa, chairman of the council and Dube's rival, was implicated in the murder and sentenced to 12 years in prison. In the midst of internecine rivalry, JORAC's protest against rent increases developed into a struggle against the repressive behaviour of the South African Police (see Challenor, 1984:75).

When, predictably, the police failed to quell the violence in Lamontville, Koornhof reluctantly met with JORAC on 8 May 1983. This was a temporary lapse since the government did not usually talk to non-statutory bodies. According to a social researcher, 'it was only after violence broke out after Dube's murder that the authorities gave the communities' representatives a hearing and then only after an urgent plea was made by Sybil Hotz' (then mayor of Durban) (quoted in Challenor, 1984:73).

On 10 May, Buthelezi said, 'Let us take the responsibility for our people in Lamontville' (NM, 10 May 83). Coming so soon after JORAC's meeting with Koornhof, this suggests that the meeting had unnerved Buthelezi, suggesting as it did a dangerous precedent for negotiation outside bantustan or statutory structures — Inkatha's influence in Lamontville was being superseded by JORAC's more energetic initiatives. According to Challenor, once it became clear that the Ningizimu Community Council and Inkatha were not channelling popular opposition, Buthelezi saw JORAC as a direct political challenge to himself and Inkatha (Challenor, 1984:100-101).

From the outset Buthelezi had been opposed to the PNDB's rent increases. Inkatha tried to stop the increases being implemented because there had been no consultation or agreement with the community council. Two councillors who were Inkatha members brought an urgent application to the Supreme Court to prevent Koornhof raising the rents and were granted an order calling on the government to show cause why the government notice gazetting the increases should not be declared null and void (Challenor, 1984:102). But, as with the 1980 school boycotts, Buthelezi's sympathy lasted only as long as Inkatha could control the direction of popular opposition.

JORAC's enthusiasm for the idea of Lamontville possibly electing councillors to the Durban City Council was a further slight to Inkatha (NM, 11 May 83) and this may have had as much to do with Inkatha's revived interest in Lamontville being administratively incorporated into KwaZulu. For the government, incorporation offered the immediate advantage of allowing it to distance itself from the problems of Lamontville and the continued violence there. In any case incorporation was in line with the long-term goal of consolidating KwaZulu.

On 31 August 1983, the government announced that Lamontville and Hambanathi would be incorporated into KwaZulu. Buthelezi welcomed the decision. A JORAC meeting held that week and attended by about 3000 people rejected incorporation into KwaZulu and reaffirmed the wish to be controlled by the Durban City Council. The Rev. Mcebisi Xundu, a JORAC leader who had come to prominence after Dube's death, said people rejected incorporation because they were worried about losing their urban Section 10 rights (which gave them preferred if limited access to jobs), about their security and about schools (DN, 1 Sep. 83). Buthelezi tried to separate the opposition to incorporation from popular response by asking, with reference to Xundu, why people from the Transkei should 'come here and break our solidarity' by not wanting to be part of KwaZulu (Challenor, 1984:106).

There does not seem to be much evidence in Lamontville prior to 1983 of overt conflict in the township, or in the council itself, between Inkatha supporters and more progressive elements. This is worth noting because both Inkatha and the UDF sometimes attribute an historical origin to their clash. This might have been nascent in Inkatha's alignment against progressive student groupings, but it was hardly a focal point of township politics before 1983, when the UDF was formed. It is possible to trace the tendency for township traders, businessmen, civil servants and many teachers to support Inkatha and to become its urban leadership, just as there was increasing support for charterist politics amongst professionals, intellectuals, clergy, students and youth (Sitas, 1986:95-97). There was friction between Inkatha supporters and those with different political ideas but this did not take the form of a stand-off between the movement and the UDF. Incorporation was the issue that polarized Inkatha and the UDF in Lamontville and Hambanathi. The central government made its announcement that the townships were to be incorporated into KwaZulu eleven days after the national launch of the UDF at Mitchell's Plain near Cape Town. Nevertheless Inkatha's growing antipathy to JORAC must be seen in the context of the national emergence of the UDF in that the UDF posed a threat to Inkatha's claim to be the most representative and largest 'liberation movement' in South Africa. It also threatened to draw popular support away from Inkatha (see above, pp.147-9). This was also JORAC'S crime.

While community councillors' allegiances were relatively undefined before incorporation was announced, it seems that the council became an Inkatha mouthpiece when those who were not Inkatha members or supporters left the council in the months following the announcement (Challenor, 1984:108). They were months marked by clashes, some violent and fatal, between pro- and anti-incorporation factions. Hostel dwellers provided Inkatha with supporters who were prepared to march on Lamontville in a 'show of force'. This potential violence was curbed on two occasions when the marchers were turned away from Lamontville by police. One JORAC leader was anxious to point out that it was a generalization to say that all hostel residents supported Inkatha though it was understandable that those who came from rural areas where 'it is difficult to do things unless you are a member of Inkatha' supported Inkatha (quoted in Challenor, 1984:108).

In February 1984 Buthelezi said Inkatha needed to concentrate on making geographical gains in parts of Natal, such as Lamontville, where it faced opposition. In September 1984 he decided to visit Lamontville to stage one of his ever more familiar mass meetings, a visual demonstration of Inkatha's appeal to the masses which have become the hallmark of Inkatha's 'show of force'. On this occasion police actually encouraged township residents to move out and many did leave for the weekend. As it turned out there was no violence (Challenor, 1984:110). Buthelezi insisted on the mass meeting all the more vigorously once JORAC had tried to discourage it. In 1985, Buthelezi told *Leadership* magazine:

. . . The UDF chairman tried to create that place as a 'no-go' area for me. First of all he persuaded the papers to print that if I went there I would be killed. That left me no choice. I wouldn't survive politically if I listened to him. [*Leadership*, 1985:27]

In Hambanathi, Ian Mkhize and Richard Gumede resigned from the community council in 1983 and joined the residents association in the area, which in turn joined JORAC. When incorporation was anounced at the end of August there was already a considerable gulf between the Hambanathi Residents Association (HRA) and the council, which was made up of Inkatha supporters.

An Inkatha memorandum on Hambanathi cited a number of incidents in which Inkatha members' homes or cars had been stoned or burned during July and August 1984. It was said that this was the HRA's attempt 'to apply the same sort of terror to the people of Hambanathi as had been applied by JORAC in Lamontville' (Inkatha, 1985a:3). A distinction was drawn between the 'people' of Hambanathi and the HRA so that attacks on HRA members could then be portrayed as justifiable retaliation by the 'people' of Hambanathi against the HRA (Inkatha, 1985a:3). Retaliation did indeed follow and it was severe. From Friday, 24 August, Inkatha supporters marched through the streets of Hambanathi burning and stoning houses. In all, 10 houses were burnt that weekend. Observers noted that two busloads of Inkatha supporters and 'kombi' loads of 'impis' came to Hambanathi from elsewhere. Hambanathi is particularly susceptible to invasion because it is situated along the major north/south highway in Natal. There is a lot of traffic along this route at weekends transporting migrant workers and commuters and Hambanathi dwellers have a long-standing experience of weekend disruption by people stopping off on their way north or south.

Inkatha's 'bussing' of supporters to defend its territory either in a show of force at mass rallies or in the deployment of force as at Hambanathi has proved to be a favourite and perhaps necessary tactic. On the one hand it suggests Inkatha's ability, whether through popularity or force, to mobilize a substantial number of supporters when it chooses to. On the other hand it also suggests that support in the townships is either tenuous or reluctant to take part in the more dangerous of Inkatha's defensive or offensive initiatives; also it appears that those bussed into trouble spots have less to lose than those with a stake in township life.

On 26 August, after a weekend of terror, many of the victims of arson and assault were afraid to remain in Hambanathi. That day Alfred Sithole, a prominent HRA leader, and two policemen who had come to the town to visit friends were murdered. Some 25 families who were involved with the HRA left

Hambanathi and sought refuge at a monastery. Numerous charges were brought by these 'Hambanathi refugees', as they became known, against Inkatha members in Hambanathi, but only one case was prosecuted.

After meetings between Dhlomo, the HRA and other Hambanathi residents represented mainly by councillors between September and December 1984, the HRA supporters finally returned to Hambanathi. Inkatha insisted that the HRA's anti-Inkatha and anti-incorporation views and lack of confidence in the community council were minority views in Hambanathi (Inkatha, 1985a:4). There has been no opportunity to test this hypothesis. The level of violence perpetrated by Inkatha supporters in August 1984 and again in May 1985, which once again caused the HRA supporters to flee the township, made fear a prominent factor in social control in Hambanathi. It is unlikely that people would continue to express their opposition to Inkatha, the council, or incorporation, for fear of invoking the same wrath that assailed HRA supporters.

At a meeting of progressive community and support groups to discuss the shortcomings of responses to the August 1985 crisis in Durban, it was noted that Hambanathi should have provided a warning of what was to come. First, the assaults on Hambanathi provided a clear reminder of Inkatha's ability to draw on support from outside the area it was defending or seeking to bring under its control. Second, there was an active involvement in violence by important Inkatha members in the community. This gave Inkatha's leadership the problem of separating leadership directives from those of its stalwart supporters: unidentified 'mobs' or 'impis' can be explained as spontaneous popular mobilization in defence of Inkatha and its followers. However, a Women's Brigade leader involved in arson and violence is more difficult to explain away: Norah Dlamini, a leading member of the Women's Brigade, was convicted and jailed for her part in the attacks on HRA members.

Third, Inkatha's actions in Hambanathi demonstrated the power of fear as a weapon against opposition. Hambanathi is a small township. It has 533 houses and a population of between three and four thousand. In such a small community a little fear goes a long way. For many people there is a simple choice of appearing to go along with Inkatha or being victimized.

Finally, by the time violence broke out in Hambanathi the PNDB had distanced itself from accountability in preventing violence or promoting conciliation because the announcement of incorporation had allowed it to shift the burden of responsibility onto KwaZulu. The government seemed increasingly content to shift the burden of policing the townships onto the KLA and Inkatha. This trend has been amply confirmed by events since August 1985.

Within the 'Liberated Zone'

Because we have conquered at the level of KwaZulu and at the level of local government, both inside and outside KwaZulu, we have developed a position of strength. We have created a springboard from which we can go forth to conquer in ever widening circles. We have created for Black South Africa a liberated zone from whence we can mount our strategies and attacks on apartheid which are vital to the country as a whole [BS, 29 Jun 85].

Barely two months after the launch of the UDF in August 1983, a violent confrontation between Inkatha supporters and students at Ngoye (the campus of the University of Zululand) left five people dead and many injured. Most of the injuries and deaths resulted from a raid by Inkatha supporters on one of the men's hostels at Ngoye in the early morning of 29 October 1983. Large numbers of Inkatha supporters had been gathering on the Ngoye campus throughout the night to attend a ceremony commemorating the death of King Cetshwayo which was to be addressed by Buthelezi. Students had asked the university authorities to prevent the ceremony from being held on campus as Buthelezi's previous visits to Ngoye, with his inevitable throngs of followers and impis, had occasioned confrontation, disruption and violence. The official commission of inquiry into the violence noted that as a result of previous troubles when Buthelezi was on campus in his capacity as chancellor, the date of graduation ceremonies had been moved to the mid-year vacation 'when the body of students is not on the campus and the likelihood of a clash between students and members of the public is minimized' [Middleton, 1985:36].

At the beginning of the commission's report it was clearly stated that:

There was no evidence that the clash was between forces of the Inkatha movement and student supporters of the United Democratic Front or that it was a planned attack launched by Inkatha supporters [Middleton, 1985:3].

It is no doubt simplistic to see the clash at Ngoye as having been one between the UDF and Inkatha when other political groupings may have been involved. But this statement was widely interpreted, and probably intended, as an exoneration of Inkatha rather than a pointer to the lack of subtlety in press allegations. In contrast, it was noted in the body of the report that:

The sum total of the evidence placed before the Commission suggests that the violence. . . on 29 October 1983 was the product of a clash between the students, or a certain body of the students, and sympathizers with the Inkatha movement [Middleton, 1985:34].

Furthermore, the commission found that:

From the evidence of Chief Buthelezi himself and other Inkatha members who testified, it appears to the commisson that, once the ceremony had been arranged the die was cast. Chief Buthelezi and the Inkatha movement could not, at that stage, allow it to be cancelled without losing credibility. The inference, therefore appears to be justified that Inkatha supporters came to the ceremony prepared to fight if they had to [Middleton, 1985:74].

The commission also noted that Buthelezi said he was not prepared to allow Ngoye to become 'a no-go area' for him and his followers (Middleton, 1985:61).

While the commission found that there was no evidence of a planned attack by Inkatha supporters, it should be born in mind that Inkatha's attacks on its opposition rarely admit links to leadership direction or conspiratorial planning. Whether those directions or plans exist is in a sense irrelevant for it is more important to Inkatha's idea of leading a popular struggle that the ferocious defence of Inkatha by its supporters should be seen as righteous popular anger. Apologists for the movement have observed that Buthelezi is never present at the scene of violence and is therefore blameless. Indeed, on 29 October, he arrived at Ngoye hours after the hostel raid had occurred. However, his insistence that he would not allow Ngoye to become a 'no-go' area for him betrays a militant approach to student opposition and, as the Commission observed, there was ample evidence that his appearance on campus was confrontational.

Inkatha's dilemma is that violence, however far from Buthelezi or other leaders it occurs, invokes considerable criticism not just from local opposition but from quarters such as international funding bodies and political or church groupings that Inkatha is less keen to confront. Inkatha has gone to considerable lengths to distribute, overseas, justifications and denials of its involvement in violent or threatening activities (see Buthelezi, 1983; Inkatha, 1984). Yet, since 1983, violence seems to have become an increasingly important weapon for Inkatha supporters if they are to establish control over certain 'no-go' areas. The mere show of force is in itself not sufficient to silence criticism or reduce the numbers attending opposition rallies.

While some in Inkatha were shocked by the violence at Ngoye and expressed concern at the way Inkatha youth had got out of hand and could not be controlled by their leaders, Buthelezi was unrepentant (see Teague, 1983: 63-64). He accused the Congress of South African Students, SASO and various staff members at Ngoye of having plotted the incident, claiming that COSAS was a front organization for the ANC 'mission in exile' (Teague, 1983:63). In fact he justified rather than regretted the violence:

I must warn South Africa that if the kind of provocation continues which we experienced on Saturday, Inkatha youth will demonstrate their strength and their prowess . . . The peoples' [sic] anger is rising and the fervour with which we pursue our objectives will deepen. Nothing will stop us and those forces of disunity which are attempting to do the National Party's dirty work in disrupting our progress will be taught a lesson or two if the denigration of Inkatha continues . . . The abuse of me must now cease. Continuing to label me as a sell-out is going to have ugly repercussions [quoted in Teague, 1983:63].

It is important to mention here that the Inkatha supporters were not unprovoked in their attack on the Ngoye students. The raid on the hostel was apparently preceded by stone-throwing and insults. The evidence in the Middleton Report suggests that Ngoye students were the first to throw stones but also mentions that there was a lack of control by the South African Police and university security officers in allowing hundreds of Inkatha supporters to leave the vicinity of Bhekuzulu Hall, where the ceremony was being held, and march towards the hostels (Middleton Report, 1985:18, 42). Two KwaZulu cabinet members, prominent leaders of Inkatha, Dr Madide and Dr Mdlalose, told representatives of the British Council of Churches (BCC) that if the students had just thrown stones and not insults there would have been no retaliation! (BCC press release, January 1984.) Evidence of who was to blame for the Ngoye violence is well documented elsewhere (Teague, 1983:58-66; Middleton, 1985). The intention here is to offer further indications of Buthelezi's and Inkatha's attitudes and responses in defending Inkatha's position where it sees opposition. The violence of Inkatha supporters is the more conspicuous because it belies the much-vaunted platform of 'non-violence' which gains Inkatha such national and international favour as the most promising moderate black political movement.

Inkatha's sensitivity to the slightest hint of opposition in KwaZulu is further illustrated by its response to a meeting of the Alliance of Black Reformed Christians in Southern Africa (ABRECSA) which was due to hold its annual conference at KwaNzimela in the middle of November 1983, shortly after the Ngoye violence. Soon after delegates arrived, two busloads of people, many of them wearing Inkatha uniforms, accompanied Dr Madide, KwaZulu minister of the interior, to the conference centre. Some of the delegates left almost immediately because they feared for their safety. Among the delegates were UDF members who had reason to feel threatened by an Inkatha 'show of force' following clashes in Lamontville and the UDF's criticism of Inkatha's role at Ngoye. The conference was aborted. A few days later Buthelezi said he had delegated Madide 'to extend our welcome to important guests who were holding a Conference *within our territory*' (emphasis added) (Buthelezi, 1983:1). Madide claimed there was never any tension between conference delegates and Inkatha supporters. The delegates clearly felt otherwise as they unanimously agreed to leave the centre in the middle of the night 'in a convoy of vehicles for self-protection'. In a statement to the BCC, the overseas delegates to the conference said they were aware of an atmosphere of tension and fear. Following a meeting between Dhlomo, Madide and the BCC in January 1984, the BCC said it was significant that black delegates to the ABRECSA conference believed themselves to be at risk and saw 80 uninvited guests as intimidatory especially in light of the recent killings at Ngoye.

The BCC also said it was disturbed by Inkatha's 'frequent condemnation of comments or actions which offended Inkatha's sense of honour, integrity and patriotism . . . the impression is conveyed that the employment of any means is justified to satisfy the honour of Chief Buthelezi and Inkatha.' The BCC went on to ask the question: 'Why is Inkatha at variance with so many black bodies committed to liberation?' (BCC press release, January 1984).

Inkatha had treated the ABRECSA Conference — a church meeting — as the creation of another 'no-go' area in KwaZulu to be challenged. The KLA and Inkatha were not officially invited to the conference and took indications that they would not necessarily be welcome as a signal for displaying, in threatening numbers, their control over KwaZulu territory. The incident provides an example of Buthelezi's need to denigrate opposition that he cannot control. In his response to ABRECSA press statements he said:

> This Holier-Than-Thou attitude in certain circles of the Church both here and overseas must come to an end . . . They now use the Church to colonize Black minds as the ABRECSA Conference showed [Buthelezi, 1983:3].

King Goodwill has recently taken up this cry with attacks on the Catholic and Anglican churches, warning followers of the Church of Nazareth (the Shembe Church), of which he is a member, of 'false prophets'. He accused Anglican and Catholic church leaders of supporting violence and sanctions (see DN, 28 Jul. 86).

'Political thuggery'

Until August 1985, the Natal townships were generally deemed to be 'quiescent' and to have avoided the patterns of popular unrest and conflict elsewhere in South Africa. On 1 August, Victoria Mxenge, a Durban attorney and executive member of the UDF, was assassinated outside her Umlazi home by unidentified assailants. The next day meetings were held by many progressive groups to discuss the implications of her death and there was a demonstration in the middle of Durban by students from the University of Natal Medical School and the University of Durban-Westville. Thirty-five students were arrested (Meer, 1985:2; Haysom,

1986:87). COSAS and AZASO called for a boycott of schools and lectures from 5-11 August as a mark of respect for Mxenge and a protest against her assassination.

The boycotts and marches which began on 5 August were initially composed mostly of students and scholars but they began to draw a number of unemployed youths, looters and opportunists in their wake. The targets of people's anger, which at first appeared to be obvious 'symbols of the system' such as policemen, policemen's houses and administrative and school buildings, soon changed to shops, businesses and trading stores (Haysom, 1986:87; Meer, 1985:2; Sitas, 1986:105). Looting and arson occurred throughout the week in Umlazi, KwaMashu and the squatter town of Inanda. By 7 August an estimated 1000 Indians had fled Inanda to seek safety in the Indian township of Phoenix after their homes and stores had been attacked and looted. According to Sitas, by 8 August 'a racial "psychosis", aggravated by the media's coverage of events, reminiscent of 1949 was gripping both Inanda and Phoenix' (Sitas, 1986:109). Indeed the media made much of the hostility of Africans towards Indians and failed to give due weight to the burning of African-owned shops in Inanda or the fact that most of the people killed in the area were African (Meer, 1985:46; Haysom, 1986:87). From 7 August Inkatha vigilantes mobilized to protect businesses and property in the townships and to flush-out and punish not only looters and criminals but large numbers of scholars, students and UDF activists and leaders. In the process many innocent bystanders were hurt, killed or left homeless. The week of violence left progressive political organizations generally, and even Inkatha itself, with glaring gaps in their ability to control or direct events or their supporters' responses to those events. Inkatha may have been better at predicting events than others. Buthelezi and other Inkatha leaders had frequently warned of the wrath that would be unleashed by their supporters against those disrupting schooling or destroying property in KwaZulu.

On 8 August Buthelezi gave his usual warning of what could be expected:

> I am troubled about the consequences of this thuggery, particularly if the anger of the people who are being terrorized expresses itself in action [DN, 8 Aug. 85].

Violence perpetrated by Inkatha supporters in August and subsequent months more than ever before begged questions about Inkatha's strategy of non-violence and the Inkatha leadership's ability to control the actions of its supporters. In common with Buthelezi's past responses to accusations about Inkatha's brutal methods he distanced the leadership from the acts of its followers. But Inkatha's recent record has made it more difficult for the movement as a whole to side-step responsibility for its supporters' actions.

The recent past has faced the UDF with problems of a different kind. First there was the leadership's inability to prevent the progression of events from relatively peaceful school boycotts and student demonstrations following Victoria Mxenge's death on 1 August to the wide-scale rioting, looting and arson between 7 August and 9 August. Second, their affiliates were faced with immense difficulty in protecting their supporters from harassment and victimization by Inkatha supporters and in reorganizing and rebuilding community organizations. Such organizations as there were in the KwaZulu townships were not strong enough to withstand a determined onslaught by Inkatha with the tacit and actual support afforded it by KwaZulu and central state structures. However, its structural advantage notwithstanding, Inkatha succeeded in mobilizing a considerable degree of popular support. There is evidence abounding for Inkatha's tactic of 'bussing-in' supporters and vigilantes from rural or squatter areas and of the coercion used to draw bystanders into their marching armies of stick-wielding vigilantes, commonly referred to as 'amabutho'. But there is not much evidence to confirm that the make-up of the large 'mobs' that have terrorized many Natal townships since August have not also relied on willing and popular support.

The unions were probably most aware of the perils of underestimating Inkatha's popular appeal. Hence their avoidance, in FOSATU unions (now part of COSATU) in particular, of adopting political positions that might have brought the divided loyalties of workers, between union and political allegiances, into conflict on the shop floor. However, the severity of the violence in August and Inkatha's recent open opposition to COSATU have played their part in forcing the unions to offer political direction.

Two of the first reports to be published on the August violence (Meer, 1985; and Sutcliffe and Wellings, 1985) were at pains to counteract the conventional views put forward by the media and various politicians — including Buthelezi — that Inkatha had intervened to control strife-torn townships and to 'protect people and property and to maintain order'. The interpretation offered by Fatima Meer that, far from containing violence, Inkatha had fanned it through pointed and sustained attacks by its supporters on UDF activists and those associated with them is backed by numerous affidavits relating to assaults, murders, arson, intimidation and harassment. Both reports also provided information on the apparent 'racial hostilities' in Inanda between Indians and Africans that contradicted the press and SABC's tendency to suggest a recurrence of Durban's riots of 1949 when, with equal alacrity, the press had exaggerated antipathy between Africans and Indians without examining the divisive government strategies that had fuelled the animosity.

Other studies have pointed to serious weaknesses in UDF organization (De Villiers, 1985; Sitas, 1986) and have attempted to look beneath the simple characterization of the August conflicts as a battle between Inkatha and the UDF (Gwala, 1985; Sitas, 1986). Of importance to the discussion of Inkatha's responses to opposition in Natal is Sitas' exploration of the increasing stratification between 'haves' and 'have nots' and the way the poorest people develop the notion of a 'legitimizing right' to attack various symbolic targets. He argues:

> The contrasts in the townships started being drawn in stark lines. That the youth and later, many ordinary people came to vent their anger by attacking all symbols of wealth and by looting is intelligible in economic terms alone [Sitas, 1986:101].

Buthelezi was not prepared to dwell for a moment on the 'felt' legitimacy of people's targets such as schools and administration buildings in August. He said:

> It grieves me that members of a certain political organization, plus the external mission of the ANC, . . . are promoting this black-on-black confrontation as well as . . . a programme of self-laceration in having blacks burn down their own facilities . . . There is no way in which we are going to accept being terrorized by other blacks, aided and abetted by misguided children and thugs. It is hogwash to present this kind of political thuggery as the black liberation struggle [NM, 8 Aug. 85].

This statement shows the usual patterns of blaming unrest on outsiders, denigrating any liberation struggle outside Inkatha, warning against attacking government buildings, and of course, the portrayal of children as misguided.

In 1980 Buthelezi made an initial gesture of sympathizing with the reasons for school boycotts, but by 1985 he seems to have realized that school boycotts in the townships could not but be a threat to Inkatha. Not only did they buck the authority of the KwaZulu department of education but they also indicated that Inkatha had failed to appeal to significant and vocal numbers of young people in the townships. It is likely that Inkatha was aware that young people were the mainstay of the UDF in KwaZulu's townships. Youth organizations were undoubtedly the most active, organized and largest UDF affiliates in the townships of Umlazi and KwaMashu and in many other KwaZulu townships in Natal (Sitas, 1986:103-104). UDF affiliates in KwaMashu and Umlazi and in squatter towns, Inanda in particular, faced enormous difficulties in raising community support except amongst scholars and students through AZASO and COSAS.

It has also been suggested that in some of the Natal townships where the UDF was more powerful, Lamontville and Chesterville for instance, the leadership was preoccupied with national rather than day-to-day community concerns and failed to consolidate grass-roots structures (see Sitas, 1986; DeVilliers, 1985). Sitas talks of the important link between scholars and unemployed youth in taking COSAS initiatives beyond the confines of schools and classrooms:

> Frustrated by the curricula, frustrated by the closing horizons of their futures, frustrated too by the political developments in other schools all over the country in comparison to Durban, they were a volatile force. Many have commented how their elder siblings were unemployed, how economic hardship was affecting their family lives and how many of their peer group were out of school and into the township with nothing to do. When they started mobilizing themselves they were bound to reach out from the classroom into the streets in an explosive way to draw in the many more youths waiting there [Sitas, 1986:104].

Initial revelations following the August violence about the methods used by Inkatha supporters to oust opposition in KwaMashu and Umlazi were viewed by many as indicating a new dimension in brutality. The unpredictability and seeming randomness of attacks, coming as they often did in the middle of the night and making no distinction between targeted political activists and babies or grandmothers, also introduced a new dimension of fear. Or so it seemed. But a reading of affidavits made during the 1980 school boycotts and of those concerning violence in Durban's townships since August 1985 suggests that the methods, including the use of fear, should not have been unexpected. There are a number of similarities in the kind of information given by victims in 1980 and in 1985.

One similarity is in the allegations of collusion between the South African Police and Inkatha vigilantes. The following excerpt is from the 1980 affidavit of a KwaMashu scholar who sought and was granted an interim interdict, 'by consent', against two prominent members of Inkatha forbidding them to assault or threaten to assault him, or to incite others to assault him:

> My family as well as my close associates and intimate friends are living in fear of our lives and realize that the police are impotent to act in the present situation more especially in that we suspect that the Inkatha movement exercises tremendous influence in police channels.

This scholar went on to say that he thought Inkatha wanted to get rid of 'all forms of opposition and other democratic forms of expression where these are in opposition to the Inkatha movement' (Durban Supreme Court Case No M/520/ 80, cited in Teague, 1983:40).

In 1985 Bheki Bright Msomi made an affidavit containing the following information:

At . . . 12.25am . . . a group of men, some of them armed with guns came to my house and demanded entry. They described themselves as policemen but I recognized two of them, Mr Winnington Sabelo an Inkatha Central Committee member and a man known only to me as Jerry who is an employee of the Executive Hotel, Umlazi . . . I was taken to the Executive Hotel and whilst we were in the Kombi the men started hitting me with sticks at the time accusing me of being a leader of the Umlazi Youth who they said had been responsible for the unrest . . . I was again beaten with knobkerries and sticks and the butts of rifles. I was thereafter taken to the police station. The police did not even take a statement from us [Black Sash Files, October, 1985].

Another man told this story:

I was victimized by Inkatha amabutho of Lindelani. They were under their leader known by the name Khanyile under the headman Thomas Mandla Shabalala. I was chased away from my house with my family of 12 children, a mother and I stayed in the bush for about 14 days. They said people of Lindelani did not want me . . . they said I am a member of the UDF. I reported the matter to police and to Inkatha officials of Ntuzuma . . . But nothing was done about it [Black Sash Files, November, 1985].

A second similarity between 1980 in KwaMashu and 1985 in the KwaZulu townships was the way vigilantes moved in large groups forcing all in their path to join with them. In 1980 a lawyer, Aubrey Nyembezi, noted the growth of vigilantism and the way KwaMashu was seen as unsafe by some opponents of Inkatha:

The violence has reached epidemic proportions. There are crowds of people hunting in vigilante groups. Several children are sleeping out in the veld because they are scared they will be beaten up [STb, 8 Jun. 80].

Members of Inkatha will further incite one another against myself and other young people . . . who have been accused of being instigators of the boycott . . . At present members of Inkatha . . . have formed vigilante groups which are patrolling the streets of KwaMashu . . . these people conduct themselves as though they are a law unto themselves [Durban Supreme Court Case No. M/520/80, cited in Teague, 1983:41; RDM, 9 Jun. 80; DN, 9 Jun. 80, 14 Jun. 80].

In June 1980 Buthelezi urged that vigilante groups be formed and that they should 'shoot to kill' anybody 'interfering' with buildings (DN, 2 Jun. 80). In 1985, there were no instructions, but vigilantes appeared to know what to do. On 7 August a memorial service for Victoria Mxenge in Umlazi was raided by a large band of 'amabutho' allegedly from the Lindelani shack settlement, which is many kilometres from Umlazi (see map). Seventeen people were killed and many were injured in the clash that ensued. On 9 August the 'amabutho' conducted house-to-house searches for activists, looted goods in KwaMashu and Umlazi and forced bystanders and chosen victims to join their marching gangs, wield sticks, and shout Inkatha slogans. Many were merely forced to march and chant but the fate for others was far more severe. The following excerpts from an affidavit concerning 'amabutho' actions in KwaMashu on 9 August, terrifying as it is, is not unusual:

. . . before I reached KwaMashu station I saw a large crowd of 'amabutho' who told me to join them. They were armed with spears, bush-knives, knobkerries and sticks. I had no alternative but to join their group . . . a portion of the group chased four young men who were standing in the road, amongst them my son . . . three of them managed to escape. My son . . . ran into my house which was close by and locked the door . . . The warriors then stoned the windows and chopped down two doors. I went inside . . . to attempt to prevent people from assaulting my son . . . he told me that he and the other young men were merely . . . watching the group of warriors pass by. I noticed that my son was bleeding badly and it appeared that he had been stabbed all over his body. In my presence he was again stabbed and . . . dragged from the house into the garden where the group stoned him and stabbed him and hit him on the head with bush-knives. I attempted to intervene but it was useless and after a short while I noticed that my son was dead [Black Sash Files, November 1985].

More typical is the story of Methodist minister and former Diakonia chairman, Wesley Mabuza. He was one of several church leaders singled out for harassment by Inkatha, and one of the many hundreds of people who were forced to march and demonstrate loyalty to Inkatha:

On the 9 August . . . between 6.00-7.00 am . . . I heard some singing of male voices outside . . . I peeped through the window and saw men armed with sticks, knobkerries and spears . . . they started calling out my surname loudly . . . 'Mabuza open the door! We have come for you.' . . . By that time, my son had started crying softly, saying to me 'Baba, baba [Father, father].' .. We started singing a hymn in Zulu in preparation for what I thought was imminent gruesome death . . . We saw that there were people at almost every window shouting at us. One person . . . accused me of conducting UDF meetings in my church. I denied this . . . I thought the mob was going to kill me. I changed my pyjamas for another pair of trousers and a coat. I opened the front door. I was escorted to a bigger group of people . . . As we walked, I was told to lift up my right hand, make a fist, and say, 'The UDF is a dog. It separates people.' . . . Despite telephone calls to the police . . . the police did not come [affidavit lodged with the Legal Resources Centre, Durban; see also Haysom, 1986:91].

From Friday night, 9 August, busloads of 'amabutho' arrived in KwaMashu and Inanda. Numberplates showed they had come from all over Natal (ST, 11 Aug. 85; Gwala, 1985:10). Over the weekend the death toll rose to 70. The police claimed to be responsible for only 37 of the deaths. Affidavits and other information available since August show that the death toll was higher. In the case of a child who was shot, the cause of death was stated on the official death certificate as 'abdominal injury'. A number of people reported that they were unable to find relatives who had been forced to march with the 'amabutho' between 8 and 11 August (Black Sash Crisis Office Files, August and September 1985). The 'amabutho' were not the only perpetrators of violence after they took control of KwaMashu and Umlazi from 9 August but they certainly had the upper hand. By 10 August Inkatha supporters, with the help of police and the South African Defence Force, had quelled the rioting and were engaged mainly in demonstrating their power by marching through the township streets and in a sort of 'mopping-up' operation aimed mostly at punishing UDF activists, particularly students and scholars.

In the months that followed, a new stratum of Inkatha leadership came to public prominence in some Natal townships — vigilante leaders; those who lead the 'amabutho' into battle against Inkatha's opponents. Some, like Winnington Sabelo and Gideon Sibiya, had long combined their official roles (KLA member and councillor respectively) with an enthusiastic preparedness to be Inkatha's spokesmen in vilifying opponents in the townships and to rally supporters in Inkatha's defence (see above, Chapter 7).

In 1980, Sabelo had called a meeting of students and parents in which he said that a boycott of exams had been masterminded by political exiles who aimed at destroying Inkatha and Chief Buthelezi's image (DN, 20 Oct. 80). He had a history of opposing student protests and was a likely candidate for leading attacks against student boycotters in 1985. Furthermore as a property-owner and businessman he had a vested interest in controlling the riots that threatened his possessions and livelihood. There have been numerous allegations concerning Sabelo's participation in violence since August 1985 (see for instance, Meer, 1985:22-23). Along with KLA deputy chief minister Prince Gideon Zulu, Sabelo led a throng of 'amabutho' to harass mourners at a mass funeral of people killed during the August 'unrest'. This event was well-documented (DN, 26 Aug. 85; NW, 28 Aug. 85; Haysom, 1986:90; Meer, 1985:16-17). In line with Inkatha's pattern of blaming 'unrest' on 'non-Zulus' or people outside KwaZulu, on 27 August Sabelo ordered UDF supporters to 'get out of Umlazi'. He cited people from Lamontville and Hambanathi as particularly at risk of reprisal if they didn't leave and added that cars without Umlazi registration plates would not be allowed to enter the townships (NM, 27 Aug. 85). His singling out of Lamontville and Hambanathi from the rest of Durban's townships is a reminder of the potential threat JORAC had posed to Inkatha since 1983 and that UDF leadership in Natal amongst Africans was perceived to emanate from these areas.

The only time Inkatha's new township leadership has been repudiated for its threatening or violent actions was when Oscar Dhlomo said Sabelo's call for UDF supporters to leave the townships had not been sanctioned by Inkatha. Buthelezi did not back up this repudiation and it has been argued that this reflects Buthelezi's reluctance to alienate the new township leaders (Meer, 1985:17; Sutcliffe and Wellings, 1985:4). Much as the outspoken and demonstrative 'war lords' publicly test the credibility of Inkatha's commitment to non-violence, they also rally and control significant support: support which Inkatha cannot afford to tamper with in a volatile economic and political climate in which Inkatha and its opposition are fighting for the same constituencies — workers, young people and the unemployed.

Gideon Sibiya, like Sabelo, has informed his strategies with a strong element of ethnic chauvinism and threats. As an Inkatha councillor in the Ningizimu Council representing S.J. Smith hostel, he was involved in challenging the sway of JORAC from its inception. In a letter to the *Natal Mercury* in July 1985 he wrote concerning an attack on an Inkatha member's home after a community meeting in a church:

> What really annoys us Zulus is these meetings are chaired mainly by Xhosa ministers who hold Transkei passports . . . I would like to warn leaders of disruptive groups and church ministers that we Zulus have now been pushed right to the wall and we are not going to tolerate their nuisance any longer [NM, 22 Jul. 85].

Other leaders demonstrating Inkatha's new confrontational style in the townships are Patrick Pakkies, the mayor of Imbali near Pietermaritzburg, and KLA member V.B. Ndlovu. On 30 August 1985 they led a march on the Federal Theological Seminary outside Pietermaritzburg, claiming that students had provoked unrest in the area. An interdict was granted to prevent the two from attacking students or the property of the seminary. Buthelezi refused to act as mediator between the seminary and the two men unless the interdict was lifted (Meer, 1985:17; NM, 3 Sep. 85; DN, 11 Dec. 85).

Perhaps more revealing of Inkatha's attitude to this new leadership is the fact that Thomas Mandla Shabalala, the 'war lord' of Lindelani, is now on Inkatha's central committee. Lindelani is a shack settlement on the north-eastern outskirts of Durban. It is within the boundaries of KwaZulu and it appears that KwaZulu authorities have made efforts to capture the allegiance of its population by promising that they would not be removed and by providing transport facilities and water. Shabalala emerged as a leader of Lindelani early in its existence. He has actively taken part in suppressing school protests and boycotts in KwaMashu since August 1985 and is alleged to have been behind the attack on Victoria Mxenge's memorial service and on Indians and Africans in Inanda. His enthusiastic support of Inkatha's goal of suppressing opposition in Durban saw him speedily co-opted onto Inkatha's central committee.

On 26 May 1986, a temporary interdict was granted against Shabalala restraining him from assaulting or threatening to assault a Lindelani couple, Belinda and Simon Mfeka. In papers before the Supreme Court, Belinda Mfeka said she had been told to appear at Shabalala's house by a group of women dressed in Inkatha and UWUSA T-shirts. She and her husband decided to go to Shabalala's house, because he had 'the reputation of being an extremely powerful and dangerous man whose orders are not to be lightly ignored' (STb, 1 Jun. 86). She went on to describe the 'war lord's' barracks:

> . . . a most sinister place. There are many armed men within the premises, many armed men with rifles and some of them wearing khaki uniforms and boots, and armed with knobkerries, spears and rifles. I gathered that the people were [Shabalala's] bodyguards . . . I saw . . . two buses, two combis and a car leaving the premises packed with men, armed with sticks, spears and bush-knives . . . [Shabalala] shouted at myself and my husband in an aggressive way accusing us of being members of the United Democratic Front . . . He said that Lindelani was a place for Inkatha people and not for people who supported the United Democratic Front . . . we did not dare to go to our houses and slept in the veld that night . . . I am aware that many members of the KwaZulu police station at KwaMashu have very close links with [Shabalala]. [affidavit lodged with the Black Sash].

Within hours of the interim interdict being granted against Shabalala a group of about 100 people wrecked the Mfekas' brick home, using pickaxes and other tools to destroy the house, trees and vegetable garden (STb, 1 Jun. 86).

Towards the end of May, in the wake of escalated conflict between Inkatha and COSATU and the UDF following the launch of UWUSA, Shabalala's right-hand man Khanyile was quoted as saying: 'I long for the day when there will be an open war between the UDF and Inkatha — it will prove who is who in this political battle.' He added that with his pistol he would 'leave hundreds of UDF supporters dead on the battlefield' and that it had been 'decided' that all councillors and Inkatha branches should set up groups to 'stamp out UDF-created unrest' (*Echo*, 5 Jun. 86).

The advantages to Inkatha of vigilante activity have temporarily outweighed the damage to its reputation of being associated with violence. Inkatha was widely credited by the press with restoring order to Durban's townships in August 1985 and Buthelezi's nomination as 'Man of the Year' by the *Financial Mail* in December 1985 indicates how little Inkatha's allies — capital and government — are disturbed by revelations of Inkatha supporters' methods.

It may be said of Inkatha, as it has been said of the South African Police and the South African Defence Force, that they 'are limited by potential publicity and hindered by legal considerations in their ability to perpetrate the deliberate terror and violence needed to combat popular organizations' (Haysom, 1986:7). The Inkatha leadership excuses itself from accountability for vigilante violence by explaining it as the 'people's anger' and saying that the prominent leaders involved are acting not as Inkatha members but in their personal capacity as angry members of a community besieged by political thugs, criminals and misguided children. If Inkatha insists on this interpretation, some questions can justifiably be asked.

First, if Inkatha members act without leadership sanction, how susceptible are they to control by an organization that prides itself on discipline and regimentation? Second, if members have been acting in their 'private capacity' can Inkatha claim credit for restoring order to KwaZulu townships? Third, does Inkatha's 'disciplined' approach to the 'liberation struggle' not include disciplinary procedures to contain the violence of over-zealous supporters? (See also Langner, 1983:139).

Many victims of threats or assaults by Inkatha supporters have sought police and judicial intervention in their cases. Because most of the 'dirty work' was carried out by unidentifiable vigilantes, there was little chance of relief through the courts, and police protection was allegedly reluctant (DN, 7 Aug. 85; Post, 21 Aug. 85), and often distrusted by victims (DN, 4 Sep. 85; and numerous affidavits in Black Sash Files, August and September 1985). Furthermore, many people were afraid of further victimization if they sought prosecutions. In fact many families were reluctant to seek help of any sort in August and September for fear of retaliation.

Recently however, there have been a number of interdicts granted against Inkatha supporters ordering them to refrain from various intimidatory or violent tactics. Notably, councillors Wilson Jwara and Napoleon Mhlongo and former KLA member Gobizizwe Bhengu were ordered by the Supreme Court not to assault or damage or threaten to damage the houses of three families living in KwaMashu (STb, 13 Apr. 86). A KwaMashu councillor, Esther Africa, was temporarily interdicted from assaulting a teacher and an interdict was granted against the Women's Brigade chairman of Ntuzuma, Victoria Shandu, restraining her from assaulting or damaging the property of an Education Crisis Committee worker (DN, 19 Apr. 86; STb, 4 May 86; also see affidavits of Samuel and Kisa Dlamini lodged with the Black Sash).

In many ways, the months since August 1985 have reflected patterns of conflict that were established long before. Attacks and retaliation between Inkatha and its opposition have checkered the years since the formation of the UDF. If the UDF has not succeeded in launching a campaign against Inkatha in the townships that is threatening in organization or numbers, it continues to hold out the potential of attracting support away from Inkatha at a time when Inkatha is less capable than ever of solving the 'bread and butter' problems of poverty, employment and education, and is increasingly reliant on force to prevent other organizations capturing the popular anger against the institutions of state control, which include bantustan authorities.

In 1985, prior to August, there were a number of attacks on Inkatha members' homes, particularly those of councillors and officials, in KwaMashu, Umlazi and Imbali. They were of a number sufficient to suggest that August's week of extreme violence was not as unpredictable as it seemed to many white Natalians, press commentators and even political activists at the time (eg NM, 18 Jun. 85; DN, 24 Jun. 85; NW, 18 Jul. 85). After the attack on the home of Umlazi mayor James Ndlovu in June 1985, Inkatha leaders in Umlazi decided to establish citizen defence units to combat politically motivated attacks on the homes of residents. Winnington Sabelo said members of these units would liaise with police in an effort to curb the attacks (DN, 25 Jun. 85). In July 1985, two Inkatha members' houses were burnt in Lamontville following three successive nights of violence. The UDF chairman in Natal, Mcebisi Xundu, and Oscar Dhlomo both called for restraint (NM, 18 Jul. 85) and there was talk of holding a 'peace meeting' between the UDF and Inkatha.

Though animosities had been brewing for a long time, the explosion of violence in August allowed Inkatha to assert more vigorous control over some townships and, at least in the cases of KwaMashu and Umlazi, to make them 'no-go' areas for open organization or action by its opposition. In Lamontville, where open and violent opposition has continued, Inkatha has called on the police and the SADF to effect a greater degree of control under the guise of an 'anti-crime sweep'. Ella Nxasana, chair of the Ningizimu Community Council and honorary life president of the Inkatha Women's Brigade, said the cordoning of Lamontville by 700 policemen and soldiers on 16 April 1986 was being carried out at the request of her council (NM, 17 Apr. 86). This action needs to be examined in the context of student and scholar opposition to Inkatha in the early months of 1986.

'Misguided children'

While Inkatha made geographical gains in August in the townships of Umlazi and KwaMashu by making them dangerous places for its opposition, it failed to contain the aspirations of young people in these and other townships in Natal. Much of Inkatha's rhetoric and violence since August 1985 has been aimed at schoolchildren and young people. Conversely, in his secretary general's annual report to the tenth anniversary conference of Inkatha in 1985, Oscar Dhlomo said that the Youth Brigade's percentage of Inkatha's membership, 38%, revealed 'the secret of Inkatha's power, ie the dominant role played by young people in the movement'. He also said the Youth Brigade's large share of overall membership exploded the myth that Buthelezi was only supported by the older generation (Inkatha, 1985).

There is so little documented evidence of Youth Brigade organization or action in Durban's townships that it must be inferred that either the press and Inkatha's various publicity drives have neglected to deal with an important area of Inkatha organization or that Youth Brigade members are unorganized, passive, or intimidated in the townships. If the various bands of 'amabutho' that rampage sporadically through townships streets are in fact the 'well-disciplined regimented impis' envisaged at the formation of the Youth Service Corps then discipline and regimentation have been lacking. According to photographic evidence and eye-witness accounts, 'amabutho' gangs have been far from disciplined and by no means comprised largely of 'youth', however loose Inkatha's definition of youth may be. The prowess and fervour of uniformed, disciplined YB and YSC members so much in evidence at Inkatha mass rallies have been notably absent in averting school boycotts and protests or in leading township students along a path of patient obedience.

Despite marked antagonism between Inkatha and progressive pupil and student organizations, relatively few KwaZulu schools were involved in the nationwide boycotts of 1976, 1980 and 1984. Whether this was due to the success of Inkatha's Education for Nationhood programmes or to the strict discipline and punishment manifest in its response to the KwaMashu boycotts in 1980, is a moot point. Whatever the reasons for their restraint in responding to national boycotts, there has been no shortage of friction between KwaZulu students and authorities and, as we have noted, they have organized many localized boycotts and protests in KwaZulu and Natal since the beginning of 1986 and earlier (see for instance Survey, 1983:467; NM, 15 Oct. 84, 13 Nov. 85). In 1984, the Ngoye campus of the University of Zululand was closed three times as a disciplinary action against boycotting students. In 1985 about 280 students were refused readmission to the university, ostensibly because they did not meet the criteria for readmission. According to students the criteria were mainly political and designed to exclude student activists. A move by the KLA requiring bursary students to sign a pledge 'never in word or deed [to] speak in contempt of the head of the KwaZulu Government . . . or directly or indirectly vilify, denigrate or in any manner speak in contempt of the Inkatha liberation movement' roused considerable ire amongst students (NW, 1 Apr. 85).

Students at school in Pietermaritzburg townships and in Lamontville were particularly active in 1984 and 1985 in protests and boycotts concerning various issues ranging from the withholding of matriculation results by the Department of Education and Training to the lack of proper student representative councils. The issues themselves were probably less important than the students' determination to participate in a broader political struggle against apartheid. While it was difficult for the Congress of South African Students (COSAS) to organize in KwaZulu schools in the face of sustained anti-COSAS rhetoric, it was nevertheless convenient for Buthelezi and Inkatha to portray the COSAS and JORAC stronghold of Lamontville as the seed-bed of the boycotts that precipitated the August violence in Durban.

However, even the banning of COSAS throughout South Africa on 28 August 1985 did little to curtail student opposition in Lamontville or the KwaZulu townships. Despite persecution of youth leaders and activists by Inkatha supporters, and the legal constraints placed on the organization of student opposition by detentions and the banning of COSAS, the months since August 1985 have shown the resilience of student and scholar opposition to Inkatha. Inkatha may have had an easy task in ousting loosely organized populist opposition, but it has since had to concentrate on more potent threats to its claim of a monolithic and obedient black constituency in Natal. These come from the democratically organized unions and school students. These two groups, united by common experiences and possessing ready-made bases in workplaces and classrooms, have an advantage over other organizations in the townships, which are exposed to cross-cutting class and interest allegiances and have no natural meeting-places.

Since the end of 1985 Inkatha has concentrated its rhetorical and physical attacks on trade unions and on the various organizations that have emerged to represent school students.

A new thrust in the protests and boycotts by black students and scholars in South Africa was signalled by the emergence of the Soweto Parents Crisis Committee (SPCC) in October 1985. In December at a conference at the

University of the Witwatersrand organized by the SPCC it was agreed that boycotting pupils, some of whom had not been at school for three years, should return to school on the condition that certain demands were met within three months. The demands included the lifting of the state of emergency, withdrawal of troops from the townships, unbanning COSAS, and the recognition of student representative councils (STb, 5 Jan. 86). A National Education Crisis Committee (NECC) was formed with the SPCC as its basis and representatives from 11 regions.

At a meeting organized by the Regional Ad Hoc Educational Committee in Natal it was agreed that students would go back to school at the end of January 1986, but that they would not pay school fees or for books. In February the secretary to the KwaZulu department of education and culture denied that KwaZulu pupils were opposed to paying fees. He said attempts to stir up trouble in some quarters had nothing to do with the pupils themselves, who were reasonably satisfied with the school system (DN, 12 Feb. 86). By the end of March, however, Inkatha was clearly perturbed by the evidence not only of numerous disturbances and boycotts within township schools in many parts of Natal and KwaZulu but also of growing solidarity among scholars, parents and teachers through the NECC.

The students' slogan of 1985, 'liberation now, education later', gave way at the beginning of 1986 to a new call under the NECC banner: 'people's education for people's power'. The national secretary of the NECC explained: 'Pupils can only organize and become a force for change, to combine with other forces, if they are at school . . . Student structures were increasingly weakened by almost two years of stayaway, and a general breakdown in discipline' (WIP, 1986:8). Zwelakhe Sisulu, who addressed the NECC national conference in Durban in March 1986, said that a significant achievement of the NECC was that it blurred the divisions between young and old, urban and rural people, and professionals and other members of the community (1986: 115). Sisulu also noted that '. . . from being youth-led, the struggle began to involve all sections of the population. Greater involvement of parents gave rise in turn to initiatives such as that of the SPCC' (1986:101).

The irony was that the rhetoric of the 'blackboard battalions', as one newspaper described scholar activists (STb, 5 Jan. 86), and their increasingly supportive parents was almost more threatening to the government and to Inkatha than the prospect of boycotts and disunity between the generations. The prospect of an organized national body which not only proposed to blur class and generation boundaries but also suggested a return to classrooms to consolidate the liberation struggle must have appeared to Inkatha as a hijacking of its own platforms and constituencies. Following an attack by 'impis' on an NECC meeting at Congella Hall, Buthelezi said:

> The NECC did not assemble itself in Durban to concern itself with matters of education . . . It suits political organizations aiming to make South Africa ungovernable to have pupils back at school where they can be mobilized . . . They chose Durban as a venue because they wanted to mobilize black pupils here to do their political work for them. The conference in Durban was aimed at giving evidence that it was possible *to attack me from bases very near to my home.* If there were Inkatha uniforms involved in the *eruption of anger,* why must I be blamed for their behaviour? The NECC itself came here to court that anger [emphasis added] [NM, 2 Apr. 86; NW, 2 Apr. 86].

Predictably, Buthelezi portrayed the holding of the NECC conference in

Inkatha's most successful recruiting ground, Natal, as an attempt to create a 'no-go' area for him. The NECC had excluded the Natal African Teacher's Union, an Inkatha affiliate, from the conference and this was probably an additional spur to Buthelezi's defensiveness. Buthelezi explained the attack on the meeting as an 'eruption of anger' in his defence, but, on that occasion, there was evidence that the attack was no spontaneous display of communal anger. It was revealed that the 'impis' had been transported in buses hired by Inkatha (NW, 3 Apr. 86). Weight is given to the NECC claim that their attackers were mobilized under false pretences by the following excerpts from an affidavit made by one of the people bused to the conference:

> On Saturday, 29th March I was at my home cleaning my yard. A large group of armed men came past. They were going from house to house ordering men to join them. I joined the group . . . the only thing I was told was that I was going to a meeting . . . At [Mandla] Shabalala's house the group gathered and chanted slogans for some time. I don't know the slogans at all. Two Putco buses arrived and we were ordered to board the buses. We were told . . . that we were going to KwaMashu Polyclinic as there was apparently violence occurring there. As the bus went towards Durban I realized that we were not going to the polyclinic at all. The bus went straight to Congella. People were asking each other on the bus if they knew where it was going . . . I have no idea whatever why I was forced to go to Congella on the bus . . . However it was clear that those on the bus expected to be engaged in fighting at our destination. Many people were armed with spears, sticks and knobkerries . . . I am a member of Inkatha. I was compelled to become a member when I lived in Umlazi . . . Although I was not given an order to attack people when we arrived at Congella I fully expected to receive such an order, and if I had . . . I would have attacked those I was ordered to attack. I say this because as we were being forced to march to Lindelani, and to board the buses at Shabalala's house, anyone who refused to come along was beaten with sticks . . . [affidavit filed with Black Sash, Durban].

NECC conference delegates alleged intimidation by Inkatha 'impis'. Even the police initially admitted Inkatha was behind the confrontation at Congella Hall, though they quickly disclaimed this admission. A prominent newspaper headline, hastily softened in the second edition of the newspaper, read: 'Two killed in Inkatha attack' (STb, 30 Mar. 86).

A spokesman for the Putco bus company not only said that the buses used to transport people to Congella Hall had been hired by Inkatha but also that the Putco drivers had been asked to fetch reinforcements and had refused to do so (WM, 4-10 Apr. 86).

The attack on the NECC conference was ugly in its premeditation and tragic in its outcome. Two of the people 'bussed-in' by Inkatha were killed. Discussions at the conference were curtailed by disruptive attacks and a frantic search for alternative venues. Inkatha was roundly condemned by the conference as an 'enemy of the people' and a 'fascist organization in league with the government' (WM, 4-10 Apr. 86; NW, 4 Apr. 86). School boycotts which had been rife in KwaMashu before the conference because of shortages or the lack of promised free stationery, were prolonged despite the conference's call for a return to the classrooms when scholars said they feared reprisal from Inkatha after the deaths at the NECC conference (WM, 11-17 Apr. 86; NM, 8 Apr. 86). In Lamontville, many scholars continued to boycott classes for a variety of stated reasons — one being the failure of the government to provide free stationery — but police heavy-handedness and Inkatha's intimidation and authoritarianism were probably more germane to their protests (WM, 11-17 Apr. 86; WIP, 1986:12).

In response to continued school protests and boycotts, the KLA sent a committee mainly of chiefs and KLA members to various schools in the Pietermaritzburg area to explain why school fees and funds need not be refunded in line with student demands (*Echo*, 24 Apr. 86). A teacher at one of these schools said the delegation blamed the crisis in the schools on the fact that teachers were not members of Inkatha, did not teach Inkatha, and that there were no Youth Brigade branches at school. Teachers were instructed to give their names and state whether they were members of Inkatha or the UDF. They were told that the principal 'should unite with the staff and build up Inkatha . . . should students then revolt, Inkatha would be sent in to support the staff and discipline students . . . if Boer students behaved in the same way as black students they would be shot by their elders' (statement lodged with the Black Sash, Pietermaritzburg, 28 Apr. 86).

Early in April 1986 a 13-year-old girl, Prudence Mngadi, died from gunshot wounds after police opened fire on a primary school in Lamontville. At least nine other pupils were wounded (NM, 7 Apr. 86). It was in this climate that the police put Lamontville under a virtual state of siege (WIP, 1986:12). While the police said they were on a mission to mop up criminals, their mandate seemed also to include a routing of political activists, youthful ones in particular. The chair of the community council, Ella Nxasana, would not pinpoint the targets of the police and SADF operation but suggested that children were on the agenda: 'I said to the community that each and every one must keep their children in after 8pm. If they do not obey what can we do?' (NM, 17 Apr. 86). This is reminiscent of Buthelezi's question nine months earlier: 'What can we recommend? That the police be removed from our townships? If we make that recommendation what would we recommend to take the place of the SAP?' (NM, 23 Jul. 85).

The launch of the Congress of South African Trade Unions (COSATU) on 1 December 1985 posed an even greater threat than that of the NECC to Inkatha's claim to represent black political aspirations in Natal. As long as the most significant and well organized unions — notably those of the Federation of South African Trade Unions (FOSATU) — avoided overt political positions and alliances, a worker could belong to Inkatha and to a union without being disloyal to either. COSATU's sympathy for disinvestment and its alignment with anti-Inkatha progressive organizations brought the divided loyalties of workers into focus. It also highlighted differences in Inkatha and unionist positions that had been a source of conflict for many years. Bus boycotts were a source of contention between workers and Inkatha and the KLA from the first year of Inkatha's existence (see WIP, 1980a:51-57; Maré, 1979:67-69). The cost of transport, in a country where most workers are forced to live at a considerable distance from the workplace, is an important issue for workers. The KLA's involvement in the ownership of bus companies in large industrial areas such as Hammarsdale and Isithebe made its claim to represent worker interests hard to sustain in the face of boycott action (Sutcliffe and Wellings, 1986 (forthcoming):27, WIP, 1980a).

Even where Inkatha has not had a financial stake in transport it has contradicted or compromised worker positions. During a bus boycott in Empangeni at the beginning of 1985 the KwaZulu cabinet initially stated its full support for commuters and there was co-operation between the commuters' committee and the KLA (Byerly, 1985:45). After two months, however, the KLA began to move towards negotiations with the Empangeni Bus Company, against the commuters' demand that various conditions be met before negotiations. Simon Conco, KLA member and now the most prominent spokesman of UWUSA, said 'the unions had their own political agenda' and 'some elements did not want to end the boycott because they were benefiting from it' (Byerly, 1985:48). The outcome of this divisiveness was that commuters were gradually forced by police intimidation and harassment, and by disunity in their ranks, to end the boycott without some of their most important demands being met (Byerly, 1985:48, 49).

These events prefigured the open conflict between Inkatha and independent trade unions that now pervades Natal's mines and industries. So too did Inkatha's response to a consumer boycott of white-owned shops in Pietermaritzburg and Howick between 15 August and 16 September 1985. The boycott was organized by FOSATU in protest at the mass dismissal of workers from BTR Sarmcol. Predictably it was rejected by Inkatha despite Buthelezi's frequent threats to unleash the boycott weapon against whites and even Indians. Inkatha representatives put pressure on the Metal and Allied Workers Union to call off the boycott (Van Niekerk, 1986:5). P.G. Gumede, the president of Inyanda (the Natal and Zululand African Chamber of Commerce) explained Inkatha's attitude:

> We informed them that Chief Buthelezi has pronounced strongly against the boycott, and if FOSATU persists with its boycott call in Natal this will mean that it will be openly challenging the Chief Minister's influence. We warned them not to push us into a corner where Nyanda [sic] will combine with Inkatha in an open battle to see who is who between FOSATU and KwaZulu leadership [NM, 25 Sep. 85; also quoted in Sutcliffe & Wellings, 1986 (forthcoming);26; and see Chapter 6, pp.130-33].

At the beginning of June 1986, COSATU presented the press with a substantial dossier documenting assaults and threats on union members and their families and associates. The declaration of the state of emergency on 12 June 1986 seems to have prevented the full horror of the dossier's contents from being revealed to the public. Whereas fear of reprisal was a major obstacle to exposing vigilante atrocities in 1985 and early 1986, by the middle of the year the emergency regulations and an over-zealous obedience of them by most of the country's newspapers continued to keep Inkatha's township policing methods under wraps.

Affidavits collected by COSATU reveal that Inkatha's vigilante activity is rife in townships throughout Natal and is probably more severe in townships in KwaZulu where the KwaZulu police have authority. Affidavits from residents of Madadeni township near Newcastle show the extent of high-level official involvement in harassment and intimidation. In one affidavit a trade unionist stated that on 19 July 1985, Dr Mdlalose, KwaZulu minister of health, and Hugh Madonsela, minister of finance, arrived at his house after midnight. He was dragged out of the house by a member of the Youth Brigade: 'I protested and Dr Mdlalose said that if I resisted he would shoot me.'

The following excerpts from another affidavit indicate the tenor of many of the documented incidents of harassment:

> At approximately 12.30 am, 24 January, 1986 I was awakened by banging on the door of the house. I . . . saw, in the front yard about 40 people, many of them armed with sticks and spears. The group was led by a policeman from the Madadeni Police Station by the name of Thusi, the mayor of Madadeni Mr Bhengu, Sipho Hadebe of the

Inkatha Youth Brigade and Temba Mdlalose who is the son of Dr Frank Mdlalose, Minister of Health of the KwaZulu Government . . . Thusi said that if I did not open the door they would burn the house down . . . A large group . . . entered the house and ransacked it . . . Thusi also questioned me at length about my relationship with . . . COSATU . . . I was then pushed into a police van . . . In the back were some Inkatha Youth Brigade members.

After various of the respondent's friends and associates were rounded up they were all taken to the police station:

> . . . We were told by Thusi to stand with our hands behind our necks. As we stood there Thusi began assaulting us one by one, by punching us in the stomach. At all times Thusi was wearing the unifórm of the KwaZulu Police and was armed with a handgun . . . We were told to stay on the verandah and wait for Frank Mdlalose and Mr Madonsela . . . After some minutes these two men arrived. They did not talk to us. I saw them talking to Thusi and after a few minutes they left.

The respondent said he was then handed over to the South African Security Branch in Newcastle, where he was tortured and told to make a statement regarding various unionists and members of the Newcastle Youth Organization.

A union member whose house was burnt down by people wearing UWUSA T-shirts said he did not report the arson directly to the police station because he felt there would be no point in doing so: 'There is a strong feeling amongst people who are affiliated to the COSATU trade unions that the South African Police at Madadeni Police Station are very strongly biased in favour of the Inkatha organization and do not take any steps to investigate matters in which Inkatha people are suspected of alleged offences' (affidavit filed with the Legal Resources Centre, and in COSATU, 1986).

'Friends of the people'

The apparent contradiction between Inkatha's posture as a liberation movement of 'the people' and its essential practice as an ethnically-based bantustan political party has proved, in the 1980s, to be not so much a contradiction as a consistent strategy. Both guises are necessary for developing a power-base in the politics of moderation and stability in South Africa. Hence Buthelezi could suggest in 1981 that KwaZulu's own police force would be 'friends of the people' (DN, 26 May 81).

Events in 1985 and 1986 have strengthened allegations of an opportunistic or conspiratorial relationship between Inkatha and the KLA on the one hand, and the South African government on the other, in policing, maintaining stability and repressing revolt in Natal's townships. While it is obvious that a bantustan government relies on the central state as much for policing and security as it does for income, it is important to examine how this reliance operates, especially where it reveals Inkatha policy.

For instance, Inkatha and the KLA have long maintained a greater distance from the South African Defence Force (SADF) than from the South African Police (SAP), though both are equally apparatuses of the central state. Involvement with the SAP, however, pertains mostly to local level politics whereas relations with the SADF encroach on national and international politics where Inkatha's claims and postures are more public and accountable.

Inkatha's willingness to develop open ties with the SAP has increased in the past couple of years but from early in its existence it has enthusiastically pursued control over the apparatuses and instruments of repression in KwaZulu. The KLA has long been keen to police its own boundaries and its reluctance to support the defence of South Africa's boundaries may have more to do with Inkatha's own strategic considerations than with intrinsic moral squeamishness about involvement with the SADF (see below).

In 1974 Buthelezi proposed that the government grant firearm licences '. . . to all chiefs for the destruction of vermin and to deserving businessmen and other Zulus of repute who need these firearms for the protection of their businesses and themselves' (KLAD, 4:333). Jeffrey Mtetwa, KwaZulu minister of justice, said in 1978 that the KLA '. . . not only aimed at taking over the police but would also ask Pretoria to give military training to tribal regiments' (NM, 12 May 78). In 1980, however, the KwaZulu cabinet turned down King Goodwill's request that he be trained as a soldier by the SADF. A number of 'ethnic battalions' were formed within the SADF. The 'Zulu' battalion — 121 Battalion — was based at Jozini close to the Ingwavuma district and the border of Mozambique (Maré, 1982a:16-17). Before Goodwill's attempt to join the SADF Buthelezi had said that the KwaZulu administration would have nothing to do with the SADF's 'Zulu' brigade (Survey, 1980:408). The king's application was made at Nongoma and it was forwarded to the KwaZulu cabinet for approval. Buthelezi said that he had already turned down an invitation to become commander-in-chief of 121 Battalion, and that the cabinet would not recruit for it (Maré, 1982a:16). He said: 'I do not think it is in the interests of the king's own image, or that of KwaZulu for that matter, for His Majesty to train as a soldier' (Survey, 1980:408). Some observers saw Goodwill's overtures to the SADF as an attempt to continue to define an independent role for himself or to challenge Buthelezi. There was speculation that South African agents could have been behind Goodwill's army initiative in a move to embarrass Buthelezi (Survey, 1980:408).

Since 1980 the KwaZulu police force has been under the control of the KLA, initially under the department of justice, and then as an independent department with Buthelezi as minister of police (KLA, nd:50). The 'Zulu' brigade, however, was simply an ethnic batallion of the SADF and beyond the bounds of KLA control. Buthelezi typically deplores the SADF presence in KwaZulu with the rhetoric of non-violence: 'If we were not a society in conflict, there would be no need for a military presence in this part of KwaZulu' (St, 25 Jul. 82). Referring to military doctors in KwaZulu, he said that although he respected the work being done by the defence force, he condemned 'the propagandistic use of army men in their attempts to seduce our young people into believing that war is the best method of solving human conflicts, because it is just not so' (St, 25 Jan. 82). Yet, as has been shown above (see p.68), Buthelezi has not been reluctant to develop the para-military aspects of Youth Service Corps training. The Inkatha constitution itself sets out that the national council shall include 'ten representatives of the security forces, once we are in a position to have them' (Inkatha, nd(a):23).

The takeover of existing police operations by the KwaZulu police began in 1980 under the command of Lieutenant-Colonel 'Tony' Fontini, who was seconded by the SAP. J. Mtetwa, minister of justice for KwaZulu, said the establishment of a security section of the KwaZulu Police would take place as soon as possible and he urged vigilante groups to join the police reservists (DN, 8 May 80). This possibly refers to the emergence of vigilante activity in response to the KwaMashu school

Inkatha impis pursuing mourners at the funeral of victims of the attack on the memorial service for the murdered lawyer and UDF activist, Victoria Mxenge. The service, held in Umlazi's cinema on 7 August 1985, was attacked by several hundred men shouting Inkatha's war-cry. The police acted only when the attackers were being driven off.

BILLY PADDOCK

BILLY PADDOCK

Umlazi 1985. Impi leader issues orders while mourners try to slip past.

Winnington Sabelo (in the foreground with gun just visible under his jacket) points to mourners and photographers in Umlazi cemetery.

Thomas Shabalala, Lindelani community leader and senior Inkatha member, threatens a KwaMashu headmaster with death for 'allowing' pupils to boycott classes, October 1985.

boycotts of 1980 and is an early suggestion of KLA and Inkatha awareness of the difficulty of supporting 'loyal' vigilantes outside their immediate and formal control. Buthelezi voiced another preoccupation of the KLA when he said the KwaZulu Police would be a '. . . unit to look after our property' (DN, 7 May 80).

In 1982, when Gerrit Viljoen, then Minister of National Education, addressed the KLA, he said that KwaZulu Police would soon be entirely responsible for policing KwaZulu (NM, 22 Apr. 82). As yet this promise remains unfulfilled: the KwaZulu Police are in charge of rural KwaZulu and most townships, but they have been denied control of the largest townships in Natal, KwaMashu and Umlazi, probably because of their proximity to the vital port of Durban and to the largest concentration of white inhabitants in Natal. Similarly, the sensitive border district of Ingwavuma, in the north, has been excluded from KwaZulu Police control even though it falls under the KLA administration.

By mid-1986 there was sufficient common interest between the central government and the KLA for Buthelezi to press for the handing over of police control of Umlazi and KwaMashu by the SAP to the KwaZulu Police (DN, 4 Jun. 86; 26 Jun. 86). The demonstration of Inkatha's willingness to police opposition in the two townships in 1985 and 1986 has now been rewarded with the granting of control over these areas, and with various concessions to the regional power-sharing between Natal and KwaZulu. The KLA's enthusiasm for controlling the police force in KwaMashu and Umlazi, despite its taint of collaboration, is probably related to its confidence in its future in regional and central politics. It is probable that Inkatha will become less sensitive to accusations of collusion, even with the SADF, if its stake in sharing the power of the central state is increased.

It is also possible that as Inkatha draws nearer to regional 'power-sharing' it may wish to distance itself from the strong-arm tactics of the 'amabutho', or at least to formalize control over them. There might be a measure of legitimacy attached to the use of 'KwaZulu-Natal Police' in the future that is lacking in the use of 'amabutho' violence at present. In May 1986, after a spate of interdicts against Inkatha members was reported in the press, Buthelezi said he and King Goodwill objected to the use of the term 'amabutho' to describe groups of armed vigilantes. He said 'amabutho' meant regiments and that in the 'Zulu' nation it was solely the king's prerogative to form regiments. He felt the term 'impi' was likewise abused and said the press could refer to these people simply as 'armed men' (NM, 28 May 86). Perhaps, in Buthelezi's view, one way to rescue 'Zulu tradition' and language from perversion is to put police uniforms on the 'amabutho'.

Unrest in Natal's townships has confronted Buthelezi with the dilemma of the South African state: that of the efficacy of violence versus the legitimacy of stability gained via a reform process. In effect, the political position of Inkatha's leadership, and the political actions of some of its supporters, can hardly be distinguished from those of the central state. Inkatha is willing to formalize its role in political repression through responsibility for the KwaZulu Police and it has indicated its desire to extend defence forces under its control. Expanded, formalized control over the policing and defending of Natal will, of necessity, accompany joint administration and proposed legislative responsibility in the region.

9. Conclusion

The Inkatha leadership has shaped and wrapped a political commodity which is being offered to various conservative takers in South Africa and internationally. This is clear in their language and strategies. The wrapping makes the political package *appear* ambiguous, but the sales patter, upon examination, does not hide the conservative and repressive direction taken within the movement.

Buthelezi's Inkatha

It must be stressed that this book deals with the Inkatha movement as initiated, directed, and presented by its leadership, especially through the central charismatic figure of Chief Mangosuthu Gatsha Buthelezi, the president of Inkatha and chief minister of the KwaZulu bantustan. Inkatha's leadership can in no way be equated with its membership. The membership is drawn to Inkatha for a wide range of 'positive' reasons — and forced to join through coercion and actual or potential sanctions. Inkatha's claimed membership probably exceeds its actual support, and that it is no monolithic organization becomes clear from a number of newspaper articles that have mentioned dissent from within. Such manifestations of discord must be the tip of an iceberg in a movement which constitutionally prohibits the public airing of dirty linen. Examples of dissent have centred around political and other advantages flowing from setting up and running local Inkatha branches (see *Echo*, 26 Feb. 81, for a case in the townships outside Pietermaritzburg; and *Echo*, 15 Apr. 85 for clashes between two Inkatha factions in KwaMashu; also Survey, 1979:31). We are not aware, however, of any large-scale mobilization of members against Inkatha's present leadership or political direction, although Dladla's popularity early in the bantustan's history probably offered that potential. Such a mobilization would, in any case, be extremely difficult, if not impossible, because of the central control over essential material, media, security, and ideological resources exercised by the present leadership and their state and business backers.

Ironically, the concentration of power around Inkatha's leadership and Buthelezi, and the sheer size of the movement, might well have resulted in a diffusion of power centres. The general points we have made, while true for *Buthelezi's* Inkatha, might not always hold true at the local level. At the branch level strong but localized 'fiefdoms' have been created that owe their power to locally specific sanctions that can be imposed, and to locally specific class configurations. At the same time there have been a small number of instances where community groups have been able to work with local level Inkatha officials, though it appears to be more common for Inkatha to have control.

Inkatha is left with few of its allies of earlier days. The South African Black Alliance exists in little more than name while even such staunch friends as PFP

217

members have had to distance themselves from Inkatha on certain issues, as they did, for example, during the national convention movement debacle. This is certainly not to say that Inkatha has not, and will not, pick up conservative support. The KwaZulu/Natal Indaba is a clear example of the cementing of new alliances, both with business and with even more conservative political interests than in the past. Internationally this is also the case, as the governments of Britain, the USA and West Germany search for black faces to undertake the task of post-apartheid collaboration. These governments see the abolition of apartheid in a similar way to the achievement of political independence in colonial Africa in the 1950s and 1960s. The hope of finding the local equivalent of a neo-colonial solution is what informs their approaches to Buthelezi and others like him.

If Inkatha is examined through the presentation and direction of the leadership, we find a picture apparently far removed from enforced membership and internal dissent. Here we have Inkatha presented as a 'national cultural liberation movement', which reflects the unity of the 'black' or African oppressed. This is the picture we have scrutinized and found to be full of flaws and misrepresentations. Despite the absence of unity, the concept of 'populism' is an analytical thread in Buthelezi's Inkatha. The rhetoric of mobilization he employs is that of populism. In the words of John Saul, the 'political rallying cries' of populism are those 'that stress . . . solidarity and the unity of sections of the populace'. He continued:

> In very many cases the stress upon solidarity will represent neither the real situation of the mass of the people, nor their views of that situation . . . *Rather it will represent an aspiration to make a particular view as to the characteristics that unite people prevail over any continuing awareness of the elements that divide* [emphasis added] [1973:173].

Of the few critical analytical evaluations of the Inkatha movement that have been published, those by Southall (1981) and by McCaul (1983) have both concluded that Inkatha is 'a populist movement making petty bourgeois demands and neutralizing class antagonisms', and that if it 'represents a class alliance, it is increasingly that between the African petty bourgeoisie and the reform-minded elements of the South African bourgeoisie' (McCaul, 1983:89-90). However, McCaul concurs with Southall's ironic earlier conclusion that:

> It seems unlikely that Buthelezi . . . will play anything but a *divisive role*, and that the only politics of compromise in which he will be likely to engage effectively will be those which serve to compromise the course of future South African liberation [emphasis added] [Southall, 1981:481, quoted McCaul, 1983:90].

The irony is that a movement that claims to speak on behalf of all 'the people', should be one of the primary factors of conflict in the struggle for a changed South Africa. However, Inkatha's populism covers a range of political positions and economic interests. Inkatha's leadership, Buthelezi in particular, has appropriated 'total' representation of a range of interests for the movement. However, despite the claim of 'neutrality', Inkatha's direction is informed by a definite class orientation and style of politics that serve the interests of both the state and of capital. As Saul warned, 'it is wiser to look to the tensions between various elements and various perspectives' within a populist movement than it is to take the rhetoric of unity at face value.

There are several dimensions to Inkatha's claim of 'total representation'. First, Inkatha claims to speak for the people, as populist movements do. Populist rhetoric usually equates 'the people' with the African population or, even more inclusively, the black population, but in Inkatha's case 'the people' effectively means the 'Zulu nation'. The historical perspective taken in this study explains why a regional 'ethnic populism' should be available to the petty bourgeoisie for mobilization and, even more important, why the constituency should be available for such a mobilization. A large proportion of Inkatha's members do respond to a cultural definition of 'Zulu', with its specific history and distinctive social and personal characteristics such as 'brave' and 'warlike'.

Divisions within this populism are secondary. When antagonisms are acknowledged they are transformed 'into simple differences' (cf Laclau, 1977) such as when Buthelezi stated that the 'bricks of black nationalism are many and varied. There are ethnic groups, there are tribes, there are trade unions, drama societies, black church groups, student organizations, cultural groups and many others' (BS, 14 Mar. 76:17; also 16 Feb. 77:3). Even, or maybe especially, when addressing class specific groups Buthelezi gives the same message. In 1976 he told migrant workers in the S.J. Smith hostel in Durban that:

> It is true that I believe in trade unions. I believe that workers can only have machinery for negotiations between themselves and management through trade unions. Having said this, let me emphasize that we are however not oppressed only as workers in South Africa. We are not oppressed only as peasants. Nor are we oppressed as an educated elite . . . we are oppressed . . . on the basis of our black skins. We have therefore to unite as blacks if we intend dealing with our problem decisively [BS, 28 Aug. 76].

In an address to the Women's Brigade conference Buthelezi spoke about 'an organization which embraces all sections of our black community without any distinction of class . . . or any other distinction', and said that there 'should be no room for fights between slaves' (BS, 29 Oct. 77).

A second aspect of Inkatha's 'total representation' arises out of overriding common oppression, and his equally frequent attacks on those who do a disservice to this unity arise out of Inkatha's populist claims — unity is possible only through Inkatha. On a simple level, if an organization represents 'the people' it is not possible for other bodies to claim the same constituency or an overlapping one.

Third, Inkatha claims to be the repository of traditions of resistance in South Africa. This is why the continuity claimed with the ANC has been so important to Inkatha's leaders, and why clashes with the 'Mission in Exile', the UDF, COSATU, and many other organizations have taken such an 'inevitable' path.

Finally, Buthelezi projects himself as the embodiment of resistance. Tordoff, writing about trends in African politics in the post-independence period, noted the tendency not only for power to be 'centralized in a single party, but also for it to be personalized in the hands of the party leader . . .' (Tordoff, 1984:5 and 105). Charismatic leadership has been found to be one of the characteristics of populist movements in Latin America as well, with 'a tendency for the leadership to bypass or "short-circuit" their own internal organization at critical moments, or indeed whenever it suits them to do so' (Raby, 1983:13). There may well be something in the parallels drawn with Peronism in Argentina, but that would take us too far from the specific reality and history of south-east Africa, and 'the Zulu nation'. Buthelezi's own representation of his position comes across clearly:

> Inkatha is Black South Africa undivided, standing together, pursuing the time-honoured traditions of Black South Africa. . . . For us, Black South African political traditions go back to 1912 when the African National Congress was formed. I stand

boldly before you and say that those are the traditions which Black South Africa serves. Those are the traditions which Inkatha serves. The struggle for liberation in our country started with history itself [sic]. It is tragic that so many new organizations arise to pretend that they only have now discovered [sic] the struggle for liberation. The struggle has endured for generations . . . I am rooted in this tradition. Dr Pixley ka Isaka Seme was my uncle. He was one of the founding fathers of the ANC. I grew up at my mother's knee learning what he and others did. When I became older, I joined the ANC . . . I knew people like Nelson Mandela, Robert Sobukwe and Oliver Tambo personally. I knew what their faces looked like. I know what their voices sound like and I know what the feel of their hands in my hands feels like. My own ambitions were to become a lawyer, but it was Chief Luthuli himself who said that my duty lay with the people and that I should not indulge in the luxury of doing what I wanted to do . . . The great leaders of South Africa when I was a young man recognized that I was destined to do what I am now doing. My father and his father before him served successive Zulu Kings as Prime Ministers and for me there was no escape from this hereditary role unless I was to betray my people and seek my own selfish ends away from them. Thus, comrades when I say that I serve Black South Africa's political traditions, I say that with sureness and with power. These traditions run in my blood and I did not create my own blood. I was born into this world with the blood coursing through my veins carrying the traditions of the people [BS, 13 May 84:5-6; also BS, 29 Jun. 85:10-12].

There is a specific style to the centralized leadership of Inkatha that is anti-democratic. It is well illustrated by Buthelezi's comment after a meeting with the Joint Rent Action Group (JORAC) in 1984, when the Reverend Xundu refused to make press comment, 'saying that JORAC would itself have to meet before any statement was issued'. Buthelezi responded by saying that 'his own people trusted him (Buthelezi) to make decisions and that he was not used to dealing with leaders who had to work in this way' (DN, 21 Aug. 84). It indicates both a political style and at the same time the 'divine right of ancestry' that Buthelezi claims for himself within 'Zulu' political history. The Indaba is being conducted in the same undemocratic style. It would appear to be an essential element of the politics of consociationalism.

The effect, then, of Inkatha's populism has been to construe nearly all alternative opposition in South Africa as threats to its claims to represent the 'wisdom of the struggle' and 'the wisdom of the ages' (BS, 29 Jun. 85:12). This is the case with other 'national liberation' movements, such as the ANC and the UDF, and also with class organizations. As Raby wrote: 'The ideology of populism is all-embracing, appealing to the idealized unity of the nation or the people; it cannot therefore tolerate class-based organizations which are truly independent, and therefore divisive.' (1983:15). As Buthelezi told the NSRAIEU sugar workers, 'when I speak as President of Inkatha, I speak with the voice of the workers' (BS, 13 May 84:4).

Inkatha has found it necessary to go beyond the rhetoric of populism and establish its own union, the United Workers Union of South Africa (UWUSA). In large part this was due to the inevitable political role of trade unions in South Africa as exemplified in COSATU. Raby referred to the *institutional expression in a corporatist structure* (emphasis added) of the all-encompassing appeal of populist movements that sometimes takes place. This means that 'sectors' such as labour, the peasantry and the middle class are represented within the movement — 'the typical populist party will set up its own union movement, or else attempt to take over existing unions' (Raby, 1983:14-15). Inkatha attempts to provide a 'home' for the organized expression of interests such as unions, teachers' organizations and professional bodies generally, and also to give form to interests without organizations, such as current attempts to link agricultural capital and farm labourers in northern Natal.

Despite the populist rhetoric of unity and common interests Inkatha displays class political and economic interests that increasingly mesh openly with the forces of conservatism in South Africa, and has in fact never challenged those forces in any fundamental way. What we find in Inkatha confirms previous contentions that populism and populist mobilization should not be taken at face value, though there can be conservative and progressive, or even revolutionary, populism.

The Inkatha leadership has shown a firm commitment to the principles and ideology of capitalism (the 'free enterprise system') as a motor of development, guarantor of democratic rights, provider of employment, and agent of desirable change for all in the country. Inkatha's economic practice has ensured the structural integration of the movement itself into capitalist enterprise (the party as capitalist), and the advancement of the direct interests of members of the African ('Zulu') petty bourgeoisie. Its economic links have to a large extent been created in cooperation with and nurtured by monopoly capital. Similarly the movement's political practice has been to work closely with individuals from the monopoly sector or with the political representatives of that sector. In the political arena Inkatha has sided with the state, if not always in intention then at least in effect, and against other organizations and individuals committed to working for a new South Africa, radically different from the present society. Inkatha has, in effect, drawn a distinction between the *apartheid* state and the *capitalist* state, in a manner similar to the Thatcher and Reagan administrations. While clearly antagonistic towards the apartheid system and working towards its abolition, Inkatha has become an integral part of the system of ensuring the survival of capitalism in South Africa. The latter course of action has meant cooperation with state agencies, the bantustan administration being one. In this sense Inkatha's resistance has been *loyal* to politicized ethnicity, to reformism and compromise, to capitalism, to anti-communism and anti-socialism, to foreign capitalism. It has also *resisted* in mounting an effective campaign against the most obnoxious elements of apartheid such as racial discrimination and total political exclusion, though in fact its resistance has served to give greater credibility and desirability to its loyalty, where nearly all bantustan leaders failed hopelessly.

Inkatha's political practice clearly serves to maintain capitalist relations of production through disciplining the working class, through the creation in May 1986 of UWUSA, with its pro-capitalist, anti-strike, anti-boycott, anti-sanctions and anti-disinvestment line. The recent move into the agricultural sector in the Natal region is an illustration of the movement's disciplinary role. Employers were approached to allow Inkatha certain concessions (recruitment for the movement, it appears) in exchange for which farm labourers would participate in securing northern border areas from guerilla infiltration, and would attempt to reinstate conservative 'tribal' and family values.

Buthelezi's Natal

The KwaZulu/Natal Indaba, an attempt to formulate a proposal for a regional legislative authority that would in effect be the first unit in a federal South Africa, was launched with a great deal of local media hype. Editorials dug up the most banal examples of the supposed distinctiveness of the Natal region. Of greater political significance than the wishful thinking about a Natal (and hence English) racial tolerance amongst whites were the frequent references to the Inkatha movement and the role of Chief Buthelezi. For a wide range of local and international interests Buthelezi has become *the* hope for regional stability.

The Indaba and the federal political direction in general allows Buthelezi's Inkatha to make a strength of its weakness as a national political factor. The Indaba allows Inkatha's ethnic base, which is predominantly confined to Natal, to open doors into national politics. As a federal 'prime minister' Buthelezi would achieve national prominence and make national claims for inclusion that would not be possible for a clearly ethnic leader competing with national, non-ethnic and non-racial organizations. The 'Natal option' would also allow the state to give Buthelezi a central position that it could not allow the other bantustan nonentities. Furthermore, it might lead to the formation of a multi-racial political party on the basis of the practical cooperation that has occurred behind the closed doors of the Indaba (at which the National Party has observer status).

On a regional level Buthelezi's populist appeals to the unity of the oppressed frequently slip into ethnic chauvinism. 'Zuluness' is the tradition from which he draws his legitimacy, and within which he has consequently achieved his political position and recognition. While some care has been taken in the past to balance the clearly ethnic 'Zulu' appeals, the dramatically more prominent role that King Goodwill is now being allowed to play on the political stage of Natal has swung the balance towards regional and 'Zulu' consolidation. In some of his pronouncements King Goodwill has displayed a level of antagonism towards non-'Zulus' that cannot but inflame even further tensions created and maintained by apartheid and does not bode well for the future.

Also on a regional level Inkatha has been constrained by the bantustan base that it claims to have adopted as an expedient strategy. Its structural involvement with this central pillar of apartheid administration has not only tainted the organization but has made it dependent on the patronage and finances that KwaZulu makes available. There is of course no reason why Inkatha control over a federal region of Natal could not fulfil the same or an extended patronage function. This is the direction in which Buthelezi seems to be moving — forming new structures would, of course, still have to be sanctioned by the central state, but there is mounting pressure from both capital and existing administrative bodies for a regional solution to the problem of instability for capital to be accepted.

The approach we have adopted has allowed us to move beyond the deserved, but ultimately shallow, moral opprobrium heaped upon Inkatha (and blatantly ignored by its backers) for its role in a highly conservative maintenance of 'law and order' in the region. It is not simply a case of bad and good but a clash of political positions and economic interests of two opposed visions for a future South Africa. To describe the conflict as 'black on black' violence is to remain on the surface of events.

Buthelezi, and initially Inkatha, gained the approval of a wide range of organizations and individuals during the first half of the 1970s, including the fledgling independent unions, the ANC and religious bodies. At the same time the state and local capital were engaged in a campaign to unseat Buthelezi or limit his powers. However, the 16 years since the Zulu Territorial Authority was formed, and especially the 11 years since Inkatha's formation, have seen a revolution in political action and political debate in South Africa. The tide of resistance since

The Chief

BILLY PADDOCK

Blood brothers: Buthelezi with Kaizer Matanzima, 'chief minister' of the Transkei bantustan.

1973 has involved trade unions, the scholars' revolts, community action, new political organizations, international pressure, and a generalized crisis of the state and of capital, and it has, in large measure, left Inkatha behind and forced its leaders to link the direction of the movement to the forces of conservatism. But Buthelezi's appetite for power will not be satisfied in a subordinate context. The drive for power will be one of disruption and reaction, of division and of attempts to protect what has no place in a democratic future.

APPENDIX 1
Inkata

Before giving a description of an Inkata I must explain that it is not at all the same as the ordinary grass pad for supporting burthens on the head which goes by that name.[1] The Inkata now described is a larger thing, made of certain fibres which are very strong and binding. The doctor specially deputed to make it knows exactly what fibres to use. He makes it in secret, sprinkles it with various concoctions, and finally winds the skin of a python round it, as this reptile is considered the most powerful of animals, coiling itself round its prey and squeezing it to death, as it does. When the Inkata is finished all the full-grown men as well as the principal women of the tribe are summoned, and are sprinkled and given powders of various dried herbs to swallow. The men then go down to the river and drink certain mixtures, bathe in the river, and return to the kraal where the Inkata is made. They are then sprinkled a second time, and return to their homes.

After this the Inkata is handed over by the doctor to the chief's principal wife, and entrusted to her and to two or three others, to be withdrawn from the common gaze. It is taken care of and passed on from generation to generation as part of the chief's regalia. The Inkata is looked upon as the good spirit of the tribe, binding all together in one, and attracting back any deserter.

The king or chief uses it on all great occasions — more especially on those of a civil nature. For instance, when a new chief is taking up the reins of government, the Inkata is brought out of its hiding-place, a circle is formed by the tribe, and it is placed on the ground in the centre. The new chief then, holding his father's weapons, stands on the Inkata while he is being proclaimed by his people. After this it is carefully put away again.

In the case of the king being taken ill the doctor seats him on the Inkata while he is "treating" him (elapa). It is also used in a variety of other royal ceremonies, and is looked upon as more sacred than the English Crown. It is, in fact, the guardian spirit or totem of a Zulu tribe. Yet, strange to say, it appears that nothing was known to the Judges of the Native High Court as to the existence of the Inkata, in a very important case[2] not long since tried there, when it was what might be termed the very essence of the case, and possibly injustice resulted from this ignorance of native laws and customs.

(From L.H. Samuelson (1974: 138-40), original published 1929).

---

1. The word seems to be almost universal in the Bantu languages:- Nyanja, nkata; Luganda, enkata; Swahili, kata; Suto, khare. What is most curious is that, so far away as the Gold Coast we find an indication of ceremonial usages connected with this article. See the *Journal of the African Society* for July, 1908, p. 407. The Fanti word for it is ekar, which may be a merely accidental resemblance, or may point to a fundamental identity of roots in the West African and the Bantu languages. Possibly the root idea of kata is 'something coiled or rolled up', and this may be the only connection between the head-pad and the charm. The Baronga (Delagoa Bay) have a similar tribal talisman called mhamba, which is a set of balls, each containing the nail- parings and hair of a deceased chief, kneaded up with the dung of the cattle slaughtered at his funeral, and no doubt some kind of pitch to give it consistency. These balls are then enclosed in plaited leather thongs. The custom of thus preserving relics of dead chiefs is found elsewhere: The Cambridge Ethnological Museum possesses a set of the "regalia" of Unyoro, which would come under the same category. — ED.

2. Rex v Tshingumuzi, Mbopeyana, and Mbombo, 1909.

APPENDIX 2
'The Statement of Belief' issued to branches of Inkatha

'We can only move from where we are on the basis of strategies acceptable to most people. I think it is relevant that I should inform members of this House about "THE STATEMENT OF BELIEF" I have mentioned above, because I would be grateful to know what members of this Assembly think of it. And here it is' (Buthelezi to KLA).

(1) We believe that respect for individuals and the value placed on cultural and large groups is synonymous with progress towards a politically stable society.

(2) We believe that political rights of all national groups should be protected within a constitutional framework which outlaws discrimination based on colour, sex or creed.

(3) We believe in individual equality before the law, equality of opportunity and equality of benefits from the institutions of the State.

(4) We believe that the identity of an individual within a particular cultural milieu is essential to his identity as a South African, but we believe also that culture belongs to all men and that no social, economic or political impediments which hinder the free movements of individuals from one cultural milieu to another are in any respect justified.

(5) We recognize that there are privileged communities and underprivileged communities and we believe that it is the very special duty of the State to provide the opportunities and back those opportunities with resources to enable every individual who is underprivileged to develop to the maximum of his ability.

(6) We believe that the resources of the country and the wealth which has already been created which is controlled by the State, belongs to all the people of South Africa, and we believe that the resources and the wealth of the country should be utilized for the greatest good of the greatest number.

(7) We believe that we are facing a grave crisis in which the poor are threatened with greater poverty and we believe it essential that all men join hands and enter into a partnership with the State to effect the greatest possible redistribution of wealth commensurate with maximizing the productivity of commerce, trade and industry, whether State-controlled or privately owned.

(8) We believe that fiscal control is essential to regulate the quantity and flow of money and near money, and we also believe that State control by equivalents of the Reserve Bank are essential for the utilization of land, water and power in the interests of the economy and in the interests of developing underdeveloped areas and populations.

(9) We believe in the elimination of secrecy in public administration and we believe individuals should have rights to appeal to the courts to protect his or her privacy in the pursuit of that which is lawful.

(10) We believe that practices acceptable in civilized nations should characterize the methods and the procedures used by the police in the enforcement of law.

(11) We believe that the enforcement of law is devoid of meaning outside of the rule of law, and we believe that there should be both a criminal code and a justice code in which rights to appeal to the highest courts of the land are the rights of all persons, and we believe that upon pronouncement of an

impartial law society, the State should bear the costs of appeal where the appellant pursued a course of action to protect his individual rights.

(12) We believe that in living the good life in a just society an individual should be free to attend any educational institution in which he has entry qualifications, reside where he wishes, own ground where he wishes, become qualified in any trade or profession for which he has the required degree of competence.

(13) We believe that the development of trade unions, guilds and associations should be encouraged by the enactment of enabling legislation and courts of arbitration.

(14) We believe that the accumulated injustices of the past and the injustice now present in the institutions of our country have created a bitterness and anger among the underprivileged sections of our populations, and we believe that growing fears of this anger and bitterness make the privileged sections of our population intransigent in the face of the need for change.

(15) We believe therefore that the transition from an unjust society to a just society will be difficult.

(16) We believe that in this eleventh hour of South Africa, responsible leadership must publicly declare its commitment to bring about a just society within the foreseeable future, and we believe that leadership must meet the demands of responsibility by taking whatever steps remain from time to time to avoid a race war.

(17) We believe that the mobilization of constituency protest and a refusal to act within the restrictive confines of race exclusively holds a promise we dare not abandon.

We, the undersigned, pledge ourselves and our constituencies to supporting a movement which for want of a better designation will be known as the PEOPLES' MOVEMENT FOR RADICAL PEACEFUL CHANGE.

(from Schmahmann, 1978:443-47, appendix VIII.)

APPENDIX 3
Description of the Mace of the KwaZulu Legislative Assembly and its Symbolic Significance

1. On top of the mace is a typical ZULU HUT, "Indlu", to symbolize the birthplace of Zulu culture and custom and the close-knit Zulu family on which the whole Zulu social structure is built.

2. This hut stands firmly on the MYSTICAL COIL — "Inkatha". The grass in this mystical coil was plucked from the thatch of the doorways of all Zulu Chiefs' huts and is known to the Zulus as "Inkatha yokusonga izwe". This is to symbolize the coil's deep power to unite and keep firm all the different tribes of the Zulu people. Each of the 285 strands around the coil represents one of the tribes composing the Zulu Nation.

3. Below the mystical coil is the black BEER-POT — "Ukhamba", adorned with the head of a white beast from the royal Zulu herd. This is to symbolize the traditional generosity and hospitality of both Zulu chief and commoner.

4. Below the beer-pot is the traditional GRAIN-BASKET, "Isilulu", a battle axe, "Isizenze", and a knob- stick, "Iwisa". This is to symbolize the Zulu's origin from the North and serves as a reminder to the rulers to see that the basket is kept full so that the Nation could be fed, and the shield warns that the Nation must be protected.

5. Below the grain-basket is a black polished HEAD-RING, "Isicoco", worn by Zulu dignitaries. This is to symbolize the wisdom and maturity of the Zulu elders and councillors, their inherent dignity, impeccable manners and respect for authority — "Inhlonipho".

6. All these symbols stand upon four OSTRICH FEATHERS, "Izimpaphe Zentshe", worn by the Zulu warriors of old.

7. Below the feathers the staff is square in shape. On two opposite sides of the square is the BROAD-BLADED STABBING ASSEGAI, "Iklwa", used by the armies of Shaka, the Zulu King. This is to symbolize the discipline and strength of the Zulu Nation.

8. On the other two opposite sides of the square is portrayed the historical EVERLASTING SPEAR OF THE ZULUS, "Umkhonto Wenkosi Oyis-imakade", kept by the Paramount Chief. This is to symbolize the close association of Royal House of the Zulus has with this governing body; and the Nation's continued existence.

9. On the scroll around the shaft appear the WORDS OF PRAISE AND RESPECT. This the Zulu Government Body will utter symbolizing its affirmation of loyalty and union with the Paramount Chief of the Zulus and the Royal House — "WENA WENDLOVU BAYETE!"

10. The mace is made of the inner heart wood of the Russet Willow (Combretum Apiculatum). This tree is known to the Zulus as "Mbondwemnyama". In the time of the Zulu Kings, Shaka and Dingane, the "Keepers of Order" (and executioners) were armed with heavy knob-sticks of this dark wood. The red wood of which the spears are made is the heart wood of the tree Rhamnus Zeyheri, known to the Zulus as "Mnini" or "Mcaka". This wood is the 'Royal' wood of the Zulus.

11. The mace is carried vertically and is known in Zulu as "INDUKU YOMBUSO KA ZULU".

(from KLA, nd.)

APPENDIX 4
KwaZulu Regulations for Chiefs and Headmen

Duties, powers, authorities and functions of chiefs and headmen

6.(1) Any chief or headman shall —

   (a) enjoy the status, rights and privileges and be subject to the obligations and duties conferred or imposed upon his office by the recognized customs or usages of his tribe;

(b)   be entitled, in the due fulfilment of his functions, to the loyalty, respect, support and obedience of every resident of the area for which he has been appointed;

(c)   subject to such lawful orders or instructions as may, from time to time be given to him by or through any competent representative of the Government, carry on the administration of his area;

(d)   maintain law and order and report to the Government, without delay, any matter of import or concern, including any condition of unrest or dissatisfaction;

(e)   exercise within his area, in relation to any resident —

    (i)   the powers of arrest conferred upon him, in his capacity as a peace officer, by Chapter IV of the Criminal Procedure Act, 1955 (Act 56 of 1955); and

    (ii) subject to the provisions of subsections (3) and (4) of section 46 of the said Act, the powers of search and seizure, relating to stolen stock, liquor, habit forming drugs, arms, ammunition and explosives, referred to in subsection (1) of that section;

(f)   ensure the protection of life, persons and property and the safety of *bona fide* travellers within his area, and report forthwith to the competent authority —

    (i)   the death of any person from violence or other unnatural cause;

    (ii) the outbreak of contagious or infectious disease;

    (iii) any pretended witchcraft or divination;

    (iv) any misuse of Government property;

    (v) any irregular receipt or use of public monies;

    (vi) the holding of any unauthorized meeting, gathering or assembly or the distribution of undesirable literature in, or the unauthorized entry of any person into his area; and

    (vii) the commission of any offence which does not fall to be dealt with under his own jurisdiction;

(g)   disperse or order the dispersal of any unauthorized assembly of armed persons or of any riotous or unlawful meeting or gathering;

(h)   if a state of lawlessness exists in his area or in his opinion cannot otherwise be prevented, order that all or any of the following shall be prohibited for any period in his discretion —

    (i)   the gathering of men in groups;

    (ii) the brewing of beer or the holding of any feast within such area as he shall specify;

    (iii) the carrying by any person of a shield or more than one ordinary stick;

    (iv) the shouting of war cries or the blowing of bugles or whistles;

(i)   make known to the residents of his area the requirements of any new law;

(j)   ensure compliance with all laws and the orders and instructions of any competent authority;

(k)   prevent cruelty to animals;

(l)   detain and, when so required by law, impound any livestock depastured unlawfully or found straying within, or introduced illegally or under suspicious circumstances into his area and report the fact to the competent authority;

(m) not be or become a member or take part in any activities or in any manner promote the objects of any organization of which the aims are the unconstitutional overthrow of the Government and shall not encourage disobedience to or resistance against any law; and

(n) generally seek to promote the interests of his tribe and of the region and actively support, and himself initiate measures for the advancement of his people.

(from KwaZulu 'Zulu Chiefs and Headmens Act (8 of 1974)')

BIBLIOGRAPHY

A Note on Sources

The bibliography has been divided into categories to facilitate access to the textual references while at the same time presenting an additional range of sources. First, there is a list of *Newspapers and Journals, and Abbreviations used in references.* This is followed by a list of *References* that appear in the book. Third are the *Speeches* made by Chief Buthelezi and by King Goodwill Zwelethini that receive mention; fourth, *Inkatha publications,* and fifth, *Kwazulu official publications* that have been consulted. *Unpublished interviews* follow, and finally we have added a *Bibliography* of some useful material that did not receive mention in the text itself.

Chief Buthelezi has delivered a very large number of speeches during the 1970s and 1980s. It would make a booklet in itself to have listed all of these. There is no single complete collection that the authors are aware of. However, a catalogue and index of some of the themes, issues and individuals appearing in these speeches has been undertaken as part of the project of which this book is part. An early decision was taken not to consult the speeches systematically before writing a first draft. Such an approach would have meant that Buthelezi's version would have shaped the form of the book too directly. The index was, therefore, consulted at a later stage to provide illustrative material or to ensure that we had not misrepresented Chief Buthelezi and the values that he holds. Obviously, with the amount of repetition that characterizes these speeches, only a limited number of references have been given. These could easily be expanded upon.

We have relied extensively on published material, in newspapers, journals, books, and of course Inkatha publications themselves. Chief Buthelezi occupies many columns of newspaper reports every year and has been repeatedly interviewed by more or less sympathetic journalists and researchers. These interviews show the same degree of consistency that his speeches display. We also wish to acknowledge all the individuals who knowingly or otherwise contributed to this book and to the store of information we have not used. As indicated in the preface we are not willing to name them in the present national and regional political climate in South Africa.

Temkin's biography of Buthelezi (1976) has been used rather reluctantly. It is often unclear and leaves a host of unanswered questions. However, it carries the approval of Chief Buthelezi, and Temkin claims to have had free access to much of Buthelezi's personal records, and memories.

Newspapers and journals, and abbreviations used in references in text

Abasebenzi
ABRECSA — Alliance of Black Reformed Churches of Southern Africa
BCC — British Council of Churches
BC Report — Buthelezi Commission Report
Bd — *Beeld*
BS — Buthelezi Speech
CC — *Clarion Call/Inhlabamkhosi*
CIIR — Catholic Institute for International Relations
Cit — *Citizen*
CT — *Cape Times*
Deurbraak
The Developer
Development Action
DN — *Daily News*
Drum
DSG — Development Studies Group
Echo — weekly supplement to NW
EPH — *Eastern Province Herald*
FM — *Financial Mail*
Frontline
Graphic
GS — King Goodwill Zwelethini Speech
IIE — Institute for Industrial Education
Ilanga
Indicator
International Labour Report
IRDATA
KCAV — Killie Campbell Library Oral History Project, University of Natal
KLA — KwaZulu Legislative Assembly
KLAD — KwaZulu Legislative Assembly Debates
The Leader
Leadership SA
LMG — Labour Monitoring Group
LRC — Legal Resources Centre
Mining Survey
New Statesman
NM — *Natal Mercury*
NW — *Natal Witness*
Pace
Post
Post Natal
R — *Rapport*
RDM — *Rand Daily Mail*
Reality
SAIRR — South African Institute of Race Relations
SALB — *South African Labour Bulletin*
SARS — South African Research Service
SASO *Newsletter* — South African Students Organisation
SE — *Sunday Express*
Sow — *Sowetan*
SP — *Sunday Post*

SPEISAN — Study Project on External Investment in South Africa and Namibia
SPP — Surplus People Project
SPRO-CAS — Study Project on Christianity in Apartheid Society
St — *Star*
ST — *Sunday Times*
STb — *Sunday Tribune*
STbH — *Sunday Tribune Herald*
Survey — Survey of Race Relations in South Africa
Die Vaderland
The Voice
WIP — *Work in Progress*
WM — *Weekly Mail*
ZO — *Zululand Observer*

References (in text)

Barker, Dr Anthony (1974) — 'The rural communities' (paper presented at the Focus on KwaZulu Conference, University of Natal, Durban).

Barrell, Howard (1985) — 'ANC Conference: "All for the Front"', in *Work in Progress,* 38.

Beall, Jo, Jeremy Grest, Heather Hughes and Gerhard Maré (1984)
— 'Conceptualising Natal: implications of a regional political economy' (working paper for Southern African Studies Seminar, University of Natal, Pietermaritzburg).

(1986) — 'The Natal Option: regional distinctiveness within the national reform process' (paper presented at the seventeenth annual Congress of the Association for Sociology in Southern Africa, University of Natal, Durban).

Bekker, J.C. (1983) — *Rol van die Regsprekende Gesag in 'n Plural Samelewing* (HSRC Report, Pol 21).

Beard, T.V.R. (1972) — 'Background to student activities at the University College of Fort Hare', in Hendrik van der Merwe and David Welsh (eds) — *Student Perspectives on South Africa* (Cape Town: David Philip).

Bengu, Professor Sibusio M.E. (1977) — 'Cultural liberation: principles and practices' (mimeo, five lectures at University of Natal, Durban).

Bennett, M. (1986) — 'Interview with Simon Conco' (original consulted — edited version in *Indicator,* 4, 1).

Benson, Mary (1963) — *The African Patriots: the story of the African National Congress of South Africa* (Chicago: Encyclopedia Britannica Press).

235

Bernstein, S.A. (1977) — 'African nationalism, black consciousness and the dialectic of Zulu participation in separate development' (unpublished BA Hons dissertation, University of Witwatersrand, Johannesburg).

Black Sash Files (various dates), held at Durban and Pietermaritzburg.

Bloch, Robin (1982) — '"All little sisters go to try on big sisters clothes": the community council system in South Africa' (paper presented at African Studies Seminar, University of Witwatersrand, Johannesburg).

Bonner, Phil (1979) — 'Focus on FOSATU', in *SA Labour Bulletin*, 5, 1.

Booysen, S.A. (1982) — 'MG Buthelezi se steunverlening aan die Suid-Afrikaanse politieke stelsel — 'n inhoudsontleding (1972-1980)' (unpublished MA thesis, Randse Afrikaanse Universiteit).

Bot, M. (1985) — *School Boycotts 1984: the crisis in African education* (Durban: Indicator Project SA).

Bradford, Helen (1984) — 'Lynch law and labourers: the ICU in Umvoti, 1927-1928', in *J of Southern African Studies*, 11, 1.

Brookes, Edgar and Colin de B. Webb (1979) — *A History of Natal* (Pietermaritzburg: University of Natal Press).

Brown, R.P.C. (1975) — 'The determinants of change in capital-intensity in the South African manufacturing sector' (unpublished MComm dissertation, University of Natal, Durban).

Brownlie, Ian (ed) (1971) — *Basic Documents on African Affairs* (London: Oxford University Press).

Buthelezi, Chief M.G. (1972) — 'The past and future of the Zulu people' (introduction by E.S. Munger), in *Munger Africana Library Notes*, 2, 10.

(1975) — 'Inkatha: extracts from the opening address delivered to the general conference of the National Cultural Liberation Movement (Inkatha)' in *Reality*, 7, 5.

(1978) — 'The early history of the Buthelezi clan', in John Argyle and Eleanor Preston-Whyte (eds) — *Social System and Tradition in Southern Africa: essays in honour of Eileen Krige* (Cape Town: Oxford University Press).

(1979) — 'Comments on the business codes', in *SA Outlook*, 109, 1295.

(1979a) — *Power is ours* (intro by Leon H. Sullivan) (New York: Books in Focus).

(1980) — 'Development — a non-starter without people involvement', in *Development Action*, 1.

(1983) — 'Response to statements made by the ABRECSA Conference and by overseas delegates to ABRECSA Conference — November 1983' (mimeo, Ulundi, 19 Nov. 83).

Buthelezi, Chief Gatsha, and other panel members (1973) — *Management Responsibility and African Employment in South Africa* (Johannesburg: Ravan).

The Buthelezi Commission Report (nd(1982)) — *The Requirements for Stability and Development in KwaZulu and Natal* (2 volumes) (Durban: H & H).

Bibliography

Butler, Jeffrey, Robert I. Rotberg and John Adams (1977) — *The Black Homelands of South Africa: the political and economic development of Bophuthatswana and KwaZulu* (Berkeley: California University Press).

Byerley, Mark (1985) — 'The Empangeni-Richards Bay bus boycott: 1985' (unpublished BSocSci Hons dissertation, University of Natal, Durban).

Carrim, Yunus (1986) — 'Working-class politics to the fore', in *Work in Progress*, 40.

Catholic Institute for International Relations (1986) — *Namibia in the 1980s* (London: CIIR and British Council of Churches).

Challenor, Martin (1984) — 'Business built on stones: a case study of responses to service charge increases in Port Natal Administration Board townships' (unpublished BSocSci Hons dissertation, University of Natal, Durban).

Charney, Craig (1983) — 'The rise of black (business) power in Natal', in *Management* (June).

Christopher, A.J. (1969) — 'Natal: a study in colonial land settlement' (unpublished PhD thesis, University of Natal).

Clarke, Liz (1978) — 'The need for a community development approach to combatting malnutrition' (paper to SALDRU Conference on the Economics of Health Care, University of Cape Town).

Clarke, Elizabeth and Dr Anthony Barker (1974) — 'South Africa's black population: a report on Nqutu in KwaZulu', in SPEISAN (ed) — *The Conditions of the Black Worker* (London: Africa Publications Trust).

Cobbett, William, Daryl Glaser, Dough Hindson and Mark Swilling (1985) — 'Regionalization, federalism and the reconstruction of the South African state', in *SA Labour Bulletin*, 10, 5.

(1986) — 'South Africa's regional political economy: a critical analysis of reform strategy in the 1980s', in SARS (ed) — *South African Review three* (Johannesburg: Ravan).

Conco, S. (1986) — 'Statement by Mr S. Conco' (mimeo, press conference, Johannesburg, 8 Mar. 86, to announce 1 May UWUSA launch. Attached is UWUSA 'Aims and Objectives', 'Principles' and 'Policy Standpoints').

Congress of SA Trade Unions (COSATU) (1986) — 'Incidents of violence, threats of violence and assaults on unionists in Natal' (mimeo, press release).

Cooper, Carole (1984) — 'Bantustan attitudes to trade unions', in SARS (ed) — *South African Review two* (Johannesburg: Ravan).

Cope, N.L.G. (1986) — 'The Zulu royal family under the South African Government 1910-1930: Solomon kaDinuzulu, Inkatha and Zulu nationalism' (unpublished PhD thesis, University of Natal, Durban).

Daniel, John (1983) — 'Swaziland: South Africa's willing captive', in *Work in Progress*, 27.

(1984) — 'A comparative analysis of Lesotho and Swaziland's relations with South

Africa', in SARS (ed) — *South African Review two* (Johannesburg: Ravan).

Daphne, Paul, (1982) — 'Tribal Authority and community organization' (Centre for Research and Documentation occasional paper, University of Zululand).

Davenport, T.R.H. and K.S. Hunt (eds) (1974) — *The Right to the Land* (Cape Town: David Philip).

Davies, Rob, Dan O'Meara and Sipho Dlamini (1984) — *The Struggle for South Africa: a reference guide to movements, organizations and institutions* (London: Zed).

Deane, Dee Shirley (1978) — *Black South Africans : A Who's Who, 57 profiles of Natal's leading blacks* (Cape Town: Oxford University Press).

Desmond, Cosmas (1970) — *The Discarded People: an account of African resettlement in South Africa* (Harmondsworth: Penguin).

Development Studies Group/Southern African Research Service (DSG/SARS) (1982) — *The Land Dispute: Incorporating Swaziland?* (Information Publication 7).

De Villiers, R. (1985) — 'UDF under attack: Inkatha and the state', in *Work in Progress*, 39.

Dhlomo, Dr Oscar D. (1979) — 'Comment', in *Reality*, 11, 2, (comment on Sheena Duncan (1978)).

(1981) 'The role of Inkatha in development: the need to overcome problems, identify opportunities and formulate strategies' (mimeo).

(1983) — 'The strategy of Inkatha and its critics: a comparative assessment', in *J of Asian and African Studies*, XVII, 1-2.

(1983a) — 'The political philosophy of Inkatha' (paper presented to Symposium 'Whither Black Political Thought', Centre for Research and Documentation, University of Zululand).

(1984) — 'Inkatha and the ANC', in *Leadership SA,* 3, 1.

Dladla, B.I. (1978) — 'The development of effective labour relations', in Hendrik W.van der Merwe, Nancy Charton, S.A. Kotze and Ake Magnusson (eds) — *African perspectives on South Africa* (Cape Town: David Philip).

Duncan, Sheena (1978) — 'A depressing picture: an account of the Freiburg Conference', in *Reality*, 10, 5.

Du Plessis, Z. (1981) — 'The role of the small trader', in *Development Action,* 3.

Etherington, Norman (1979) — 'Labour supply and the genesis of South African confederation in the 1870's', in *J of African History,* 20, 2.

(1985) — 'African economic experiments in colonial Natal, 1845-1880', in Bill Guest and John M. Sellers (eds).

First, Ruth (1972) — 'Foreign investment in *Apartheid* South Africa' (United Nations, Unit on Apartheid, Notes and Documents, 21/72).

Frankel, Philip (1980) — 'The politics of poverty: political competition in Soweto', in *Canadian J of African Studies*, XXIV, 2.

Freund, Bill (1984) — *The Making of Contemporary Africa: the development of African society since 1800* (London: Macmillan).

Gastrow, Shelagh (1985) — *Who's Who in South African Politics* (Johannesburg: Ravan).

Gerhart, Gail M. (1978) — *Black Power in South Africa: the evolution of an ideology* (Berkeley: University of California Press).

Giliomee, Hermann (1982) — *The Parting of the Ways: South African politics 1976-82* (Cape Town: David Philip).

Giliomee, Hermann and Lawrence Schlemmer (eds) (1985) — *Up Against the Fences: poverty, passes and privilege in South Africa* (Cape Town: David Philip).

Godwin, Peter and David Lipsey (1985) — 'Sanctions: black support grows', in *Sunday Times* (London), 25 Aug. 85.

Gordon, Dennis (1982) — 'The people of heaven: a warrior race enters the industrial environment', in *Mining Survey*, 1/2.

Grest, Jeremy and Heather Hughes (1983) — 'The local state', in SARS (ed) — *South African Review one* (Johannesburg: Ravan).

(1984) — 'State strategy and popular response at the local level', in SARS (ed) — *South African Review two* (Johannesburg: Ravan).

Guest, Bill and John M. Sellers (eds) (1985) — *Enterprise and Exploitation in a Victorian Colony* (Pietermaritzburg: University of Natal Press).

Guy, Jeff (1979) — 'The British Invasion of Zululand, some thoughts for the centenary year', in *Reality*, 11, 1.

(1982) — 'The destruction and reconstruction of Zulu society', in S. Marks and R. Rathbone (eds) — *Industrialization and Social Change in South Africa* (London: Longman).

(1982a) — *The Destruction of the Zulu Kingdom* (Johannesburg: Ravan).

Gwala, Zilondile (1985) — 'Rebellion in the last outpost: the Natal riots', in *Indicator*, 3, 2.

Haarhoff, Dr Errol (1985) — 'Where the workers live', in Crispin Hemson (ed).

Hackland, Brian (1982) — 'The Progressive Party, 1960-1980: class agents in a capitalist society' (paper presented at the Conference on South Africa in the Comparative Study of Class, Race and Nationalism, New York).

Hamilton, Carolyn and John Wright (1984) — 'The making of the Lala: ethnicity, ideology and class-formation in a pre-colonial context' (paper for History Workshop, University of the Witwatersrand, Johannesburg).

Hanf, Theodor, Herbert Weiland and Gerda Vierdag, in collaboration with Lawrence Schlemmer (c1981) — *South Africa: the prospect of peaceful change* (Cape Town: David Philip).

Haysom, Nicholas (1983) — *Ruling with the whip: Report on the violation of human rights in the Ciskei* (Johannesburg: DSG/SARS, London: CIIR).

(1986) — *Mabangalala: the rise of right-wing vigilantes in South Africa* (Johannesburg: Centre for Applied Legal Studies, University of Witwatersrand, occasional paper 10; British ed: *Apartheid's Private Army* (London: CIIR).

Hemson, Crispin (ed) (1985) — *Natal/KwaZulu: the political and social environment of the future* (Durban: Centre for Adult Education and *Indicator*, University of Natal).

Hemson, David (1978) — 'Trade unionism and the struggle for liberation in South Africa', in *Capital and Class*, 6.

Hill, C.R. (1964) — *Bantustans: the fragmentation of South Africa* (London: Oxford University Press for the Institute of Race Relations).

Horrell, Muriel (1968) — 'The rights of African women: some suggested reforms' (Johannesburg: SA Institute of Race Relations).

(1978) — *Laws Affecting Race Relations in South Africa 1948-1976* (Johannesburg: SA Institute of Race Relations).

Huntington, Samuel P. (1982) — 'Reform and stability in South Africa', in *International Security*, 6, 4.

Inkatha — see Inkatha publications listed separately below.

Institute for Industrial Education (IIE) (1974) — *The Durban Strikes 1973* (Durban/Johannesburg: IIE/Ravan).

Kane-Berman, John (1982) — 'Inkatha, the paradox of South African politics', in *Optima*, 30, 3.

Karis, Thomas G. (nd(1980)) — 'Buthelezi and Inkatha' (mimeo, at Inkatha Institute).

Khanyile, Z.A. (1982) — 'What is a trade union?', in *SA Labour Bulletin*, 8, 1.

Khoapa, B.A. (ed) (1973) — *Black Review 1972* (Durban: Black Community Programmes).

Kiernan, Jim (1982) — 'Authority and enthusiasm: the organization of religious experience in Zulu Zionist churches', in J. Davis (ed) — *Religious Organization and the Religious Experience* (London: Academic Press).

Kotze, D.A. (1975) — *African Politics in South Africa 1964-1974: parties and issues* (with a foreword by Chief M. Gatsha Buthelezi) (New York: St Martin's Press).

KwaZulu Legislative Assembly (KLA) — see separate entries below.

Laband, J. and J. Wright (1983) — *King Cetshwayo kaMpande* (foreword by Mangosuthu G. Buthelezi) (Pietermaritzburg: Shuter and Shooter and KwaZulu Monuments Council).

Labour Monitoring Group (LMG) (Natal) (1985) — 'Monitoring the Sarmcol struggle', in *SA Labour Bulletin*, 11, 2.

Laclau, Ernesto (1977) — *Politics and Ideology in Marxist Theory: capitalism — fascism — populism* (London: New Left Books).

Langner, E.J. (1983) — 'The founding and development of Inkatha Yenkululeko

240

Yesizwe' (unpublished MA dissertation, University of SA).

Laurence, Patrick (1984) — 'South African black party politics', in *Africa Insight*, 14, 4.

Lawyer, A. (1983) — 'Homeland labour laws', in *SA Labour Bulletin*, 8, 8 and 9, 1.

Legal Resources Centre (Durban) — various affidavits.

Le Grange, Louis (1984) — 'Interview', in *Leadership SA*, 3, 3.

Lewis, John and Estelle Randall (1985) — 'Survey: the state of the unions', in *SA Labour Bulletin*, 11, 2.

Lodge, Tom (1983) — *Black Politics in South Africa since 1945* (Johannesburg: Ravan).

Lombard, Professor J.A., Profs J.A. du Pisani, G.C. Olivier and W.B. Vosloo (nd(1980)) — 'Alternatives to the Consolidation of KwaZulu: progress report' (University of Pretoria, Bureau for Economic Policy and Analysis).

McCaul, C. (1983) — *Towards an Understanding of Inkatha YeSizwe* (Johannesburg: SARS/DSG, dissertation series 2).

(1984) — 'Inkatha's new labour wing', in *Work in Progress*, 32.

Maré, Gerhard (1978) — 'Class conflict and ideology among the petty bourgeoisie in the "homelands": Inkatha — a study', in *Conference on the History of Opposition in Southern Africa* (DSG, University of Witwatersrand).

(1979) — 'Bus boycotts', in *Work in Progress*, 10.

(1980) — *African Population Relocation in South Africa* (Johannesburg: SA Institute of Race Relations).

(1981) — 'Old age pensions and the bantustans', in *Work in Progress*, 17.

(1982) — 'Monopolies, marginalization and "homeland" underdevelopment' (unpublished MA dissertation, University of Witwatersrand, Johannesburg).

(1982a) — 'Repression in/through the bantustans', in DSG/SARS (ed) — *'Homeland' Tragedy: function and farce* (Johannesburg: DSG/SARS, information publication 6).

Marks, Shula (1970) — *Reluctant Rebellion: the 1906-1908 disturbances in Natal* (Oxford: Oxford University Press).

(1975) — 'The ambiguities of dependence: John L. Dube of Natal', *J of Southern African Studies*, 1, 2.

(1986) — *The Ambiguities of Dependence in South Africa: class, nationalism, and the state in twentieth-century Natal* (Johannesburg: Ravan).

Maylam, Paul (1986) — *A History of the African People of South Africa: from the early Iron Age to the 1970s* (Cape Town: David Philip).

Mbata, J.C.M. (1960) — 'The operation of the Bantu Authorities system in the northern Transvaal' (report for SAIRR, Johannesburg).

Meer, Fatima (ed) (1985) — *Institute for Black Research Special Report: Unrest in Natal August 1985* . . . (Durban: Institute for Black Research).

Middleton, Prof A.J. (1985) — *Report of the Commission of Inquiry into the Violence which occurred on 29 October 1983 at the University of Zululand* (2 volumes) (Pretoria: Government Printer).

Moodie, T. Dunbar (1980) — *The Rise of Afrikanerdom: power, apartheid, and Afrikaner civil religion* (Berkeley: University of California Press).

Munger Africana Library Notes number 56 (December 1980) — Issue on the Buthelezi Commission.

Nattrass, Jill (1985) — 'The impact of underdevelopment, poverty and inequality on the development of KwaZulu/Natal', in Crispin Hemson (ed).

Nattrass, Jill and R.P.C. Brown (1977) — *Capital Intensity in South African Manufacturing* (interim research report 4, Department of Economics, University of Natal, Durban).

New York Correspondent (1985) — 'Disinvestment and black workers: a critique of the Schlemmer Report', in *SA Labour Bulletin*, 10, 6.

Ngubane, Jordan K. (1976) — 'Shaka's social, political and military ideas', in Donald Burness — *Shaka King of the Zulus in African Literature* (Washington: Three Continents Press).

Obery, Ingrid and Karen Jochelson (1985) — 'Industry and government: "Two sides of the same bloody coin"', in *Work in Progress*, 39.

O'Meara, Dan (1983) — *Volkskapitalisme: class, capital and ideology in the development of Afrikaner nationalism, 1934-1948* (Johannesburg: Ravan).

Orkin, Mark (1986) — *Disinvestment, the Struggle and the Future: what black South Africans really think* (Johannesburg: Ravan).

Peires, J. (ed and intro by) (1981) — *Before and After Shaka* (Grahamstown: Institute for Social and Economic Research, Rhodes University).

Platzky, Laurine and Cherryl Walker (1985) — *The Surplus People: forced removals in South Africa* (Johannesburg: Ravan).

Pretorius, Louwrens (1981) — 'Plans for the reorganization of society: the reports of the Buthelezi Commission and the Constitutional Committee of the President's Council', in *Social Dynamic*, 7, 2.

Prinsloo, M.W. (1984) — 'Political restructuring, capital accumulation and the "coming corporatism" in South Africa: some theoretical considerations', in *Politikon*, 11, 1.

Raby, David L. (1983) — *Populism: a marxist analysis* (Montreal: McGill University, Centre for Developing Area Studies, Studies in International Development, 32).

Randall, Peter (1973) — *A Taste of Power* (Johannesburg: SPRO-CAS).

Rich, Paul B. (1984) — *White Power and the Liberal Conscience: racial segregation and South African liberalism* (Johannesburg: Ravan).

Roux, Edward (1964) — *Time Longer than Rope: a history of the black man's struggle for freedom in South Africa* (Madison: University of Wisconsin Press).

Roux, Marianne, Andre Roux and Paul Steward (1982) — 'East London and the politics of decentralization' (paper for SAIRR Urbanization Conference, Johannesburg).

Samuelson, L.H. (Nomleti) (1974, original published 1929) — *Zululand: its traditions, legends, customs and folklore* (reprint Durban: T.W. Griggs).

Saul, John S. (1973) — 'On African populism', in Giovanni Arrighi and John S. Saul — *Essays on the Political Economy of Africa* (New York: Monthly Review Press).

(1979) — *The State and Revolution in Eastern Africa* (New York: Monthly Review Press).

(1985) — 'Nkomati and after', in John S. Saul (ed) *A Difficult Road: the transition to socialism in Mozambique* (New York: Monthly Review Press).

Schlemmer, Lawrence (1980) — 'The Stirring Giant: observations on the Inkatha and other black political movements in South Africa', in Robert M. Price and Carl G. Rosberg (eds) — *The Apartheid Regime: political power and racial domination* (Cape Town: David Philip).

(1982) — 'The report on the attitude surveys', in Buthelezi Commission Report (nd(1982)).

(1984) — 'Black worker attitudes: political options, capitalism and investment in South Africa' (Document and memorandum series, Centre for Applied Social Sciences, University of Natal).

Schlemmer, Lawrence and Tim Muil (1975) — 'Social and political change in the African areas: a case study of KwaZulu', in Leonard Thompson and Jeffrey Butler (eds) — *Change in Contemporary South Africa* (Berkeley: California Press).

Schmahmann, Bella (1978) — 'KwaZulu in Contemporary South Africa: a case study in the implementation of the policy of separate development' (unpublished PhD thesis, University of Natal, Durban).

Schulz, Brigitte and William Hansen (1984) — 'Aid or imperialism? West Germany in sub-Saharan Africa', in *J of Modern African Studies*, 22, 2.

Seidman, Ann and Neva Seidman (1977) — *South Africa and United States Multinational Corporations* (Westport, Conn: Lawrence Hill).

Seidman, Ann and Neva Seidman Makgetla (1980) — *Outposts of Monopoly Capitalism: southern Africa in the changing global economy* (Westport, Conn and London: Hill/Zed).

Simon, Bernard (1984/5) — 'Looking at the Codes' in *Leadership SA* publication *Human Resources*.

Sisulu, Zwelakhe (1986) — 'People's education for people's power', *Transformation*, 1.

Sitas, Ari (1986) — 'Inanda, August 1985: "Where wealth and power and blood reign worshipped gods"', in *SA Labour Bulletin*, 11, 4.

Sitas, Ari, John Stanwix and Cathi Shaw (1984) — 'Trade unions, monopoly power and poverty in Natal's industries' (paper for the Second Carnegie Inquiry into Poverty and Development in Southern Africa, University of Cape Town).

South African Institute of Race Relations (SAIRR, Natal) (1982)
— 'The Buthelezi Commission: requirements for stability and development in KwaZulu and Natal' (information sheet 2/82).

South African Institute of Race Relations (various years) — *Survey of Race Relations in South Africa* (Johannesburg: SAIRR).

South African Labour Bulletin, 1, 1 (1974) — 'IIE News'.

1, 3 (1974a) — Editorial.

8, 4 (1983) — 'Organizing small towns: an interview with Matthews Oliphant and Vincent Mkonza, organizers of the National Iron, Steel, Metal and Allied Workers' Union . . .'.

11, 3 (1986) — 'COSATU launch'.

South African Research Service (ed) (1983) — *South African Review one: same foundations, new facades?* (Johannesburg: Ravan/SARS).

Southall, Roger (1981) — 'Buthelezi, Inkatha and the politics of compromise', in *African Affairs*, 80, 321.

(1982) — 'The Buthelezi Commission Report: consolidation, consociationalism — collaboration?' (paper for the Conference on South Africa in the Comparative Study of Class, Race and Nationalism, New York).

(1983) — 'Consociationalism in South Africa: the Buthelezi Commission and beyond', in *J of Modern African Studies*, 21, 1.

Stanwix, John (1983) — 'A study of the Natal regional economy' (Report for the Natal Town and Regional Planning Commission).

Steenwijk, Drs Reina R. (1984) — 'Europe's perspective on (Black) politics in South Africa' (Amsterdam: Information Centre on South Africa, mimeoed briefing at the SAIRR, Johannesburg, 3 Jul. 84).

Study Project on Christianity in Apartheid Society (SPRO-CAS) (1973) — *South Africa's Political Alternatives* (Johannesburg: SPRO-CAS).

Surplus People Project (1983) — *Forced Removals in South Africa* (5 volumes) (Cape Town):SPP) (Volume 4, Natal: volume 3, The Western and Northern Cape and Orange Free State).

Sutcliffe, Dr Michael O. and Dr Paul A. Wellings (1985) — 'Attitudes and living conditions in Inanda: the context for unrest?' (Durban: Built Environment Support Group).

(1986) — 'The widening rift: Buthelezi, Inkatha and mainstream black opposition politics in South Africa', in *Transafrica Forum* (forthcoming).

Teague, Peta-Ann (1983) — 'A study of Inkatha YeSizwe's approach to the youth, with specific reference to the movement's Youth Brigade' (unpublished BA Hons dissertation, University of Cape Town).

Bibliography

Temkin, Ben (1976) — *Gatsha Buthelezi: Zulu Statesman* (Cape Town: Purnell).

Thomas, Wolfgang (1986) — 'Miljoene sonder werk: ons kan hier begin', in *Die Suid-Afrikaan*, 6.

Tordoff, William (1984) — *Government and Politics in Africa* (London: Macmillan).

Turner, Richard (1980) — *The Eye of the Needle: towards participatory democracy in South Africa* (Johannesburg: Ravan).

Van Niekerk, Phillip (1986) — 'Inkatha and COSATU: drawing the battle lines', in *Work in Progress*, 42.

Venter, T.P. (1982) — 'Die rol van Inkatha Yenkululeko Yesizwe in die Suid-Afrikaanse politieke proses' (unpublished MA dissertation, Potchefstroomse Universiteit vir CHO).

Walshe, Peter (1970) — *The Rise of African Nationalism in South Africa: the African National Congress 1912-1952* (London: C. Hurst).

Webster, Eddie (1977) — 'The 1949 Durban "riots" — a case study in race and class', in P.L. Bonner (ed) — *Working Papers in Southern African Studies: papers presented at the ASI African Studies Seminar* (Johannesburg: ASI, University of Witwatersrand).

(1979) — 'A profile of unregistered union members in Durban', in *SA Labour Bulletin*, 4, 8.

(1984) — 'New force on the shop floor', in SARS (ed) — *South African Review two* (Johannesburg: Ravan).

Welsh, David (1971) — *The Roots of Segregation: native policy in Natal* (Cape Town: Oxford University Press).

Wentzel, Jill (1977) — 'Black United Front: an interview with Dr Nyembezi and Mr Mavuso', in *Reality*, 9, 3.

Willmer, Brendan (nd) — 'Buthelezi and Inkatha: the truth exposed' (Durban: South Africa First Campaign Pamphlet).

Work in Progress, 12 (1980) — '"Jo the Cow" comes home'.

13 (1980a) — 'Bus boycotts: Madadeni-Osizweni'.

15 (1980b) — 'Natal education boycott: a focus on Inkatha'.

15 (1980c) — 'Rents: Mondlo'.

42 (1986) — 'People's education: creating a democratic future' (I. Rensburg interviewed by Ingrid Obery).

Wright, John (1983) — 'Politics, ideology, and the invention of the "Nguni"' (paper for Southern African Studies Seminar, University of Natal, Pietermaritzburg).

Zulu, P.M. (nd) — 'The rural crisis — a look into authority structures and their role in "development"' (mimeo).

Buthelezi and other speeches (referred to in text)

Buthelezi Speech (BS 16 Jan. 74) — 'White and Black nationalism, ethnicity and the future of the homelands' (Hoernle Memorial Lecture, University of Cape Town).

(BS, 11 Aug. 74) — 'The federal formula as the next step in the development of a greater South Africa' (Address to the Conference of Young South Africans of the United Party, Cato Ridge, Natal).

(BS, 14 Mar. 76) — 'In this approaching hour of crisis: a message to South Africa from black South Africa' (Jabulani Ampitheatre, Soweto).

(BS, 7 Aug. 76) — 'Speech at the inauguration of the regional branch of the Hlanganani regional area: Nxamalala tribal authority offices' (Impendle).

(BS, 28. Aug 76) — 'Visit to riot-torn Soweto' (Soweto).

(BS, 26 Oct. 76) — 'Human rights and constitutional development in South Africa' (Address to the Institute of International Affairs, Nigeria).

(BS, 16 Feb. 77) — 'A short presentation at UCLA'.

(BS, 29 Oct. 77) — 'Statement made as part of the opening address to the Women's Brigade Congress'.

(BS, 27 Jun. 78) — 'Opening address: Youth Brigade leadership training course' (Mahlabatini).

(BS, 7 Feb. 79) — 'The bias of historical analysis' (Opening address at a conference on the 'Anglo-Zulu War — a centennial reappraisal', University of Natal, Durban).

(BS, 21 Oct. 79) — 'A black perspective of realism in the black struggle for liberation' (Speech at the annual rally of Inkatha at the Jabulani Ampitheatre, Soweto).

(BS, 18 May. 80) — 'Speech at KwaMashu prayer meeting and youth rally' (Princess Magogo Stadium, KwaMashu).

(BS, 20 Jun. 80) — 'Presidential address: sixth ordinary conference of Inkatha Yenkululeko Yesizwe' (Ondini).

(BS, 18 Jul. 80) — 'Opening remarks: central committee meeting: Inkatha Yenkululeko Yesizwe' (Ondini).

(BS, 10 Oct. 80) — 'The struggle is right where you are at home' (Women's Brigade fourth annual conference, Ondini).

(BS, 23 Nov. 80) — 'Address to the National Executive of the Inkatha Youth Brigade' (Ulundi).

(BS, 29 Aug. 82) — 'Address at prayer meeting to commemmorate "the last leader of the banned ANC who was democratically elected before the organization was banned — Chief Albert Mvumbi Luthuli"' (Groutville).

(BS, 3 Sep. 83) — 'Official opening of the Sobonakhona Makyanya tribal authority headquarters and offices' (Umbumbulu district).

(BS, 24 Sep. 83) — 'King Shaka Day speech' (King Zwelethini Stadium, Umlazi).

(BS, 5 Nov. 83) — 'Speech at prayer meeting' (Esikhawini).

(BS, 8 May. 84) — 'Federal and confederal futures for South Africa' (265th Wilton Park Conference, Wilton Park, Sussex, England).

(BS, 13 May 84) — 'Address to the National Sugar Refining and Allied Industries Employees Union' (Esikhawini).

(BS, 6 Aug. 84) — 'Black politics in and around and outside the new constitutional dispensation' (Address to Stellenbosch University).

(BS, 27 Nov. 84) — 'Speech at Emandleni-Matleng Camp: passing out parade' (Ulundi).

(BS, 10 Jan. 85) — 'A few remarks on the occasion of a meeting with Senator Edward Kennedy' (Royal Hotel, Durban).

(BS, 29 Jun. 85) — 'Inkatha's 10 year existence as a movement — and reflections on what Inkatha has done in non-violent strategies for liberation and the increasing temptation and pressure of mindless violence as a strategy of desperation in the absence of a viable basis for peaceful negotiation' (Presidential address: Inkatha annual general conference, Ulundi).

(BS, 24 Aug. 85) — 'Surviving between the devil and the deep blue sea — the liberation struggle in the midst of black-on-black confrontation' (Presidential address to the 10th conference of the Youth Brigade, Ulundi).

(BS, 8 Jan. 86) — 'A few remarks' (Visit to Mondi Paper Mill, Richards Bay).

(BS, 14 Mar. 86) — 'Address' (Natal conference of the Stainless Steel Industry, New Holiday Inn, Durban.

(BS, 14 Apr. 86) — 'Fourth session of the fourth KwaZulu Legislative Assembly. Statement (on Chief Minister of KaNgwane, Enos Mabuza, press interview) by the Honourable the Chief Minister' (Ulundi).

King Goodwill Zwelethini Speech (GS, 16 Jun. 86) — 'Address to the Zulu Nation' (Mona Saleyards, Nongoma).

Inkatha publications (pamphlets, booklets, newspapers, etc.)

Inkatha (nd) — Meeting between Chief Gatsha Buthelezi President of Inkatha and Mr J.T. Kruger, Minister of Justice, Police and Prisons. Pretoria — 19 September, 1977.

(nd(a)) — Constitution of the National Cultural Liberation Movement or Inkatha (with amendments).

(nd(b)) — Letters from Black South Africans to the President of Inkatha.

(nd(d)) — Inkatha replies to UDF pamphlet.

(nd(e)) — Ongoye: what happened? 29 October 1983.

(nd(f)) — The Aims and Objectives of Inkatha (appendix B, Langner, 1983).

(1978) — KwaZulu Elections 1978 Candidates' Manifesto (appendix IX, Schmahmann, 1978).

(1979) — Evidence submitted to the Commission of Inquiry on the Constitution.

(1980) — 'A rationale for para-military developments within Inkatha — paper presented for discussion by the central committee'.

(1983) — Inkatha: its viewpoints on change and liberation in South Africa.

(1983a) — Inkatha's reply. ANC and PAC.

(1983b) — Inkatha's reply to AZASO.

(1984) — Press statement (on European trip), by Dr Oscar Dhlomo (sec gen); Dr Dennis R.B. Madide (chair political, constitutional and foreign affairs committee); Hugh T. Madonsela (chair disciplinary committee); Macdonald September (member of central committee).

(1985) — Report of the Secretary General.

(1985a) — Memorandum on the Problems in Hambanathi township.

Inkatha Institute (1980) — 'A development for progress and peace' (telex).

The Nation (1976-1979).

Inkatha (1976-?).

Inkatha (various years) — Inkatha Conference Brochures.

Inkatha (various years) — Conference Resolutions.

Inkatha (various years) — Conference Reports and Memoranda.

KwaZulu official publications

Bhengu M.J. (nd) — *In Search of Black Unity* (Ulundi: Bureau of Communication).

Bhengu, M.J. (ed) (1982) — *A Man for All Seasons . . .: Mr M.G. Buthelezi: President of Inkatha* (Ulundi: Bureau of Communication).

Development Action (1980-?) — Journal of the KwaZulu Development Corporation.

Inhlabamkhosi/Clarion Call (1983-) — published by the Bureau of Communication, Department of the Chief Minister, KwaZulu Government.

KwaZulu Government Diary (various years) — published Durban: Edupress, for the KwaZulu Government.

KwaZulu Legislative Assembly (KLA) (nd) — *KwaZulu Legislative Assembly: 1972-1982* (Ulundi: Bureau of Communication).

KwaZulu Legislative Assembly Debates (KLAD) —

vol 1 : 22 May 1972

vol 2 : 17 January 1973

vol 3 : 4-14 May 1973

vol 4 : 3-17 May 1974

vol 5 : 28 August 1974, pp 1-73
        18 February 1975, pp 74-91
        9-18 April 1975, pp 92-340

vol 6 : 21-30 April 1975, pp 341-676

vol 7 : 1-6 May 1975, pp 677-876
        13-17 October 1975, pp 877-969
        19 January 1976, pp 971-1055

vol 8 : 7-18 May 1976, pp 1-309

vol 9 : 19-25 May 1976, pp 310-531
        1-4 June 1976, pp 532-655

vol 10 : 16-30 March 1977, pp 1-338

vol 11 : 31 March-22 April 1977, pp 339-700

vol 12 : 18-28 April 1978, pp 1-334

vol 13 : 1-17 May 1978, pp 335-767

vol 14 : 18 May-1 June 1978, pp 768-1246

vol 15 : 23 May-8 June 1979, pp 1-305

vol 16 : 11-19 June 1979, pp 306-624

vol 17 : 20-26 June 1979, pp 625-819
         6 August 1979, pp 820-879

vol 18 : 17 April-2 May 1980, pp 1-377

vol 19 : 5-21 May 1980, pp 378-751

vol 20 : 22 May-12 June 1980, pp 752-1165

vol 21 : 22 April — 5 May 1981, pp 1-401

vol 22 : 6-20 May 1981, pp 402-792

vol 23 : 21 May-4 June 1981, pp 793-1068

vol 24 : 5-18 June 1981, pp 1069-1354

vol 25 : 21 April-11 May 1982, pp 1-320

vol 26 : 12 May-3 June 1982, pp 321-682

vol 27 : 4-28 June 1982, pp 683-1017

vol 28 : 2-16 March 1983, pp 1-345

vol 29 : 17 March-15 April 1983, pp 346-748

vol 30 : 25 October-15 November 1983, pp 1-269

vol 31 : 16 November-6 December 1983, pp 270-470

vol 32 : 3-27 April 1984, pp 1-343

vol 33 : 30 April-15 May 1984, pp 344-682

vol 34 : 16-28 May 1984, pp 683-938

vol 35 : 12-15 November 1984, pp 939-1216

KwaZulu Ministry of the Chief Minister (1985) — Letter to South African leaders, 22 April 85; appendix of Buthelezi KLA policy speech on power-sharing (April 1985), and press statement. Follow-up letter 10 June 85; appendix of further KLA speech given 27 May 85.

Umxoxi (1985-) — published by the Bureau of Communication, Department of the Chief Minister, KwaZulu government; editor in chief Suzanne Griffin, editor John Bhengu.

Unpublished interviews

Killie Campbell Oral History Project material (KCAV) — Killie Campbell library, University of Natal, Durban. Interviews consulted listed below:

KCAV ? — Zephaniah Mahaye (interview conducted 11 Nov. 81), businessman, Mtubatuba.

KCAV 130 — J. Moeli (3 Apr. 79), businessman, treasurer KwaMashu region of Inkatha.

KCAV 142 — C.C. Majola (20 Jun. 79), Urban Foundation organizer KwaMashu, ex-councillor.

KCAV 156, 190 — Professor C.L.S. Nyembezi (28 Aug. 79), academic, writer, publisher in Edendale.

KCAV 157, 176 — Dr. F.T. Mdlalose (5 Oct. 79), minister of interior KwaZulu.

KCAV 158, 166 — Oscar Dumisani Dhlomo (6 Sep. 79), KwaZulu minister of education and culture.

KCAV 159 — B.E. Nzimande (11 Sep. 79), taxi-owner and KLA member, ward chair of Inkatha.

KCAV 168, 169 — C.D.S. Mbutho (25 Oct. 79; 1 Nov. 79), ex-councillor, businessman.

KCAV 171, 173 — P.H. Simelane (16 Oct. 79; 14 Nov. 79), mayor Chesterville. Died early 1982, funeral attended by Inkatha dignitaries, speech by Dhlomo.

KCAV 181 — A. Hlongwane (24 Aug. 79), secretary to the Cele people, Umlazi.

KCAV 184, 185 — S.K. Ngobese (28 Nov. 79), businessman, mayor of Umlazi.

KCAV 188 — W. Yengwa (24 Nov. 79), councillor, KLA member, Inkatha Women's Brigade executive.

KCAV — 104 — E. Nxasana (10 Nov. 79), councillor, Women's Brigade executive.

KCAV 311 — Thembi Khomo (18 Jul. 81).

Swart, R (1984) — 'Interview with Dr Oscar Dhlomo'.

Teague, Peta-Ann (1983a) — 'Questions for the Chief Minister' (mimeo, reply from Chief Buthelezi to questions posed by Teague, dated 18 Nov. 83).

Additional bibliography (not directly referred to)

Africa Confidential, 27, 5 (1986) — 'Inkatha vs COSATU'.

Africa Institute of SA (1982) — 'The Buthelezi Commission Report and the Lombard Plan', in *Bulletin* (of the Africa Institute), 22, 8.

Africa Report (March-April 1973) — '"The Ablest Politician": Chief Gatsha Buthelezi' (interview).

Africa Today, 18, 3 (1971) — 'The Buthelezi factor: hope for the bantustans'.

Bengu, S.M. (1975) — 'The National Cultural Liberation Movement', in *Reality*, 7, 4.

Bernstein, Ann (1978) — 'Inkatha Yesizwe', in *The Black Sash*, 19, 4.

Booysen, Susan (1983) — 'Buthelezi — collaborator or liberator? An assessment of attitudes and opinions', in *SA International*, 13, 3.

Bosman, J.P. (1985) — 'Die kulturele simboliek van die Inkatha-ring by die Zulu' (unpublished MA dissertation, Randse Afrikaanse Universiteit, Johannesburg).

Botha, P.R. (1980) — 'Die "Lombard-verslag": 'n bespreking', in *Development Studies Southern Africa*, 3, 1.

Boulle, L.J. (1982) — 'The Buthelezi Commission recommendations in the light of current constitutional trends', in *The Comparative and International Law J of Southern Africa*, XV, 3.

Boulle, L. and L. Baxter (eds) (1981) — *Natal and KwaZulu: constitutional and political options* (Cape Town: Juta).

Brewer, J. (1981) — 'The modern Janus: Inkatha's role in black liberation', in Institute of Commonwealth Studies — *The Societies of Southern Africa in the nineteenth and twentieth centuries,* 12.

(1985) — 'The membership of Inkatha in KwaMashu', in *African Affairs*, 84.

Brown, Peter (1978) — 'Reflections on Graaff-Reinet', in *Reality*, 10, 3.

Buckland, Peter (nd) — 'The Buthelezi Report: education policy and the discourse of reform' (mimeo, University of Cape Town).

(1982) — 'The education crisis in South Africa: restructuring the policy discourse', in *Social Dynamics*, 8, 1.

Buthelezi, Chief M.G. (1972) — 'Independence for the Zulus', in Nic J. Rhoodie (ed) — *South African Dialogue: contrasts in South African thinking on basic race issues* (Johannesburg: McGraw-Hill).

(1972) — 'KwaZulu development', in S. Biko (ed) — *Black Viewpoint* (Johannesburg: SPRO-CAS/BCP).

(1973) — 'My role in separate development', in *Sechaba*, 7.

(1977) — 'Open letter to Ambassador Andrew Young', in *SA Outlook,* 107, 1272.

251

(1977) — 'Bevryding van swartman is ons prioriteit', interviewed in *Deurbraak*.

(1979) — 'Christian perspectives of the black liberation struggle in South Africa', in *SA Outlook*, 110, 1299.

(1981) — 'A short speech of welcome to the Hon the Deputy Minister', in *Development Action*, 3.

(1982) — 'Politics and change in South Africa', in *Africanus*, 12, 1 & 2.

(1982) — 'Acceptance address', on receipt of AFL-CIO Human Rights Award, in AFL-CIO *Free Trade Union News*, 37, 10.

(1983) — 'The colored Labor Party and proposed constitutional reforms', in AFL-CIO *Free Trade Union News*, 38, 1.

(1983) — 'South Africa — the enduring struggle', in AFL- CIO *Free Trade Union News*, 38, 2.

(1984) — 'Aide memoire for discussion with Mr Irving Brown of the AFL-CIO. . .' in *SA Labour Bulletin*, 9, 4.

(1984) — 'Investment in South Africa', in *SA International*, 14, 4.

(1984) — 'Statement on the surveys by Michael Sutcliffe and Paul Wellings of the Natal University. . .' (mimeo, Ulundi).

(1984) — 'The distinction between living history and views about history', in *Reality*, 16, 6.

(1986) — 'A black critique of the South African constitution', in J.A. du Pisani (ed) — *Divided or United Power: views on the new constitutional dispensation by prominent South African political leaders* (Johannesburg: Lex Patria).

Carrim, Yunus (1985) — 'Unions take the lead', in *Work in Progress*, 39.

Church, Joan (1983) — 'A new dispensation for black women? a note on Act 6 of 1981 (KwaZulu)', in *The Comparative and International Law J of Southern Africa*, XVI, 1.

Claassens, Aninka (1979) — 'The Riekert Commission and unemployment: the KwaZulu case', in *SA Labour Bulletin*, 5, 4.

Colenbrander, Peter (1984) — 'The "Year of Cetshwayo" revisited', in *Reality*, 16, 2.

(1984) — 'A reply to Dr O. Dhlomo', in *Reality*, 16, 4.

Clegg, Jonathan (1981) — '"Ukubuyisa Isidumbu" — "Bringing back the body": an examination of the ideology of vengeance in the Msinga and Mpofana rural locations, 1822-1944', in P. Bonner (ed) — *Working papers in Southern African Studies*, vol 2 (Johannesburg: Ravan).

Counter Information Service (1979) — *Buying Time in South Africa* (London: CIS).

Dhlomo, O.D. (1980) — 'Role of Inkatha in community development', in *Institute for Public Service and Vocational Training Bulletin*, 4, 2.

(1980) — 'The changing political context within which such matters as homeland consolidation and a constellation of southern African states must be considered' (mimeo, Pretoria, 17 Jan. 80).

(1981) — 'Education in KwaZulu', in *SA Outlook*, 111, 1320.

Bibliography

(1983) — 'Inkatha and the reform proposals', in Fleur de Villiers (ed) — *Bridge or Barricade? the constitution — a first appraisal* (Johannesburg: Jonathan Ball).

(1984) — 'A reply to Peter Colenbrander', in *Reality*, 16, 3.

(nd) — 'Inkatha: its origin, policies and strategy' (mimeo).

Dladla, B.I. (1974) — 'Problems of African labour' in *Reality*, 6, 2.

Du Pisani, J.A. (1980) — 'Samevatting van die "Lombard-verslag" oor Natal en KwaZulu', in *Development Studies Southern Africa*, 3, 1.

Ensor, Linda (nd) — 'Inkatha YeNkululeko YeSizwe — a sketch towards a possible analysis' (mimeo).

Felgate, Walter (1981) — 'Cooperation between Natal and KwaZulu — an Inkatha view', in Boulle and Baxter (eds).

Financial Mail (6 Jul. 79) — 'Gatsha Buthelezi: the Inkatha phenomenon'.

(25 Mar. 83, Soweto supplement) — 'Inkatha — ethnic or no? '.

(6 Dec. 85) — 'Man of the Year: Mangosuthu Buthelezi'.

Frederikse, Julie (1985) — 'Inkatha collaboration in Natal', in *AfricAsia*, 22.

Gardner, Colin (1973) — 'Chief Gatsha Buthelezi speaks to Colin Gardner', in *Reality*, 5, 4.

Glaser, D. (1986) — 'Regionalization: the case of KwaNatal' (paper presented to seventeenth annual Congress of the Association of Sociologists of Southern Africa, University of Natal, Durban).

Hayes, Grahame (1979) — 'Inkatha: an analysis' (paper presented to Southern African Studies Seminar, University of Natal, Pietermaritzburg).

Haysom, Nicholas and Modise Khosa (1984) — 'Trade unions in the homelands' (paper for Second Carnegie Inquiry into Poverty and Development in Southern Africa, University of Cape Town).

Information Centre on South Africa (the Inkatha office in Amsterdam) (1984) — 'South African townships: a case study of Lamontville'.

Jaffee, Georgina (1984) — 'Living with unemployment: strategies for survival', in *Work in Progress*, 34.

Jansen van Rensburg, N.S. (1978) — 'Inkatha — werktuig of wapen?' in *Woord en Daad*, 188.

Johnstone, A.M. and F. McA. Clifford Vaughn (eds) (1978) — *Devolution — Natal's Case* (Department of Political Science occasional paper 1, University of Natal, Durban).

Judge, Joseph (1971) — 'The Zulus: African nation in the land of Apartheid', in *National Geographic*, 140, 6.

Kane-Berman, John (1981) — 'KwaZulu: a new way to save a nation', in *Observer* magazine (29 Nov. 81).

Langner, E.J. (1983) — 'Inkatha se beleid en strategie: welslae en terugslae', in *Africanus*, 13, 1 & 2.

Lijphart, Arend (1979) — 'Consociation and federation: conceptual and empirical links', in *Canadian J of Political Science*, XII, 3.

McCarthy, Jeff and Mark Swilling (1985) — 'Empangeni bus boycott', in *SA Labour Bulletin*, 10, 6.

Makhapele, Lungile (1980) — 'Analysis of Inkatha and the Urban Foundation' (mimeo).

Maré, Gerhard (1984) — 'Inkatha: what content to populism?' (paper presented to Southern African Studies Seminar, University of Natal, Pietermaritzburg).

Maritz, Prof Chris (1982) — 'Die Buthelezi Kommissie
1. — vernaamste bevindings en aanbevelings', in *Woord en Daad*, 239
2. — konsensus en konsosiasie die uitgangspunt', in *Woord en Daad*, 240.
3. — hoe realisties?', in *Woord en Daad*, 241.

(1983) — 'Inkatha Yenkululeko Yesizwe', in *Oenskou*, 1, 3.

Molteno, Frank (1977) — 'The historical significance of the bantustan strategy', in *Social Dynamics*, 3, 2.

Morris, Mike (1986) — 'UWUSA, Inkatha and COSATU: lessons from May Day', in *Work in Progress*, 43.

Mphalala, S.J. (1981) — 'Inkatha (National Cultural) Liberation Movement', in *Institute for Public Service and Vocational Training Bulletin*, 4, 2.

Mpumalanga Township, Hammarsdale (nd) — 'Inkatha: in the throat of a whirlwind' (mimeo).

Munger, Edwin S. (1971) — 'Chief Gatsha Buthelezi of the Zulus', in *American Universities Field Staff Reports*, XV, 9.

Naidoo, G.R. (1964) — 'Buthelezi — the man with the key to Zulustan: the rebel chief of Zululand', in *Drum* (May).

National Federation of Workers (1981) — 'Report on the work stoppage at Richards Bay Minerals', in *SA Labour Bulletin*, 7, 3.

Nattrass, Jill (1981) — 'Natal and KwaZulu: an economic profile — its relevance for a new dispensation', in Boulle and Baxter (eds).

Newsweek (23 May 77) — '"We want power sharing"', interview with Buthelezi, with introductory article 'Any hope for peace'.

Ngubane, Jordan K. (1979) — *Conflict of Minds: changing power dispositions in South Africa* (New York: Books in Focus).

Nicholson, Jillian (1984) — 'The pension crisis in KwaZulu' (paper for second Carnegie

Bibliography

Inquiry into Poverty and Development in Southern Africa, University of Cape Town).

Page, Prof D. (1981) — 'Die Natal-KwaZulu (Lombard) Plan: 'n evaluasie', in *Woord en Daad*, 222.

Rouseau, Prof Jacques (1978) — 'Biographies of prominent Fort Harians: Mangosuthu Gatsha Buthelezi', in *SA Outlook*, 108, 1288.

Sibanda, Z.M. (1984) — 'Inkatha replies to UDF', in *Sash*, 27, 3.

Sinclair, Michael (1982) — 'In search of the political middle ground in South Africa', in *Politikon*, 9, 1.

South African Institute of Race Relations (SAIRR, Natal) (1977) — 'The National Cultural Liberation Movement' (information sheet 1/77).

(1980) — 'The Inkatha syllabus' (information sheet 4/80).

Southern African Research Service (SARS) (compiled by) (nd) — *Know the Facts: information about South Africa's extra-parliamentary groups* (Pretoria: SA Catholic Bishops' Conference).

Swart, Richard (1984) — 'Can Inkatha be a national cultural liberation movement with its predominantly Zulu base?' (unpublished BA Honours dissertation, University of Natal, Durban).

Third World Forum, 9, 1 (1982) — supplement introducing Inkatha.

Thula, Gibson (1980) — 'A basis for the constitutional transformation of South Arica', in H.W. van der Merwe and Robert Schrire (eds) — *Race and Ethnicity: South African and international perspectives* (Cape Town: David Philip).

To the Point, 8, 46 (1979) — 'Pathway to power or a road to confrontation'.

Van der Merwe, Hendrik W., Nancy C.J. Charton, D.A. Kotze and Ake Magnusson (eds) (1978) — *African Perspectives on South Africa* (Cape Town: David Philip), (contains several contributions by Buthelezi, Dladla and Bengu).

Van der Merwe, Hendrik, Marian Nell, Kim Weichel and Jane Reid (eds) (1980) — *Towards an Open Society in South Africa: the role of voluntary organizations* (Cape Town: David Philip).

Van Schendelen, M.C.P. (1983) — 'Critical comments on Lijphart's theory of consociational democracy', in *Politikon*, 10, 1.

Van Wyk, J.J. (1977) — 'Politieke onafhanklikheid vir KwaZulu: 'n empiriese analise van studentehoudings', in *Politikon*, 4, 1.

Venter, T.P. (1978) — 'Student participation in KwaZulu politics', in *SA J of African Affairs*, 2.

(1981) — 'Inkatha Yenkululeko Yesizwe en die beweging se betrokkenheid in die Suid-Afrikaanse politiek: 'n oorsig' (Instituut vir Suid-Afrikaanse Politiek, Potchefstroomse Universiteit vir CHO, Aktualiteitsreeks 19).

(1981) — 'Die betrokkenheid van Inkatha in die Suid-Afrikaanse politiek', in *Woord en Daad*, 223 (Part 1 of article) and 224 (part 2 of article).

(1981) — 'Inkatha: Spanningsfaktor in ons swart politiek', in *Woord en Daad*, 225.

(1981) — 'Inkatha: quo vadis?', in *Woord en Daad*, 226.

Viljoen, F.V. (1985) — 'Review: seminar on Natal/KwaZulu: the political and social environment of the future', in *Development Southern Africa*, 2, 4.

Watt, John (1982) — 'KaNgwane and Ingwavuma: the Swazi view', in *Reality*, 14, 5.

Welsh, David (1976) — 'Inkatha', in *Reality*, 8, 1.

(1982) — 'Review of the Buthelezi Commission', in *Reality*, 14, 4.

Whisson, M.G. (1980) — 'The Sullivan principles: striking a lost chord', in *Social Dynamics*, 6, 1.

Wits Student (1978) — 'Where to Inkatha?' (12 June)

Work in Progress (WIP), 5 (1978) — 'School unrest in KwaZulu'.

5 (1978) — 'Strikes: Isithebe'.

24 (1982) — 'Trade unions: America steps in'.

25 (1983) — 'Labour Party: a constitutional decision?'

43 (1986) — 'Natal vigilantes: "At war with UDF, COSATU and the ANC"'.

SELECT INDEX

ABRAM-MAYET, S., 160
Adelman, Sammy, 173
Africa, Esther, 206
African communalism, 98-100
African humanism, 23n, 99
African nationalism, 29, 30
African National Congress (ANC), 28, 32-3, 35, 36, 41, 152, 159, 162, 163, 165, 176, 178, 184, 197, 200, 219-20, 222
    Inkatha and, 45-6, 77-8, 136-49
    pre-1940s, 21, 23-4, 50, 54
African National Congress Youth League, 24, 28, 141
Africans, government of, 27-8
Afrikaanse Studentebond, 70
Aggett, Neil, 126
Alliance of Black Reformed Christians in South Africa (ABRECSA), 197-8
Alusaf refinery, 121
Amabutho, 181n. See also Vigilantes.
American Federation of Labor/Congress of Industrial Organisations (AFL-CIO), 126, 128-9
Anglo American, 115
Anti-SAIC, 158, 159-60
Apartheid policy, 6-7, 11, 13, 15, 27-32, 83-4, 95
Apollos, Reginald, 157
Ardington, Tony, 49
Arenstein, Rowley, 33, 49, 137
Arnold Bergstraesser Institute, 178-9
Azanian Congress of Trade Unions (AZACTU), 117
Azanian People's Organization (AZAPO), 19, 151
Azanian Students Organization (AZASO), 199, 201

BADSHA, Omar, 120
Bambatha Rebellion (1906), 18-19
Bantu Authorities Act 1951, 21, 28-9, 33
Bantu Homelands Constitution Act 1971, 41
Bantu Investment Corporation, 10, 100, 108-09, 111
Bantu Laws Amendment Act 1973, 108
Bantustan policy, see Apartheid policy
Barayi, Elijah, 116-7, 133
Barclays, 115
Bata Shoe Company, 103
Bengu, Sibusiso M.E., 64, 98-9, 100, 142, 158, 183-4, 186
Bhengu, Ewart, 73
Bhengu, Gobizizwe, 206
Bhengu, H.J., 77
Biko, Steve, 150, 187
Black Advisory Council, 164
Black Allied Workers Union (BAWU), 130, 132
Black consciousness, 149-52
Black Consciousness Movement of South Africa, 143, 144

Black local authorities, 37-8, 153-4
Black People's Convention, 150, 168
Black Sash, 92, 168
Black Unity Front (BUF), 79, 157-8
Blaustein, Albert, 178
Bolton, Harriet, 120
Boraine, Andrew, 173
Botha, Fanie, 127
Botha, M.C., 64
Botha, P.W., 149, 164, 156-7, 158, 165-6
Bowring Barclays and Associates (SA), 115
Boycotts
    bus, 189-90, 211-2
    consumer, 130-1
    school, 182, 185-9, 201-2, 204, 207-11
British Council of Churches, 197-8
Brookes, Edgar, 33
BTR Sarmcol, 103, 212
Bureau for State Security, 108
Buthelezi Commission (BC), 11, 85, 106, 146, 163-7
Buthelezi, Mangosuthu Gatsha
    and founding of Inkatha, 54-60
    leadership style, 64, 92-5, 173-4, 219-20
    political career, 32-41
    political strategy, 5, 15, 41-4, 89, 218-25
    and the press, 1, 175-6

CALATA, James, 21
Campbell, Marshall, 50
Capitalism, 6, 10-11, 98-102, 106-16, 221
Central Administration Services, 120
Champion, A.W.G., 23-4, 53, 77
Cheadle, Halton, 123
Checkers, 108
Chemical Workers Industrial Union, 121
Chiefs, 18, 21-2, 27, 33-6, 59-60, 88-92
Chinsamy, Yellan S., 158, 160
Christian Democratic Union, 178
Christian Institute, 151
Civil servants, 91-2, 93-4
Coady Institute, 70
Codes of conduct, 102-4
Coetzee, Johann, 3
Coloured Persons Representative Council, 157-8, 160
Committee of Ten (Soweto), 153-4
Community councils, 28, 153-4, 155
Conco, Simon, 67, 113, 124, 130, 131-2, 140, 212
Congress Alliance, 29, 126, 159-60
Congress of South African Students (COSAS), 85, 197, 201, 208-9
Congress of South African Trade Unions (COSATU), 3, 53, 71-2, 116-7, 128, 130-1, 132-3, 200, 211-3
Consociationalism, 167, 220
Cooper, Saths, 151
Coronation Brick and Tile Company (Corobrick), 118-9, 121

257

Corporation for Economic Development (CED), 111-3
Corruption, 90-2, 93
Council of Unions of South Africa (CUSA), 117, 130, 132
'Cultural nationalism', 30
Cyprian Bhekuzulu, Paramount Chief, 34, 40, 45

DAVIDSON, Peter J., 115, 132
Democratic Turnhalle Alliance, 171
Development Bank of Southern Africa, 111
Dhlomo, Oscar, 61, 84, 85, 125, 143, 150, 163, 169, 175n, 195
Diakonia, 70
Dikwankwetla party, 158
Dinuzulu, Zulu king, 19
Disinvestment, 101-6
Dladla, B.I., 83, 109, 120-4, 217
Dlamini, Norah, 195
Dookie, Baldeo, 159
Dube, Harrison, 191-2
Dube, John L., 4, 19, 21, 50, 53, 54
Durban Chamber of Commerce, 131
Durban City Council, 193

EDENDALE Bakery, 111
Education, 85, 182-9
The Employment Bureau of Africa (TEBA), 49-50
Erwin, Alec, 130
Ethnicity, 28-9, 30, 31, 32, 64, 57-8, 170
Executive Hotel, Umlazi, 115n.

FEDERATION, 169-70
Federation of South African Trade Unions (FOSATU), 125, 130-1, 200, 211
Felgate, Walter, 49, 175
Fisher, Foszia, 120
Fontini, Tony, 214
Frame group, 123
Freedom Charter, 141-2, 147

GASA, 'Moonlight', 192
General Factory Workers Benefit Fund, 120
Goodwill Zwelethini, Zulu king, 4, 36, 42, 50, 53, 57, 76, 118-9, 149, 222
Greatermans, 108
Griffin, Suzanne see Vos, Suzanne
Gumede, Archie, 147, 148
Gumede, Philemon, 131, 132
Gumede, Richard, 194

HADEBE, G., 132
Hadebe, Reggie, 186
Hahn, Lorna, 178
Hambanathi Residents' Association, 194-5
Hartke, Vance, 178
Heaton Nicholls, George, 46, 49, 53
Hemson, David, 120, 123
Hendrickse, Alan, 153, 158, 159, 160, 161
Heunis, Chris, 161

Hlatswayo, M.V., 132
Horwood, Owen, 166
'Homelands' see Apartheid policy.

ILANGA, 4, 19, 176
Improper Interference Act, 172
Inala Party, 110n.
Indians
  attacks on, 205
  brought to Natal to work sugar plantations, 9, 19
  tension between Africans and, 33, 152
Industrial and Commercial Workers Union (ICU), 23-4, 49, 53
Ingwavuma, 73-5, 95
Inkata kaZulu, 32, 45-53, 59
Inkatha
  branches, 64-6
  economic policy, 5-6, 97-116, 220-1
  and the media, 174-7
  membership, 64-6, 70-3, 217
  origins of, 24, 45-8
  political strategy, 6-8, 56-60, 78-88, 135-79
  populist appeal, 217-27
  reaction to opposition, 189, 195-8, 206-7
  statement of belief, 227-32
  structure, 61-4
  and students, 207-11
  and working class, 97-8, 116-33, 211-3
Inkatha (headring), 227
Inkatha Bulletin, 175
Inkatha Development Office, 70
Inkatha Institute, 68, 129, 131, 155, 165, 176-7
Inkatha Women's Brigade, 66-8, 80, 187
Inkatha Youth Brigade, 66, 68-9, 70, 76, 81, 85, 149, 183-5, 187-9, 207
Inkatha Youth Service Corps, 69, 188-9, 214
Institute for Industrial Education (IIE), 120, 124, 126
Inyanda (Natal and Zululand African Chamber of Commerce), 110, 111, 113, 130-1
Inyandza movement, 158, 159, 163
Isizwe-Sechaba, 175
Ithala Savings Bank, 113

JEUGKRAG SA, 70
Johns, Tony, 112, 128
Joint Consultative Committee, 166
Joint Rent Action Committee (JORAC), 149, 192-3, 204
Jwara, Wilson, 206

KANYE, W.S.P., 66-7, 83, 152
Khanyile, Z.A., 112
Khulani Booksellers, 113
Khulani-Brown Wholesalers, 113
Khulani Holdings, 108, 113-6, 124
Khulani Insurance Brokers, 115
Khumalo, M.Z., 113-5
Konigkramer, Arthur, 49
Konrad Adenauer Foundation, 178

258

Koornhof, Piet, 156, 165-6
Kruger, Jimmy, 75, 83, 142, 150
KwaZulu cabinet, 85
KwaZulu Constitution, 41-3
KwaZulu Development Corporation, 108, 110, 111-3
KwaZulu education department, 188, 189
KwaZulu Finance and Investment Corporation (KFC), 104, 108, 112-3
KwaZulu Legislative Assembly (KLA), 3-4, 13, 34, 41, 55-60, 62, 72, 84-8, 89-95, 108-10, 111, 182-4, 191
KwaZulu-Natal Indaba, 1, 3, 10, 44, 169, 218, 222
KwaZulu police force, 1, 3, 213-5
KwaZulu Savings Bank, 213-5
KwaZulu Shoe Company (KSC), 112

LABOUR Party, 157-63
Labour tenancy, 75-6
Land Act 1913, 8, 10, 21, 23, 27
Larkan, Bill, 50
Le Grange, Louis, 144, 161
Leon, Sonny, 153, 159
Lindelani, 205
Lloyd, Anson, 112
Lobban, R.B., 112
Lobolo, 67
Lombard Commission, 164-5, 171
Lugongolo-Mtolo, S.S., 77
Lusaka Manifesto 1969, 61
Luthuli, Chief Albert, 21, 23, 24, 35, 41, 45, 77-8, 137-9
Luthuli, Albertinah, 41, 138
Luthuli, Nokukhanya, 138
Luthuli, W.T.V., 112, 113, 115
Luthuli Memorial Foundation, 138

MABHIDA, Moses, 77
Mabuza, Enos, 158, 163
Mabuza, Wesley, 203
Madide, D.R.B., 84, 130, 151, 197
Madlala, Msuthu, 156
Mafole, Ntwe, 70
Magnum group, 115
Magnum National Life Assurance, 115
Magogo, 53
Mahlabatini Declaration, 170, 172
Malunga, P., 132
Mandela, Nelson, 41, 77, 133, 136, 146, 147, 149
Mandela, Winnie, 152
Mangosuthu College, 50
Mansfield, Peter, 177
Maphumulo, Mhlabunzima, 110n.
March and McLennan, 115
Martin, Frank, 171
Mashinini, Tsietsi, 143
Mcwayizeni, Prince Israel, 36
Mbatha, Picton, 138
Mdlalose, Frank T., 58, 73, 84, 85, 112, 125, 128, 189-90, 197, 212

Mdlalose, Thusi, 213
Meer, Farouk, 151
Meer, Fatima, 39, 41, 152, 200
Mfeka, Belinda and Simon, 73, 205
Metal and Allied Workers Union, 103, 120, 124, 131, 212
Mhlongo, Napoleon, 206
Mhlungu, S.J., 113-5
Middleton, Norman, 117, 120, 161
Middleton Report, 196-7
Mkhize, Ian, 191, 194
Mkhize, Musa Arnold, 68, 70
Mkhwanazi, A.P., 113, 115
Mopeli, K., 158
Motlana, Ntatho, 143, 153, 156
Mpetha, Oscar, 147
Mshiyeni kaDinuzulu, 21, 78
Msimang, H.S., 77
Msomi, P., 132
Mtetwa, C.J., 83
Muil, Tim, 49
Mxenge, Victoria, 199

NATAL African Teachers' Union (NATU), 73, 210
Natal Alliance, 172
Natal Code, 66-8, 89
Natal Indian Congress, 33, 158
Natal Provincial Council, 166
The Nation, 4, 174-5, 177
National convention, 168-9
National Convention Movement, 174-5
National Education Crisis Committee, 209-11
National Forum, 97, 151
National Iron, Steel, Metal and Allied Workers Union (NISMAWU), 128
National Party, 24, 28, 58, 70, 115, 159, 165, 166, 173
National Statutory Council, 3, 156
National Sugar Refining and Allied Industries Employees Union (NSRAIEU), 127, 130, 132
National Union of South African Students (NUSAS), 38, 70
National Union of Textile Workers, 112, 121, 124
Native Administration Act 1927, 49, 88
Native Advisory Boards, 28
Native Affairs Act 1920, 27
Native Representative Council, 21, 28, 29
Native Trust and Land Act 1936, 19, 27
Native Urban Areas Act 1923, 28
Naudé, Beyers, 102, 104
Ndlazi, Bennet, 161
Ndlovu, P.S., 132
Ndlovu, V.B., 204
Nel, M.C. De Wet, 29, 30
Nel, Trevor, 50
New Republic Party, 166
Ngcobo, Isaac, 128
Ngcobo, M.A., 84
Ngobese, Edward, 55

Ngobese, R.S., 55
Ngobese, Solomon, 123
Ngubane, Jordan, 33, 34, 37, 77, 178
Nicholson, J.H., 46
Nqutu, 20, 32
Nsibande, Selby, 127
Ntsanwisi, Hudson, 102, 157, 158
Nxasana, Ella, 66, 211
Nxumalo, J.A.W., 83, 124
Nxumalo, Otty, 55
Nyembezi, C.L.S., 55, 127, 156
Nyembezi, S.M., 157
Nzo Alfred, 138

PAKKIES, Patrick, 204
Pan Africanist Congress, 139, 143, 152-53
Phatudi, Cedric, 157
Phalabora Mining Company, 102
Population relocation, see removals.
Populism, 6, 218-9
Premier Milling, 111
President's Council, 160, 164
Progressive Federal Party, 106, 159, 163, 166, 168, 169, 172, 217-8
Progressive Reform Party, 172
Promotion of Bantu Self-Government Act 1959, 13, 29, 36

QOBOZA, Percy, 154

RAJBANSI, Amichand, 159
Reddy, J.N., 159, 160
Reform Party, 152, 158, 159, 160, 163
Regional Advisory Committees, 156
Release Mandela Campaign, 168
Removals, 8, 19-20, 95
Rents, 189
Representation of Natives Act 1936, 21
'Retribalization', 49, 53
Rio Tinto Zinc Corporation, 102
Robinson, Brenda, 49
Robson, Gavin, 175
Rudden, Roy, 49
Rupert, Anton, 115
Rupert, Johan, 115
Rupert family trust, 115

SABC, 85, 176
Sabata Dalindyebo, Paramount Chief, 145
Sabelo, Winnington, 154, 202, 204
Salaries, 92-4, 98, 107
Sanctions, 101-2, 117, 158
SANLAM, 115
Sarmcol strike, 130
Sasko Milling, 108
Saunders, Chris, 49, 165
Schlebusch Commission, 164, 170
Schlemmer, Lawrence, 49, 102, 112, 120, 176-7
Schreiner, Deneys, 165
Schwarz, Harry, 170, 172
Seme, Pixley kaIsaka, 140, 141

Separate development policy see Apartheid policy.
September, M., 112
Shabalala, Thomas Mandla, 62, 73, 205
Shaka, 17, 57
Shaka's Spear Party, 86
Shandu, Victoria, 206
Shepstone, Theophilus, 67
Sibeko, Paul, 59, 149
Sibiya, Gideon, 203, 204
Sishi, R.D., 103
Sisulu, Albertina, 147
Sisulu, Walter, 139
Sithole, Alfred, 194
Sithole, Nomathemba, 65
Sithole, Chief S.O., 83, 151
Slabbert, Frederick Van Zyl, 165, 169
Sobukwe, Robert, 152-3
Solomon kaDinuzulu, Zulu king, 45, 46-50, 51, 54
South African Allied Workers Union (SAAWU), 128
South African Black Alliance (SABA), 79, 152, 157-63, 169, 171
South African Communist Party, 77, 146
South African Congress of Trade Unions (SACTU), 29, 126
South African Council of Churches, 151
South African Defence Force, 203, 213-4, 215
South African Indian Council, 154n., 158, 159, 160
South African Information Department, 108
South African Institute of Race Relations, 120
South African Native National Congress, 21
South African Planters' Union, 46
South African Police, 192, 199, 203, 212-4
South African Students Organisation (SASO), 39, 119, 150, 197
South African Sugar Association, 164, 165
South African Youth Foundation, 70
South West African People's Organisation (SWAPO), 143
Soweto Civic Association, 154
Soweto Parents Crisis Committee, 208-9
Special Cabinet Committee on Urban Blacks, 156
Spies, Marius, 112
Stanger Businessmen's Association, 58
State President, 88-9
Steenwijk, Reina, 179
Stellenbosch, University of, Students Representative Council, 70
Steyn, G.L., 73
Strikes, 28, 118, 162
Sugar industry, 9-10, 46, 50
Summerley family trust, 115
Surplus People Project, 31
Swart, Ray, 49
'Synthesis', 55

TAMBO, Oliver, 138, 139, 144, 145, 147, 149

Thatcher, Margaret, 101
Thebehali, David, 155
Thula, Anastasia, 66
Thula, Gibson, 63, 69-70, 98, 141, 154, 156
Tidwell Housing Company, 103-4
Tiger Oats, 111, 113
Tolbert, President of Liberia, 138
Tomlinson Commission, 20
Trade Union Advisory and Co-ordinating Council, 120-1
Trade Union Council of South Africa, 126
Trade unions, 97, 116-8, 119-33, 211-3
Transkei, 29, 124
Transport and General Workers Union, 120
Tribalism, 31-2, 60
Tripartite companies (tripcos), 100, 108-13
Turner, Richard, 38
Tutu, Desmond, 153, 156, 168

UBHOKO, 45, 55
Ubuntu-Botho see African humanism.
Ulundi, 95
Ulundi Trading Company, 115n.
Umkhonto, 78
Umlazi Bakery, 108
Unemployment, 69
Unification Church, 173
United Democratic Front, 19, 71, 73, 97, 125-6, 147-9, 193-200, 203-4, 206-7
United National Independence Party (Zambia), 55, 61
United States Government, 1
United Workers Union of South Africa (UWUSA), 73, 97, 119, 124, 129-33, 220
Urban Bantu Councils, 28, 153
Urban Foundation, 106
Usuthu, 34

VAN DEN BERG, G.J., 113
Verwoerd, Hendrik, 28, 29, 30, 34
Vigilantes, 199-207, 210, 212-3, 214-5
Vilane, Jeffrey, 131

Viljoen, Gerrit, 172
Violence, 135, 181, 194
  Federal Seminary Imbali, 204-5
  Hambanathi, 149, 194-5
  Inanda, 199
  Phoenix, 199
  University of Zululand, Ngoye, 147, 162, 186-7, 196-7
Vorster, B.J., 56, 120, 157, 158
Vos, Suzanne, 49, 144
Vulamehlo Vukani Peoples' Party, 161

WAGES commissions, 120-1
Wattle Industry, 9
Webster, Eddie, 120
Western Industrial and Trading Company (WITCO), 112
W.G. Brown, 113
Whyte, Quintin, 35
Wiehahn Commission, 124
Working class, 6, 97, 116-33, 211-2

XOLO, Chief E.T., 83
Xuma, A.B., 24, 77
Xundu, Rev. Mcebisi, 193

YENGWA, W., 66
Young, C.B., 46
Young Christian Workers, 120
Young Pioneers (Malawi), 70

ZALABISA Savings Account, 113
Zambian Youth Service, 69-70
Zulu, Bishop Alpheus, H., 37, 46, 55, 77, 111, 112, 127
Zulu, Prince Clement, 42
Zulu, Prince Gideon, 55, 204
Zulu King, 34, 41-2, 88
Zulu National Fund, 46, 55
Zulu Territorial Authority, 35, 37, 38, 41, 43, 83
Zululand Coloured People's Committee, 157
Zululand Planters' Union, 46